CRAZY GOOD

The True Story of Dan Patch,
the Most Famous Horse in America

CHARLES LEERHSEN

Simon & Schuster
New York   London   Toronto   Sydney

SIMON & SCHUSTER
Rockefeller Center
1230 Avenue of the Americas
New York, NY 10020

First Simon & Schuster hardcover edition June 2008

SIMON & SCHUSTER and colophon are registered trademarks of Simon &
Schuster, Inc.

For information about special discounts for bulk purchases,
please contact Simon & Schuster Special Sales at
1-800-456-6798 or business@simonandschuster.com.

Designed by Nancy Singer

Manufactured in the United States of America

10 9 8 7 6 5 4 3 2 1

Library of Congress Cataloging-in-Publication Data
Leerhsen, Charles.
  Crazy good : the true story of Dan Patch, the most famous horse in America / Charles
Leerhsen.
    p. cm.
  Includes index.
    1. Dan Patch (Race horse) 2. Harness racehorses—United States—Biography.
3. Messner family. I. Title.
SF343.D3L44 2008
636.1'750929—dc22

                              2007045165

ISBN-13: 978-0-7432-9177-4
ISBN-10:   0-7432-9177-8

Photo Credits:
Collection of the Harness Racing Museum and Hall of Fame: 1, 2, 4, 6, 8, 9, 12, 14
Courtesy of the Dan Patch Historical Society: 3, 5, 7, 10, 11, 13

To Charles Edward Leerhsen, my dad

CRAZY GOOD

At the Razor's Edge

ONE AFTERNOON IN JULY of 2005, Diane Kleinsteiber, a fifty-something pottery-store clerk from Watertown, Wisconsin, arrived without appointment at the Razor's Edge hair salon in Savage, Minnesota, and asked to see the proprietor, Jens Bohn. Besides being a master barber, Bohn, who is in his mid-sixties, is the president of the Dan Patch Historical Society, a group that means to keep alive the memory of the racehorse. It was in this latter capacity that Kleinsteiber addressed him, saying immediately after introducing herself, "I have something you might want to see."

Bohn looked up from the customer whose hair he was cutting. "Uh-huh," he said, cocking an eyebrow. It was not unusual for people to drop into his shop toting a Dan Patch sled, the wringer from a Dan Patch washing machine, a cube of Dan Patch pool-cue chalk, or a Dan Patch tobacco tin, certain that they were about to hear an appraisal, or receive a check, of life-changing dimensions. But this, he sensed, was something different. The woman standing before him was extending both hands and presenting him with a small, blue patent-medicine tin. On its lid were the words "Cascaret's Candy Cathartic, 25 Cents, Liver Stimulant, Strengthens the Bowels, Makes Pure Blood."

"Open it," Kleinsteiber said.

Bohn did, and saw what looked like a small scrap of dark brown canvas or fiberglass—something thickish but flexible— perhaps an inch long and half an inch wide, with a neat hole at one end through which someone had looped a tiny, deep blue ribbon that was tied into a knot. The object was sitting on a folded piece of lined, yellowing paper. "It's a note," Kleinsteiber said. "Go ahead, read it."

Written in pencil in a boyish old-fashioned scrawl, it said, "This is a piece of hoof off of Dan Patch, champion pacer of the world." The writer was Kleinsteiber's grandfather, Sylvester Redford, now long dead after a life of Wisconsin farming but fourteen at the time. When she was little, Kleinsteiber explained, the old man would occasionally take out the Cascarets tin, open it up, and tell the story of how he had gone to see Dan Patch at the Wisconsin State Fair in 1904. Dan had thrown a shoe while warming up, and had been guided by his driver to the blacksmith's shed to get a replacement, while the curious Sylvester followed close behind. The smitty picked up Dan's foot and mindlessly shaved off the slightly ragged edge of Dan's hoof in preparation for putting on a fresh shoe. Young Sylvester scooped up the fragment as it fluttered to the ground—but not before Dan's pet stable dog rushed at him, snarling viciously. "My grandfather always said he barely got out of there alive," she said.

By the time she had reached that point in her story, the barbershop was silent. All of the chatter about the Vikings, the Twins, youth hockey, politics, the weather, and the guy who had just left—all that had come to a halt, and the man in the chair and the half dozen waiting customers were looking at Kleinsteiber and Bohn, who were looking at each other.

It is interesting, if not exciting, exactly, to watch Dan Patch aficionados in action. This was obviously an important find. First-degree relics of Dan Patch are extremely rare. A woman in upstate New York owns a few strands of hair from the horse's mane that long ago were braided and put into a locket, and a vice president of Bohn's Dan Patch Historical Society has a tail, dyed red for unknown reasons, that may have belonged to the once-famous horse—but that is about it. Since Bohn is a serious collector—he has a display at the Razor's Edge that includes vintage photographs, as well as a Dan Patch pocket watch, a Dan Patch padlock, and several posters from *The Great Dan Patch,* a movie starring Dennis O'Keefe and Gail Russell that came out in 1949—one might expect that he and Kleinsteiber would at that point have commenced a negotiation. But Bohn, being a Dan Patch person himself, understood that Kleinsteiber had not come to him to sell her treasure. In displaying the hoof clipping to the president of the historical society, she was merely doing what members of the Dan Patch community seem compelled to do: that is, to keep reminding themselves and one another that the great Dan Patch really existed (if you're not in the presence of another enthusiast, it's easy to forget), and that he was, in fact, great. So the meeting was brief, ending as abruptly as it had begun. Once Jens had said how special her relic was ("You've got just about the only part of Dan Patch above ground," he told her), and how wonderful it was to see, Diane smiled, snapped the tin closed, got in her car, and drove the five hours back to Wisconsin, her 101-year-old horse hangnail in her purse, her mission accomplished.

CHAPTER ONE

The 1900s was an age of Charisma, and some of the healthiest personalities, those with a natural endowment of the stuff, radiated their own heat—a few seemed like walking planets. They had a gravitational heft that had nothing to do with physical size.

—Darin Strauss, *The Real McCoy*

THE CROWD ROSE AS one to stare at the horse, and the horse, as was his custom, stared back.

It was 4:35 p.m. on October 7, 1905, a brilliant fall Thursday at the Breeders Track in Lexington, Kentucky, and Dan Patch, a big mahogany-brown stallion, had just finished an attempt to lower his own world record for the mile. He was still blowing hard, but after wheeling around and jogging back to the finish line—on his own, with no guidance or encouragement from the small, mustachioed man sitting in the racing sulky behind him—he had come to a dead stop and, with his head cocked slightly to the left, was slowly and deliberately surveying the assembled.

This was a trademark move, something he did not do automatically, like a circus animal mindlessly performing a trick, but often enough, when the mood struck. People waited for it, and felt like they had gotten their money's worth when it came. Dan Patch's fans used to say—when they talked about him in taverns and barbershops and at dinner tables all over America—that the horse liked to count the house.

A dramatic silence fell over the scene. An official clocking would come down from the judges at any moment, and a quarter of a second either way could mean the difference between the front page and the sports section. Had Dan done the impossible once again? In the press area, a finger hovered above a telegraph key.

From where the horse stood, he could hear the three timers in the judges' stand, a few feet behind and about twenty feet above him, murmuring confidentially as they consulted their chronographs; if their individual hand-timings differed, as they might easily by a fraction of a second or so, they needed to reach a consensus on an official clocking. In an age when horse speed, and the mile record in particular, mattered to a mass audience, these racing judges were men of gravitas, doing important work. They wore suits and ties and natty straw boaters. They hefted 17-jewel stopwatches that had the power to transform a day at the races into an historic event. If Dan Patch had gone as fast as some in the packed grandstand guessed he had, everyone there would have a story to tell, maybe for the rest of his life. Tens of thousands who weren't there would also claim to have seen the beautiful brown horse power down the homestretch of the perfectly manicured red-clay racetrack in the lengthening autumn shadows. It was a golden age of sports, horses, ladies' hats, and bullshit.

Seconds ticked by, tension increased, but the horse, as a reporter said later, was the calmest person on the grounds. Nine years old and at his physical peak, Dan Patch stood at almost the exact midpoint of a long career spent, for the most part, touring the country in a plush private railroad car and putting on exhibitions of speed. He knew the drill: first there was the Effort, the race against the clock, one mile in distance, with the galloping prompters to urge him on and stir his competitive spirit. Then there was the Silence, as judges checked their watches. After the Silence came either the Roar—a world record!—or the Sigh—alas, not this time. The Roar invariably involved flying hats and a surging wave of well-wishers.

Dan Patch preferred the Roar. Which was odd, because why would a horse choose hysteria over a quiet walk back to the barn? What did he care about world records and the endless hype? The preference wasn't horselike. Dan Patch was an odd horse.

He was different to a degree, in fact, that experienced horse handlers found amazing, even hateful (jealousy being a big part of the racing game). For example, though stallions tend to be skittish, lashing out with teeth and hooves at the slightest provocation, Dan Patch—an intact male who had already shown he had no problems in the breeding shed—exuded calm, allowing strangers to approach him and small children to run back and forth beneath his belly. He wasn't frightened by the world human beings had made. He did not waste energy worrying, or see danger where there wasn't any, or fret about things he could not change. He trusted—a quality humans found terribly flattering, and loved him for. As for the racing and touring, he seemed to get it, to understand that his job was to be this new thing in America: a superstar. Whenever he saw a photographer, he stopped.

That evening in Lexington, Dan Patch would be led into the lobby of the Phoenix Hotel, where happy drunks would pat his nose and perfumed women would want to nuzzle. Whatever he was thinking when people pressed around him, Dan remained charming and affable; the boors and the rubes always went away feeling noticed and cared-for. Fans sometimes pulled hairs from his tail to twist into key chains or put into lockets; in such cases, Dan might spin his handsome head around and cast a sharp glance, but he never kicked. He had an admirable sense of his own might, and others' vulnerability. The only person Dan Patch ever bit was a young Minnesota boy named Fred Sasse, who would grow up to write an appallingly bad book about him. You just had to love a horse like this.

And people did. They turned out to see him, 80,000, 90,000, 100,000 strong, paying usually a one-dollar admission, a day's wage for the average Edwardian Joe. Sometimes when Dan would amble out, unannounced, for a few warm-up laps, hours before he was scheduled to race, the crowd would erupt in a sustained huzzah that would not subside until he headed off twenty minutes later—sometimes but not always taking a little bow at the top of the exit ramp, stirring up his fans even further. Teddy Roosevelt, the president during Dan Patch's prime, bragged about having a Dan Patch horseshoe at his home in Oyster Bay, Long Island ("A gift

from his owner—from the race in which he broke the two-minute
mile!"). The actress and courtesan Lillie Langtry visited Dan in his
gleaming-white custom-built railroad car with his almost-life-size
picture emblazoned across both sides; as famous as the Jersey Lily
was (mostly for being the mistress of both Edward VII and his
nephew, Louis of Battenberg), the meeting clearly meant more for
her career than his.

On days when the horse wasn't performing, people would
wait in line for hours just to see him standing in his stall, sometimes looking less than regal with his pet rat terrier perched atop
his head. Dwight Eisenhower recalled queuing up with his parents
to see Dan at the Kansas State Fair in 1904; Harry Truman, in his
postpresidential dotage, remembered sending Dan a fan letter.

People exaggerated their connection to the horse to make themselves seem more important, or better human beings. A common
boast in the 1920s, '30s, and '40s—a kind of urban myth com-
parable to saying you were at Wrigley Field when Babe Ruth hit
his famous "called shot" home run—was to say you were once
at a racetrack someplace, leaning on the fence and watching Dan
Patch warm up, when his trainer drove the horse over, picked you
out of the crowd, and asked if you'd like to take ole Danny boy
for a spin. The story, which was told all over the country, had two
seemingly contradictory points: that Dan, like Jesus, moved among
the common folk, and that you were somebody special for being
picked to drive him. (Some said they jumped at the chance to sit
behind him in the sulky; others, unwilling to weave a more tangled
web, claimed to have demurred.) In their obituaries, many who
had never met Dan Patch—or who had perhaps only the slightest
connection, having mucked out the stall next to his at a state fair
one morning, say—were identified as his trainer, owner, breeder,
horseshoer, or groom, their impressive fibs following them relent-
lessly to the grave. So many people lied about having groomed
the horse that one Dan Patch Web site lists as a FAQ, "How can I
verify that my relative was Dan Patch's caretaker?" (The answer:
You can't, because the poor soul almost certainly wasn't.) In 1923

an early author of self-help manuals, Harry Heffner, published a pamphlet called *Dan Patch: The Story of a Winner,* in which he revealed how to become a more highly effective businessperson, friend, spouse, and Christian by acquiring the virtues of the by-then-deceased horse. In the introduction to a book called *The Autobiography of Dan Patch,* written by a publicist named Merton E. Harrison and published in 1911, the author writes, "The work of his caretakers, trainers and drivers has always been high class, but it has always been supplemented by the self-esteem, the care and thoughtfulness of the horse himself. Dan Patch has come to be spoken of as 'the horse that knows.'"

Even John Hervey, the preeminent turf writer of the early twentieth century, a florid scribe at times but usually a sober one, fell hard for the horse. "A kinder, a wiser, a finer dispositioned spirit in equine form never lived," Hervey wrote of Dan in the 1930s. "He was goodness personified. And wisdom. That he knew more than most of the men then on earth was the firm conviction of those who knew him. It was almost unbelievable that a horse with so mighty a heart, so dauntless a courage, such endless masculine resolution, strength and power, could at the same time be so mild, so docile, teachable, controllable, lovable. Those constantly with him worshipped him—would have died for him, I veritably believe, had it been necessary."

In this one animal, humbly bred and congenitally malformed, had come together all the virtues the horse-drawn world had ever imagined. To use the parlance of the day, Dan was crazy good. Dan Patch madness was still approaching its peak that day in October of 1905, when the horse, with tremendous fanfare (which is to say, the usual fanfare), came to Lexington. The local hardware store by then might have a Dan Patch calendar hanging on its wall, and anyone could buy Dan Patch cigars and sleds from stores and mail-order catalogs, but the great wave of Dan Patch merchandise, the washing machines, breakfast cereals, rocking horses, dinner plates, pocket watches, pocketknives, pancake syrup, automobiles—even Dan Patch real estate and the Dan Patch stallion shield, to prevent the family carriage horse from masturbating—all these fine products and more had yet to hit the marketplace.

Further in the future, too, was a certain morbidly cold, rainy day in Los Angeles, when the track was slippery, the crowd was thin, and the party was long past over.

At Lexington in 1905, though, life was good, and the rose was still blooming. Dan Patch, that day, was all about hope and promise and a possible payoff in the betting for those who had wagered, at even money, that he would beat his famous world record for the mile.

At last, a man in the judges' stand stood up and lifted a megaphone to his lips.

In the grandstand, women leaned forward clutching the souvenir Dan Patch horseshoes that their husbands and beaux had bought them for a dollar on the way in. Men leaned forward too, and touched the brims of their straw boaters, aware that hats might have to be flung.

Dan Patch stopped panting and pricked up his ears.

"The time for the mile . . . ," said the judge, and then he shouted the numbers, declaiming them clearly in the direction of the crowd. But for once there was neither the Roar nor the Sigh. There was only more silence. The crowd seemed not to believe what it had heard.

The judge, bemused, lowered his megaphone and waited five or six heartbeats. Then he raised it up and shouted the numbers again, hitting each one hard, until his voice rasped.

Silence, still, for another heartbeat.

And another.

Now came the Roar.

The events of this book may seem as if they transpired on another planet.

Harness horses have not made front-page headlines across the nation since fast food meant oysters. Racehorses of any ilk don't linger in the mass media these days unless they have terribly cute names or sad stories involving shattered cannon bones or kids with cancer. The sports and pop cultural paradigms have shifted so radically in the interim that it is difficult to wrap one's mind around the truth: this pacer was the most celebrated American sports figure in the first decade of the twentieth century, as popular in his day as any athlete who has ever lived.

Who even knows what a pacer is anymore?

Backward leaps the imagination trying to comprehend it all. America was already sports-mad when Dan Patch made his public debut at a little country fair in Indiana in 1900—but only boxing, baseball, and horse racing really mattered. The latter, which mattered most of all, was divided into two distinct, and deeply rivalrous, pastimes: Thoroughbred racing, in which horses run various distances carrying various weights, most famously for the roses each spring—and harness racing, in which they don't run at all, but compete rather at either of two gaits, the trot or the pace, pulling a two-wheeled rig called a sulky, almost always at the distance of a mile, the weight of the passenger being of relatively small significance.

Before Dan Patch's day, and dating back to colonial times, the Thoroughbreds were the closely watched breed; it was their major races that tentpoled the sports calendar (such as it was in the pre–Civil War years), their hard-charging champions whom the masses cheered; if you said "horse racing" before 1885 or so you meant the sport of kings, the galloper's game. By the time of Dan's death in 1916, the same rules applied: the Thoroughbred had reclaimed the throne, which he has retained into this inglorious era of 3,000-person "crowds" at Belmont Park; "racinos," where people literally turn their backs to the horses while pumping quarters into video slot machines; and Yum Foods Presents the Kentucky Derby. America's sports fans, let it be acknowledged, have clearly shown their overall preference for this handsome, hyper, powerful-yet-fragile breed that the English confected in the eighteenth century and still so steadfastly admire.

Yet between its two lengthy marriages to the Thoroughbred, America had a passionate fling with the light harness horse, or Standardbred, as he is more formally known. For the final fifteen years of the nineteenth century, and the first fifteen of the twentieth, it was him they clearly loved best, and they followed his sport—known generically as trotting, despite a plethora of pacers—more fervently than any other.

   Trotting and pacing races highlighted hundreds of city, county,
and state fairs during this period, and rich men paraded their prized
harness horses down Manhattan's Third Avenue every Sunday,
rain or shine, sometimes competing in informal "speed brushes"
for side bets—a cask of oysters, say, or maybe a case of wine,
a Florodora girl, or dinner at Luchow's; the "Sealskin Brigade,"
the drooling masses called the rotund, mustachioed millionaires
who sat behind the dappled bays and grays. In 1873, a group of
Standardbred owners and breeders started the Grand Circuit, a
traveling race meet for the best stock, a kind of movable major
league. The first example of an American sport organizing itself
into a business with published schedules and standardized rules—
baseball's National League would follow shortly—the "Roarin'
Grand" became an instant hit, stopping in New York, Buffalo,
Chicago, Indianapolis, Lexington, Detroit, and other major cities
where thousands packed the stands to watch the premier Standardbreds compete for purses of $1,500 to $5,000—serious ragtime-era cash. Newspapers reflected the burgeoning public interest, providing race results, reporting on the sale of harness horses
and the birth of foals, and passing along gossip with a Standardbred slant ("Kennedy is thinking of shipping his trotter Dorothy
S., whom he named for his pretty sister-in-law, to the state fairgrounds. His wife will not accompany him on the journey"). The
Thoroughbreds got attention, too, during this period, of course—
just not half as much. "Thoroughbred racing settled individual
differences between horses," wrote the racing journalist Dwight
Akers. "It no longer measured a leveling up of the breed," the way
harness racing did.
   What made the phenomenon all the more remarkable is that
harness horses, then and now, have a lot going against them as
crowd-pleasers. For one thing, they are, generally speaking, less
comely than their more finely featured and curvaceous Thoroughbred cousins. For another thing, they are, although able to carry
their speed for long distances while going at a trot (a diagonal gait
in which the right front moves with the left rear, then vice versa)
the pace (think parallel: right front and rear move together, then
left front and rear), not as fast. Even their name—"standard" as

compared to "thorough"—seems to render them second-class citizens, unexceptional animals, though the standard in question is not a slight but refers rather to an impressive minimum speed (2:30 for the mile) that was required of the breed's charter members.

The saving virtue that more than offset these considerable faults was that the Standardbred had a practical application; he was something more than what the Thoroughbred had become—more, that is, than merely a bettor's plaything. He was—along with the incandescent lightbulb, the slot machine, the gramophone, the typewriter, and other wonders of the age—a life-changing American invention. A loose network of equinophiles in the eastern United States had set out, circa 1835, to produce the great American driving horse—and within three decades they had, to their own amazement, succeeded brilliantly, compounding the Standardbred, a completely new breed, out of equal parts Thoroughbred bloodstock, common farm nags, and dumb luck. Some of these horses trotted naturally at relatively high speed others preferred to pace, but they were in either case a perfect fit for the changing times, when a network of well-engineered roads began snaking across America and our great-great-grandfathers got more sophisticated and citified, climbing out of the saddle and into the driver's seat. The world suddenly was a world on wheels—the mid-nineteenth-century racing historian Frank Forester thought it worth noting that five out of six people he passed on the road in those days were driving, not riding. "The pleasure or spring wagon," Forester noted, "appeared in many carriage houses long before the piano supplanted the quilting frame in the parlor." And, he added, "speed, which was formerly little regarded, is now an indispensable requirement in a good horse." New types of well-sprung vehicles rolled from factories daily; Anthony Trollope, traveling through Rhode Island in 1861, commented on the "general smartness" of the carriages he observed. And what would a smart and stylish person hitch to his buggy, barouche, or coach (not to mention his cabriolet, random, berlin, victoria, surrey, herdic, hansom, rockaway, cariole, britzka, tilbury, chaise, phaeton, sluggy, gharry, coupé, curricle, trap, growler, gig, dos-à-dos, landau, limber, brougham, vis-à-vis, or whim)? Why, never some lurching galloper, as handsome as he might be. No, you wanted a smooth-going gaited horse—a Standardbred—between your shafts.

The first official Standarbreds, registered in 1879, were considered minor miracles. "The Standard-bred light-harness horse," wrote John Hervey in his classic 1947 work *The American Trotter,* "is America's great contribution to the ranks of the world's most valuable domestic animals . . . universally recognized as the only separate and distinct breed of light horses which has originated with the memories of persons now living." Ralph Waldo Emerson, the sage of Concord, was spotted frequently at the harness racing track in Cambridge, Massachusetts; Ulysses S. Grant became an early enthusiast, buying and breeding trotters and, after he went broke, watching other peoples' trotters and arguing bloodlines with his friends. The elder Oliver Wendell Holmes wrote a wildly popular poem called "The Wonderful One-Hoss Shay," an ode to the kind of vehicle a Standardbred might pull, and an equally adored companion piece titled "How the Old Horse Won the Bet" that contained this couplet celebrating one of harness racing's first star drivers:

Budd Doble, whose catarrhal name
so fills the nasal trump of fame . . .

Showing their keen sense of what the masses liked to look at—and more specifically what kinds of images they would pay between twenty-five cents and four dollars to own in lithograph form—Nathaniel Currier and his partner James Ives (their motto: "colored engravings for the people") turned out nearly seven hundred prints (10 percent of Currier & Ives's total output) with a harness-racing theme, simultaneously reflecting and fueling the Standardbred craze.

As time went on, and the breed started sorting itself out, a natural hierarchy developed: the swifter specimens tended to find their way to the racetrack while their more common relations pulled the nation's passenger vehicles, trucks, fire wagons, and ambulances. Thus on a visit to the Grand Circuit or state fair, people often saw the latest, fastest models of what they had in their home stables—and they tended to form rooting interests based on horses who might be related by blood, albeit distantly, to their own. It was, in other words, a lot like NASCAR, though the enthusiasts were much better dressed.

Even in an age rife with record-smashing champions (Star Pointer, Lou Dillon, Anaconda) and a fawning press to burnish their images, Dan Patch was without dispute the flesh-and-blood beau ideal of his beloved breed. Just look at him! Yes, he had his physical abnormalities back toward the rear, so extreme in fact that anyone might wonder how he ever became a racehorse— but his head was as pretty as any Thoroughbred's. His adventures on the racetrack were the stuff of which Victorian-era children's books were made, and he was fast enough to get the public excited about the trickle-down effect he might have on the breed, and hence American life, once he retired to stud duty. (As a stallion, Dan Patch himself figured to be prohibitively expensive for most people, but middle-class folks might, for $50 or $100, breed to one of his offspring—and get, with luck, a horse who could help them cut ten or fifteen minutes off their daily commute.) What's more, Dan Patch had exquisite timing, appearing at the precise midpoint of the Standardbred boom, just after the two-minute mile was broken (by the sorry-looking, patched-together pacer Star Pointer) and, more important, just before the automobile reached its tipping point and rendered the whole science of buggy-pulling forever moot. What he was doing on the racetrack—extending the limits of equine achievement—seemed genuinely important, not just mere sport. His fame spread to the castles of Europe, and American children (like Harry Truman) wrote him 50,000 fan letters a year. In Dan's heyday, it almost seemed as if his P. T. Barnum–ish owner was being a bit modest when he proclaimed his pacer, in posters, handbills and newspaper ads, to be "The Most Wonderful Horse in the World!"

Because there is no one alive who saw Dan Patch race, and because there is scant film footage of him in action, I realize the modern reader, even one who has spent a lifetime devoted to sports, is likely to ask herself, Really? The most wonderful horse in the world, you say? I thought that was Seabiscuit—Hollywood assured me it was so. How come I've never even heard of Dan Patch? If there are no firsthand memories, because of the passage of time, where at least are the secondhand ones? Where is the monument to this beloved crazy-good athlete? Ruth has Yankee Stadium, and a plot in Hawthorne, New York, where people still shed a tear and leave a beer bottle. Man o' War, the still-remembered Thoroughbred champion of the 1920s, is buried beneath a larger-than-life bronze of himself, in the Kentucky Horse Park. When Messenger, the great foundation sire of both the running and trotting horse breeds, died in 1808 in the Long Island hamlet of Buckram (now Locust Valley), "news of the death of the old patriarch spread with great rapidity," wrote John H. Wallace, a distinguished historian of the American horse. "Soon the whole countryside was gathered to see the last of the king of horses and to assist at his burial. His grave was prepared at the foot of a chestnut tree and there he was deposited in his holiday clothing. In response to a consciousness that a hero was there laid away forever, a military organization was extemporized and volley after volley was fired over his grave." America loves to memorialize its hero animals. Balto, the brave sled dog who carried desperately needed diphtheria serum between Nome and Anchorage in 1925, has an annual race—the Iditarod—in his honor, and a statue in Central Park, buffed to a high sheen by the *tuchuses* of tens of thousands of New York tykes. Where is the simple headstone—or the bronze statue or the towering shaft of granite—that marks the grave of the great Dan Patch?

A good question. So is this:

"Why is it that Dan Patch, the greatest horse, to my way of thinking, that harness racing has ever produced, should be forgotten to such an extent that one scarcely ever sees his name mentioned nowadays in the turf papers?" So goes a query posed by a reader of the *Horse Review*—in 1923. It is not easy today to find someone who has heard of the horse who was once a household name, who at least twice drew crowds of more than 100,000 just to watch him race against the clock—and who earned roughly $1 million a year at a time when the highest-paid baseball player, Ty Cobb of the Detroit Tigers, was making $12,000.

During the time I worked on this book I ran the name of Dan Patch by a random sampling of friends, acquaintances, work colleagues, relatives, cabdrivers, and yoga teachers. Outside of Oxford, Indiana, where the horse was born, and Savage, Minnesota, where he spent most of his life, very few knew who Dan was. People in New York City, where I live, were particularly clueless. A couple of them instantly came back at me with a line from "You've Got Trouble (Right Here in River City)," a song from Meredith Willson's *The Music Man* ("Like to see some stuck-up jockey boy sitting on Dan Patch? Make your blood boil, I should say."). But they admitted that they had no idea what the words meant; they might as well have been reciting the lyrics of "Louie, Louie." Of the handful of other New Yorkers who said they recognized the name, one person identified Dan as a pre-Ruthian baseball player, and another had him confused with the two-legged nineteenth-century bridge-jumping daredevil Sam Patch. Still another said, "Isn't Dan Patch a name for the devil?"—but he must have been thinking of Old Scratch, a fairly common synonym for Satan that occurs, for example, in Stephen Vincent Benet's short story "The Devil and Daniel Webster."

Alone among my Manhattan respondents, Bob Wallace, an old friend who has been the managing editor of *Rolling Stone* and is now an executive at ESPN, knew exactly who the horse was, and how deeply he had infiltrated the culture. "Oh, sure, the old harness-racing horse," he said. Bob, who grew up in Arizona in the 1950s and '60s, told me a story about watching dancers do the Pony (a minor offshoot of the Twist that involved a kind of prancing step; Chubby Checker had the hit single) on the weekly rock-and-roll show *Hullabaloo* when he was about ten. His parents, passing through the room at the time, pointed at the TV and laughed. "Why, that's just the ol' 'Dan Patch Two-Step,'" his father had said, citing a hit song of the early 1900s, the sheet music for which occasionally crops up on eBay. Shortly before he related this tale, Bob, it turned out, had also watched—and hated—*The Great*

Dan Patch, a black-and-white B movie that is as bad in its own twisted way as Fred Sasse's 1957 book. (You can buy the DVD on eBay most days for a buck. The book, which surfaces infrequently, usually goes for about $20.)

After a while it dawned on me that Bob was the only person I'd encountered who knew of the horse but felt neutral about him. Virtually everyone else I polled was either ignorant of Dan or passionately devoted to collecting Patchiana. Dan Patch lunch boxes, pedal cars, Irish mails (four-wheeled toy scooters powered by a hand lever), flour sacks, tobacco tins—that and all of the bric-a-brac mentioned previously and more: the members of the Dan Patch cult sucked it off eBay or out of auction houses and added it, as often as not, to their household shrines. "My living room," more than one has told me, "looks like a museum." (This declaration is usually made in the presence of a spouse or other life partner who personifies the term *long-suffering,* and who stands a bit to the side and behind the collector, smiling wanly and rolling his or her eyes.) Dan Patch aficionados operate not in the just-tell-me-what-it's-worth spirit of *Antiques Roadshow* but more like devout Irishwomen determinedly making a case—relic by relic, discarded crutch by discarded crutch—for the canonization of a beloved parish priest. They don't just accumulate, they advocate. And in this way, I realized, Dan Patch is set apart from every other champion who trod the turf. For you can say what you want about Man o' War, Seabiscuit, Citation, Native Dancer, Secretariat, Funny Cide, Smarty Jones, or even Barbaro—as gallantly as they ran, as regal as some looked draped in Kentucky Derby roses, no one would give you $50 today for a hunk of their mummified manure. Dan Patch is another matter entirely.

The physical evidence of Dan's life is scattered throughout North America in the homes of—at most—three hundred serious collectors. I have met a man who showed me a mock-bamboo walking stick worn smooth at the handle by the hand of the obscure Hoosier farmer who was Dan Patch's first trainer, and another man who owns an authentic left rear shoe (the Holy Grail of Dan Patch footwear), and a married couple who owns the barn where the horse lived from 1896, the year of his birth, until 1902.

George Augustinack, the retired Burnsville, Minnesota, printer who owns the tail that may be Dan Patch's, also has the horse's harness, a not-so-miniature scale model of the farm where Dan lived from 1902 until 1916, and photographs of virtually everyone who worked there and their significant others; he has even, for some reason, acquired, when possible, the clothing those people were wearing in those photographs. "Sometime over the last forty years," George notes unnecessarily, "I got carried away." George has moldering currycombs that may contain Dan Patch hair and dander and boxes of canceled checks from the horse's third and final owner, a Minneapolis entrepreneur named M. W. Savage—and George wants more. He wants, for example, M. W. Savage's belt buckle and false teeth. "And I think I can get them, too," he says, with a mysterious wink. As for Dan Patch dung, there is, unfortunately, none known to exist, but more than one of the faithful has shared with me his fantasy of owning some, and I've been assured by insiders that, at a well-advertised auction, a single turd with the proper provenance would go—quickly—for $800 to $1,000.

So, to pick up on a thread left dangling many paragraphs back, where is the headstone that says "The Most Wonderful Horse in the World"?

I think I know where Dan Patch is buried, approximately.

On a perfect late-summer afternoon in Scott County, Minnesota, I walked, escorted by an entourage of butterflies, past several No Trespassing signs and over railroad tracks and found a spot down by a creek, a particular bend in the stream that certain people had described to me. To check my location, I took from my pack an eight-by-ten aerial photograph of the area that I had been given by a great-grandson of a man who helped bury the horse on a steamy July day in 1916. That photo, on which a large, orange X had been drawn, had been passed along with considerable trepidation. "I hope no one is going to disturb the grave after all these years," my source, who wishes to remain anonymous, had written in an accompanying note. His concern was understandable, if only because, in the late 1980s, a Savage man who told Jens Bohn the exact location of the horse's remains had died suddenly a few days later. Since then, some people in Savage have theorized about a Dan Patch curse.

It struck me, as I stood there in three-foot-high grass, that I was not sure what I was doing. Why did it feel so necessary to seek out this place? The setting, to be sure, was paradisaical, and it's always fun to trespass, especially in middle age, but what did I expect to find? I knew that the horse's grave was unmarked, and an unmarked grave that is not set between two marked ones looks, ninety years later, like . . . nothing at all, really. So what was there to see? Even if I were a grave robber looking for bones to peddle to the Dan Patch cult, it seemed impossible that anything would be left in the muddy earth along this winding stream. For, you see, the great horse had been hurriedly stuck in a shallow, wet hole—I looked again at the photograph, then over toward an old cottonwood tree, then down at my boots; yes, this could be the spot—without even a simple pine box.

CHAPTER TWO

Horses sometimes run for cups, but not half so often as men do.

—*Oxfordite,* January 10, 1863

THE WAXING OF THE teats, the softening of the vaginal opening—to Dr. Frank Scott, the veterinarian on duty at Kelley's Livery Stable in Oxford, Indiana, on the evening of April 28, 1896, that could mean only one thing: it was time to ask his faithful assistant John Kelley, the son of the stable owner, to go to his brother Michael Kelley's tavern, just across the alleyway and down past the Opera House, for a quart of Hunter rye whiskey.

"Here's a dollar," Dr. Scott said, glumly, as he stared at the very pregnant mare, whose name was Zelica. "I believe it's going to be a long night."

But it was a long night only for poor Zelica. Scott and Kelley were both passed out drunk within a couple of hours, thus missing the birth of the mare's deep brown and exceptionally large son, who would become known to the world as Dan Patch, early on the balmy morning of Wednesday, April 29.

This, of course, had not exactly been the plan going in.

Daniel Messner Jr., the thirty-five-year-old son in Messner and Son, the town's principal dry-goods store, had brought his mare to Kelley's Livery because he wanted her to have the best possible care—to have someone knowledgeable standing by to clean and disinfect the stall, to snip and tie off the umbilical cord, and to watch for possible complications when Zelica gave birth, at the age of seven, to her first foal. He didn't absolutely need the livery stable's services. Messner owned a perfectly fine barn with a spacious foaling stall and good light and ventilation on South Michigan Street, about a half mile from Kelley's stable; it had been Zelica's home for the last three years, and she could have stayed there and delivered in familiar surroundings. Yet Messner was not a horseman by any stretch of the term; with his custom-made clothes, uncallused hands, and fastidious ways, he was more like the traveling businessmen who arrived by train from Indianapolis or Chicago and stayed a few nights at Oxford's Ohio House hotel—more like them than the field-tanned locals who shopped at Messner and Son for work boots, bridal gowns, husking gloves, yards of gingham, and swatches of lace. He realized he had no experience delivering horse babies, or whatever they were called, and because he had lately become the butt of jokes around town for his animal-husbandry skills, he wanted to minimize the possibility of even the slightest mishap. The livery stable was marginally closer to the veterinarian's house than his own barn, and it had a reputation for fair dealing and dependability (Kelley's rental horses, it was said, would always bring a traveling salesman back to the center of town if he got lost or drunk or dozed off at the reins). Putting his mare there had looked, from every angle, like the most prudent plan.

But now pretty much everything had gone wrong. Not only were his handpicked caregivers unconscious at the critical moment, but as the cock crowed Zelica's colt was floundering in his own birth mess, too crippled in his left rear leg to stand up and take that first nourishing draft of mother's milk, called colostrum, so necessary to a newborn because it contains vital antibodies.

It was, in fact, the colt's frantic life-and-death thrashing that finally woke Scott and Kelley. The dynamic duo, to their credit, instantly realized what was wrong and moved in on the colt, joining their hands around his still-wet body and hefting him up as best they could to his mother's teat. "He had trouble sucking," Kelley would recall fifty-three years later, when he was interviewed by a reporter from the *Fort Wayne* (Ind.) *Journal-Gazette* as part of the hype for the movie *The Great Dan Patch*. "But when he started he never stopped."

The men, sweating and panting, were still holding the colt up to nurse when Dan Messner appeared in the doorway. Messner could be a stern boss; though he had a pleasant counter-side manner with customers, and was liberal about extending credit to local farmers, he could, as one former employee told me, remembering a tense encounter more than sixty years earlier, "look at you when he was displeased in a way that you didn't soon forget." When Scott and Kelley saw Messner's expression, they smiled sheepishly and both let go at once, allowing Dan Patch to fall back onto the foul straw. The colt, his bad leg askew beneath him, looked up innocently through large brown eyes. "He was," Kelley remembered at age seventy-three, "as gentle as a big dog."

But he was also seemingly doomed, like any horse who could not stand up to take nourishment. "Do you want me to get a hammer?" Kelley asked.

It was a loaded question, a euphemism for euthanasia—though that was precisely how people might put an animal out of its misery in that time and place: by bashing in its skull. They genuinely loved horses, those old Hoosiers, but often with a tough love that came from watching so many horses get born, work hard, and die. In this case, a bullet might have done the job more neatly and humanely, but they were too close to the center of town for guns.

History has left us with conflicting accounts of exactly what happened at Kelley's Livery that morning, but it appears that Messner considered, but never responded to, the suggestion of blunt force trauma. Certainly he wasn't going to splatter any brains on his fancy made–in–St. Louis shoes, but there was so much more going on than that. He later would say, for public consumption, that the struggling horse had looked into his eyes in a way that made it impossible to put him down. John Wattles, a sixty-eight-year-old farmer and part-time horse trainer who arrived on the scene shortly after Messner, would say, in his version of the tale, that he was impressed by the exceptionally wide space between the animal's eyes, and strongly urged Messner to put all thoughts of the hammer aside. To an old-school horseman like Wattles, a wide eye span indicated a large brain pan and thus high intelligence. Wattles believed that if the colt in the straw was half as smart as his eye spacing indicated, he would find a way to stand up and survive. But when Wattles spoke up that morning to spare the horse's life, he made a point (he later told his son Ray) of emphasizing brawn over brains, knowing that what Messner wanted most was a fine physical specimen—a sleek, impressive-looking stallion who could pull the family buggy around town with a bit of panache, and silence the skeptics who had been criticizing the storekeeper's horse sense. He had no interest in something ugly and ill made, no matter how smart it might be.

An untitled and unpublished account of Dan Patch's early days, written by Ray Wattles many years later, records the scene in considerable detail.

"Congratulations!" Wattles said. "You've got yourself a horse colt!"

"But look at him, John," the storekeeper replied. "He's all crooked."

"Sure, he's crooked," Ray's father said, stroking the long white beard that marked him as a member of Oxford's pioneer set. "You'd be crooked, too, if you'd been rolled up in a ball these past several months. Just give him time to get the kinks out of his legs!"

Messner shot Wattles one of his withering stares. Even a man who wore cuff links to work could see this was more than a matter of getting kinks out.

"Oh, I'll admit he's scraggly looking, with those rough hocks and rounded curb joints," Wattles allowed. "But there's nothing wrong with him that he won't outgrow. And no matter what he looks like, Dan, he's got the frame. That's what counts. You can dye him another color if you don't like the one he's got, but you can't grow a chest and shoulders like those."

Just then the sound of hoofbeats made everyone turn toward the open door. A farmer named Beecher Gwin was driving his two-horse team down Howard Street. "Beecher!" Messner called. "Got time to help us a minute?"

In her charming and valuable book *Two Dans . . . And One Was a Pacer,* self-published in 1984 and based in part on interviews with aging eyewitnesses, Oxford native Mary Cross writes that Gwin said, "Whoa," to his team and "carefully tied the lines to the whip on the dashboard and alit from the wagon. He followed Mr. Messner into one of the stalls. There, he saw in the flickering light a newly born bay colt lying in the bedding on the floor." With some help from the others, Gwin and Messner propped the colt up so he could resume nursing.

The sweet smell of disaster had by then drawn a small crowd to Kelley's 120-by-120-foot barn. "After one glance," Cross writes, the onlookers "began to tell Mr. Messner and Mr. Kelley how dreadful and unattractive [Dan Patch] appeared to them." Jasper McConnell, a lawyer and the town judge, pulled Messner aside and said, "I don't think that colt will ever make a horse." The consensus was clear: it was not too late to reconsider the hammer.

Surely, it would have thrilled the gossips to watch Messner or some eager volunteer lay waste to what almost everyone saw as the latest in a series of shockingly expensive horse blunders; Messner probably could have sold tickets to the execution and recouped some of his losses. But what the storekeeper did next actually pleased the onlookers even more: he boldly stepped over his malformed colt and strode to the corner of the stall, where Zelica stood staring out a little cobwebby window and shivering with exhaustion. Messner gently rubbed the mare's nose and, speaking loudly enough for all present to hear, said, "Well done, old girl!"

The spectators looked back at the horse splayed in the straw. *Well done?*

How shocking—and scrumptious—to watch Dan Messner, the faux city slicker who profited from their need for coats and boots and underwear, the smiling storekeep to whom so many were in debt, dig himself in ever deeper. For when you're stuck in the Indiana flatness, eking out an existence from a 100-acre patch, aided but even more encumbered by eight or nine sniveling children, with only whiskey and religion and quilting bees and potluck suppers to ease the agony, it is comforting to know the fates are screwing someone else royally, too.

Later, when schadenfreude had morphed into braggadocio, a kind of Christ myth grew up around the birth of Dan Patch. Perhaps because the horse took himself to such heights, people felt compelled to balance his tale by adding flamboyantly humble origins. But how do you put a false bottom on what is already the story of a stable-born king? The answer: You say he was born on a manure pile. That pungent lie had wide currency for several decades and found its way into sober historical texts like *Tales of a Prairie Town*, an otherwise authoritative history of Oxford and its environs written in the early 1930s.

Around Oxford you can still hear a sanitized version of the myth, as I did late one March afternoon in the brightly lit taproom of the no-frills Oak Grove Country Club, on the east end of town.

"The word in these parts," a man named Coonie Morris told me when he heard I was interested in Dan Patch, "is that the old horse was born in a coal bin."

"That's odd," I said. "Was there coal in the bin at the time?"

Coonie drained his beer can. "No, sir," he said. "It was an empty coal bin, about twenty feet by ten feet, about from here to the wall. They just led the mare right in there and she eventually gave birth."

"Really? But why would someone do that?"

Coonie paused, annoyed, I'm pretty sure, by my question. "Don't know," he finally said. "But that's what people around Oxford have always maintained."

From behind the bar a man spoke up: " . . . And I believe that coal bin was there until the 1950s."

The speaker was John Messner, the grandson of Dan Jr., who brought Coonie another beer and sat down at our card table. John is the golf pro at the country club, a handsome and personable man in his early fifties, an ex-high-school athlete grown a bit beefy who moves with a vaguely sorrowful air. Like his grandfather, he is not a horseman and doesn't pretend to be. About his only con-

nection to horses, if you can call it that, is that fifteen years or
so ago he and a bunch of Oxford buddies occasionally made the
four-hour round-trip drive to Balmoral, a nighttime harness-racing track in Chicago; he would pay his way in, sit anonymously
in the grandstand, drink beer, and bet on horses Dan Patch could
have beaten while dragging a bank safe. John noted that he'd been
hearing the stories about the manure pile and the coal bin all his
life, but had no idea how they got started or if they contained a
germ of truth. He was not, he hastened to say, a Dan Patch expert;
he had never read the Fred Sasse book or seen the movie, though
he'd heard the latter was awful.

I was glad to meet John. I had by this time been wondering for
a while how the horse was regarded within the Messner family. Dan
had brought them a certain measure of fame, but relatively little
fortune. If you know the Dan Patch story, it's hard to avoid the conclusion that John's grandfather cashed out too soon, and—maybe—
spent the rest of his life feeling a bit foolish about his timidity.

"Dan Patch just never was a subject of much discussion around
my house when I was growing up," John said, opening his own
can of beer. "I never really talked to my father about the horse,
and I don't think he talked to his father much about him. We
didn't have any pictures or trophies or memorabilia or anything
like that around the house—maybe just a horseshoe above the
refrigerator. It's not like it was taboo, like anyone in my family felt
bad about the way things turned out—it just wasn't a topic."

He shrugged, and took a hit of beer.

Of course, the horse wasn't a topic in many American house-
holds after about 1920, when "Dan Patch" was just a name fading
from the tub of a washing machine or the slats of a sled. The difference is, the subject of which the Messners did not speak wasn't
just a trivia answer; it was, rather, something—an opportunity? a
miracle?—that a fellow Messner had once held in his hands, then
let slip through his fingers.

Symbolizing the family's lack of interest, the Dan Patch barn—
where Zelica no doubt should have given birth, and where Dan
spent the first years of his life—stood boarded up and largely
ignored for most of the twentieth century. John Messner's father,

Dick, who was born in 1912 and who lived his entire life in Oxford, working in the family store, died in 1992 without ever having gone inside. John, whose house sits about seventy-five feet from the barn's back door, has kept up the exterior of the ancient structure, doing minor repairs and having the horse's name repainted on the roof every five years or so in large white letters. When people driving through town get out to have a closer look—which can happen half a dozen times on a fine summer's day—they may find John puttering around, and he may wind up talking to them and answering some of their questions as best he can. But he, too, had never entered the barn until recently.

Down in the Kentucky bluegrass country, the horsey folks like to say—as they sit on their verandas sipping Jim Beam, plucking the crease in their madras slacks, and flicking imaginary lint off their Lilly Pulitzers—that to get a champion you breed the best to the best and hope for the best. Compared to other systems that humans attempt to impose on the breeding and betting of horses, that one is unusual in that it occasionally works. What more can you do, after all, but breed the best to the best? But that is not the way Dan Patch came about.

His story starts with a bad case of indigestion.

At the age of thirty-three, Dan Messner Jr. started suffering from stomach problems, nagging headaches, and insomnia (even though one local history guarantees that a day of honest labor in bucolic Benton County invariably results in "refreshing slumber"). It was 1893, the year aspirin was invented and Charles and Frank Duryea built the first American gas-powered motorcar. Although Messner was working hard in the store from eight in the morning to at least nine or ten at night, six days a week, refreshing slumber eluded him; his symptoms persisted and worsened, and he eventually went to see one of the town's half-dozen doctors.

Messner appears to have had a classic case of what neurologists were then calling "American Nervousness." The malady affected tens of thousands, at the very least, as the population of the United States began shifting from rural areas to cities in the mid-1870s, and the pace of life palpably quickened. Trains, telephones, telegraphs, typewriters, electric lights, and all sorts of steam-driven, soot-belching machines suddenly allowed people to accomplish more than ever before—but, alas, never as much as their hearts desired. This new and persistent yearning for more time to make more money to acquire more things had a harmful effect on the national health. Writing of the period in his landmark 2005 biography *Mark Twain: A Life,* Ron Powers notes that "with hyper-mechanization, hyper-capitalism and hyper-urbanization came hyper-anxieties." The archetypical businessman of the Gilded Age, the celluloid-collared go-getter, kept piling on the stress and popping (mostly useless) patent medicine pills like Dr. Kilmer's Swamp Root and Kickapoo Indian Sagwa (and Cascaret's Candy Cathartic) to address previously unknown ailments of the liver, heart, lungs, kidneys, skin, blood, and bowels. Carefully worded ads for (bogus) erectile-dysfunction remedies proliferated in the sports pages and rates of alcoholism, divorce, and suicide shot upward. Naturally, the "increased mental activity of women" was said to be partly to blame for the mess, though women were thought to be at risk from similar "neurasthenic" illnesses. Some saw all this as a sign of God's displeasure with a world suddenly crowded with kinescope machines and dance halls and aswirl with rumors of radio. But the burned-out look that came with American Nervousness soon became a badge of honor; just as a portly stomach had signaled success in the previous decade, when Chester A. Arthur represented the masculine ideal, to have a pale, clammy pallor, a Martinez cocktail in one hand and a Sweet Caporal cigarette dangling from the other, meant you were a Twentieth Century Man, succeeding not with your muscles but with whatever the Second Industrial Revolution, and all of the accompanying fin de siècle folderol, had spared of your poor, frazzled mind.

Dan Messner's anxieties centered, of course, on the big store that sat on the corner of Justus and McConnell streets, bulging with merchandise. The business had blossomed since Daniel Sr. had moved the family five miles north over rough roads from the tiny hamlet of Pine Village to Oxford, the jewel of—and the only town in—Benton County in 1877. Messner and Son occupied two floors in the largest building on the town square, with men's clothing down the right aisle, ladies' down the left, and footwear for both sexes arrayed along the rear (the "cloak" department consumed the entire upstairs). On a good Saturday the store would do $1,000 in sales, a tidy sum in those days. But it was never easy selling to farmers, who were frugal by nature, clever at clothing repair, and at the mercy of volatile crop and livestock prices.

Certain new trends were also worrisome to Messner. One was the growing number of freelance peddlers who poured off the railroad and fanned out over the countryside, selling the same articles Messner stocked but in the convenience of farmers' living rooms, and often for cheaper prices. Messner also faced competition from the catalog companies: Sears Roebuck, Montgomery Ward, and a fast-rising Minneapolis outfit run by a certain M. W. Savage. But Messner's biggest, if perhaps not his most immediate, concern was the nationwide migration from farm to city, a shift that was bound to erode his base of potential customers. People weren't packing up their butter churns and pedal-driven sewing machines and abandoning Oxford en masse quite yet. But the restlessness of the younger generation was palpable. He and the other astute merchants of Oxford could feel the change a-coming, and the prospect withered their spirits.

Messner didn't just fret, though; he addressed his business problems the modern way—with advertising. His frequent ads in the *Oxford Tribune* stressed low prices, especially when farmers couldn't get much for their hogs and corn, and he had a big annual sale (a very twentieth-century merchandising concept) each fall. But in tough times and flush, he shaped his copy to create a sense of excitement, seeming to understand that Americans were developing a craving for entertainment, and that shopping could be not just a means but an end in itself, as stimulating and diverting, in its own way, as vaudeville, the legitimate theater, or the suddenly booming spectator sports (thousands would now turn out for a "base-ball" game between the Oxford Eurekas and the Plow Boys of Union Township). Sometimes Messner stressed the thrill of shopping to the point of overlooking the merchandise he sold. "Follow the crowds and come to our store!" urged a typical full-page Messner and Son advertisement on the back of the daily *Tribune*. "Come to the fountain head where fashion's latest is placed before the people and see the masses standing on line to get waited on! Hotshot bargains! Drive up in your buggies! Bring in your wagons and we will load them to the brim with over 49,000 items on sale!"

Other times he was more succinct: "Fine silk handkerchiefs are just the cookie for your beau."

He had an instinct for that new thing called publicity, too. When a prairie chicken wandered into town one afternoon and stared in his store window for a while before dashing off to the west, Messner let the *Tribune* know about it, and used his leverage as an advertiser to make sure such worthy news made it into print. The chicken may have been drawn by one of the fascinating items Messner displayed behind the plate glass, the better to lure the curious into his orbit— a pair of slippers, fashioned from sea-lion fur and trimmed with caribou hide, that a local man had bought in Dawson City, Alaska, during the Klondike gold rush; a globe five inches in diameter made from 500 pieces of wood; photographs of the International Correspondence School of Scranton, Pennsylvania, in all its glory; a 120-year-old hat. Once Messner cosponsored a contest with the Wooltex coat company: At 2:00 p.m. over a stretch of Saturdays, grade-school girls would stand on a box in Messner's cloak department and recite a six-to-eight-line poem about Mary's little lamb that worked in a plug for Wooltex. The winner of the first prize, a $10 cloak, was Miss Mable Confer, who wrote: "I live in Oxford, proud to say / where Wooltex coats are sold / I'm just as good as Mary's lamb / Although not quite as old." Mabel went on to become a stenographer, and never married.

A more action-packed event took place on Messner's state-of-the-art concrete sidewalk, with the help of Sweet-Orr. The well-known clothing maker offered free work pants to any two men who, by taking hold of a leg each, could rip the trousers apart at the seams. The *Tribune* reported that a large crowd gathered to watch and cheer as three teams of farmers tried in vain to murder a pair of overalls.

More than a place of business, Messner and Son had become, by the early 1890s, a locus of the community. The town philosophers sat on two benches just inside the front door discussing politics, sports, local scandals like the Ada Atkinson murder (the fifteen-year-old Oxford girl was hacked to death in her home by an unknown intruder), and the controversial 1893 U.S. Supreme Court decision declaring the tomato a vegetable. Professors from Purdue dropped by when taking agricultural students on tours of the Benton County cornfields. Once a week, after closing time, the Women's Christian Temperance Union held meetings in the back, amongst the high-button shoes; as Messner said good-bye and headed off to the tavern of an evening, he would remind the good ladies to lock the door behind them on the way out.

It was, in truth, a very prosperous and well-run place—a Benton County institution. Messner, father and son, "stand equally high in the social and business circles of the county," an Indiana business journal wrote at the time, owing to their "very handsome, tasty, and attractive-appearing store."

Still, Dan Jr. always could find something to get his stomach roiling: excess inventory, slow cash flow, mice, thieves. Second-story men came through the upstairs window one night and made off with $19.05 from the cash box, a black-and-white-striped blanket, and a handsome beaver shawl. ("Even sneak thieves know where to get the best," Messner's *Tribune* ad said a few days afterward.) On another occasion several Ku Klux Klansmen paid Messner a visit, appearing, unhooded, at his office door to ask him to help them stop a Catholic church from coming to Oxford (he let them have their say, paused, then told them to go away, quickly; he needed all the customers he could get). One morning two of the storefront philosophers got into a heated debate over the merits of newly elected president Grover Cleveland, and Messner said, "Take it outside, boys"; they did, but presently John P. Ross pushed James H. Bell through Messner's plate glass window. Although a judge eventually ordered Ross to pay Messner $9.00 in compensation, unscheduled expenses were always worrisome to the storekeeper, who insisted, correctly, that he was hardly as well-to-do as some people around town assumed.

Messner in those days lived in a modest wood-frame house next door to the Presbyterian parsonage, and though he owned a barn for some reason, he had no horse. His was a middle-class striver's life: he had amassed two small parcels of farmland not far from town and, in 1892, had married well; the former Maud Dodson was a local girl who had graduated from Luray's Female Institute, in Luray, Virginia. But, being something of a proto-yuppie, he lived a bit higher on the hog than the average Oxfordite, spending about as much as he made—on vacation trips to Atlantic City, on custom-made clothing, on swings up to Indianapolis to see the new opera *La Bohème,* and on entertaining business colleagues and civic leaders. He had, in other words, a big churn and a very thin cushion.

Hence the headaches, the neuritis, the neuralgia. The doctor listened to Messner explain what was keeping him awake nights, then said, "Dan, I really think you need to go on drives with a horse."

Messner reacted like a fat man who has been told to take up exercise. He said he didn't have time, didn't know how to get started, and had no natural affinity for that kind of thing. "But I walk to the store for exercise and fresh air, and walking is supposed to be the best exercise," he told the doctor, adding, "I have no driving horse."

"Get one," said the doctor. "Right now you are ruining your health."

It is curious that at a time when horses were everywhere—pulling plows, taking taxis full of debutantes to the Plaza, dropping dead on street corners, providing the background noise of daily life in the form of clip-clops, whip cracks, whinnies, and neighs—they were also seen as a tonic and a relief from the norm. But thus it was, and perhaps always had been. "There is nothing so good for the inside of a man," says an English proverb, "as the outside of a horse." Magazines like the *Horse Review* and the *American Horse Breeder*—vibrant, jam-packed weeklies that were something like a cross between *Sports Illustrated* and *Time*—sang the physical and mental benefits of "the management of a fine horse." Speaking of "doctors, dentists, lawyers, merchants and manufacturers," the *Horse Review* said, a bit ungrammatically, that "as health insurance, these men will tell you that jogging, training and racing a horse has golf hopelessly distanced and that it is no more expensive [an abject lie]. If you are underweight and run down, a few months' jogging and a few spring work-outs will add many pounds. If you are overweight, and your equator is out of bounds, the same treatment will put you in condition fully as fast as your horse shows improvement." Such titans of the turf as California governor Leland Stanford, *New York Herald* publisher Robert Bonner, and lumber heir George Ketcham had all been first turned toward horses by their concerned physicians, just as Messner was now.

"My prescription," the doctor told Messner, "is to get out in the fresh air with a horse, and you will soon feel fine."

Taking his hat down from the hook, Messner left the office saying he would think about it.

The Ray Wattles manuscript—which is the gnostic gospel of the Dan Patch canon, a newly surfaced document that doesn't jibe with the received wisdom at certain key points—contains no mention of Dan Messner's doctor's appointment. And that is not surprising. Wattles's is a most midwestern brand of narrative; it is above all else upbeat—and polite: neurosis, conflict, and anything that could possibly be construed as unpleasant or reflecting badly on anyone or anything is absent from its fifty typewritten pages. So instead of a trip to the doctor's, Ray Wattles begins with an account of Messner, old Uncle Johnny Wattles ("uncle" being a term of endearment in nineteenth-century Indiana), and four other unnamed men driving eighteen miles along the hot, dusty road from Oxford to the Remington fair "on that fateful morning in September of 1893." Messner, who is described as a "tall, broad and fine-looking man in a linen duster and flat straw hat," suddenly sees "a half-grown colt, playing along in a pasture" and watches with glee as the little black horse "kicks up his heels and breaks into a queer bouncing run." Ray Wattles writes that "Father could tell that the colt had made an impression on Dan. He knew that the big man ached to get out and fondle the velvety muzzle that the colt thrust over the fence."

A page or so after this thrusting, aching, fondling, and velvet we read, perhaps not surprisingly, that "Dan turned to Father
with an odd light in his eyes.

" 'John, I'd like to own a horse some day,'" he says—but then
Messner quickly adds that he can't, of course, because "horses
and dry-goods stores don't mix."

In response to that well-worn truism, old Wattles snorts,
shakes his head disgustedly, and says, "You and your store! Give
me a slick piece of horse-flesh like my Oxford Girl [a filly Wattles
owned] and you can keep your store. A store can't whinny every
time it sees you. It can't stick its nose in your pocket and hunt for
apples. You can't feel the surge of its muscles as it makes a break
for the lead in a race!"

From a shopper's point of view, that may be a good thing.

At least the Wattles version eventually gets Messner to the
sunbaked Remington fairgrounds, where there are "tented con-
cessions, rides of all sorts along the midway, hastily constructed
pens holding hogs, sheep and cattle of all breeds." Messner and
John Wattles did in fact go to Remington on the last day of
the fair and, toting a picnic basket packed by their wives (and
probably augmented with a couple of flasks they had slipped
in themselves), wandered into a tent where, as was traditional
on closing day, horses and other livestock were being sold off
at auction.

Messner sat down on a bench as the horses of Dr. David Henry
Patton began entering the sales ring—a sad parade that signaled
the complete dispersal of Patton's nearby Rensellaer Stock Farm.
A fifty-six-year-old physician who had just finished a term in Congress, Patton may have been hurt by the Panic of 1893, the worst
financial crisis to hit America up to that point. A run on gold in the
last days of the Benjamin Harrison administration, combined with
the failure of the Philadelphia and Reading Railroad and the bank-
ruptcy of the National Cordage Company (the most actively traded
stock on the New York Stock Exchange), had caused widespread
bank and business failures. Patton was selling everything, including
his land, and moving to the Indian Territory, which would later
become Oklahoma. Or at least he was trying to turn his horses into

ready cash. The bidding that afternoon was painfully slow, with some decent animals being gaveled down for $35 or $50.

Then Zelica, a two-year-old filly Patton had bred himself, limped into the sales ring, and the auctioneer said that he had an announcement to make before bidding began: Henry Y. Haws of Johnstown, Pennsylvania, had telegraphed in a starting bid of $250. Did anyone care to offer $255?

Those who were paying attention were shocked.

Haws was a connoisseur of prime horseflesh, a manufacturer of what he called "fine bricks" and cement who had survived the famous flood that ravaged his hometown in 1889, and branched out to become a small-scale coal magnate and the president of the Johnstown National Bank. He would later, for a brief interval, own the famous "Iron Horse" Joe Patchen, a charismatic—and breathtakingly beautiful—jet-black pacer who started 100 times in his career, won 52 races, and was described by the *American Horse Breeder* as "the most magnificent horse we have ever seen in harness." Named for an obscure character in Irish poet Thomas Moore's 1817 epic *Lalla Rookh: An Oriental Romance,* Zelica, by contrast, was among the most nondescript animals anyone could ever expect to see—not bad looking, exactly, but very light in the bone, as horsemen say, especially below the knee. Given the level that Haws usually operated on, his interest in Zelica—to the point where he was offering more than $100 above the average sale price that day in hopes of preempting the bidding—was nothing if not mysterious.

It remains so to this day.

Did he see her as a racing prospect? How could he?

Although she was bred to be a trotter, and a good one of those could compete for purses of several thousand dollars, even in those financially depressed times, Zelica was not going to be tearing up any racetracks; that much had already been decided. In the first start of her life, earlier that year, the filly, racing as a pacer, a gait she presumably preferred, had injured a front ankle, finishing far up the track, last by at least a quarter mile. The damage to her leg had turned out to be permanent, and the hitch in her step—easily observable as she walked back and forth before the

fairgrounds auctioneer—left the observers at Remington to wonder if she could even make a decent carriage horse.

That left the breeding shed as an option for Zelica in Haws's
plan.

For that theory to make sense, she would of course need
bloodlines that promised speed and mixed well with the fashionable sires of the day. But the best that could be said about Zelica's
pedigree was that it was obscure.

Her great-grandfather on her mother's side, Abdallah, had
been killed in Kentucky during one of the many Civil War raids
in which Union and Confederate soldiers stole horses back and
forth from each other. Her father, Wilkesberry, the grandson of a
famously mean stallion named George Wilkes, had died in a rain-
swollen Indiana creek, dragged under by a wagon that could not
be unhitched fast enough to save the young, still-unproven stud.
Zelica's maternal grandmother, meanwhile, was a rough-looking
Morgan farm mare that folks called Fanny.

The audience in the Remington sales tent that day wasn't
aware of this backstory—all they knew was that she was already
lame, that she had the flawed conformation of a filly who was
likely to go lamer still, and that she was from a sire and dam that
no one except the failed horse breeder Dr. Patton had ever heard
of. Meanwhile, some rich guy from out of town was offering the
highest price of the day for her.

While they were puzzling over that, something even stranger happened: Zelica was quickly gaveled down—to Messner—for $255.

What in the world did he see in her?

The truth is, nothing. A neophyte at horse auctions, Messner had no intention of buying the mare. He was not even paying attention to the sale when he waved, at a most inopportune
moment, to an acquaintance he saw entering the tent. But the auctioneer was all too pleased to take his gesture for a bid. The gavel
fell, and the filly was now Messner's.

"Sold! To the man in the linen duster!"

The sales tent fell silent for a moment, then started to buzz.
Messner could have protested and explained to the auctioneer what
had happened, but he was too embarrassed. Instead he stifled his

horror and feigned pride. With the eyes of the assembled weighing heavily upon him, he signed the sales slip, signifying that he had bought the mare, with a flourish and a frozen smile.

"My doctor's been keen on me to get a horse," he muttered to no one in particular.

"Come pretty high, didn't she, Dan?" a man who knew Messner asked with a wink. "What's she supposed to be, some kind of champion?"

"No, I don't think so," Messner said. "I just happened to want her. If I got skinned, it isn't the first time that's happened."

While Zelica waited in a holding stall, a stunned Messner sat in a shady spot with Wattles and their four friends and lunched on fried chicken and angel food cake. Then the group walked over to the track to see the trotting and pacing races. At some point Wattles noticed that Messner had disappeared.

They found him about an hour later back in Zelica's stall. "He had borrowed a brush from the attendant," John Wattles told his son, "and he brushed his prize until every hair was in place." Messner was standing in the stall, fanning himself with his straw hat and admiring his handiwork, when the others walked in.

Johnny Wattles could only shake his head and smile.

Then the old horseman hitched Messner's filly to the back of his wagon, and Zelica limped the eighteen miles back to Oxford. Years later John Wattles recalled that on the return journey Messner kept swiveling his head around and asking him over and over if he thought he had bought a decent-looking animal (Wattles, a good friend, kept saying he did, indeed, think so) and if she was okay back there by herself ("Believe so, Daniel").

But word of mouth was one of the many things that traveled faster than Zelica. By the time she arrived in her new home, people around town were already tsk-tsking, shaking their heads and saying, "Two hundred and fifty-five dollars?" Later, after Messner had bought Zelica an expensive buggy with red wheels and fancy rubber tires, and a harness that glistened with ornaments of German silver, the locals started calling the mare "Messner's folly," unaware, of course, that the quintessential nineteenth-century slur—remember Fulton's Folly (the steamboat) and Clinton's

Folly (the Erie Canal) and Seward's Folly (Alaska)?—had a way of coming back to bite the people who used it.

Messner's way of dealing with the whispers was to dig in his heels. He felt he could never stop acting proud, treating Zelica like a princess, smiling broadly and bravely.

"I was in Oxford on the day that Dan first drove Zelica," Ray Wattles wrote in his manuscript. "Down the street from the livery barn he came, his big face beaming proudly. Zelica shone from a recent brushing. The harness gleamed like burnished metal. The buggy had been freshly polished until it sparkled in the morning sun. Zelica stepped daintily. Her fine head was held high, as if she were conscious of her grace and beauty."

Ever the polite narrator, he declines to mention her limp.

CHAPTER THREE

What avail your pedigrees? What boots it, Ponticus, to be valued for one's ancient blood? . . . Tell me, thou scion of the Trojans, who deems a dumb animal well-born unless it be strong? It is for this that we commend the swift horse whose speed sets every hand aglow, and fills the Circus with the hoarse shout of victory. . . . The slow of foot, fit only to turn a miller's wheel, pass for a mere nothing from one owner to another and gall their necks against the collar.

—Juvenal

THE HARD NUGGET OF history is this: in May of 1895, Dan Messner Jr. took Zelica to be bred to the stallion Joe Patchen.

The question is, why?

Why would a stressed-out storekeeper who had been reluctant to acquire even one horse decide, about twenty months later, to try for two? And why, to get this superfluous hayburner, this added responsibility, would he cross a nationally renowned Grand Circuit champ with his gimpy, ill-bred mare, an animal barely suitable for routine domestic duty?

This is no exaggeration. Joe Patchen was frighteningly fast (he had paced a mile in 2:01 ¼), admirably consistent (the "Iron Horse"), darkly handsome, and already, at three years of age and with only one season of racing on his résumé, a notable presence on the American harness turf. Within a few years, the jet-black stallion, utterly forgotten today, would be a household name to rival John Philip Sousa and Gentleman Jim Corbett. "There comes Joe!" was the signature greeting that the crowd would roar when he stepped onto the track. If Dan Patch was the Messiah, Joe Patchen (who inspired his own minor hit songs, the "Joe Patchen Two-Step" and the "Joe Patchen March") was John the Baptist, testing out the highway along which the first American superstar would tread. Meanwhile, no one was writing odes to Zelica. Very few knew she existed, and, despite the fancy way Messner had fitted her out, the sight of her galumphing around Oxford tended to make people snicker, not break into song.

The popular biographical material on Dan Patch is of no help in figuring out why Messner would make such a bizarre match-up. In hundreds of newspaper stories written about the horse over the years, in books and in yellowing articles from *Reader's Digest,* the *Saturday Evening Post, Esquire,* and such, you will find no discussion of how the great horse came to be bred. Writers simply report the pairing without comment, as if it made sense. It doesn't. Comment is required. Let us start with the price.

Joe Patchen's stud fee was $150. That is not as much as it might have been if he were already a full-time stallion with a long list of accomplishments as a racehorse and sire. In 1895 Joe was merely a budding superstar taking a spring break, as it were, and getting his toe (let us say) wet before returning to the racetrack for what the sportswriters, then as now, liked to call "a sophomore campaign." Still, $150 was serious money for a breeding service in those days, probably among the ten highest such fees in the nation, and about three times as much as poor Zelica, and everything in her tack trunk, was worth.

But apart from the matter of why Messner would spend so much, there was the question of why anyone would breed a mare to Joe Patchen in the first place. For as admirable as he was as a racehorse, there was an unsightly—and obvious—flaw in his pedigree: a streak of meanness bordering on murderousness that came down from his grandsire, the famously hot-tempered trotter George Wilkes. Even for a stallion, George Wilkes (who was named after the editor of the popular sporting journal *Spirit of the Times*) was one nasty son of a bitch, perhaps because, after his mother died giving birth, he was raised on a diet of cow's milk laced with sugar and Jamaica rum. And mixing his blood did not temper the trait, but only seemed to activate it; many of his off-spring, astonishingly, proved even more violent. One of George Wilkes's sons, Patchen Wilkes, was, according to the writer John Hervey, a "regally handsome horse, quite a 'picture horse,'" but "the most savage [member] of the entire Wilkes family [to date]. Along in his 'last phase' he used to be kept literally in chains and nobody thought of entering his stall without a pitchfork or some-thing like that to keep him at bay. It was said that he had almost killed more than one man."

Why would anyone breed to this monster? I don't know, but someone did—and got a shrieking, wild-eyed filly they named Patchen Maid. Known as "the driving elk," for her habit of career-ing from inner to outer rail during races, scattering entire fields in the process, she was eventually banned from most tracks. "Her antics at the post and on other patches of the racetrack," Hervey wrote, "used to give sensitive female spectators hysterics, and caused the actuaries to mark down the age-limit of trotting horse drivers." Patchen Maid was one of only two offspring of Patchen Wilkes to achieve any sort of notoriety. The other was Joe Patchen.

As a colt growing up on a farm in Peabody, Kansas, Joe Patchen was curious, mischievous, and not at all mean. A stable hand named Henry L. Allen, who would go on to become the edi-tor of the *Horse Review,* recalled that Joe Patchen, in the spring of his two-year-old year, was turned out in a paddock that had a "high board fence that he couldn't see over." The inquisitive colt found the situation intolerable and attempted to scale the barri-er—only to somehow get his left front foot stuck between the two uppermost boards. The 1,200-pound beast hung there, thrashing and screaming, for several hours before Allen, while bringing the farm's other horses in for the night, heard the cries of distress. "Traces of the long and violent struggles he made to free him-self were plainly visible," Allen wrote years later. "Help was sum-moned and he was finally extricated—with the supposition that his leg would be found broken or else that he was crippled for life. But not so—aside from superficial scratches he was unhurt."

The Iron Horse, indeed.

Joe Patchen began racing the next year, when he was three, an early debut for horses of that era. Those who noticed Patchen Wilkes in his pedigree no doubt braced for antisocial behavior, but none came—at first. "I for one used to consider him quite harmless," Hervey wrote of the young Joe. "Many a time Jack Curry [Joe's trainer and driver at the time] has taken me into his stall and he has been all urbanity—and I recall once taking two very fair damsels to see him race John R. Gentry [Joe's longtime archrival], and whip him, after witnessing which nothing would do but they must have a close-up of the lordly victor. So I chaperoned them over to where [Joe Patchen] was holding court, the center of a throng of idolators; and . . . they patted his nose and smoothed his satin neck and got the thrill of their lives. Yes—in them days Joe Patchen was a gentleman."

And in them days, turf writers got paid by the word.

But Joe Patchen's violent nature blossomed steadily as he aged. By the time he was four, he had become exceedingly hard to handle, and his beleaguered, nicked-up grooms grew hoarse shouting at visitors, "Get back—keep away!" The Thoroughbred pacemaker who accompanied him on races against the clock so often incurred his "hatred" and "wrath," wrote the historian Dwight Akers, that the poor running horse had to brought onto the track "by stealth." One groom, or "swipe," was said to have lost an ear to the pacer. "It is unnecessary to be too explicit," Hervey wrote. "Suffice to say that the paternal temperament became uppermost—decidedly . . . and his demeanor toward visitors was such that they found distance lent enchantment to the view." For the good of humanity, Joe Patchen, too, soon had to be draped in heavy chains and—like the stereotypical raving lunatic in magazine cartoons of long ago—shackled to the wall of his cell.

Logic would suggest that people would rather let their mares go fallow than breed to a fire-breathing dragon from the George Wilkes line. Fie on those Wilkes genes—let them wither and die! But the Wilkeses had produced some speedy offspring, and to be fair, it is possible that someone might see an opportunity there—he might think, "Wait now . . . If I match a really mellow mare to Joe Patchen, perhaps, with a little luck, I can get his speed and her personality. Or maybe it'll be like putting milk in coffee; maybe I can take a bit of the edge off without losing too much of the kick." Neither is an outlandish notion, and both, for better or worse, represent the way at least some professional breeders think.

But if Messner was plotting along those lines, he had the wrong mare for the task. For while Zelica herself was a calm, even-tempered animal, she and Joe Patchen shared the same dangerous blood. They were something like second cousins once removed: the mare's paternal great-grandfather was Joe's granddaddy—none other than George Wilkes. Instead of complementing each other, Zelica and Joe Patchen compounded the family's worst trait. Milk into coffee? No, gasoline onto fire.

In his extensive writings, Hervey addresses the strange Zelica–Joe Patchen pairing only once, as far as I can tell (in the *Harness Horse* weekly in 1936), and he portrays it as a marriage of convenience. It wasn't the pale moon that excited Messner, he says, but the nearness of Joe Patchen—the stud was, Hervey notes, standing just across the state line from Oxford, in Chebanse, Illinois.

The Ray Wattles manuscript proffers a contrasting view: the younger Wattles contends, predictably, that his all-knowing and saintly daddy was responsible for Dan Patch's conception. In Ray's deeply corny account, old John has some kind of spontaneous eureka moment, realizing suddenly and for reasons never stated that Zelica and Joe Patchen would produce a champion pacer—and he urges his buddy Dan Messner to act on his advice. ("Father explained to Dan that an analysis of the pedigrees of the great pacers had shown that the highest results had come from the use of sires who were themselves fast pacers." Really, Raymond? You don't say!)

But let us get real. Chebanse, up near Kankakee, was still a fairly long haul from Oxford—more than forty miles—and Messner needed a racehorse in his life about as much as he needed an additional hundred pairs of unsold Pingree & Smith high-button shoes. Besides, even if his intention was to get an animal who could go all the way to the Grand Circuit, there were probably a hundred stallions placed more conveniently and priced more reasonably than Joe Patchen—it was not for nothing that Indiana was known even then as the Cradle of the Pacer. No, "What really happened," John Messner told me one fine fall day, roughly 110 years after the fact, while we were leaning on the back of the Dan Patch barn in Oxford, "was that my grandfather and Johnny Wattles got drunk one night and decided to haul their mares up to Chebanse and breed them to Joe Patchen."

As soon as he said this, I stopped scribbling and looked up from my notebook. This was a startling revelation, something never before reported or even hinted at in the Dan Patch histories. It was also very believable. Many of us would not be here today if it weren't for alcohol, and so it is with the great Dan Patch. With drunkenness as the explanation, the events of that long-ago spring begin to snap satisfyingly into place.

Something else occurred to me at that moment: John, in dropping this bombshell, had just executed a shocking violation of the code of small-town middle America, which says one never speaks ill of the dead—especially, for some reason, members of the ownership class, and most especially the prominent citizens from Dan Messner's era, who must, under these unspoken rules, be portrayed in public forums as being as staunch and upright as their celluloid shirt collars. To this day in Oxford, the working-class men call each other Bob or John or Jim, or Coonie or Cootie or Scronedog, but the first owner of Dan Patch is invariably (barely perceptible bow of the head) "Mr. Messner." It's as if he were still alive, and might hire or fire them or a member of their family. In Minnesota, Dan's latter-day owner is always "Mr. Savage," the "genius" who "made Dan Patch what he was"—a "wonderful, wonderful man." It makes you wonder: Isn't this America? Why doesn't anyone ever say, just on principle, "That rich bastard. Screw him"?

John seemed to realize he was crossing a line, but didn't care. "I mean, people are just people, right?" he went on. "My grandfather was a good guy, but he was a normal human being who liked to take a drink now and then. And this Joe Patchen business was just one of those things that happens on a night when you've had a few too many and you get yourself a little stoked up." He paused, pushed back the brim of his Oak Grove Country Club gimme cap, and looked toward the sky. "At least, that's the way the story was always told in my house."

In that brief coda, I realized, there was another dollop of news: an admission that despite his earlier insistence that the horse was seldom mentioned in his home, young John and the other Messners had indeed discussed Dan Patch some nights over pork chops and succotash. This, too, seems only human. Dan Patch stirred many emotions, including pride and jealousy, and when he was gone, some Oxfordites—even, I would venture to say, some of the most jealous ones—felt a piercing sense of loss. Some still do. When a tornado roared through the old Benton County Fairgrounds, six miles west of town, in 2003, at least a few people's thoughts went immediately to the decrepit, long-since-abandoned stable that still stood there, hard by the site of the half-mile track where Dan Patch had his first race. Dan Patch once stayed in that stable, they used to tell visitors and passers-through, and maybe even told themselves when they drove by on State Road 352. After the storm passed, their worst fears were realized: the stable had been flattened, its rotting shards flung around the neighboring cornfields. No one had been hurt, no valuable property damaged; still it was heartbreaking, for some, to see nature beating a dead horse.

When John said that his grandfather had gotten "stoked up" on that fateful night, he was no doubt referring to whiskey's well-known ability to first soothe and then, as the evening progresses, inflame an unhealed hurt. Dan Messner was by that time thoroughly sick of the "curbstone critics and the livery barn loafers" (as Ray Wattles calls them) who were perpetually on his case, mocking him for paying so much for Zelica. Didn't they have anything better to do? (Actually, in Oxford, maybe not.) But Messner had been stifling his feelings, and not just because that's what people did in those parts. As a retail merchant he felt it prudent to be on pleasant terms with everyone in town because everyone was a potential customer with other options—he might go to one of Messner's competitors; he might repair the worn item he was thinking of replacing; he might make it through one more winter with the same sad long johns. But ever since Messner had come home from the Remington fair with Zelica almost two years before, it had been harder and harder for him to play the role of the smiling storekeep. He heard, or at least heard about, the snickering and snorting, and he yearned to get revenge, even if that meant some took their custom elsewhere. After a few drinks that night, he felt it not just advisable but absolutely necessary to breed his mare to that big bull of a stallion who, in the previous year, had made page-one headlines by lowering his personal best for the mile from 2:19 to 2:04 and winning a slew of heats. It was a classic this'll-show-those-bastards move, right down to the detail that, as a way of showing those bastards, made no sense. If anything, he was playing into the bastards' hands.

Messner's decision to seek out Joe Patchen came, like many regrettable instincts, with a sense of urgency that is hard to account for in retrospect. He and Wattles not only had to go to Chebanse, they had to get there that night. (Wattles, feeling a warm surge of brotherhood, had thrown in with Messner, saying he would take his Oxford Girl to Joe Patchen as well.) So, after going home to get some cash, they hitched Zelica and Oxford Girl to Wattles's two-horse buggy and, as midnight approached, set off on a north-westerly tilt. They and their mares could have taken the train to Chebanse, a much faster and more sensible way to cover the same ground, but that would have meant waiting until the next day. And that, in their state, was unthinkable.

It was a warm, dry night, which was fortunate because the pilgrims had to sleep outside along the way. When they finally reached their destination, late into the steamy afternoon of the next day, the men were in rough shape, and Zelica's bad ankle was throbbing. "But at least we made it," said Wattles, who at sixty-seven may have wondered if this was his final journey.

Joe Patchen was doing business that spring at a stock farm that its owner John Taylor called the Horse Home, in rural Iroquois County, Illinois, several miles outside of downtown Chebanse. When they saw the stallion—who had recently changed hands for the almost unheard-of price of $15,000—standing regally in his

stall, Messner and Wattles were, despite their exhaustion and dehydration, deeply impressed. "He was a giant black with four white
feet and a splash of white in his face," Wattles later reported. "His
every move was like that of a king." Ray Wattles writes that Joe
Patchen "gazed at Dan and Father with bored apathy, like a true
monarch viewing a pair of ragged beggars. He had the reputation of
being a killer, but made no move in their sight to warrant it."

"Good Lord, John," Messner says in the Wattles manuscript.
"If we get a pair of colts that have half that fellow's fire, we'll
really have something, won't we?"

The farm's owner, J. B. Taylor, looked the rumpled men over
once or twice, took their $300, then told them to come back in
a month, by which time they could be sure that both Zelica and
Oxford Girl had, as horsemen say, "caught." For $150 you were
guaranteed a live foal, but not, as Messner would find out, a well-
constructed one.

That same night the two men—now horseless—caught the
railroad home. For the most part they sat in silence, feeling grungy
and guilty about ducking out on their lives. But as their train
pulled into the Oxford depot, Messner turned to Wattles and said
he had a question.

"Certainly, Dan."

"How long," said the man who was now officially a horse
breeder, "does it take for one of these babies to get born?"

CHAPTER FOUR

The spirit of the time shall teach me speed.

—Shakespeare, *King John*

A FEW HOURS AFTER he was born, Dan Patch did something that temporarily silenced the critics—or at least the ones who were still hanging around Kelley's Livery, basking in the afterglow of that morning's disastrous delivery: he struggled to his feet and, with a deep exhale, unfurled his body like the dark brown flag of some proud, new nation.

It was a ta-da moment. One gawker whistled through his teeth. Standing up straight like that, the horse looked entirely different, and damn good. He was, as anyone could see, a deep mahogany bay with black feet (or "points"); he had a small splash of white on his face and another white spot on his right hind foot. "Magnificent" was too strong a word for him at that moment—he was still a rather wet and wrinkled brown flag—but he was remarkably well muscled and fine of face, especially for a Standardbred of that still early era, many of whom look in old photographs like *Sopranos* actors or mashed-up middleweights: at best, cuddly-ugly. He had an air about him that is sometimes called "the look of eagles," though in personality he would remain the "big puppy dog" that John Kelley saw lying in the straw. Gaining his balance, the colt "wobbled around the stall for a few minutes," favoring his badly formed left leg, Kelley remembered. Then, suddenly, the wobbling stopped—for good.

Messner took it all in, but he didn't quite know what to make of it. There had been several pendulum swings in the last few hours, and as someone who had never paid much attention to horses before, he felt confused and emotionally exhausted. Did this kind of thing happen all the time?

He had woken up that morning with the thought that if Zelica delivered what Johnny Wattles called a "horse colt" and he called a baby boy, he would proudly name it Dan Patchen, after himself and the sire. In the last couple of hours, though, he had reconsidered that, wondering if he should save that name for a better prospect—one that might, for example, live. Now the patient was standing up steadily, looking like he would probably survive and need to be fed and cared for and housed. Should he be happy about this?

Wattles, standing just across the stall, was wrestling with no such questions. When Messner looked over, he saw the old man beaming at the sight of the standing colt.

"Dan, if this fellow ever grows into those legs," Wattles said, "he'll be the fastest horse in the world."

That, in any case, is what Wattles said he said in his numerous retellings of the tale over the remaining twelve years of his life. If he really did make that statement, it no doubt frightened Messner, who was not looking for the fastest horse in the world, and wouldn't know what to do if such an animal came into his life.

Messner, to put it mildly, was not a racetrack sort of guy. God in His infinite wisdom had given Dan Patchen to one of the very few adult males in Oxford who was not excited by the idea of fast horses competing for the pleasure of the betting public. Like a lot of people who have never paid much attention to horse racing, Messner found the track intimidating, an arcane demimonde of gamblers, hustlers, and pickpockets with its own language, customs, and dress codes, holding infinite possibilities for faux pas. He had met enough customers and salesmen who owned racehorses, though, to know this much: at just about any level beyond the country fairs, it was a rich man's game; given the cost of training, shipping, shoeing, entry fees, and veterinary care, even the owners of the fastest horses rarely turned a profit. Indeed, a few years later the *Horse Review* would publish a survey that showed that of 50,000 horses put into training annually, only about 500 earned their expenses. Those odds made it a game that Messner—who fretted much about money—did not want to play.

So if Dan Patchen was not to be a racehorse, what did Messner, who already had Zelica to pull his buggy, plan to do with this new arrival? The truth is, he had no clue. He would, he supposed, figure that out later. For the time being he was just glad that Dan Patchen wasn't Dead Patchen.

The horse himself was sublimely untroubled by the lack of a clear career path. Dan Patchen's first year was, but for one afternoon in the fall of 1896, an idyllic period, the only time in his life when he was totally and blissfully unemployed. ("My first memories are pleasant ones," begins Dan's 1911 *Autobiography*. "They are of comfort and sunshine in a pasture with plenty of feed and wooded with picturesque old oak trees.") No one was asking him for speed or sex; life was simple—and grand. He spent the rest of April and all of May 1896 living in the livery-stable stall with Zelica, looking back at the curious townsfolk who came to see one of two horses in town now known as Messner's Folly—but who often went away talking about how special the horse seemed. It wasn't his athletic ability that struck people—who knew at this point if he could even walk fast?—but his warm demeanor and the gentle look in his soft brown eyes. Little Dan seemed interested in his visitors in a way that sometimes made them slightly ill at ease, especially those who had come to mock him. "I feel like he's looking right into me," one of them said.

By June the colt had grown too large to share a stall with his mother, and Messner moved him and Zelica to the Wattles farm, three and a half miles northwest of town. After his bad experience with "the slurring loafers and neglectful attendees" at Kelley's (to quote Ray Wattles), Messner had no desire to prolong his arrangement there. Besides, he, as always, wanted the best for Dan and Zelica, and from his layman's point of view it seemed like a good idea to give a baby horse the chance to run in the fields with his mom.

He turned out to be right about the mother, wrong about the running.

Dan Patchen was a classic mama's boy, hanging so close to Zelica wherever she went that he sometimes irritated her—and made the workers at the Wattles place chuckle. When Messner, following doctor's orders, came out to the farm occasionally to hitch up Zelica and drive her around Oxford, little Dan would stay close behind the rig, untethered because there was no danger of him running away. The colt tended to tuck himself in cozily between his mother and the side of the road. "Watch that pole horse!" hecklers would yell, mimicking a racetrack judge trying to get a field of horses off to an even start.

While putting together her *Two Dans* book in the 1970s, Mary Cross found an old-timer named Mickey Maguire, who told her that as a boy he would, at Messner's request, take Zelica to graze at various spots near town, leading her on a rope, and that Dan, when very young, would shadow them closely. In time, the colt grew more playful, taking off into the pasture and daring Maguire to chase him on foot. The game was fun for a while—Dan would always allow himself to get caught, eventually—but Maguire one day decided that the next time Dan zipped away, he would surprise him by leading Zelica in the other direction, toward town, turning the tables and daring Dan not to follow along. The first time Maguire tried it, Dan did what you might expect—he at first feigned indifference, allowing Maguire and Zelica to get almost out of sight; then, his bluff called, he came charging after them. It was all just harmless fun—except for the shocking and almost unbelievable speed with which Dan closed the distance, pulling up in front of Zelica with a loud whinny, not even breathing hard. Mickey Maguire could only stand there with his mouth agape. He would remember that great whoosh for the rest of his days.

Yet it wasn't Dan's speed alone that was so impressive; it was the particular way he covered ground. Messner's colt did not run— that is, he didn't push off his back legs with the springing leap we call a gallop. Instead, he paced, moving his left front and rear legs in tandem, then doing the same on the opposite side. Most pacers, even if they descend from pacers going back many generations, need to be taught the gait, usually over a period of two weeks to three months. Then they have to be kept at it in training, almost always while wearing leg straps called hobbles that encourage the step, in order to retain the muscle memory that will allow them to drop into the pace, and stay in it when they are asked for speed. Dan Patchen, in contrast, paced naturally in the pasture, without schooling or straps of any kind.

"Good Lord!" Messner said to Wattles one day, when they were watching the four-month-old Dan Patchen zip around his paddock. "Do they really pace that young?"

"Why not?" the old man replied. "It's born in him. He's a natural-born pacer. He does it as easily as he breathes."

But Wattles, who knew that a natural-born pacer was as rare as a triple-yolk egg, must have been more impressed than he let on.

Why would anyone want a horse to pace? If it sounds like an odd idea, it is an old one, too. "Speed at the pace is older and has been longer in process of development than speed at the trot," wrote the horse historian George P. Floyd, who noted that marble friezes from the Acropolis, which date back to 437 BC, show horses in "the pacing attitude." The four bronze horses on St. Mark's in Venice, cast in Roman times, are also pacing. George Washington owned a pacer that, according to his diary, he saw race at Accotink, near Mount Vernon, on September 29, 1768. And seven years later Paul Revere borrowed a Narragansett pacer for a certain nocturnal ride through every Middlesex village and farm.

Revere, of course, rode astride his pacer, a little mare called Brown Betty (or Brown Beauty, depending on your history book). Pacing, until the mid-nineteenth century, was considered primarily a saddle gait, good for marathon distances because it allows a horse to conserve energy (compared to the gallop) and provides a smooth trip for the rider (were it not for the hills and dales along the fabled silversmith's journey, he could have brought along a cup of tea).

Spunky Narragansetts like Betty enjoyed a vogue in America as early as 1700, fifty years before the first Thoroughbred, Bulle Rock, landed in Virginia. But it was the Narragansett's lack of hauling power that was his eventual undoing; the breed became extinct by the 1850s as drivers replaced riders on the nation's roads. And that might have been the end of it for pacers, who at the dawn of the horse-and-buggy era were unloved and unwanted.

The quest for the Standardbred, it must be remembered, was initially the quest for the American trotter, who was in theory suited best of all to carriage work because of the beauty of his stride and because his off-setting, diagonal action provided a smooth, even pull. Americans had been focused on the idea of fast trotters since at least 1806, when a horse of unknown origin named Yankee made news by breaking the three-minute-mile barrier, trotting under saddle in 2:59 in what is now the Bronx. But there had never before been a distinct breed of trotting horse, one with beautiful knee action that trotted squarely and bred true, passing along the gene for his gait. Was it even possible to create such a horse through selective breeding? Some experienced horsemen had their doubts. But by the time the smoke cleared after the Civil War, the answer was a resounding yes. The American trotter, by the late 1860s, had begun to step lively over at least the eastern portion of the landscape, where the roads were best, going the mile in 2:40! no, 2:35! no, wait, 2:30!

New York Tribune writer Junius Henri Browne called the Standardbred "a revolution in horse flesh." The breed evolved so quickly that English equiphiles, who were trying to develop their own line of trotting horses at this time, couldn't believe the reports they were hearing from across the ocean. After reading an account in the *Philadelphia Inquirer* of a trotting horse going a mile in 2:35, English racing historian John Lawrence wrote, "American miles must be shorter than English miles. I apprehend no horse ever did, or could, trot over the measured English mile in that short space of time. From the excessive rapidity of his trot his feet would be apt to strike fire and set him in a blaze."

A handful of horses, none of them distinguished trotters themselves, were responsible for this revolution. The founding father of both the American Thoroughbred and Standardbred lines was a big, ungainly, cantankerous gray stallion named Messenger. Foaled in England in 1780, he won eight of fourteen races (most of them two-horse matches for large side bets) before retiring and dropping out of sight after a loss at Newmarket in 1785. He resurfaced three years later, "charging down the gangplank," as the horse histories like to put it, in Philadelphia, where he had been brought for stallion duty (at first at a Market Street inn called the Sign of the Black Horse, where his fee was $15, with another dollar to the groom). While some have denigrated Messenger as a racehorse, saying he was not a stouthearted "stayer" because he never won at more than two miles (four miles was the classic Thoroughbred distance then; today it varies between a mile and a mile and a half), no one could fault him for his work at stud. Before he died at the age of thirty-three, Messenger produced about eight hundred children, including such renowned runners as Honest John, Potomac, and Sir Solomon; he also sired the broodmare Miller's Damsel, the dam of the undefeated American Eclipse, who in 1823 beat Sir Henry in the historic North vs. South match race at the Union Course on Long Island. One of the few high-quality Thoroughbred stallions north of the Mason-Dixon line, Messenger moved often but never far—he stood in New Jersey; Bucks County, Pennsylvania; Jamaica, Long Island; Goshen, New York, and other spots—covering dozens of mares each year. But his life got especially plummy in 1796—his fee shot to $30, and he enjoyed 106 breedings—when word started to spread about the significant number of his offspring who liked to trot in a fine, square manner and who miraculously held the gait at high speed, even while being hollered at to go faster still, and whipped. (Why was this so? John Hervey, in *The American Trotter*, raises the question, then invokes the names of Shakespeare, Homer, Newton, Napoleon, Goethe, and Darwin on the way to concluding that "nature works in ways and with materials mysterious, far beyond our comprehension.") Harness racing was not yet an organized sport, so it can't be said that any of Messenger's progeny won more than the admiration of the people who saw them pulling vehicles down the road; there were virtually no formal trotting races in those days. But a son of his old age, the bay-colored Mambrino (one of the rare non-grays that Messenger produced) made himself significant by siring a horse named Abdallah, who himself did one noteworthy thing in his life, which was to sire a horse named Hambletonian 10.

Abdallah, before we brush by him, should be memorialized briefly for having a hard-knock life of extravagant proportions. For starters, he was, in an age of truly ugly, ill-made horses, the worst-looking animal that many people had ever seen. His ears were shockingly "long, thin and sharp," wrote one eyewitness, and Hervey noted that Abdallah had a "large, heavy head," a thin, rat-like tail, a hollow back, and scrawny "cat hams," all of which combined to make him look like he was two different hideous horses "joined by an attenuated cylinder." Abdallah possessed a horrible temper, too, and his early get, said the great nineteenth-century horseman Alden Goldsmith, "were nervous and lacked brain balance." Rejected by the broodmare owners in his native Orange County, New York, Abdallah was sold, for $1,000, to interests in Lexington, Kentucky—to which he was ridden under saddle in the dead of winter in 1840, nearly dying along the way. He quickly flopped as a stallion in the bluegrass, and in the winter of 1842 was sold, and ridden back, to a farm in New York, again coming close to death from exhaustion and exposure. Back in the Northeast, he passed through numerous owners and covered a smattering of mares. A high percentage of the resulting children, mentally deficient as they may have been, showed trotting speed as they matured. But it wasn't until he was too old to take on more mares that breeders fully realized what he had accomplished at the stud, and by then it didn't matter. In the spring of 1854, when he was thirty-three, he was sold for $35 to a Brooklyn fishmonger, who used the grotesque-looking stallion to pull his wagon. In November of that year, the equine artist Henry H. Cross was sketching at the Union Course when, Cross wrote, "a man drove in, bringing the news that old Abdallah had just been found dead on Gravesend Beach. I accordingly drove over with other horsemen to get a look at this celebrated stallion. The sight that met our eyes was indeed a grewsome one. The old horse had been turned loose in the wind and weather all the fall, subsisting as best he could upon beach and marsh grass and such other forage as he could pick up. Finally he had taken refuge in an old shanty on the beach, which he had grown too feeble to leave. There he literally starved to death. He had died standing, game to the last.

In his struggles he had dug a deep hole with his forefeet, in the endeavor to escape the torments of the sandflies and mosquitoes, and appeared as if half buried, his fore parts being three feet lower than his hind ones. . . . He had never lain down. Instead he had leaned against the side of the shanty for support, and in that position had drawn his last breath. I can never forget the spectacle he represented. It was one of the most extraordinary and at the same time the most pathetic I have ever seen—his strange posture, his gaunt, skeleton-like frame covered with long woolly hair and the ghastly surroundings. I believe he was given decent burial and his hoofs, his tail and some other portions of his anatomy were preserved."

"Nobody knows nothing," screenwriter William Goldman famously said about Hollywood, and the same applies to the horse-breeding crowd. Every Standardbred who has ever lived traces back to that sad, bug-bitten old nag.

The turning point of Abdallah's life, it would become apparent in retrospect, occurred in 1848 when, back on his native ground of Chester, New York, at the age of twenty-five, "near the very nadir of his career," as John H. Wallace wrote, "an old and battered outcast," he was bred to a mare owned by a farmer named Jonas Seeley. The Charles Kent mare, as she was called, after her previous owner, had already borne two foals by Abdallah, fillies whose fates are unknown. Putting up another $5 for the stud service, Seeley this time got a colt he named Hambletonian, perhaps after the English village of Hambleton, but more likely because Hambletonian was a popular horse name at the time. Hambletonian 10, as he was to be known in the stud book to differentiate himself from the others, was, needless to say, a homely individual, but from the moment of his birth he held a powerful sway over Seeley's hired man, William M. Rysdyk. Eager to strike out on his own with a stud horse, and fixated on Hambletonian, Rysdyk badgered his employer until Seeley sold him the horse for $125, with the most important broodmare in Standardbred history thrown in as an afterthought. Hambletonian started his stud career at the tender age of two. He never raced, but Rysdyk exhibited him annually at the county fair, and the horse's offspring did whatever else was necessary to advertise the sire's unprecedented ability to produce fast trotters, no matter what kind of sketchily bred country mares he covered. Rysdyk turned down no one, charging a $100 stud fee in 1864 and getting 217 takers. (The next year he raised the fee to $300, and booked 193 mares; in 1866 105 breeders paid the unheard-of price of $500.) In all he covered 1,908 mares and got 1,331 foals, who for all practical purposes defined the American trotter. "The further he recedes from us," Hervey wrote in the 1940s, "the more colossal he appears."

But leave it to nature to foil the well-laid plans of the agriculturally inclined: a fair percentage of horses carrying Hambletonian's precious blood, and thus having every genetic incentive to be trotters, preferred, for some mysterious—and often maddening—reason, to pace. Joe Patchen and Zelica, for example, both carried the purest trotting blood in their veins, each tracing back to Rysdyk's stallion several times, but both were pacers, and their most famous offspring, Dan Patch, was such a natural that later in his life he would be seen fleeing a stable fire on the parallel gait. You could not train Dan Patch to gallop.

For the men who strove to create the American trotter, the pacer was the proverbial turd in the punch bowl. The trot, with its delicate bend of the front knee and offsetting diagonal action, was, at least to upper-crust eastern tastes, the more beautiful gait by far. Hervey tells us that pacers were seen by the smart set as lacking "style and action, being . . . stiff-kneed and low-going, while they were characterized by a wide, swinging habit of action which won for them the derisive nickname of 'side-wheelers,' the allegation being made that one required the whole width of the road to navigate in." Robert Bonner, the publisher of the *New York Herald,* famously said, "No gentleman drives a pacer."

To make matters worse, an increasing number of pacers were being fitted by their handlers with leather hobbles: four loops, hanging down on suspenders from the harness, that encouraged the beasts on their vulgar way. Not only were these straps offensive to the eyes of more refined observers, they were seen as a cheap substitute for the scientific breeding and proper, patient training that was supposed to make a horse do what humans desired. A debate about whether the equipment was unsafe, unnatural, and even immoral raged in the pages of the horse papers before and after the turn of the twentieth century—and it eventually shaped the career of Dan Patch, even though he never wore the straps. Men judged each other's character by their position on pacing hobbles, just as today they might make assumptions after hearing someone speak about stem-cell research, presidential politics, or Barry Bonds. The American Trotting Association, one of the sport's governing bodies, outlawed the equipment (the ban would not be lifted until 1907). Civil authorities got involved, too: on May 17, 1903, a Broadway actor named Harrison Armstrong was arrested by New York City police for driving a hobbled pacer on the Harlem River Speedway.

Hobbled or not, pacers were the perennial in-laws of the harness-horse world, saddled with the suspicion that they descended from shady, inferior stock. If you shone a bright light into any pacer's pedigree, the brahmins believed, you would find traces of the crude Canuck "ambler" from French Canada, the puny if patriotic Narragansett, and all sorts of mongrels with, as Hervey says, "objectionable color schemes" and "goose rumps." Sportswriters of the day denigrated pacers not just as "sidewheelers" but also "squirmers" and "wigglers." But in terms of names, their owners and breeders didn't serve them much better. Hervey points out the leading trotting sires "as a rule bore names indicative of dignity and value": Hambletonian, Black Hawk, Chancellor, Commodore, Columbus, Champion, American Star, Volunteer, Grey Eagle, Napoleon, and Washington. The prominent pacing stallions? How about Bald Hornet, Copperbottom, Crazy Nick, Clinker, Crook Neck, Gossip Jones, French Charley, Hoosier Tom, Stump the Dealer, Shoo Fly, Little Sam, and Nigger Baby?

And yet the pacer endured, and eventually prospered, for what enraged and disgusted the eastern elite failed even to register with the farmers, merchants, farriers, and other less pretentious types from the interior United States. Pacers were just hunky-dory with those bumpkins. When they looked at a pacer, they saw a horse who was (a) slightly faster, as a rule, than a trotter, and (b) considerably cheaper than the Sunday dress-up steeds that men like

Bonner owned not for transportation or sport (Bonner saw racing as beneath his dignity), but merely to impress their fellow swells. If your typical midwestern farmer had wanted to impress New York swells, would he be living in the Midwest? Or farming? So what if the pacer was not the absolute perfect carriage horse? Perfect was a foreign concept to men who battled the elements to grow corn and raise hogs, or sold socks and served whiskey to those who did. Good enough was good enough for them. Nor was this crowd likely to be put off by a horse named Crooked Neck or Nigger Baby—not when the frost heaves that interrupted the Midwest flatness were joshingly known as niggerheads. No, bring us your tired-of-trotting and your poorly gaited, your weirdly named and bizarrely colored, your unfashionably bred and decidedly goose-rumped, said the Buckeye, the Hawkeye, and the Hoosier. And so the easterners did, putting aside the whips and straps and heavy toe weights they had been using to try to convert their pacers to a godlier trotting gait and selling their wigglers to the West.

Indiana was a pioneer of this newfangled notion of breeding pacers on purpose. "The Cradle of the Pacer," it was already being called in the 1890s, after a number of pacing sires started doing brisk business there, and hobbles, anathema elsewhere, came to be known as "Indiana pants." The word *pacer* still meant enough in those parts in 1967 for the upstart American Basketball Association to name its Indianapolis franchise after the horse. But today when people speak of the Indiana Pacers (who've since migrated to the NBA), their thoughts are surely as horse-free as the team's logo.

In Dan Patch's day, hoops were just being dreamed, and harness racing was the state's number-one sport, with baseball a distant second. You could not go from Oxford to, say, Otterbein, a town nine miles distant, without passing a couple of training tracks, alive with the clip-clop of pacers (and no doubt a few trotters) getting in a bit of speed work, perhaps in preparation for a nearby town fair, or just for the exercise. Anyone you stopped on the way would probably be able to spout off the current trotting and pacing records for the mile (virtually the sole distance that Standardbreds race), and if it was summertime, they could probably tell you where the Grand Circuit was camping just then. This leaves only the question of why you would ever want to go to Otterbein, a marshy berg plagued by noisy little frogs.

In the fall of 1896, with his colt coming up on six months, Messner still had no idea what he was going to do with his Dan Patchen, though he may have been starting to feel that he had side-stepped disaster. The colt, who shuttled between Messner's barn, Kelley's Livery, and the Wattles place in his first few months, was making a name for himself on the farm thanks to what Ray Wattles remembered as "his personality, magnetism or some other indefinable quality." Dan was perhaps the happiest horse anyone had ever seen, sometimes annoyingly so. He loved to splash around madly in a small brook while Wattles's other horses stood calmly drinking, and to nuzzle and roll through the spicy mint that grew down by the water. He especially enjoyed rubbing noses with a colt of Wattles's named Prosperity Bill—"to Bill's patient disgust," Ray noted. Sometimes Dan would "rear up on the fence like a goat," standing on his hind legs and watching the barrel-chested, broad-rumped work horses on the farm go through the drudgery of pulling a plow or hauling lumber. Then Dan would let out "a whinny of sheer joy," perhaps glad that he wasn't one of them.

The colt's speed was still astounding people, but what about that bad back leg? A horse with that kind of physical flaw often breaks down when put on a serious regimen. As they say around the racetrack, speed kills.

Old man Wattles was certainly aware of the dangers, but the trainer in him yearned to explore the possibilities. Aware that horse racing made Messner nervous, he decided to approach the subject gingerly.

"Dan," he said to Messner one morning, after they had to pull apart Dan Patchen and another colt who was no longer able to bear the former's constant exuberance. "This here is a horse."

Messner nodded. He knew that Uncle Johnny meant a race-horse. "But that colt's legs won't ever be any straighter, will they?" he said.

"What of it?" Wattles snorted. "If those crooked legs went any faster, he couldn't keep up with them."

The trainer then went on to offer a trade. If Messner wasn't satisfied with Dan Patchen, he could swap him for Wattles's colt Prosperity Bill, who was by an obscure stallion named General Smith.

Just as on that morning when he'd heard the suggestion that he put the horse down, Messner considered the offer, but did not respond.

Then Wattles said plainly what had been on both men's minds. "You're going to run races with him, ain't you, Dan? Ain't going to use him for an artist's model, are you?"

Again Messner remained silent.

It is not clear when, or if, Messner ever said to Wattles, "I would like you to train Dan Patchen and see if you can make a racehorse out of him." But the two decided to go down that road, albeit tentatively, in the winter of 1896–97. Still, they put off all serious thought of training until that spring, figuring that when Dan reached his first birthday, they would reassess his physical and emotional development and decide whether to begin an experiment that was guaranteed, given the weird arc of the horse's left rear leg, to raise eyebrows around town and restart the gossiping and snickering.

Not that it was such a big deal to train a horse for speed in those days, when there was a fine line between the racetrack and the road. The pacer or trotter who won by a nose at the fair on Saturday might pull the butcher's cart on Monday evening, then go back to racing the following weekend. If they were less aristocratic-looking than Thoroughbreds (their detractors called them "jugheads"), Standardbreds, generally speaking, were heartier and calmer and more cooperative than the runners; they would apply themselves honestly to whatever they were asked to do, their very gaits showing that they were willing to meet a human being halfway.

Wattles started Dan Patchen slowly, getting him accustomed to the bulky sixty-five-pound training cart and the relatively tight turns of the half-mile Chiquesalonghi track. Trainers of that era often took what today seem like absurd amounts of time to get their pacers and trotters ready. The Standardbred set had a more relaxed approach than the people who prepped the Thoroughbreds. Since 1875, Thoroughbred racing had structured its season around the Kentucky Derby, a race for three-year-olds that has never been won by a horse who did not begin training and racing at the tender age of two. The idea, which originated with the Thoroughbred breeders of the bluegrass region, was to have horses peak early, and thus get worn out early, forcing owners to return frequently to the yearling sales to replenish their stock. Harness racing had no such juvenile stakes races until 1926, when the Hambletonian, the "Kentucky Derby for trotters," was inaugurated (the pacing equivalent, the Little Brown Jug, began in 1946). But even then it was not unusual for a Standardbred to make his debut at the age of five or six, when he was fully grown into his body and his joints were better able to take the stress of competition and the endless preparation that comes with it.

The harness held no perils for Dan Patchen; he was broken to it easily. Soon after his first birthday in the spring of 1897 he was pulling Messner's wagon around town, alternating with Zelica, and also spending periods of time at the Wattles place, where he had little to do but grow and gambol. People still shook their heads when they noticed Dan's malformed leg, and said it was a shame, since he was otherwise bigger and better-looking than the average colt, and of course so gentle, more like a dog than a stud horse. Even those sympathetic to Messner assumed that given Dan Patchen's physical limitations, he could never be much more than a pet.

Messner, though, was starting to think bigger. Sometime in the first months of 1897 he took the notable step of registering the colt's name with the American Trotting Register Association, something a man wouldn't do with a horse he had no plans for. Messner wasn't sure how to submit an application, and perhaps John Wattles, who was more of a hands-on horseman, wasn't either, because Messner asked a friend from the dry-goods realm, a shoe manufacturer and wholesaler named C. L. Foster (who may have raced a few Standardbreds himself) to send in the proper documents. On July 30, the organization wrote back to Messner with a brief letter saying that the name Foster had submitted, Dan Patchen, was "contrary to the rules," though the nature of those rules was not stated and is hard to imagine. (Could it be that it was too close to Joe Patchen? Or that someone named Dan Patchen might object? The registrar's office at the U.S. Trotting Association, harness racing's governing body since 1939, professes to be baffled by its predecessor's explanation.)

The letter also said that the alternative choice Foster had submitted, Dan P., was already taken (by two horses, as it turns out, neither of which was more than mediocre). Foster had apparently told the ATRA in his letter of application that if those two names didn't work out they should just go ahead and use their imagination. Surprise me, he said. And so they did. The letter concludes: "As you request us to select a name in this event, we have registered this colt as Dan Patch, with the No. 0392 . . . and enclose a certificate of this registration."

In retrospect, right about here, you can see Messner's luck beginning to change. He was still blundering around in the world of horses, going 0 for 2 in the name department, but "Dan Patch" was a better name than either of the ones he submitted, and it still looks proud and sassy on the certificate, which today hangs, simply framed, in John Messner's kitchen. Dan Patch: it's a name somehow redolent of the ragtime era, a snappy, show-bizzy moniker, one fit for a hero of the emerging pop culture; maybe it's because we know what happened, but it even sounds fast.

But even with a new, improved name and a few more months to grow and mature, Dan Patch was the same always-in-motion, too-curious-for-his-own-good colt. One day that September the teenage Ray Wattles was driving a horse-drawn mowing machine through the pasture at his family's farm, intending to cut some weeds in an adjoining fenced-in field. When he reached the entrance to the field, he got out and lowered the mower's sickle bar, "with its row of wicked-looking, razor-sharp blades," and climbed back into the driver's seat. Ray tells the tale in his manuscript:

> The colts had been in the far corner of the pasture with their backs turned toward me. But I hadn't reckoned on Dan.
>
> I had not even noticed him when I opened the gate into the field. Yet he must have even then been sprinting across the pasture toward me. For I had no more than lowered

the sickle bar when I heard the drumming of hooves on the ground behind me and turned to catch a flash of mahogany bay bearing down on me.

It was over in a split-second—the shrill squeal of agony and surprise from Dan, the quick spurting of blood from sliced tissue.

Somehow the colt had gotten one of his front ankles—Wattles doesn't say which one—caught in the blades of the mowing machine.

"I leaped from the seat and grabbed the leg. He had withdrawn it from the sickle-bar and was holding it up. He had stepped between two of the triangular blades. Evidently, feeling the sting of the first incision, he had jerked his foreleg back, cutting it even more."

In an eerie echo of what had happened to his fence-climbing father, the machine had given him a series of deep cuts just above the ankle, but no tendons had been severed. Ray Wattles wrapped his handkerchief around the wound, then led Dan back to his stall.

"Fortunately, Father happened to come by in a little while; he took over the treatment of the injured colt. . . . The injury healed quickly. Yet Dan bore the scars to his grave."

Well, maybe. Wattles is just guessing about that. When it was time for the grave, the simple life in Indiana, and the folks who went with it, were long ago and far away.

CHAPTER FIVE

There is one turf abuse upon which we have for some time been desirous of 'speaking our mind.' We refer to the deplorable and detestable practice of naming horses after criminals, or notorious reprobates, of both sexes. There is scarcely a day that the reader of the turf press is not confronted with a succession of Harry K. Thaws, Evelyn Nesbits, Cassie Chadwicks, Nan Pattersons, Oscar Wildes, Josephine Pollards and others of the same ilk which smell to heaven of foulness.

—*Horse Review*, August 10, 1909

AND THERE THE RAY Wattles manuscript ends.

Or not quite.

It does go on for a half-dozen more lines in which the younger Wattles writes about having Dan Patch "taken from me" in the fall of 1897 and brought back to Kelley's Livery. The narrative finally halts abruptly, in mid-sentence, at that point not because the author stopped writing, but because the pages are missing and probably lost for good. Joe Morris, the burly, bearded fifty-something Oxford plumber who is John Wattles's grandnephew, and who generously allowed me to photocopy the original yellowing pages, said the manuscript came down to him, decades ago, in its current truncated state.

Ray Wattles's whine about having Dan Patch taken away from him—if in fact it is a whine—is an aberration in an otherwise saccharine, conflict-free script, and thus to the Dan Patch scholar something deeply intriguing. Was there rancor between Wattles *père* and *fils* over the horse? Between Messner and the Wattleses? Did Messner blame either or both of the Wattleses for allowing Dan Patch to get his foot caught in the mowing machine? After fifty pages of almost unabated sunny skies, buzzin' bees, and sweet Hoosier harmony, one positively aches for rancor. But while we will probably never know where Ray was going with that thought, there is, alas, no corroborating evidence of the protagonists getting testy with each other. If Messner took Dan off the farm for any significant length of time in the horse's second year, it was probably because he enjoyed having him near—and wanted to show him off around town. He might have even wanted to make a few bucks with Dan—not for the money so much as to show that his horse dealings had finally resulted in something with some market value. We just don't know. But however the arrangement came about, Dan was soon seen pulling the wagon of Oxford's grocer, Conrad Zeis, around town with some regularity, and standing patiently at the hitching post while pickups and deliveries were made. Indeed, from that point until the day he left Indiana, Dan Patch was a staple of the downtown Oxford scene, harnessed to Messner's wagon or the grocery cart. In summer, he looked considerably darker because his caretaker, Cyril Altpeter, lovingly coated him from tail to nose with coal oil, a crude but fairly effective method of keeping the mosquitoes away. In winter, sporting his natural mahogany coat grown out for the cold weather, he might be seen pacing happily through the town square, pulling the cutter of his increasingly proud owner, who would puff a cigar and blow smoke at the passing scene. If Messner paid little attention to the reins, that was no problem; except for Dan's habit of speeding up every time another horse began to approach him on the road, the colt drove himself.

In his old age a retired farmer named Ray Steele recalled that Messner once granted him permission to hitch his sled to the back of Messner's sleigh with a length of rope. "I felt," said Steele, "like I was flying."

Messner and Wattles certainly made for an odd couple. While the storekeeper presented himself to the world as a man of the new century, Wattles, by 1900, was very much the wizened sage, a throwback to pre–Civil War times. The small, sinewy old sodbuster wore a knee-length black frock coat and a flat, wide-brimmed hat, and his white hair and beard were both unfashionably long and shaggy—a look that clearly marked him as a man of the Jacksonian era. In his long life Wattles never ventured far from Oxford, where he was born in 1828, and where he attended a log-cabin schoolhouse, a rude structure where the desks were slices of tree trunks teetering on four iron legs and the windows were greased paper. He looks grim in his few extant photographs, but ancient Oxfordites remembered him to Mary Cross as the class clown, a "real boy" with a taste for mischief. When Wattles was growing up, Oxford was no more than a cluster of houses at the confluence of several cow paths that wound through a forest. Cross tells us that "children actually became lost in the middle of the town because of the density of the trees and undergrowth." Wattles himself liked to reminisce about the herds of deer, sometimes fifty or more, that would wander through town, not realizing that they were in the midst of civilization. Occasionally, Wattles would walk up to one of the naive critters, club it over the head, and drag it home for dinner. Curbed streets, railroad depots, fancy carriages, and crisply gaited carriage horses—all those things were still far in the future.

In 1850 Wattles married Elizabeth Gray, a distant relative of the Messner clan. The Wattles had five daughters in addition to Ray, an average-size family in those days when just about everyone needed all the help they could get to work the family farm. Wattles worked 120 acres, a fairly large spread by local standards, its size attributable at least in part to the patriarch's side dealings with horses, both for racing and for farm labor. Horses, for any turn-of-the-century farmer, were part of the bargain, the only power source beyond moving water, the occasional ox or mule, and human muscle. But some farmers, like Wattles, had an interest in the animals that went beyond the mundane; they bred, trained, and raced horses, hurrying along the evolution of the Standardbred and in the process adding a few thrills to their hard country lives. Two years before Dan Patch came along, Wattles had a crack trotting colt named Cottonwood who won a big race at Milford, Illinois, then won again a few weeks later at the Benton County Fair, just down the road from Oxford. That December Wattles sold Cottonwood to a man from Frankfort, Indiana, for $1,000. Uncle Johnny may have been a part-timer, because of his farm work, but in matters equine he was no dilettante.

As a trainer the old man was decidedly old school: he believed, like a lot of the early harness men, that horses thrived on work and that hard labor was often the best medicine for whatever ailed them. Is ol' Stewball lame? Let him jog out his kinks, get the blood flowing to those muscles. Is Stewie rank and hard to handle? Extra miles will wear off those sharp edges and calm him down. Is the Stew-meister off his feed? Let the sumbitch work up an appetite. A Standardbred does in fact need plenty of foundation miles to build up his lungs and his legs, as well as quick sprints to foster speed. But an old-timer like Wattles would jog a trotter or pacer ten or twelve miles of a morning before getting down to serious training.

In the spring of 1898, when Dan had just turned two, Wattles brought him, along with several horses in his racing stable, to Chiquesalonghi Park, a former fairgrounds about two miles east of downtown Oxford, near the town of Templeton. Chiquesalonghi, a Pottawatomi Indian name meaning "beautiful place," was now part of the Paul Kennedy farm, but Kennedy had preserved the fair's half-mile track as an oasis in his cornfield, and he graciously allowed anyone who had trotters and pacers to come around and give their animals a workout, free of charge. Kennedy had the harness-horse bug as bad as any Hoosier, and like a lot of people back then, and some now, he found the sight, the sound, and even the smell of racehorses bracing.

Wattles was excited by the prospect of finally hitching Dan to a training cart and jogging him around a track. A harness horseman never knows what he's got, really, until he gets an animal rigged up and asks for a bit of speed. That first morning, though, Wattles didn't get more than a quarter mile with Dan before realizing that something was seriously wrong.

There were in fact two problems. One was that as soon as Dan reached any kind of speed, even a clip as slow as 2:45 for the mile, the action of his crooked left rear leg became exaggerated, and he started striking the axle and, sometimes, the inside left wheel of Wattles's conventional, one-size-fits-all training cart. Dan's fetlock, or ankle, quickly became bruised by the force of the blows, which were strong enough, Wattles knew, to knock the wheel clean off a lightweight racing sulky—that is, if the foot didn't get mangled in the metal spokes first.

The second problem, related to the first, was that Dan was "crossfiring"—hitting the back of his front leg with his diagonally offsetting hind hoof. Fairly common in pacers, crossfiring can be especially pronounced in horses who don't wear hobbles (which tend to keep the legs in line) and who are "off behind," as Dan was, severely: the leg that swung too far to the left and back would also tend to come too far to the right and forward. Thus, the same leg that was being punished (by whacking the cart) was also inflicting punishment (savaging the right front). Despite Dan's abundance of natural talent, Wattles saw that, as a racehorse, the colt was a mess.

Harness-racing trainers may spend a lot of time tinkering with a horse's gait by experimenting with shoes, toe weights, knee boots, and other equipment. They will observe a trotter or pacer in action, either by sitting behind him or watching from the rail, then try something, maybe changing his shoes or using different bits and bridles. After such an adjustment is made, they will put the horse back out on the track so they can observe further, and decide whether to put on or take off yet another piece of tack. The trial-and-error process can take months, or in some cases years, and not every mystery is solvable. But Dan Patch's case didn't lend itself to a trainer's thoughtful tinkering. Wattles, hearing the sickening thwack of horseflesh against wood, and sensing the horse's pain, had to pull Dan up immediately and assess the damage. He leaned to the right to look around the horse's rump. There was blood on Dan's right front leg and more blood on his left hind hoof. There was blood on the track.

Wattles knew what to do about Dan hitting the wheel with his left rear hoof. The horse's physical deformity dictated how far his leg went out; there was no way a trainer could alter that—but he could change the cart. Wattles either built, or more likely had Guy Taylor, the blacksmith, build him a custom cart that was forty-four inches wide, four inches wider than the standard model. To be extra safe, he decided that the spokes on the left wheel should be made of wood, not steel, so they would shatter if struck by the horse's errant hoof.

When it was ready a week or so later, the new vehicle worked just fine. A wider wheel base might put Dan at a bit of a disadvantage when trying to negotiate the hairpin turns of a country half-mile track—if he ever got to the stage where he was racing—but his hoof now had at least an inch of clearance, even when his leg was fully extended. Obviously, if Dan were to start in a race, where lighter-weight sulkies were used, the same accomodation would need to be made.

The crossfiring proved a much tougher challenge for Wattles. It's unclear whether the trainer tried some remedies himself or took Dan directly to the Taylor Blacksmith Shop on the town square, and perhaps other smittys, but his first attempts at solving the problem did not work, and Dan continued to interfere with himself severely every time Wattles tried to pick up the pace. The horse was able to train after a fashion, but he could only grind out the kind of long, slow distances that build foundation. Speed work was impossible. If Dan was going to continue to make progress, something had to be done.

It was probably in the early summer of that year, 1898, that Messner brought Dan Patch to the blacksmith shop of Thomas Eleazor Fenton in Pine Village, the community where the Messner family had run a store before moving five miles north to Oxford. (Wattles, it seems, did not come along; the old man may have simply been busy at the farm, but he may also have pooh-poohed the visit, perhaps out of loyalty to the town farriers.) Fenton, then in his mid-forties, had a reputation as a curer of hard cases, a man who could get creative with an anvil and forge. In this instance, he was also a blacksmith of last resort.

Though Dan had pulled his owner's wagon to Fenton's door (the crossfiring didn't occur at normal road speed), the smithy asked Messner if he wouldn't mind going half a mile farther, to the track outside Pine Village, which had a reputation as one of the best racing surfaces in the state. There, Fenton told Messner to drive the horse no more than a quarter mile or so, going as fast as he could before the crossfiring kicked in. Messner shook the lines, Dan Patch stepped off, and after only about twenty seconds Fenton waved his arm, signaling that he had seen enough. "Okay," he said. "Let's go back to the shop."

On the return trip, Fenton and a helper whose name is lost to history rode together in their own wagon and conferred quietly. Back at the shop, after about an hour of heating, hammering, and checking Dan Patch's left hind hoof, Fenton stood before the forge, holding a bizarre-looking shoe, still white-hot, in his pincers: it was shaped like a highly asymmetrical U, three inches longer on the left prong than on the right, with the extended side flipping up slightly at the end—not the most beautiful piece of steel ever hammered, to be sure, but perhaps a useful one. Fenton nailed it to Dan's bad foot, the group made its way back to the track, and voilà: by slowing down that left hind foot ever so slightly, it allowed Dan to pace a quarter mile in the middling time of forty seconds without savaging his own foot. Assuming the problem didn't come back when he tried in training to push beyond that point, a major obstacle to Dan's success had been surmounted.

Fenton was so proud of his accomplishment—horses that interfere with themselves to the extent Dan Patch did often have to be retired—that a few years later, after the pacer began his rise to glory, he set a pair of the already famously off-kilter "Dan Patch shoes" in a block of concrete outside his place of business, where they became a minor tourist attraction. Fenton died in 1929, but the monument remained until his shop was bulldozed and replaced by a private home in the 1960s. No one knows what became of the concrete-encased shoes.

With his gait corrected, Dan could—in theory, at least—travel as fast and as freely between the shafts of a training or racing vehicle as he could out in the pasture. He still behaved greenly on the Chiquesalonghi track, weaving on the straightaways and suddenly slowing down to look at other horses—or at clouds or shadows or squirrels or blackbirds—but when he kept his mind on business he could flash breathtaking speed on the pace. Partly to siphon off a bit of his excess energy, Messner and Wattles concocted a plan to breed the colt, then two, to Wattles's mare Oxford Girl. (It was not unusual then to breed horses before and during their racing careers; European horsemen do it to this day.) The union would result in a filly Messner named Lady Patch, another mouth to feed in his in-town barn, and another horse Messner had no certain plans for.

Meanwhile, Dan Patch continued to show signs that he might make at least a good country-fair racehorse. One day in the late summer of 1898 a Templeton man named Benjamin Lee brought one of his better colts to Chiquesalonghi to train. Lee had his horse—name unknown—hitched to a somewhat ridiculous-looking high-wheeled sulky of the sort seen in Currier & Ives prints (highwheelers were already obsolete for racing purposes). After a few warm-up miles, Lee, eager to show off his pacer against the local stock, began cruising around the track, looking for a horse to challenge. "Want to go a lap?" he said, drawing up inside Wattles, who moments before had been tapping his colt with the whip and saying, not for the first time that day, "Stop clowning, now—get serious." Wattles didn't have time to respond to Lee. As soon as the horses looked each other in the eye, they quickened their strides and took off racing. Lee's pacer was a speedball who knew how to hug the turns, and the two stayed nose to nose for a brisk quarter mile—until Dan, on the outside, slid into another gear and pulled away so suddenly that the other horse startled and broke into a gallop. As Lee struggled mightily at the reins, trying to get his horse back on stride, Dan Patch pulled away and kept going. His margin of victory in the impromptu half-mile dash was about two hundred yards, the explosion of speed more than a little impressive. Two of the old men who came to Chiquesalonghi to watch the horses train stood up and cheered.

Before long, no one in Oxford was calling Dan Patch "Messner's Folly" anymore. The colt was blossoming into a big, imposing stallion with obvious athletic gifts. The first formal acknowledgment of his growing renown came from the Benton County tax office, which in July of 1898 assessed Dan Patch at $200, an extraordinary amount at a time when horses, regardless of their actual worth, were routinely assigned a tax value of $35 or less. In her *Two Dans,* Mary Cross says that this high evaluation, when reported in the newspapers, "hurt the feelings of other horse owners in the county."

Word of Messner's colt was soon spreading beyond Oxford.

In September of 1899, Harry Y. Haws, the Johnstown, Pennsylvania, businessman who had briefly owned Joe Patchen and who had been Messner's only rival in the auction for Zelica four years before, telegraphed Messner with an offer of $1,000 for Dan Patch. As with Zelica, Haws had never laid eyes on the horse he was angling for, but he obviously thought well of Dan's breeding. Haws was hearing good things about him, most likely from the businessmen who passed through Oxford.

A thousand dollars was a lot of money for an unproven horse with a twisted leg. But to the surprise of many, Messner sniffed at Haws's offer—which was no doubt intended to bowl over a Benton County bumpkin—and instead told the *Tribune* that he had wired back the Pennsylvanian, demanding $1,200. Was he really willing to part with Dan Patch? Or did he see that as a dazzling, deal-breaking number that would, as a fillip, elicit a gasp from the groundlings?

If the latter was the case, he may have been surprised when Haws agreed to pay his price—if Messner threw in the filly Lady Patch. But Messner promptly said no to that, and Haws wound up instead buying John Wattles's Joan—the filly Wattles had gotten as a result of bringing Oxford Girl to Joe Patchen—for $1,000. Wattles, in retrospect, made a sharp deal. Joan—a name not exactly designed to strike fear into the hearts of the competition—was never heard from again.

The summer fairs of 1899 came and went without an appearance by Dan Patch, who remained in training at dusty old Chiquesalonghi. The colt was still growing and maturing, and Wattles saw no purpose in rushing Dan's development. When winter came, Dan pulled a sleigh again, and delivered groceries. In the spring Altpeter resumed rubbing him all over with coal oil. But even between the shafts of a grocery cart, wearing the equivalent of blackface, Dan looked like something special.

It was on or about the Fourth of July, 1900, that Dan Patch did something that shocked Johnny Wattles, already his biggest fan. As the horse and trainer were making yet another circuit of the old training track in the morning heat, Dan, with no prompting, grabbed the bit, lowered his head, and began striding out in a way that was not just fast but also, for the first time, fierce and purposeful. The silliness that had always been part of Dan's personality was suddenly gone: he was bending his knees deeply, he had his chest low to the ground, and he was surging inexorably forward. Wattles was at first suspicious: was this the advent of stallionish behavior, the first sign that the horse was undergoing a personality change, the way Joe Patchen did at about the same age, when the black horse morphed from curious to carnivorous? Wattles let Dan go for one lap, two laps, three laps, and more in the heat and then, with some apprehension, lightly pulled on the reins. Would he stop with just this tap on the brakes? Dan, who had always been the most obedient horse Wattles ever drove, slowed down instantly, dropping into a jog. Wattles sighed with relief. The colt wasn't getting rank, he was just getting, as the horsemen say, racey.

Wattles was so excited by the development he drove Dan Patch directly from the training track to Messner's store. There he swung out of the cart, hitched Dan to a post, and ran inside to tell the owner to meet him at Chiquesalonghi the next morning at eight; there was something he needed him to see.

Messner arrived right on time, accompanied by a friend, a furniture merchant named Charles Shipps. In his vest pocket, Shipps carried a stopwatch which, it if could ever be located, might bring a fortune on eBay.

They didn't know what to expect. A horse who could pace a mile in 2:30 in those days could be competitive at the smaller fairs, and every second below that was significant in terms of the class you raced in, and the purse money you could win. A 2:20 horse, for example, could bring a man considerable local prestige, and pick up four or five hundred bucks in the bargain. Conditions at Chiquesalonghi were far from ideal for speed; the track was rocky and rutted, and Dan's extra-wide training cart weighed seventy-five pounds, about twice as much as a stripped-down racing sulky; those things would tend to add quite a few seconds to the clocking. But that was okay; Messner understood and was willing to settle for a rough estimate of what Dan could do.

After giving Dan a couple of warm-up miles in a clockwise direction, Wattles pulled the horse up at the head of the homestretch and wheeled him around, drawing gently on the right rein; he was ready to begin the demonstration.

The old man chirped to get his horse going, and then Dan took it from there, picking up speed steadily and smoothly. As they swept past the starting marker, Shipps clicked his watch.

"Let's hope for two minutes thirty seconds," Messner said to his friend, smiling nervously and holding up crossed fingers. That would be pretty fast, but then Uncle Johnny had been pretty excited.

The horse's gait was still not perfect—his knees brushed each other occasionally—but his stride was terrifically long, allowing him to gobble up ground like no horse Wattles had never seen. Yet perhaps the most remarkable thing about Dan Patch's mile that day was that the horse started out fast, then got faster every quarter, something that almost never happens in an actual horse race. The last quarter mile in particular would never be forgotten by the small group of witnesses at Chiquesalonghi that day. By the time Wattles turned Dan Patch into the bumpy homestretch for the second time, the horse was moving so fast that Wattles's hat blew off, and his long white beard flowed back on either side of his pink and wizened face, wrapping around his ears and flapping wildly in the wind.

This was indeed something that had never been seen before in those parts: beard-splitting speed.

Shipps clicked the watch again as Dan charged past the finish line, then, without saying anything, turned the face toward Messner.

It said 2:14.

Now there was no doubt about it: Dan Messner had himself a racehorse.

But there were reasons to be cautious. While Dan Patch seemed much more grown up than he had been just a few weeks before, and suddenly able to concentrate and carry his speed, he was also a four-year-old who had never raced, or ventured beyond a very small world. Messner, and to a lesser degree Wattles, worried about Dan embarrassing himself, and both of them, if they entered him even in the novice class at the county fair. Distracted by the crowd and the new surroundings, by the sights, sounds, and smells of the midway, he might easily revert to the green colt he had been just a month ago. In the heat of the moment, finding himself in close quarters with eight or nine other horses for the first time, anything might happen: he might break into a gallop; he might change his stride and resume thwacking his bad leg against the side of the sulky and crossfiring. A horse as sensitive to his surroundings as Dan might actually be less able to keep his cool if something unexpected happened; he might panic. Wattles and Messner weighed the pros and cons, then decided it would be best to give Dan a test run under racelike conditions instead of just dropping his name in the entry box. Together they hatched a plan to stage an "exhibition race" at a town picnic scheduled for a few weeks hence at Chiquesalonghi. The race would feature Dan against three or four of Wattles's other horses for a token prize they would figure out later.

It seemed like a perfect way to ease Dan into the racing scene and check on whether he was really as good as they thought. If he didn't behave like a professional, they could skip another summer of fair racing and allow him to get more seasoning. Many horses then raced until they were ten or twelve years old or more; there was no rush. They could claim, should things not go right, that it had always been their intention to wait for the 1901 season. Wattles and Messner both liked the plan, and felt relieved. But when the appointed day, August 18, arrived, the skies opened and the rains came. The track was a swamp, the picnic a washout, and with it, the exhibition race.

Now, if they wanted to race Dan Patch in 1900, as a four-year-old, they would have to gamble that he could handle himself. The Benton County Fair was set for August 29 through September 2. It had all the things they feared: a couple thousand noisy (and nosy) spectators; older and more experienced horses; fireworks.

They considered the possible pitfalls.

They considered Shipps's stopwatch.

They decided to take a chance.

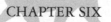

CHAPTER SIX

LAND FOR PACER Will trade 80 acres of land in the best drain-
age district of Wisconsin for a pacer that is now ready to race.
Must be young, sound and straight in every way, and be able to
show five heats fast enough to get the money in his class.

    H. J. Finch, Stevens Point, Wis.

           —classified ad in *Horse Review,* July 27, 1909

A CURIOUS THING HAPPENED around the time that Messner and
Wattles decided to enter Dan Patch to race at the Benton County
Fair: the Taylor Blacksmith Shop, on the Oxford town square,
hung out a sign that read, "We Do Dan Patch's Shoes" (which
they did, following the prescription set forth by Tommy Fenton of
Pine Village). In case you missed that notification, Taylor's took
a large display ad in the *Oxford Tribune* making the same boast.
Thus the horse did his first endorsement, in a manner of speaking,
before he ever went to the post. He was, in fact, still delivering
groceries.

    Sporting events do not come any more small-time than the
county-fair horse race in which the four-year-old Dan Patch made
his debut on August 30, 1900. Wattles, now acting as the horse's
official trainer and driver, entered Messner's colt in a best-three-
out-of-five heats contest in the 2:35 class at the Benton County
Fairgrounds, which meant, under the long-since abandoned classification system of the day, that the event was open to pacers who
had never gone a mile that fast in a winning effort. The purse was

$230, a healthy sum, but one that was in large part the horsemen's own money in the form of nomination and entry fees, with some supplementary cash from the fair association; half went to the winner, with the rest normally split among the second- through fifth-place finishers. (The winner's share of any purse was hung in a sack near the finish line, and after the deciding heat the winning driver would steer his horse back there, dismount, and remove it to varying levels of applause. The custom is no more, but turf journalists still write about a horseman or horse "taking down" the purse money at a particular race.)

The 2:35 race was the slowest division at the most minor-league level of racing, and thus accessible to every green-as-grass maiden, genuine grocery horse, and broken-down buggy nag who desired admission. Or to put it another way: a horse who had accomplished anything at all on the racetrack was not eligible for that particular contest. Marginal races like that usually were carded early in the fair—as this one was—and they often featured a large, motley field of wannabes and never-wases, veering all over the homestretch, acting up and sometimes breaking down: a comic mob scene. This particular 2:35 race, though, shaped up differently than most events of that class. There were only two other horses in it besides Dan Patch.

It is not difficult to imagine why: in a small town, as we have seen, people talked, and the horse's reputation preceded him. Speaking to a reporter for the *Indianapolis News* in April 1948, Wilber G. Nolan, who was described by the paper as a prominent Indiana attorney, remembered the electric days leading up to Dan's first race, when everyone was talking about "the Messner horse." Nolan, who had grown up in Boswell, Indiana, recalled a spirited rivalry between his hometown and Oxford, and pointed out that Boswell had "its own 'people's choice horse' at that time," a promising but untested sorrel mare named Merrygo, so highly regarded by her connections that she was entered to start against Dan Patch.

A few mornings before Merrygo and Dan would face off, Nolan, then ten, was leaning on the rail of the Boswell track with Merrygo's trainer; both were watching Dan Patch work out over the half-mile oval, and the trainer had a stopwatch on Messner's buzzed-about colt. "At one point the man looked down at his watch," Nolan recalled, "and his hair about stood on end. 'We're not going to be able to race him,' the man said. 'He went his last half mile in 1:04, my boy, and we can't race that stuff!'"

Merrygo stayed in the race, though. Only she and a gray gelding named Prince Medium were not intimidated by Dan Patch.

The thirtieth of August fell that year on a Thursday, traditionally one of the slower days at the Benton County Fair (which always ran Wednesday through Sunday). On a typical fair Thursday, one might catch the bearded lady napping in the half-empty sideshow tent, and the mule-drawn merry-go-round would have plenty of empty seats. On Thursdays fair organizers staged special attendance-boosting promotions like Banana Day tropical fruit being a rare treat in Indiana, especially at the loss-leader prices found at the fair—the prospect of seeing tarantulas scampering across the stalks an irresistible draw for the young male set. (The tarantula myth, like the alligators-in-the-New-York-sewers myth, persists in some quarters to this day.) An Oxford woman named Elizabeth Hall stated for publication that the high point of the 1900 Benton County Fair was peeling and eating a banana, not seeing Dan Patch race.

And so it may have been, depending a lot on Ms. Hall's waist-to-hips ratio, yet it must be said that her preference for fruit over horses put her in the minority. Largely because of Dan Patch, the entire fair that year hummed with a heightened sense of possibility. On August 29, opening day, a crowd of almost 2,000 turned out, most paying $1.50 each for a five-day fair pass, plus another fifty cents for one-day horse parking. On the half-mile track, Prosperity Bill, trained and driven by John Wattles for owner James Petree, a local man of leisure, survived a thrilling stretch duel in the final heat and won the featured race, a trot. (There were also a few "novelty races" for runners, the sport of kings being a mere curtain-raiser in the Cradle of the Pacer.) After Prosperity Bill's race, the band played "For He's a Jolly Good Fellow," and several hundred people cheered and sang—until somebody's carriage horse got spooked by all the hoopla, and backed up and sat down on somebody else's fried-chicken-and-watermelon picnic, which had been spread just-so on a quilt beneath a shade tree. Children ran from the scene, screaming. A broken dish cut the panicky animal, and a veterinarian was summoned to administer stitches. In other news, racehorse trainer Matt Cooper of Boswell was fined $10 for "talking sassy" to the starting judges.

A more innocent time? Not really: it was almost a Benton County Fair tradition that somebody's house got ransacked and robbed while everyone was off strolling the midway, or watching the internationally renowned parachutist Professor Echert jump out of a hot air balloon into a hot cornfield (one of the major attractions, after Dan Patch, that year). In 1900 the unfortunate fairgoer was John Wattles's brother Charles, who also worked a farm on the outskirts of Oxford. Break-in artists took clothing belonging to Charles's hired man and a dollar or two that Mrs. Wattles had hidden in a teacup, which to some, said the *Tribune*, indicated an inside job. The case remains unsolved.

Still, August 30, the day of the three-horse 2:35 pace, was the most exciting day in Oxford's history. "This Thursday! Dan Patch Day!" screamed headlines in the *Tribune*. Every business in town except for the post office closed, and virtually the entire population of 1,674 went to the fairgrounds racetrack, seven miles east of town. People drove from Lafayette, and some came by train from as far away as Indianapolis and Chicago. The newspaper gave the attendance at 8,000, or more than double the combined populations of Oxford and Boswell. Most of those who turned out, their chests swelling with pride, were, of course, the same people who had been badmouthing Messner, Wattles, Zelica, and Dan for several years running. It didn't matter; they had all done the Christian thing and forgiven themselves—then got dressed up, as if for church, and gone to the fair to cheer their hero. At noontime, Oxford's town square probably looked as deserted as it does today, in the post-Wal-Mart era. Said the *Tribune*: "Only Postmaster James Pickering and his office cat remained behind."

As I was working on this book, I kept sticking at this point in the story. Sure, people like horses, I thought, and it was a long time age in a faraway land and all that. But people are still people, and people have things—such as their children, their jealousy, their jobs—that tend to prevent them from playing extras in someone else's movie. Even though the evidence is there in the old newspapers and in the oral tradition, it all sounded so impossibly corny: a mass migration to the county fairgrounds to see the once-crippled colt who just might, by golly, put Oxford, Indiana, on the map! With a little imagination one can see the scene up there on the big screen, as part of a mediocre 1950s musical: Doris Day and a bunch of women in bonnets, kicking up their petticoats and singing their hearts out; John Raitt and his buddies in derbies, snapping their suspenders, clicking their heels and looking suspiciously like the Jets and Sharks from *West Side Story* because, for whatever reason, the same six bachelor gents used to get all the good dance parts. I felt, in the early stages of my research, that it couldn't have really happened that way, to real people and a real horse. It was only after more digging and thinking that I came to accept that—save for the singing and dancing—it actually did.

It happened because conditions were ripe for the emergence of someone—or something—to rally around. The attentive reader will have noticed that before Dan Patch came along there was not a hell of a lot in Oxford to kick up one's petticoats or snap one's suspenders about. The town's one legitimate claim to fame—well, significance—was that it appeared in the footnotes of legal history as the site, in 1873, of the first murder trial in Indiana in which circumstantial evidence resulted in a conviction.

Oxford's only other moment of semi-fame concerned the so-called Benton County Lion, a sort of landlocked Loch Ness monster that terrorized the area starting in the spring of 1868, when pigs and sheep went missing without explanation, and some steers were found with their hindquarters chewed off. Looking at the evidence, the town fathers quite naturally came to the conclusion that a lion was about, and organized search parties to comb the cornfields. No lions were found, but cattle continued to be savaged. When Spinger and Henderson's Circus came to town that summer, some prominent Oxfordites implored the lion tamer to take one of his beasts on the prairie to see if he could smoke out its African cousin. The trainer declined, but a few months later, with anxiety still high, "one man put out some poisoned meat," wrote Howard C. Gillespie in a 1935 history of Oxford called *Tales of a Prairie Town*. "The next morning he found an enormous timber wolf. He brought the animal to town, got a room and showed it for twenty-five cents a look. Everybody wanted to see the 'lion.' He then took the wolf to Lafayette, and in all, cleaned up a couple hundred dollars by exhibiting the carcass." The story received widespread newspaper coverage throughout what was then still known as the West. "Great stories had been told," Gillespie wrote, "and one paper was even received from Germany giving an account of the beast and telling of the wild life of the frontier."

Ha, some wild life. If the Germans had only known how fusty the American frontier could be: waltzing and two-stepping were frowned upon in Oxford, on the theory that they led to additional waltzing and two-stepping. Dances of any sort were rarely held, and social events seemed to revolve around the vigorous manipulation of vegetable matter—there were flax pullings, wood choppings, apple parings, pumpkin cuttings, and corn huskings. "Courtin' or keepin' company was an informal proceeding and a universal custom," Jesse Birch writes in *History of Benton County and Historic Oxford*, "yet a flirt was soon found out and given the mitten."

And yet the history books, so Midwest-polite, tell only part of the tale. The people of Oxford did have more than flax pullings and fake lions to focus on for mental stimulation: they had one another. One thing I came to realize early in the writing of this book, and which I had never realized in ten years of working as an editor at *People* magazine and *Us Weekly*, is that what we call the "celebrity culture" is not confined to the territory staked out by those show-bizzy glossies. The celebrity culture crops up everywhere across space and time. It is something that occurs naturally, when a minimum of two beings come together: one will become intrigued, if not obsessed, with the other, or more likely, they will exhibit a mutual interest. And I also learned this while probing the history of Oxford: the smaller the town, the more celebrities per capita.

In Oxford, Indiana, in 1900 you could be a celebrity—that is, you could be the subject of widespread gossip, speculation and criticism, and coverage in the local press—merely by breaking your ankle, throwing a party, coming down with an unsightly skin rash, or buying a pair of shoes. If you took a trip to Lafayette, twenty-three miles distant, the *Oxford Tribune* would take note of it, and the men who sat on the benches outside Messner and Son would ask each other if they had seen the item and discuss at length what you might be doing there, and perhaps why you thought it necessary (one eyebrow cocked here, meaningful pause) to stay the night. An Oxfordite named Phoebe W. Baldwin achieved a brief but real celebrity for making suits of clothes for two men who left town in 1849 to join the California gold rush, her pay being reported in the newspaper as a white hog weighing 150 pounds and two bushels of wheat. A man named Hartley T. Howard became more than a little famous in Oxford for bringing the first sausage grinder to pork-centric Benton County in the 1850s (the exact date is a subject of scholarly debate), and he was memorialized in a poem composed by Alexander Campbell, one of John Wattles's classmates at the old one-room schoolhouse. I quote from the *Tribune*:

Of all the sausage grinders in the west,
Harley T. Howard's got the best.
Just step in and give him a call,
And see him grind up pig, tail and all.

A sixty-something soldier, Jacob Nelling, became a household name in Oxford after he was lynched in 1883 for the previously mentioned murder of sixteen-year-old Ada Atkinson. Removed from jail by an angry mob, he was taken to the scene of the crime and unceremoniously hanged. "A man of wonderful nerve," one witness called him, "who passed into the great unknown without a murmur or a plea for mercy."

By the turn of the twentieth century, John Wattles was a celebrity just for being seventy-something years old. Dan Messner was an A-list celebrity for owning the town's biggest store; his paying

too much for Zelica and breeding her to Joe Patchen for an exor-
bitant fee were framed in conversations as the foibles of a man out
of touch with practical wisdom. The 1,600 souls who inhabited
Oxford circa 1900 have all long since departed—many without ever
tripping the wires strung by government, hospitals, and banks—
and no one visits their untidy graves; for all practical purposes, they
never existed. Yet for a time they were, almost all of them, deeply
fascinating to all the nobodies now moldering in the surrounding
plots, all the more so if they were good looking.

Dan Patch was extremely good looking. "I remember him,"
Mrs. Evan Eastman told Mary Cross nearly seventy years later, her
voice hushed with wonder. "He was a beautiful satiny brown."
But he was more than just a pretty face; he was the kind of celebrity that Oxford had never seen before: he had the potential to
be talked about, lied about, and criticized far beyond the town
limits. Everyone in Oxford understood that, and it made their
hearts pump.

Along with the thriving celebrity culture, the annual fairs, which
mixed innocent frivolity with naughtiness, provided Oxfordites
with much-needed relief from the mind- and soul-numbing prairie
propriety. In a good year at the fair you could see cooch shows,
fortune-tellers, dice games, card games, Elizabeth Hall eating a
banana, booths selling hard cider—and, thanks in large part to
the latter, plenty of fistfights, with various people's daddies getting
down in the dirt with other people's daddies and causing scenes
of delicious and enduring embarrassment. The church ladies were
always outraged and the local constable always shocked, just
shocked, to hear reports of such illegal goings-on. Annually, he
vowed to investigate and give perpetrators the mitten.

Horse racing, which was always a big draw, came and went
as a source of controversy—or, rather, because it was a source of
controversy, it came and went. Back in 1851, for example, Asbury
Keenan and Israel Doyle were each fined $2 for placing bets, and
a few years later racing was banned—only to be reinstated in the
late 1850s, with officials winking at the trackside bookmakers
who conducted well-organized betting pools. And then suddenly
racing was banned again, and preached against as evil ("Under the

deceptive title of 'Agriculture Fair,'" said Brooklyn, New York, pastor Thomas De Witt Talmage, "are the same cheating and the same betting, the same drunkenness and vagabondage and the same abominations that were to be found under the old horse racing system")—until the day it was once again brought back with much fanfare. (This was the pattern nationwide during the nineteenth century.) During periods when the antiracing forces had the upper hand, you could show a pacer or trotter in competition at the Benton County Fair in hopes of winning a blue ribbon, but the animal by law had to remain absolutely still; technically, the owner could be arrested if it moved.

Dan Messner and his wife, Maud, arrived at what was officially the Benton-Warren Agricultural Association Fair on August 30 in the elaborate red rig that he had bought for Zelica—who was limping along good-naturedly between the shafts, wearing her harness trimmed in German silver. The Messners alit from the vehicle, the crowd parted for them, and the couple who owned an untested horse in the lowest-class race on the afternoon's program were escorted, like royalty, to special seats in the grandstand. Messner looked around him. So this is horse racing, he surely thought. This isn't so bad. I could get used to this.

From where they sat they could be seen by all, and could themselves see, down on the half-mile track, Dan Patch being warmed up by John Wattles. (Harness horses always work several miles on the day of a race, usually starting a couple of hours before post time.) The old man wore a cap of bright blue silk and a white silk jacket trimmed with gold piping; it had been sewn for him by his wife of nearly fifty years, Elizabeth. For this special occasion, the coal oil had been squeegeed off Dan by his new groom, James Stephen, and the horse's beautiful bay coat danced with dapples.

Since the 1940s, harness racing has employed the mobile starting gate—basically a car fitted with retractable wings that a field of horses lines up behind in post-position order. In 1900, though, the tedious score-down system was still in place. That meant that the three horses in the 2:35 class convened upstretch at a spot about 300 yards ahead of the starting point, lined up in post-position order (it is not known what position Dan started from in his first race), then swept before the grandstand from the top of the homestretch, picking up speed as they went. The goal was to reach the start in something resembling a straight line, at which point the starting judge, standing on a platform near the start/finish wire, would holler "Go!" through a megaphone. And they would be off. If, however, the imaginary line was too raggedy for the judge's taste, or if any of the horses was ahead of the inside, or pole, horse, he rang a bell. The horses then pulled up, returned to the top of the stretch, caught their breath, and the process began again. Sometimes thirty minutes passed before an exhausted field was finally sent away. The intimate group in Dan Patch's race got off to a more routine start, trying four times before the judge said "Go!"

The race, which started just after two in the afternoon, had the crowd on its feet and cheering, though it offered little in the way of strategic maneuvers or suspense. In the first heat, Dan Patch glided directly to the lead and stayed there for the required two laps around the track, drawing away at the end of the mile to win in 2:24 ½, with Merrygo second (by an unrecorded margin), and Prince Medium bringing up the rear. Dan Patch was so superior he may not even have realized he was in a race. "He paced home," an eyewitness named Warren Davis told the *Merrillville* (Ind.) *Herald-News* in January of 1938, "without sweating a hair."

In the next heat, according to Davis, the other drivers in the race conspired to box in Dan Patch and prevent him from getting the lead. This was a common enough tactic among the hard-bitten harness horsemen of that era, but Davis's account is undercut by his memory of a full field of rivals—he talked about one man refusing to go along with the plot, but the others forming a flying wedge around Dan Patch—while it is clear from several other sources that there were only two others. Perhaps we can split the difference and say that in the second heat Dan came from off the pace to win in 2:22 ¼, and Prince Medium beat Merrygo for second place. In the final, conducted about an hour later, Dan Patch led all the way around again, and won again in 2:24 ¼, with Merrygo outpacing Prince Medium in what seemed like their own private match race.

In each heat, to the delight of the crowd, Wattles's beard wrapped around his ears and flapped in the breeze as he came down the homestretch, even as he struggled mightily against the reins to slow the horse down. The object for the driver, under the old classification system, was to win in as slow a time as possible so as to remain eligible for the next slowest class. Astute horseman that he was, Wattles wanted to climb the class ladder with Dan rung by rung, picking up as many purses and trophies as possible along the way. Dan, however, quickly made a hash of that plan by blowing all the way down to the 2:20 class in his debut. Wattles, for all his skill, was simply not strong enough to make Dan go slower.

Back in Oxford that evening, the town's two rival drugstores cosponsored an impromptu party for the horse. A crowd of several hundred people gathered in the town square to sip pink lemonade and (on the sneak) hard cider and wait for the sky to get dark enough to set off fireworks. The pyrotechnics didn't last long; they amounted to just a few Roman candles left over from the Fourth of July, but they provided a nice, festive punctuation. As Mary Cross writes: "Thus ended the perfect day as people started off for their homes for bed and pleasant dreams of many more such celebrations in honor of their favorite son. How fortunate they lived with such good neighbors, warm friends, and a race horse who looked like a sure winner."

What a pretty picture. And yet the horse, as it turned out, was not universally beloved. The next day—when every man in town seemed to be driving his rig at top speed, in imitation of Dan and Uncle John Wattles—the *Tribune,* besides complaining that it was not safe to cross the streets anymore, carried an item in which an unidentified someone "lowed that the frost would soon be here to nip the vegetation. So would the frost of disappointment soon nip the tender leaves of expectation for Dan Patch." It sounded like the witch from Snow White had moved to Oxford, but the remark is worth noting.

Still, there is no denying that it was an idyllic moment. Oxford that evening was approaching its peak of influence and prosperity, such as it was; things have gone decidedly slack in the interval. The population has dipped about 25 percent, to 1,200, and the town square, with its mostly vacant buildings, its apologetic-looking pizza place, its storefront golden-oldies radio station festooned with plastic used-car-lot pennants, suggests an Edward Hopper painting not quite come to life. Messner's store closed in the early 1980s—no one, not even John Messner, seems to remember exactly when; it was a florist shop, and then a sandwich shop, and now it's empty. Once Oxford was a place where the strait-laced and the easily unlaced maintained a symbiotic relationship, but the center did not hold. The presumably permanent depression there represents several trends in American society, not the least of which is the (Pyrrhic) victory of the flax-pulling puritans over the purveyors of good, semi-clean fun. Horse racing departed the scene in the 1930s; a bowling alley, which was located above Messner's store, came and went after a few years in the 1950s; the movie theater, talked about briefly decades ago, never arrived, and now never will. The last saloon in town closed its doors a couple of years ago. It was called the Dead Horse.

The same thing that killed the horse killed Oxford: the automobile. Once everybody had a car, moving away became much less of a psychic struggle because one could always get back so quickly, and the world offered so many more reasons to move away than to stay. Even those who remained could use their cars to shop in Lafayette, formerly a once-a-year destination, or at a Wal-Mart planted on some arbitrary spot along the highway, so another downtown withered and died.

Social life of a sort does go on, though. On an early autumn evening I attended an Oxford Lions Club potluck supper. In a room so fluorescently lit that my fillings vibrated, I dined, without the aid of alcohol, on premolded pork and beef patties swimming in each other's juices, a casserole made from canned string beans and canned onion rings, and, for dessert, a white cube of Betty Crocker can-frosted cake. It was a meal best taken with a dab of Wildroot in one's hair. Various citizens were being formally thanked for their volunteer efforts, including Bob and Thelma Glaspie, a warm and gracious couple who for more than forty years have been the keepers of the Dan Patch flame in the community and who display their collection of memorabilia and edu-

cational materials at Oxford's annual Dan Patch Days festival.
The speeches that evening were as preformed as the patties—until
Thelma rose (it was Bob's bowling night, and I'd come as her
guest) and sharply criticized the Lions for not advertising the Dan
Patch Days, with the result being, she said, that the event had
attracted a total of only sixty people over the course of two lan-
guid afternoons. As she spoke, her voice quavered with emotion,
and the audience appeared stunned. What she was doing was simply not done at a Lions Club potluck supper, but Thelma, whose
ancestors were among the first white settlers along the nearby
Wabash, is no outsider. White-haired and fair-skinned, she is a
strikingly beautiful and extremely well-spoken woman: the kind
you want on your side. When she finished her brief but unexpected blast, she sat down abruptly, and for a long moment we
all stared into our brightly colored canned punch while the fluo-
rescent lights hummed. Then, without comment from the chair,
the meeting resumed, with the acknowledgment of a man who
had run the very-well-attended rodeo. My gaze wandered, and I
noticed—how could I have not seen this before?—a painting of
Dan Patch hanging on the back wall: there the great horse was,
ready to race, with his nattily dressed driver sitting proudly behind
him, the scene slightly faded but as large as life.

Thelma, sitting across from me, saw me looking. "That's something, isn't it?" she said. "It hung in the bank for many years."

The bank, which in past times put little likenesses of Dan Patch
on its signage, its stationery, and its checks, now had a modern,
abstract logo as well as a smaller, more functional space befitting
the ATM era and, I'd noticed that day, a homemade banner in the
window that said "Go Blue Devils," a shout-out to the high school
football team. For a long time now, football and, of course, basketball have been the main Hoosier games, and racing has meant
the Indy 500. The nearest harness track to Oxford is 113 miles
away, at Hoosier Park. Oxfordites prefer rodeo now, and, judging
by my car radio, country music. Indiana is the West again.

"Good ol' Dan . . . ," Thelma said, sighing.

The mahogany horse, his head cocked to the left, looked back
at us from a more beautiful age.

CHAPTER SEVEN

I never knew a man yet who could give himself to the pleasures of the turf for a long reach of time, and not be battered in morals. They hook up their spanking team, and put on their sporting-cap, and light their cigar, and take the reins, and dash down the road to perdition. The hotels are thronged, nearly every kind of equipage is taken up at an almost fabulous price, and there are many respectable people mingling with jockeys, and gamblers, and libertines, and foul-mouthed men and flashy women. The bar-tender stirs up the brandy-smash. The bets run high. The greenhorns, supposing all is fair, put in their money soon enough to lose it.

—Thomas De Witt Talmage

DAN PATCH'S SECOND RACE—ANOTHER marathon affair involving a minimum of three and a maximum of five one-mile heats—occurred on September 5, 1900, just six days after his maiden victory. Grueling as that schedule may sound by today's standards—Thoroughbred trainers often complain that there are only two weeks between the first two Triple Crown races—it was not out of line with what other turn-of-the-twentieth-century athletes, human and equine, routinely endured. The sports world in the ragtime age was certainly not as spartan and barbaric as it had been in pre–Civil War times. Gone were the blood-soaked, for-men-only spectacles—the dogfights, the rat-baitings, and the ugly, bareknuckled, pre–Marquess of Queensberry brawls—that had transpired in the back rooms of smoky taverns and slimy oyster houses during what academics call the "bachelor period of American sports," fifty years earlier. Sports, during the Second Industrial Revolution, had been cleaned up and made into a big business, entertainment for the masses, a spectacle rife with rules and standards, suitable for the whole family. But athletes still led a relatively Hobbesian existence: their shifts were nasty, brutish, and long.

Horses, especially the durable Standardbred, were held to the same Herculean standards as humans. Hence the now all-but-abandoned heats system, which downplayed speed in favor of endurance—or, as the English called it, "bottom"—as the supreme virtue of the day. The idea was usually to win three heats, or to have the best combined placings in a maximum of five heats, all conducted on the same often-broiling afternoon. Between starts there was constant travel—sometimes by rail, sometimes on foot—and endless training miles, often ten or more per day. Work was thought to be good for horses, and in fact many lived long and prospered, either in spite of or because of their regimens. A pacing mare named Effie Powers had a twelve-year career during which she competed at ninety-five different tracks in sixteen different states and Canada, going a total of 629 competitive miles. I know that not because Effie Powers was famed for her durability and longevity—she was not famed for anything—but because I stumbled upon her stats in the April 6, 1905, *Van Wert* (Ohio) *Daily Bulletin* in a short item that was buried under a story headlined "Van Wert Bowlers Win Over the Lima Blue Ribbons." Effie was a real trouper, a tough old babe, a Tad's Steakhouse steak of a pacing mare, nothing more.

And yet Dan Patch's early schedule was unusual in one way: his second race, which took place at the Lafayette, Indiana, fairgrounds, constituted a steep and, to some of his newfound fans, scary step upward. Lafayette, the seat of relatively prosperous Tippecanoe County, was, in terms of racing and most other matters, the legitimate semi-big time. It had a population of 18,116 in 1900, making it about twelve times the size of Oxford, and it sits just across the Wabash River from West Lafayette, the home of Purdue, then the largest and most prestigious university in the state. Twenty-seven miles to the southeast of the Benton County fairgrounds, it was a destination point for shopping, culture, and catting about beyond which few Oxfordites ever felt the need to venture. "You went there once a year," Bob Glaspie, the local Dan Patch historian, told me. "Maybe twice if your family had the means." (Now some people who live in Oxford work in Lafayette.) Lafayette was not Indianapolis, a metropolis of 169,000 experiencing boom times thanks to nearby natural gas fields and a nascent automobile industry. But compared to Oxford, everything was up-to-date in Lafayette, and everything was on a grander scale, including the $300 race in which Wattles, even before the Benton County triumph, had entered Dan Patch.

It was a bold move any way you looked at it. Entering your horse at the Lafayette fair was, in one sense, not the sort of thing that was done in Oxford: striving openly to show you were better than others, making a statement that you were ready for prime time, such as it was—that kind of behavior was just a bit too show-offy for some folks. The Greek chorus of philosophers who warmed the benches outside Messner's sang a song of Wattles and Messner getting carried away with themselves, feeling invulnerable, and in the process getting poor Dan Patch, the pride of Benton County, in way over his head. We all know what pride cometh before.

From a betting person's perspective, that was not an unreasonable position to take. The still very green pacer—he hadn't learned much about racing, after all, in three easy wins—would be meeting an exceptionally large field of ten challengers at Lafayette, almost all of whom were battle-scarred veterans of the racing wars. Some had even raced on the lower levels of the Grand Circuit. The latter group included a hard-knocking chestnut gelding named Milo S., who seemed to be rounding into form and, simultaneously, taking the kind of class drop that makes horse players salivate; he loomed as the heavy favorite in the brisk (and illegal) betting that was sure to take place on the track apron and throughout the grandstand.

Though Milo S. was a certifiable plug—the Lafayette race was still in the pokey 2:35 class, after all; Dan was eligible because he still hadn't gone that fast on the day when entries closed—the seven- or eight-year-old gelding (reports vary) seemed to have the advantage, if only because he was a veteran campaigner, as sports-writers still like to say. Milo S. was all business, a no-nonsense professional who came to the fairgrounds to do a job of work—and not, like Dan Patch, to learn how to race while checking out the crowd and the other horses and stopping occasionally (at least during warm-ups) to smell the popcorn. The week before at Boswell many had watched in amazement as Dan calmly accepted nose pats and rump slaps from the mob that had poured down from the stands and flowed around him after the final heat. The horse's willingness—nay, eagerness—to mingle impressed every-one, but it made some wonder if Dan wasn't simply too nice an animal to succeed against tough, cold, out-of-town competition. Where was the inner rage that seemed to fuel the fastest stallions? "He's more like a pet," one Oxfordite told the *Tribune,* noting Dan's deep brown eyes and affection for penny candy. And it was true: standing still and crunching butterscotch, young Dan Patch did not look all that intimidating.

Dan Patch in motion, though, was a most different tale, as the horsemen who had seen him train and race already knew. He stood 15.3 hands high now, tall for a Standardbred of that day. He was slightly taller in fact than he was long (15.2 hands), which was not classic conformation, but everyone agreed that his 1,100 pounds were distributed in handsome fashion. He was hardly a perfect-gaited pacer; his orthopedic shoe and extra-wide sulky could not correct what John Markey, the legendary racing writer who signed himself "Marque," later called "a rolling gait that was always the subject of criticism from fastidious horsemen." He sprawled behind, and wasted energy. Yet he covered ground effortlessly, despite his physical quirks; *Horseman* magazine once estimated that he traveled an amazing 44 feet per second and that, even in "the teeth of a stiff wind . . . his stride did not vary for many rods." He had won so impressively at Boswell that the back-stretch types at Lafayette—the trainers, grooms, horseshoers, and owners—were all looking out for "the Messner colt" when Dan arrived a few days before the race. Clair Cutler Wolverton, an Indiana horseman of that era, remembered in his memoir *Fifty Years with Harness Horses* that at Lafayette Dan was stabled in the same barn as the Standardbreds trained by him and his father, Philip. "Accompanied by my father," wrote Wolverton, who was fifteen at the time, "I was a visitor to [Dan Patch's] stall, where I hung on every word of his friendly caretaker. I believe that even then people realized he was a great horse."

For everyone who was there to witness it, though, the first heat at Lafayette was a most perplexing event.

The large field made it necessary to have two tiers of horses in the starting formation: six across in the front tier and five across behind. None of the few extant reports from that day tells exactly which post position Dan Patch drew, but we do know that he was one of the five in the rear tier of pacers and stuck out toward the middle of the track, a highly disadvantageous position, especially for a horse new to racing. With another, slower horse starting directly in front of him, Wattles had no choice but to be conservative at the start, the result being that he and Dan promptly got shuffled back to ninth or tenth place as the field went around the first turn.

The pole horse, Milo S., meanwhile, had grabbed the lead. For three-quarters of a mile, Wattles, dressed as usual in his blue-and-gold driving colors, his beard flapping in the breeze, sat calmly toward the rear as the field, in the preferred racing style of the day, hugged the rail behind Milo S. in "Indian file," saving ground for one climactic rush. Dan didn't seem to mind pacing along in heavy traffic, but would he ever make a move?

Yes, he would. As Milo S. led the way around the fourth and final turn of the half-mile track, Wattles guided Dan Patch from the rail and began passing horses. The crowd gasped, then cheered as he reached the middle of the pack. "He appeared for all the world," wrote Wolverton, "like a big schoolboy pushing a lot of little boys out of the way on a playground." A judge who timed Dan separately, and unofficially, later said that Messner's colt had traveled the final quarter mile in 30 ¼ seconds, one of the fastest fractional times ever recorded to that date—and Wattles had yet to even flick his whip.

But it was a star-crossed heat. Wolverton, watching from the backstretch, recalled a half-century later that he saw Dan, just as he was gathering momentum, throw a hind shoe, probably the left one with the extended shank. "It had sailed away up high much as one would sail a pie plate," Wolverton wrote in his memoir. Certainly that made Dan's last quarter mile all the more impressive. Yet his effort still fell short; at the finish line, he was a neck back of Milo S.

The crowd reacted with silence—odd because the betting favorite had won. But what shocked the assembled was that the horse who was clearly much the best hadn't. What had happened? Was it a case of human error? Had Wattles simply driven him poorly, making his move too late?

The horsemen, and the savvier fans, thought not. Their immediate assumption was that Wattles, one of the cagiest drivers in the state, a man who could judge the pace of a race perfectly and time his moves precisely, had lost the race on purpose so he could either cash a bet on Milo S. or raise the odds on Dan for heat number two, or most probably both. A certain level of skullduggery has always been part of the racing scene, and it is tolerated the way the owner of a restaurant might passively condone a headwaiter's bribe-taking, as part of the culture, as the way things have always worked. Yet horse people, like everyone else, can get greedy or careless, and sometimes the cheating gets a bit too blatant. Then the perpetrators must be punished, or at least publicly called out and slapped around for the good of the game. The racing judges, in this case, felt that Wattles had gone too far and was insulting their intelligence; he clearly had enough horse between his sulky shafts to have won by open lengths had he made his move at an appropriate time.

As soon as the race was over, the Lafayette officials summoned Wattles to their stand on the finish line. With their mustaches twitching in anger, they grilled him about his tactics—the initial lack of aggressiveness, the impressive but ultimately insufficient surge. They also reminded Wattles that they had the power to fine or suspend him from racing—permanently, if they saw fit.

Wattles, standing there with his blue silk driving hat in his hand, staring down and scuffing the sole of his boot on the floorboards, looked like a very old bad boy. He knew this was more than just a ritual dressing-down, done mostly to impress the locals and to show the authorities that racing was an honest, self-policing sport deserving of its place at the fair. No, this time Wattles had the suits in a state of high dudgeon.

Still, he was not overly worried. Though bumpkinesque and laconic by nature, a small, frail man with a permanent sadness in his eyes, Wattles knew how to handle the situation and still have time to get down a bet on Dan Patch in the second heat. There was a way these things were done. First, you expressed dignified surprise at the accusations made against you. Wattles said he was shocked, really, to have his integrity impugned after all the races he had driven on the Indiana fair circuit. Why, he was racing when these judges were boys in short pants, coming to the fairs with their fathers—and how were their daddies, anyway?

The next step, if you were accused of "laying up," or not trying to win, was to remind the officials that you had faced tremendous adversity. Wattles spoke of how far back he had to start in the heat, and noted that he was driving a fast but inexperienced pacer not accustomed to weaving his way through traffic on a narrow half-mile track. Wattles also added some new, inside information—a smart strategic move. He said a broken buckle had forced him to switch to a new harness that very morning, and he hadn't quite gotten used to the feel of the way the horse was rigged, and that this had, alas, affected his driving. Wattles seems not to have thrown in the excuse of the lost hind shoe that Wolverton observed, perhaps because it flew off behind him and he hadn't noticed it himself yet, having been summoned to the judges' stand so abruptly. He did insist, though, that he had not bet on Milo S. (which may have been true) and that he was not trying to manipulate the odds for heat two (which, based on the testimony of people who knew Wattles and were there that day, almost certainly wasn't).

The three judges listened, harrumphed, conferred among themselves, harrumphed again—then issued a stern warning to Wattles, telling him he had better not pull any fast ones with Dan Patch in heat two or they would find someone else to drive the horse (ordering a driver switch was then a common judicial practice).

Messner, meanwhile, watched the scene play out from the

grandstand with annoyance verging on anger. Surrounded by the inevitable well-wishers and backslappers, he had been embarrassed by the sight of Dan coming up short. Messner wasn't interested in artificially inflating the odds by making Dan Patch lose; he wanted to win, win, and win again, and go home to more fireworks and another party. The more he thought about it, and the more people who came over to console him during the awkward postrace moments, the madder he got. Clearly, Dan Patch could have won the heat if not for Wattles. In his mind, this was a strike against the old man—and not the first one, either.

Success can be hard on any partnership, public success all the more so. As Dan Patch flashed signs of being something special, people began forming opinions about who was responsible for "making" the horse and expressing those opinions, regardless of their value, in the *Tribune*, in taverns, and sometimes in face-to-face talks with Messner and Wattles.

The majority of Oxfordites assumed that the credit for Dan Patch should go to Wattles, for the simple reason that he knew a lot about horses and Messner, as recently as a few years earlier, knew almost nothing. Paying $255 for Zelica, paying $150 to breed to Joe Patchen—only Ziegfeld had more follies than Messner. Early in the process, before Dan started flashing racehorse speed on the Chiquesalonghi track, Messner would have probably agreed that Uncle Johnny had made the horse what he was, and laughed at the idea that he could have anything to do with molding Dan into a professional pacer. But as time went on, and it began to appear that fame and money might be part of the equation, Messner started to see things differently, and to act differently as well. For one thing, he began to act more like Dan's manager (in the sense that Sarah Bernhardt and Harry Houdini had managers), insisting, for example, that the pacer go to Tom Fenton's shop in Pine Village for corrective shoeing, a decision that Wattles, apparently, opposed to the point of not coming along on the trip.

By the time of the Lafayette race Messner was no longer the bumbling, humble naïf who shied from the racetrack and deferred to Wattles on all horse matters. Now he snapped open his news-paper to the racing page each morning. Forgetting that he had not known the gestation period of a horse when Dan Patch was con-ceived, he had begun referring to himself as "a breeder." At the same time, he stopped telling the self-deprecating story of buying Zelica by mistake, and started saying—out of Wattles's earshot and usually after a cocktail or two—that it was he who had broken Dan Patch to harness and given him his first training miles. (There was a germ of reality in this: Messner had participated, in a dilettantish way, in Dan's early training, sometimes spelling Wattles in the jog-ging cart while Dan circled the track at Chiquesalonghi.)

Wattles, meanwhile, had begun to feel a bit like the biblical Abraham: dazed by the blessing of a golden child coming along so late in the game. Dan Patch made him feel like the true horse-man he had always aspired to be. In the federal census of 1900 Wattles stated his birth year, as always, as 1828, but for the first time gave his occupation as "trainer." Previously he had hung, out of modesty, with the chorus of those who said "farmer" when the census taker asked.

Wattles didn't want praise for Dan Patch; praise just made a man like him nervous. But neither did he like anyone saying that it was not John Wattles who had made a racehorse out of Dan Patch.

A vexing question now colored dealings between trainer and owner: if the horse was headed to the big time, as so many guessed he was, would Wattles be making the journey with him? He had the training and driving skills, to be sure, but he also still had a very large family farm to manage, and, of course, a lot of years on him. What would that look like, a seventy-something rookie on the Grand Circuit? Messner had asked himself that question, and he worried that Wattles might cut a kind of comic figure in the big cities along the Roarin' Grand (as it was called): fantasti-cally old, fully bearded, and stereotypically backwoodsy—just the sort to restart the snickers about Dan Messner's horse sense. Of course, Wattles wasn't the only good horseman whose services could be had for a monthly fee and a percentage of the purse money. The rumor around Oxford was that Messner was scouting for a replacement.

Meanwhile, back at the Lafayette race, Wattles had Dan Patch reshod and perfectly situated for the second heat. His second-place finish meant he would be starting from a much better spot this time (second from the rail in the first tier). It also meant that, because he had introduced a trace of doubt about Dan Patch, he could lay down a bet on the horse at slightly higher odds than he would have gotten if Dan had been first across the finish line. All wagering went unreported, of course (Indiana did not legalize betting until 1994), but the best guess is that Dan Patch went off at odds of something like 3–1.

Milo S., also hovering around 3–1, was again the pole horse because of his first-heat victory. He left alertly, but this time was quickly passed on his right by Dan Patch, who circled easily around the gelding and settled into his more familiar spot in the lead. The two top betting choices remained in that order the entire first lap, and most of the second; then just before the three-quarter pole, driver Vincent Sillick moved Milo S. away from the rail, putting himself in position for a closing surge. That surge never happened, though. As Wattles eased up on the bit, Dan paced away from the field and crossed the wire more than four lengths ahead of Milo S., in a personal-best time of 2:16.

Dan, not even breathing hard after the heat, seemed unbeatable— unless the rest of the field conspired to box him in, or someone with bad intentions hooked a wheel around one of Wattles's. Such dirty tactics were standard for the day and, like Wattles's "laying up" in the first heat, were tolerated at the discretion of the officials.

Heat three, in fact, provided an example of just what the judges might allow on a day when it would not break their hearts to see John Wattles roughed up on the racetrack. Dan once again paced out to the lead, but at the half-mile point three horses charged up wildly and, catching Wattles off guard, managed to form a kind of box around Dan (two raced ahead of him, another hung just to his right). They paced on like that for more than a quarter mile, with the crowd booing, and Dan remaining trapped along the rail—until deep in the homestretch, when a seam of daylight suddenly opened and Wattles guided his horse through it, going on to win the heat by a length in 2:18 ¾.

In heat four the nasty tactics changed—Dan grabbed the lead, but now, one by one, challengers loomed up alongside him, pressing the pace in an attempt to tire him out. "Nothing personal, Uncle Johnny," one driver said to Wattles as he pulled wheel-to-wheel. Nothing doing, either. Around the last turn, Dan sprinted away, winning by open lengths in 2:16 ¼. Taking that heat meant that he had won the race, too.

Instead of being intimidated by Lafayette, Dan had left a powerful impression. A day or two after he shipped out, young Clair Wolverton began a ritual that he called "my little superstition." For many years afterward, he would, before he started to train a new horse, bring the animal into the stall at the Lafayette fairgrounds that Dan had occupied and simply let him stand there for a few moments, on hallowed ground.

Dan Patch's southward journey from Lafayette to Crawfordsville, Indiana, the site of his third race, was not the most storied traversing of that particular fifty-mile route. On August 17, 1859, hot air balloonist John Wise had set out from Lafayette for New York City with a large sack of letters, intent on making the first airmail delivery in the history of the U.S. Mail. He didn't quite make it, landing instead in the hometown of General Lew Wallace, author of the renowned—and just about unreadable—novel *Ben-Hur*. Dan Patch, though, remains the most celebrated figure who ever went from Lafayette to Crawfordsville on purpose.

A smattering of Oxfordites also made the trek (ten hours by horse, two by train, each way) to cheer on the pacer when he went to the post for the 2:35-class race on September 12. Dan Patch qualified for this easy class because, as with his previous race, the entry box had closed weeks before, when he was still an untested commodity. Assuming that the other nine entrants were true 2:35 horses, he figured to be the prohibitive favorite. But no; because fifty miles was a long way for buzz to travel in those days, the favorite's role in the $300 purse went to a pacer named American Belle, a locally popular but mediocre mare who was not even the best of the several American Belles racing in that era, when the registration process, meant to prevent duplicate names and "ringers," obviously had its failings.

As spectacle, the Crawfordsville race did not offer much; it was no *Ben-Hur*. Dan Patch went immediately to the front and won three straight heats, leading every step of the way, the fastest time being 2:19 ¾. Under the enthusiastic urging of her driver, Harry Nixon, American Belle tried hard but simply couldn't keep up, finishing second all three times by increasingly wide margins with the eight other horses scattered behind her, gasping. If Wattles had anything to be concerned about as he led his horse off the track and past the dozens of trainers, grooms, horseshoers, and hotwalkers who had left their posts to gawk at his pacer, it was that Dan Patch had not gotten so much as a good workout.

The trip was educational in one way, though. It was Dan's first experience riding the railroad—he had walked the twenty-three miles to Lafayette several days before his race there, hitched to the back of Wattles's wagon—and he had proved to be a tranquil traveler, relaxed as ever, eager to look out his boxcar window at the passing scenery and willing to eat, drink, and doze along the way. This was extremely good news for Wattles and Messner. Not every horse, certainly not every stallion, traveled well. Some became distraught at even the sight of a train, sweating heavily as soon as they entered the yard.

There was good reason for this. Horses have delicate temperaments, and train travel for them in that era could be downright cruel. The misery would start when they stepped into a freight car that was stiflingly hot and even less well ventilated than usual because grooms had to construct makeshift stalls in the stripped-down cars, and the wooden walls cut off virtually all air flow. While a train was being prepared for a long journey, a car loaded with sixteen horses might stand all day in the sun. "It seemed that the horse cars were always spotted where there was no access to water," wrote the Standardbred historian Ken McCarr, whose father, Ned, trained in this era, "and the yards were generally located in some isolated spot where there was no way for the grooms to get food." The cars, while being coupled in the rail yard, would clash together fiercely, often causing the horses to fall down. It's not surprising that many horses lost their finely honed athletic edge on the journey, or that despite dehydration some became too distraught to drink or eat at the next stop, compounding their distress. Many a fast horse had to curtail or abandon his racing career because he couldn't take the stress of train travel. One reason that Grand Circuit purses were so high—a run-of-the-mill stakes went for $2,500—was because trainers needed an incentive to get onto trains.

Dan, as we've seen, would eventually have his own private car, as posh as anything J. P. Morgan ever saw. But for now the Crawfordsville race showed that Dan was adaptable enough to reach Chicago, Detroit, New York, and similar metropolises with a minimum of wear and tear. But was he good enough to win once he got there?

To get a better fix on their colt, Wattles and Messner decided to finish out the 1900 season by stepping Dan up into the 2:20 class for a race in Brazil, Indiana—and then taking him on to Terre Haute, where the competition was even classier than in Lafayette. In Terre Haute, Dan would start in a race that was for all but official purposes a midlevel Grand Circuit stake. The word around Oxford was that if Dan won at Terre Haute, he would be off to the big time and probably never show his handsome brown face in their little town again.

Oxford people had mixed emotions about Dan going to Terre Haute. They wanted him to teach the world what a Benton County horse could do, but they didn't want to see him win his way right out of their lives, at least not so quickly. They weren't finished loving him yet. George Gillett, the tobacconist who kept a shop on the second floor above Messner's store, introduced the Dan Patch cigar, and watched it instantly become his best seller. Children skipped after Dan Patch as Wattles drove him back from Chiquesalonghi following his daily training miles. When Wattles walked Dan in circles in front of his barn to cool him down, he would hoist the kids up on to Dan and let each one ride a while, bareback. The pacer was never broken to saddle, and the one time a grown man attempted to mount him, years later, Dan reared up and dumped the wise guy hard. But children could ride all day.

With everyone focusing on, and fretting over, that Terre Haute race on Friday, September 28, the Brazil race, scheduled for one week earlier, went almost ignored, even though it would be against the fastest horses (the 2:20 class) and for the most money ($400) that Dan had ever encountered. No one from Oxford except Messner, Wattles, and James Stephen, Dan's groom, made the ninety-nine-mile journey to the future birthplace of Jimmy Hoffa. (Dan went there directly from Crawfordsville—the future birthplace of Dick Van Dyke—by rail.) Instead, Oxfordites talked about Terre Haute and an extra "Dan Patch Train" that the Chicago and Eastern Illinois Railway had lined up for the day of the climactic race. The "special excursion," the C&EI announced, would leave Oxford at 5:40 a.m. and depart Terre Haute at 7:00 that evening; round-trip fare was $1.00. Though it meant spending a dollar on a day when you were taking off from work and not earning one, there was steady business at the depot's ticket office on Michigan Street (now Dan Patch Drive).

The Brazil race indeed proved to be missable. Over a newly laid red-clay track that was uneven in firmness and thus not particularly fast, Dan took care of business as his backers in Oxford assumed he would. In three unspectacular and interchangeable heats, the fastest of which was timed in 2:16 ¾, he beat a field that included a certain Baron B., a mare named Star Girl, and three other horses. As at Crawfordsville, he led from wire to wire in each heat and was never challenged, the others not being able to keep up. After racing three miles he was still eager for work, throwing his head and whinnying loudly as Wattles steered him back to the barn following the clincher. In the *Autobiography,* Dan dismisses the Brazil race as "a workout."

Terre Haute, though, would be a test. The one-mile track there, built just the year before, was a unique and thoroughly modern "four-cornered" affair with "scientifically constructed" grades on the turns that supposedly kept horses from tiring. Leading trainers brought their best horses to Terre Haute in hopes of lowering their record for the mile (an animal's personal best became part of his identity, as well as part of his name, as in Happy Jim, 2:08 ¼) and thus increasing their value.

The next week the *Oxford Tribune*, normally published on Fridays, came out a day early so the editor could make the trip to see Dan compete in what was now widely regarded as, said the *Tribune*, "his last race as an Oxfordite." On the twenty-eighth, more than 500 people packed the excursion train that pulled out of the Oxford depot under steely gray skies. One avid fan of the horse, though, was not on board. James Howarth, a fifty-three-year-old Oxford farmer, espoused a theory that "special" trains relied on seldom-used equipment and thus frequently broke down. He couldn't abide the thought of missing Dan Patch's coming-out race, he said, so he went the day before, on a regularly scheduled train. That, of course, meant spending the night in Terre Haute, a raucous port on the Wabash with a Bangkokian policy toward gambling, liquor, and whores—but for Dan Patch, he was willing to make the sacrifice.

It was not a pretty day in Sin City. Rain, which had threatened in Oxford, came down cold and hard in Terre Haute, as only a sad September rain can. The 500 chilly pilgrims slogged from the rail station to the racetrack to find that racing had been canceled for the day, the week, and, because it was late in the season and the crops had to be brought in, the rest of the year. The crudely graded all-clay racetracks of that era could take only so much moisture before they became a quagmire; in the wake of a drenching two-day rainstorm such as Terre Haute had just seen, it could take several days of baking sun to make the surface raceable again. The Oxford contingent, which included Dan Messner's older brother Sam, in from Danbury, Nebraska, for the race, had to wait around till seven in the evening for their train back. Some who had come with their families tried to take a walking tour of the town's stately houses, others slogged around the tenderloin district, but the conditions put everyone in a foul mood. Wrote Mary Cross: "The mud, muddier than Oxford mud, clung tightly to their shoes and its color was even different!"

No one in Oxford was more disappointed than Wattles and Messner about the washout in Terre Haute. Wattles especially had no
doubt that Dan Patch could have won there, against the kind of
slick, hard-knocking racehorses who "pumpkin-vined" their way
around the country (as the horsemen used to say), scuffling for
purses worth as much as $2,000 and $3,000. The Terre Haute
race would have been worth $1,000, making it the richest purse
that Wattles had ever driven for (in addition to a monthly training
fee of about $30, he received 10 percent of the horse's share, which
in this case would have meant another $50 if Dan had won). Now,
because there was hardly any racing beyond early autumn, Dan
would have to end his first season with a 4-for-4 record, $625 in
purse earnings—and a lot of energy to burn.

The racing season may have been over, but there were still decisions to be made, starting with the question of when Dan Patch
would return to Oxford. He could have caught a train leaving the
next evening, been back home by afternoon, and gone into hiber-
nation, as far as the racing world was concerned, until the following year. The morning after the canceled race, though, Messner,
now plotting the moves for Dan, decided to salvage something
from the trip to Terre Haute; he would keep Dan at the big-city
track until the surface dried out sufficiently for his pacer to go a
one-mile time trial. Dan would be racing only against the clock,
and whatever time he posted would be unofficial. There would
be no cheering crowd, no purse money, no chance for Messner to
play the role of proud owner. There would not even be a running-
horse prompter, as many horses had in such situations, to help
them go their best miles. But testing Dan that way might tell Messner how he ought to regard next season.

     Not long before it had been Wattles's job to decide when Dan
trained and raced, and advise the owner accordingly. But now, with
the rain still coming down hard on the shed-row roof, Messner and

Wattles came to a sad understanding. Messner never said, "You're too old—I'm making a change, Uncle Johnny." Instead he talked about all the time it would take for the track to dry, and how Wattles had a farm to manage and how a man his age couldn't be running back and forth across the state just for a one-horse time trial. "Don't worry. I'll find someone else to drive him, Johnny," Messner finally said.

Wattles said, "Okay, Dan," and walked away.

He caught the next evening's train back to Oxford. And that was that.

They both knew they were talking about more than just the time trial. Wattles had seen that moment coming. His old friend had for months now been reading about and talking about the men who dominated the Grand Circuit—glamorous, whiskey-drinking, cigar-chomping "sultans of the sulky" like Pop Geers, Knapsack McCarthy, Budd Doble, Billy Dick Dickerson, Long Shot Cox, Myron "Wizard of the Homestretch" McHenry, and Scott Hudson, who in one afternoon at the old Glenville track in Cleveland had swept every race on the card and won $40,000 in purses, despite a killer hangover. On more than one occasion, Messner had asked Wattles about the expense of campaigning a horse on the Grand Circuit and if any of those famous trainers were really trustworthy. Wattles had to say he could offer no opinion on the famous horsemen; he had never even met any of them. And Messner had let that response hang in the air.

Five days after the canceled race Dan Patch stepped out onto the Terre Haute track with the thirty-three-year-old trainer named John L. "Johnny Dick" Dickerson sitting in the sulky behind him. Dickerson had broken in with the famous Budd Doble in the early 1890s, and later displayed the considerable physical strength and patience required to train and drive Dan's rambunctious sire Joe Patchen. Well versed in the ways of green colts, he found the exuberant but willing Dan Patch easy to handle. With Dickerson sitting coolly in the sulky, Dan warmed up for about twenty minutes, traveling clockwise. Then Dan came to a stop at the top of the homestretch and, following Dickerson's gentle tug on his left line, slowly circled around. The horse understood the change in direction as a request for racing speed.

Dickerson was one of those naturally talented drivers who, as the expression goes, have "a clock in their head." Although Dan Patch slowed ever so slightly on the tight (and still slippery) turns, his quarter-mile splits were almost perfectly balanced, and he came home strongly—in exactly 2:10. He wasn't all-out by any means, but he had never gone that fast before. A lot of horses hadn't. Two minutes and ten seconds was Grand Circuit time.

About a week after that impressive mile at Terre Haute, the *Chicago Daily,* in a column called "Harness Horse Gossip," ran an item about two Chicago-area stallions who were showing signs of panning out as sires. One was a trotter called Saccharine, who had a son named Walter E. who had won a race in 2:31 ½. The other was Joe Patchen, who "had Dan Patch, 2:16, to his credit." This was the first mention of Dan in a big-city newspaper, and several salesmen who did business with Messner clipped the column and brought it in to show him on their next trip to Oxford.

Dan Patch took the train home from Terre Haute early in the second week of October 1900. Some people in town were still cranky about the canceled race and the muddy mess of the week before. But word of the time trial had also spread. A welcoming committee of about fifty fans met Dan at the depot, applauded as he came down the ramp, and walked him back to his barn on South Michigan Street. Caretaker Stephen held the lead shank. Wattles was nowhere to be seen.

A couple of days later, a pacing colt he was trying to get ready for the 1901 racing season kicked Wattles hard in the left ankle; the old trainer went down in a heap. He couldn't walk for a few weeks and afterward had a permanent limp that required him to use a cane.

Horses.

As the Mexican proverb says, "It is not enough for a man to know how to ride. He must know how to fall."

CHAPTER EIGHT

THE WIZARD OF THE Homestretch turned over the letter in his short fingers and laughed—or, rather, snorted.

Though the seal remained unbroken, Myron McHenry knew what the envelope contained as surely as if it were one of those pastel, perfumed missives that arrived postmarked from some recent Grand Circuit stop, and which, if left lying about their house in Chicago, caused a frown to darken the brow of Ida, his long-suffering wife. "Must be another Myron E. McHenry," he'd had to say, with a shrug, on more than one occasion.

This, too, was a love letter of sorts. The pathetically careful quality of the script and the postmark of Oxford, Indiana, both indicated that it was most probably a plea from some horse-owning rube—some big fish in a small pond, most likely—who imagined he had a world-beater and wanted McHenry to drive it. McHenry received a steady trickle of such mail, and no wonder: in a golden age of harness-racing trainer-drivers, he had a reputation for being the best. "I call him the greatest driver of horses of this or any period," wrote the always astute Marque. John Hervey, using a poetic term for reins, once referred to McHenry as "the only real superman of the ribbons that we have seen in action."

The letter McHenry held in his hands at that moment was written by someone who had never met him, and knew him only through his legend as it was molded by the hero-making sportswriters of the day. McHenry could infer all this merely from the method of address: "Mr. Myron McHenry, Freeport, Illinois." The letter had, after a postal forwarding or two, found him, in October 1900, in Chicago, where he had been living for several months. But years before, he had acquired, in addition to "the

Wizard of the Homestretch" (it was a nickname-crazed age) the moniker "the Man from Freeport." He became that to the multitudes who followed harness racing even though he had lived in "Pretzel City, U.S.A." (as Freeport was known after the Billerbeck Bakery opened in 1869) for only a brief period, before he gained fame as the driver of "the Little Red Horse," John R. Gentry. (As everyone knew, Gentry was a plucky pacer who had engaged in many heartstopping stretch duels with Dan Patch's sire, the "Iron Horse" Joe Patchen.)

So those who believed McHenry actually lived in Freeport, Illinois, did not know him well. Not that anyone did, really—nor did anyone know what "the Man from Freeport" meant, exactly. Every man was a man from someplace, right? Still, it was better than calling him "the brilliant but alcoholic forty-four-year-old asshole whose attitude kept him in a perpetual state of financial distress"—though that did have the advantage of being true.

Myron McHenry was more or less impossible. In a profession known (then and now) for peevish personalities who could barely abide the presence of the people who paid the bills, he stood out as a vicious biter of the hands that fed him. He also bit the hands that didn't feed him, and more than a few ladies' earlobes. Despite a lack of formal education, McHenry had taught himself to speak well, and he dressed nattily, his clothes flattering his tiny frame. But he was always poised to attack. Profiling McHenry in the 1930s, John Hervey, who had known his subject as well as anybody, recalled, "If so disposed he could be a pleasant companion with whom to spend an hour or an evening. But behind this there was quite another man. When not in the mood he was hostile, chilly, brusque to the point of intentional impoliteness and commanded one of the most biting veins of conversation to which one could care to listen, his words literally [sic] blistering the men and horses against whom they were directed—for as well as being crisp and epigrammatic they bit like a razor's edge."

Still, occasionally, when the drinks were flowing, McHenry could tell a story on himself. One of his favorite such tales involved a race that happened early in his career. The trainer found himself, as the field headed into the homestretch, trapped behind a wrinkled old driver, a man of John Wattles's age, who was refusing to budge from his path. "Get out of the way, you old coot!" McHenry shouted. "I can't hold this horse and he'll go right over you!" The elderly driver was not intimidated. Calmly he turned and, as McHenry finally got loose and sped by, said, "Next time, better hire a full-grown man to drive that horse." McHenry always said that he laughed so hard coming to the wire that he nearly lost control of his horse. But he never would have told the story if he hadn't (a) bested the old man and (b) won the race. McHenry's self-deprecation was subject to certain terms and conditions, and his repertoire lacked stories in which he did not ultimately come out on top.

McHenry stood all of five feet, one inch tall—although there are no weight restrictions in harness racing, the best drivers have always been small, nearly jockey-size men—but even in repose he looked pugnacious. With his tightly clenched square jaw, he bore a slight resemblance to Vice President Theodore Roosevelt; he had a bushy, sandy brown mustache that twitched when he got angry, and cold blue eyes that were, to steal a line from an F. Scott Fitzgerald short story, "a sort of a taunt to the whole human family." "His guard was never truly lowered," said Hervey. "Just when people supposed they knew him best they were apt to find him an enigma and a mystery. He was not open to the ordinary influences that affect human nature. He 'dwelt apart' in the full sense of the phrase and tolerated no encroachments upon that inner citadel."

McHenry always had the same reaction to the small-town horse owners who wrote to him about their "quite good" horses and their dreams of Grand Circuit glory: contemptuous disgust. "Stay in the sticks, you chawbackon, and don't presume that you or your horse could ever be good enough for the Grand Circuit," he wanted to tell all of those groveling supplicants. Sometimes he did tell them precisely that, in letters or in person, with a characteristic show of haughtiness, though he himself was a product of a very small town, a town that had in fact shriveled up and disappeared from the map—Pink Prairie, Illinois. He also vented his anger in spite of being perpetually horse-poor, owing to the insulting way he treated even those free-spending big-city horse owners he deigned to take on as clients. Horse owners took his rudeness for only so long before sending a caretaker around to walk their trotters and pacers to another trainer's barn. When turf journalists asked about his empty stalls, McHenry would say, "I have decided to concentrate on just one or two horses for now, and I haven't yet encountered any who meet my standards." The writers knew the reality, but printed his lies.

It was a shame, really. While McHenry sat and waited for another future ex-client to come along, much hard-won horse wisdom went to waste. McHenry had begun driving trotters and pacers in the late 1870s, when the breed and the sport were still on the verge of coalescing into the multimillion-dollar industry that harness racing would become in the next thirty years. His first drive of note came behind an unregistered mare named Princess on July 4, 1880, in Galva, Illinois. Young McHenry, still work-ing as a groom, or "swipe," had heard that the town sponsored a race on Independence Day, so a few days before he hitched up Princess to a high-wheeled cart and drove her twenty-five miles over rough roads from Pink Prairie. When he got to Galva, he learned that there was no racetrack there; instead, the field of trot-ters would race four times around the town square, doing as best they could with the flat, 90-degree "turns." Hitched to the same four-wheeled wagon that she had hauled on her journey, Princess trotted to victory.

McHenry had pursued the horseman's life over the objections of his parents, Daniel and Rachel, staunch Methodist farmers who saw their eldest son's occupation as an affront to the Lord. Myron and his father fought bitterly over the morality of horseracing and its ancillary dangers. Father and son didn't speak for more than twenty years, and the elder McHenry didn't see Myron drive in a race until his boy was one of the famous reinsmen invited to compete at the 1893 Chicago World's Fair, when Daniel was a very old man. By then Myron had become everything his father feared he would be if he stuck with racing—a drinker, a gambler, and the pawn of loose women. Myron's behavior depressed and frightened the petite dark-haired beauty Ida Gierhart, the belle of

Atkinson, Illinois, whom he had married in 1878. Her father-in-law gave her sympathy and support, Hervey said, but McHenry "went his way, deaf to everybody and everything and for the most part with such absolute, icy indifference that even his closest and most loyal friends were baffled and confounded." The one person McHenry stayed devoted to his whole life was Miss Mary Hammer, his first-grade teacher at the Old Salem School in Geneseo, Illinois; he kept in touch with her through his apprenticeship in the horse business, and through his many trials and triumphs and scandals and setbacks and comebacks, and she would reenter his life at a critical moment. The maiden schoolmarm was the only person he ever forgave for not knowing much about horses.

The Wizard seemed to have been born with a preternatural sense of pace—he could tell whether a quarter mile had gone in 34 or 34 ½ seconds without consulting his stopwatch. He was also, like the other elites in his game, a veritable horse whisperer who, even in mid-race, could communicate with a trotter or pacer in ways beyond the powers of mortal men. But not everything about McHenry's horsemanship was so natural or so subtle. He would hook a wheel around someone else's, or "accidentally" hit a fellow driver in the face with his whip as quickly as he would kiss the hand of that same fellow's wife at a party. He was also the most physical—indeed, the most histrionic—driver most people had ever seen, and many of his victories could be chalked up to sheer force of will. "I'll drive her tail off," McHenry once said to the trainer Monroe Salisbury, when Salisbury (another famous crank) asked if he would handle a timid, runty mare named Ann Direct in the annual Merchants' and Manufacturers' Stake at Glenville, Ohio. And so McHenry did—shouting to the mare, rattling the bit, cracking the whip, and doing everything but getting out of the sulky and dragging his little longshot across the finish line. "If ever a mare was forced home a winner," said the *Horse Review*, speaking of Ann's performance that day, "it was that daughter of Direct."

McHenry pushed himself as hard as he pushed his horses. Once, after one of his typical homestretch eruptions, he managed to get a skinny gelding named Frazier home first in the sixth heat of a cheap race at Oakley Park in Cincinnati. The horse had reached his physical limit, and so had McHenry. As two grooms ran out toward the winner, McHenry called, "One of you prop Frazier up and the other help me." Over and over, Hervey wrote, "we witnessed him pull first money out of the fire when apparently it was in ashes."

His homestretch "wizardry," though, was often all about the whip. "At times he never pulled the whip, even in a severe finish," wrote Hervey. "At others he would ply it with slashing blows that fell so thickly as to be like a rain of them upon the horse's back." Some horse lovers criticized McHenry for his cruelty, urging him to use the whip, if he must, not on the horse's flank but on the sulky's wooden shafts, where it would be more of a threat than a punishment; but others admired what they saw as his swashbuckling style. A staff writer at the *Review,* after seeing him more than once drive the trotter Phoebe Wilkes to "unlikely victories," was moved to pen this paean to McHenry's habit of "reefing" (archaic slang meaning "to hit with excessive force") the less-than-eager mare:

> *I'm sorry for these Autumn days, they fill me full of pain, for I can't see McHenry "reef" on Phoebe Wilkes again*
> *Until next year and by that time perhaps I cannot go to see the races trotted, though I hope 'twill not be so*
> *There are trotters swift and trotters slow, and trotters 'twixt and 'tween; but for trotters that stand reefing, Phoebe's the best I've ever seen*
> *She always seems to linger when she strikes the distance pole, for Mc to pick her up and lift her onward to the goal*
> *Not that I intend to argue that she quits—she don't go back; she just waits to get a lifting and a bat across the back*
> *Then she steps along as lively as the best of them can go; and in the end is likely to get her share of the "dough"*
> *There is nothing more exciting than this pair from Illinois; they've upset a pile of good things several times—just ask the boys*
> *I'm sorry for these Autumn days, they fill me full of pain, for I can't see McHenry "reef" old Phoebe Wilkes again.*

I pause now to let the reader dry his eye.

McHenry probably felt like reefing this D. A. Messner, the return-addressee of the letter he held in his hands. "Dream on, you fool!" he no doubt thought as he tossed away the still-sealed envelope. It didn't land in the wastebasket, though. McHenry had put just enough English on it so that it sailed over the bed and into his leather satchel.

Dan Messner was deeply worried about his letter. He imagined some Pretzel Town U.S.A. postal worker dropping the envelope in the Freeport mud—so different from the Oxford mud—after all the care he had taken in its preparation, going through several drafts until he felt the penmanship leaned expectantly and perhaps optimistically but did not kowtow. Messner, in his request for McHenry's services, had tried to convey what a phenomenon Dan Patch had become, sticking to harder evidence like his genetic connection to Joe Patchen, his mile times, the number of heats the pacer had won, and the endorsements of certain perhaps impressive Indiana horsemen. Without knowing anything about the choleric character of Myron Emmer McHenry, he realized he risked rejection. After all, he was daring to approach the man whom everyone said was the best. McHenry's standards were no doubt high, his barn brimming with potential champions, his days full. A turndown was possible, even probable. But no response at all? That he didn't expect, though for weeks he heard not a word.

It was in November of 1900—coincidentally right around the time that the first automobile show in America opened at Madison Square Garden—that Messner finally got a letter back from McHenry. It has been lost, along with virtually all of Messner's (and McHenry's) correspondence, but Messner described it many times over the years. McHenry's reply reeked of sarcasm and contempt. The famous horseman opened by noting that he received many requests interchangeable with Messner's plaintive note. He said he didn't know if word had reached Oxford, Indiana, that harness horses are going a whole lot faster these days. He asked if Messner had perhaps seen the newspaper items (actually screaming, 24-point front-page headlines) that had appeared a few years earlier when the pacer Star Pointer broke the two-minute-mile barrier? Did Mr. Messner understand, McHenry wondered, how extraordinarily fast his horse would have to go to have even a chance of picking up any kind of money on the Grand Circuit? Furthermore, did the esteemed storekeeper from Oxford, Indiana, have even the slightest notion of what it cost to train and ship and keep a horse eligible for the major-league races, not to mention the bills from the veterinarian and the horseshoer? It is no insult to you, McHenry added, insultingly, to speculate that few people of Oxford, Indiana, are in a financial position to handle the demands of the big time.

McHenry's letter surprised Messner, but it didn't scare him off. Although he still had a lot to learn about horses, he was a businessman who negotiated for a living. He could look beyond McHenry's blustering and posturing and see that he indeed had some interest in Dan Patch—why else would he have taken the trouble to write this letter?

Messner didn't want to play games, though; he answered by return mail, saying that he had faith in Dan Patch, based on the ease with which he had made his personal records, and that, yes, he understood and could handle the costs.

McHenry, who was suffering from his usual horse-flow problems, couldn't afford to be too cute, either. He wrote back quickly this time, saying in a brief, brusque note that Messner should jog Dan Patch ten miles a day all winter long—no speed work, he emphasized—and be prepared to ship the horse to Cleveland, where he did his preseason training, some time in mid May.

Messner took Dan out of the grocery business that winter, but he still drove him around town on appointments and errands, while Stephen took him on his daily training miles (about eight more than a horse taking a winter break would get today). For months, Messner managed to keep his plans to himself. But a cheer went up when, on a bright March day in 1901, he stood in front of his store and announced to a crowd of townsfolk that Dan Patch would be traveling the Grand Circuit with the famous McHenry. Not long afterward, *Western Horseman* magazine sent

a reporter from Indianapolis to do a story on Dan Messner's "racing operations," which consisted of Dan Patch, Lady Patch, and a
bandy-legged baby Zelica had recently given birth to, a colt by the
champion trotter Allerton that Messner had named after himself.
The writer barely acknowledged the filly and four-legged Messner
but called Dan "the prettiest and fastest horse I have ever seen."

John Wattles was absent when Dan Patch pulled out of the
Oxford depot on May 13, 1901, on a train bound for Cleveland.
Most people in town understood the break Messner had made with
Uncle Johnny—Dan Patch was just too big a deal for a local man,
they agreed—but the storekeeper was once again called foolish for
the travel arrangements he had made. His critics' reasoning went
something like this: not only had he elected to go in the famously
unlucky month of May, but he tempted fate doubly by traveling on
the thirteenth. Did this man have even a lick of common sense? To
some who spoke to the *Tribune,* such gaffes were beyond justifica-
tion, and another sign that Messner should stay away from horses.

The next day Messner's wife, Maud, gave an interview to the
Tribune, defending her mate. "You have never been superstitious,"
she said that she had told her husband several days before, when
he asked her if she thought it was true what people were saying
about the departure date putting a hex on the horse. "If Dan Patch
is a winner, thirteen will be good luck. Follow your plan to send
him to Cleveland on the thirteenth. Horses and people make their
own luck. If any horse ever wanted to win, that horse certainly
does. He is smart. He will make his own luck."

In Cleveland the next day, Messner's heart sank. McHenry had
given him a gruff nod of welcome and informed him that their
arrangement was not at all set, as Messner had thought, but
hinged on how the great man felt about Dan Patch after driving
him a few miles.

"Don't unpack—you just might be back in Oxford, Indiana,
in time for a good dinner," McHenry said. "After the horse is
warmed up it takes me just a few miles to tell if he can make it up
here. And let me tell you, few can."

Dan was brought out of his stall and stood calmly as he was hitched up by the stablehands. If McHenry noticed the extra-wide axle—or the strange left hind shoe—he didn't say anything about them. Having created, in his expert fashion, an air of tension and misery, he swung into the cart, chirped to the horse, and drove off toward the racetrack.

He had wanted to go "just a few miles," so, allowing time for warm-up laps, Messner expected he would know his and Dan's fate in perhaps twenty minutes. Instead McHenry was back with the horse in under ten.

He spun out of the sulky, threw the reins down on the seat, and stalked to the horse's head.

He looked Dan Patch in the eye and cocked his fist.

"You are either the fastest horse in the world," McHenry said, "or the biggest counterfeit."

CHAPTER NINE

ON A STICKY DAY in June I went to the Meadowlands racetrack to find out what separated a horse like Dan Patch from the plodding herd. Why did one child of Joe Patchen become, like his daddy, a crazy-good world-beater, while all of the many others, as fate would have it, turned out to be basically furniture for flies? How could Myron McHenry know, after just a few minutes in the sulky seat, that Dan might be "the fastest horse in the world"?

I came bearing these questions as a baffled horseplayer (to risk redundancy). I am a city person; I have seen hundreds of thousands of racehorses as a spectator but smelled, I don't know, twenty-six? I was more than familiar with the number-based theories and the magical thinking that casual racegoers bring to their seats in the grandstand. Now I was seeking advice from the other side of the fence. I wanted an agricultural perspective—for the training of a racehorse, lest we forget, is a form of animal husbandry, even if a lot of the customers will tell you they make a fortune going strictly by the names.

In a barn area housing five hundred Standardbreds (every one a descendant of Hambletonian) I was to meet John Campbell, the premier harness driver of modern times. When we made the appointment via cell phone ten days earlier, I had been in Minnesota, standing ankle-deep in the Credit River, a few feet from where Dan Patch had been buried on July 15, 1916. Campbell had been somewhere in this paved-over northern New Jersey marshland where harness racing—once miles ahead of baseball, football, boxing, and basketball in the sports world pecking order—was making an increasingly desperate last stand.

I was in the middle of the river looking for bones—the bones of Dan Patch, and perhaps (in my boyish fantasy) a finely made elkhide whip that someone had placed in the grave to speed the great horse on his way to the afterlife. Or maybe (I thought, just as fancifully) I'd find an exquisite pair of silver bridle rosettes that had been laid lovingly near Dan's head, to alert the specters beyond the River Styx that this was indeed the King of Pacers. Such treasures as these, I had half convinced myself, might have migrated from the grave into this shallow little river, and still be here, eighty-nine years and eleven months later, waiting to be discovered by me. At one point my foot touched something bonelike. My heart raced. In cool mud I found a shard of flower pot, circa now.

I was, of course, on a fool's errand: bones would almost certainly have disintegrated after all this time, and Dan's burial rites would have been Methodist (headline in a yellowing newspaper clip, "Dan Patch Is a Methodist"—explanation ahead), not, it goes without saying, ancient Egyptian or Greek. In all likelihood, as I already knew, there had been absolutely no ceremony conducted on the steaming-hot day that Dan went hurriedly into the hole—unless one considers, as one must, the silent prayers of the frightened grave diggers.

Still, it was a lovely pre-mosquito morning in south-central Minnesota, and the spot—once the property of M. W. Savage and now owned by Cargill, which describes itself, with world-class opaqueness, as "an international marketer, processor and distributor of agricultural, food, financial and industrial products"—is paradisiacal: lush and serene, far enough from Route 13 that you can't see the NASCAR-themed Eisen Brothers Sports Bar or the billboards for McDonald's McFlurry or hear the hum of the tires. Mr. Savage, the last owner of Dan Patch, used photographs of the Credit in propaganda he published around 1906, perfect bound booklets describing his supposedly perfect life. But I couldn't help thinking that this corner of what was then called the International Stock Food Farm, after one of Savage's several companies, resembled nothing so much as a 1930s Hollywood heaven—minus, of course, the producers' girlfriends wearing wings and strumming harps. Cottonwood trees rise at pleasing intervals in the unmowed grass. Boulders occur with terrific feng shui. There are butterflies everywhere, but not too many butterflies. And, oh, the water.

The meandering Credit is sparklingly clear, prime trout territory; to sink one's feet into its velvety bottom is bliss. Mr. Savage,
who is frequently described by his fans in the Dan Patch community as a marketing genius, once siphoned off the Credit, put it in
bottles labeled with a picture of a comely Indian maid, and sold it
as Tah-Wah-Nee Mineral Spring Water, a "radio-active" cure for
diseases of the liver, kidneys, sinuses, bowels, and bladder. Each
gulp, Savage claimed, contained pure, life-prolonging radium, one
gram of which was "worth over one hundred thousand dollars
cash." Just think: for a quarter or so you could drink from the
river from which Dan Patch drank! Got diabetes, malaria, insomnia, rheumatism, and gout? This stuff would have you up and
pacing in a trice. Tah-Wah-Nee bombed at the box office, though.
Perhaps people surmised that the Credit was also the river where
Dan Patch bathed, peed, and shat.

That didn't bother me, though. As someone trying to find the
real horse and the real people behind the cardboard characters
who've been propped up in all the moldy old tales, I must confess
that I rather liked the idea of standing in what might be considered, with some poetic license, liquid Dan Patch. I splashed some
on me like cologne. I dribbled some down my forehead, baptizing
myself. I drank some. I worked my feet in deeper, and turned my
face to the sun.

The vibration in my pants had nothing to do with my reverie.
It was Campbell calling. He had received my message, he said
cheerfully, and would be delighted to talk to me about Dan. Apart
from being harness racing's all-time leading money winner, with
more than $250 million in purses to his credit—no active Thor-
oughbred jockey has won that much—Campbell, a handsome
and youthful fifty-two, serves as the unofficial spokesman for the
sport, a quotable, camera-ready personality who steps up to perform diplomatic duties whenever the New York or national media
shows the slightest interest in his game. Which means he doesn't
need to step up very often.

"Boy, when I was a kid I was very excited about Dan Patch,"
Campbell said toward the end of our phone conversation. "I had
that book about him, and I must have read it three or four times."

I said nothing in response; I knew he was talking about the Fred Sasse book.

"Oh, I'm sure it wasn't very . . . ," he added, correctly interpreting my silence and trying to be polite (he is Canadian) to a rival biographer. "It's just that, you know, that's all there was at the time."

When Campbell was born, in 1955, harness racing was going through its second golden age. The automobile and the Great Depression had one-two punched the Standardbreds clean off center stage and into the boondocks; probably no other major pastime has ever seen such a precipitous decline in popularity. Of course, this wasn't just a matter of a horse sport falling out of favor; the horse itself was being summarily abandoned by the American public. The grassroots support that had made harness racing the NASCAR of its day was suddenly gone, as average folks converted their stables into one- and two-car garages, albeit with a horseshoe still nailed above the door. Some diehards held on as long as they could, railing against the horseless carriage. "Automobiles will cause a panic in this country yet," predicted former Maryland governor Frank Brown in the early 1900s. "I could keep four horses and two men on the box for what it costs to maintain a machine. People are crazy, fascinated, hypnotized by these infernal things. They are the ruination of young people." The racing community spent years deluding itself; horse magazines fought back with anticar poetry ("O, woe is the man who drives / where the automobilist sweeps / his horse butts into the wayside wall / and smashes the cart for keeps") and a barrage of editorials and letters to the editor smugly predicting that because automobiles were so unsafe and uncivilized, lawmakers would inevitably ban cars from the highways. Things didn't quite work out that way: there were about 8,000 automobiles in America in 1900, and about 20 million at the onset of the Depression. It was Warren G. Harding, though, who drove a stake through the horse's heart when he broke with tradition on March 4, 1921, and became the first American president to ride to his inauguration in an automobile; Harding did for the horse what Kennedy would do for the hat. In its very next issue, the *Horse Review* (which would go bust several years later) acknowledged that the war between horse and horseless was over, forever lost.

The harness-racing historian Phillip A. Pines has called the 1920s and '30s "lean and desperate years" for the sport. Race-track attendance shrank, stallion fees plummeted, and the advertisements for dispersal sales were about the only thing giving the horse magazines any cash flow. With the Grand Circuit all but collapsed, the game retreated during those hard decades to the county and state fairs, which were themselves struggling for relevance and a share of the entertainment buck.

But then a pint-sized Long Island lawyer named George Morton Levy swooped in and changed everything. Levy, who had risen to national prominence as defense counsel for Charles "Lucky" Luciano, guiding him successfully through a case involving the always-headline-friendly white slave trade, had the wide-open eyes of a successful entrepreneur. Noting with interest that the Cincinnati Reds had introduced night baseball to the major leagues in 1935, and seeing the common sense in staging spectacles when people were available to behold them, he got the idea that harness racing, which had once resonated so strongly with the populace, might enjoy a revival as an after-work and weekend gambling game in the about-to-boom county of Nassau, New York. With a small group of investors he took over a failed auto racing track on a far-flung corner of Roosevelt Field, steps from where Charles Lindbergh had lifted off on his pioneering flight to Paris in 1927. Refurbishing the abandoned grandstand and rechristening it Roosevelt Raceway, Levy introduced nighttime harness racing to Westbury, New York, in 1939. After a few stumbles (some horsemen refused to participate, fearing the lights would scare or blind their stock) and a few innovations—most notably the moveable starting gate—the idea gained traction. Once the GIs returned from World War II, it took flight, as a new wave of middle-class couples poured into the area, and the part of the island near New York City got Levittowned and strip-malled to within an inch of its life. Average nightly attendance at Roosevelt in 1964, by then engulfed by a huge shopping center, was 26,042. On weekends, when the track reached its capacity of about 40,000, you could witness a sight that, it seems safe to say, is as far gone as the stampeding of the buffalo: racetrack customers slouching back to their big-finned Chevy Bel-Airs and Fairlane Fords after being turned away out of fear of overcrowding. Yonkers Raceway duplicated Roosevelt's success under similar conditions in lower Westchester, and before long people in Chicago, Detroit, Cleveland, and other big northern cities were also going to the nighttime "trotters." Practically every newspaper in the country wrote about its renaissance, and in 1968 Stanley Dancer, a superstar trainer-driver, brought the champion pacer Cardigan Bay, sulky and all, onto Ed Sullivan's stage, rounding out a bill that featured Sugar Ray Robinson and the Beach Boys. "The trotters" was for many couples the kind of glossy, glamorous evening that would not be tolerated today—Roosevelt's elegant, dress-coded dining room atop the clubhouse turn was called the Cloud Casino. And probably half the spectators believed the races were fixed. But the glam and the sham just toned up the titillation—a night at the track was a heck of a lot more fun, and a far superior way to flaunt one's newfound affluence, than sitting through a double feature.

I walked in on this party in 1962, thirteen years old. Yonkers Raceway by law did not admit anyone under twenty-one in those days, but my father, who had brought me along on the special racetrack bus from the Bronx—we had no car, as he was a horse player of long standing—stuck a White Owl cigar in my mouth as we approached the gates; I suppose he felt it negated the baby fat and the pimples. My father had no experience with cigars—smoking was the only bad habit he never acquired—which probably accounts for this cigar still being in the wrapper as it was inserted without warning into his only son. I can to this day recall the mingled tastes of cellophane and fear as my stomach hit the turnstile—and then suddenly I was through, and into another universe. In those days of mostly black-and-white TV, the colors, when you walked into a sporting event, could at first overwhelm the ocular nerves; it took a few minutes to get used to, and during that time you couldn't do much else but stagger around slack-jawed. Why did the grass in the outfield of Yankee Stadium—or in the infield of Yonkers Raceway—look twice as green as the grass in the park? This is one of those questions to which the answer is either fertilizer or magic.

My father and I walked down the sloping track apron toward the rail. It was almost summer and still quite light. The scene to me, a boy who had never been farther from my home in the south Bronx than this place, was mind-boggling: I loved the drivers' racing colors and the way the horses reflected the changing light and the way so many were whirring around the track, scoring down several miles—as Standardbreds do, and Thoroughbreds don't— in preparation for their upcoming races. I especially loved how the slashing and chugging of the horses' legs translated into the smooth (and at my remove, coolly silent) spin of the sulky wheels. In the ensuing decades it has been maligned, ignored, and horribly mismanaged, but at bottom it is a most beautiful game.

Campbell caught the tail end of what Levy had wrought, first at Windsor Raceway in Ontario, where his father raced a modest string of trotters and pacers, and eventually at the Meadowlands, where he was recruited by the management for his talent and his reputation for integrity when the track opened in 1976—and where he promptly became king.

It was especially good to be king in those days when the Meadowlands, tapping into yet another prosperous New York City suburb, was drawing mobs and making millions for the quasi state agency that oversees it. But with casino gambling coming to Atlantic City in 1977, and off-track betting spreading rampantly through New York State, the seeds of a downturn had already been sowed. Today the most successful tracks tend to have slot machines, which mesmerize the customers (and provide most of the revenue) while the horses go about their business out there somewhere beyond the glass doors. The Meadowlands, for reasons having to do with New Jersey politics, has not yet been granted the right to install VLTs, or video lottery terminals, as they are called. The now barely profitable track will draw perhaps 35,000 for the Hambletonian, which has been contested there since 1981, but despite good racing and superior horses, average attendance has sunk to 3,963, down about 75 percent since the high point in 1978. As capitals go, the Meadowlands is now much more Montpelier than Moscow.

The horses don't care about any of this. In favor or out, they must be fed, watered, bathed, groomed, housed, shod, doctored, and exercised. The morning I met up with Campbell, he was driving four pacers in qualifying races, nonbetting events involving horses who have taken a break from racing for any number of reasons, or who have been ordered to the qualifiers by the judges for acting badly during nighttime races. With a good performance in a qualifying race, horses are deemed worthy of starting in a regular pari-mutuel race. Fans could walk in and watch the morning races for free, but nobody does; the number of fans who come at the proper hour is small enough these days. The only witnesses, apart from the judges, on this unseasonably warm day were a gaggle of horse people, most of whom had some connection to the animals in the qualifiers as owners, trainers, assistant trainers, or grooms. They stood near the paddock entrance, looking, in the early stages of each race, apprehensive, and then, if their horse stayed on gait and made at least a halfway decent move at some point in the mile, relieved. I recognized a few of these people from when I had worked briefly for a harness-racing trade magazine called *Hoof Beats*, almost thirty years earlier.

In a group this small and parochial I stood out, and it was not long before Campbell came over to introduce himself. Instead of his driving colors of maroon and white with light blue accents (harness drivers wear their own registered silks rather than those of the owner, as Thoroughbred jockeys do), he had on a worn zip-front jumpsuit of UPS brown; it was the outfit of a man working in his own basement or garage. In a way he was at home; if the Meadowlands had a master bedroom, it would, after all these years, be his. He had a drive coming up in a few minutes, he said, and then about an hour free before he needed to drive again. He suggested that we talk during his break, then reconvene if more time was necessary. "I can give you all the time you want," he said.

Campbell's schedule isn't what it used to be. There was a

period in his career when he would drive in seven or eight races at Freehold Raceway, a little afternoon track forty-eight miles down the New Jersey Turnpike, in the birthplace of Bruce Springsteen, then drive back to the Meadowlands and handle another seven or eight Standardbreds in the evening. Sometimes he would split his evening, helicoptering over to Yonkers after a few races in New Jersey, or vice versa. (The people who were betting on his horses because of their names might have been interested to learn that Campbell often didn't know what those names were, though he usually procured a few fast facts from their trainers about their various preferences and foibles.) He had decided to focus on driving over training because it was more exciting and because that's where his edge lay: he has the fighter-pilot-size body that fits so well in a sulky (Campbell is five feet, seven inches tall and weighs 155 pounds) and a unique talent for, as I once heard a trainer say about him, "getting every bit of toothpaste out of the tube." He knew how to squeeze the most out of each horse, and he rarely did his squeezing too early or too late. In this way, and probably only in this way, Campbell resembled the misanthropic Myron McHenry.

Campbell has won more than 9,900 races. But since reaching his mid-forties he has, to the relief of his wife, Paula, slowed down and begun picking his spots, not bothering with the $3,000 claimers at Freehold, focusing instead on the stakes horses who, despite the sport's tribulations, often race for purses in the six figures and, once or twice a year, for seven. He has won the Hambletonian six times, the Little Brown Jug three times, and Meadowlands Pace, which carries a purse of $1 million, seven times. Campbell's reflexes, he insists, have not slowed since he entered middle age (harness drivers can and do compete into their seventies and sometimes beyond), his will to win has not abated, but there is no longer reason for him to take unnecessary risks, and driving Standardbreds, like riding Thoroughbreds, can be a dangerous occupation. Bill Haughton, one of the sport's all-time leading drivers, was killed in a collision at Yonkers Raceway in 1985, and not long before I talked with Campbell, another driver, a journeyman named Hans Belote, had died in a racing accident at Harrington Raceway in Delaware. Campbell himself has been in several serious spills; one that occurred at Toronto's Woodbine racetrack about four months after our interview broke his leg so badly that it put him out of commission for the better part of a year. In retrospect it was telling that the first thing we talked about, when Campbell joined me at a picnic table under a tree in the deserted spectator area, was how pacing hobbles can so easily trip up a horse who goes off gait, sending him down and setting up a domino effect that can bring down trailing horses. In cases like that, the sulky can become a catapult, launching a driver in front of horses he might otherwise be safely behind. (This is more or less what happened to Campbell at Woodbine.)

"There's no question about it," Campbell said, taking a seat, "hobbles make driving more dangerous. But they're not going anyplace, so we have to live with them. They've become completely accepted now, because without them there would be a whole lot more horses breaking stride." That harness horses are apt to do that, and virtually eliminate themselves from competition, is often cited by racegoers as a reason they prefer Thoroughbreds. "The trainers have come to rely on hobbles and the horses themselves rely on them because they understand when we humans want them to pace, and they want to do it—a lot of them, anyway—and though they're already bred in that direction, the hobbles help them do it."

I presented him with a scroll—actually, a large, rolled-up print of a photo taken in about 1905. As he spread it out on the table, he could see it was a full-body profile, taken from the right side, of Dan Patch rigged up and ready to race. Campbell's eyebrows went up behind his wraparound driving glasses. Compared to the horses that he had been driving, and driving against, that morning, Dan Patch looked naked. The King of the Pacers of course wore no hobbles, and no special equipment except for knee boots—leather pads about the size of a man's hand that protect a horse's inner front knees from being struck by his opposite foot, especially around turns. Knee boots are common, especially on pacers, and Dan's may have been there because of his crossfiring. They didn't, in any case, seem to rate any demerits from Campbell.

"Wow," he said, staring at the picture. "This is one good-look-ing horse."

I asked him to elaborate.

"Well, for one thing he stands up off the ground."

"Meaning?"

"Meaning his legs are nice and long, see? And he has a long barrel, or midsection, and you can see that his head is more refined than most horses of that era. The breed has changed so much, even in the time since I was a kid. You go back all the way to Dan Patch's day, and some of those horses could look more than a little rough. Not him, though. He's got the kind of qualities that would be impressive even today, after a hundred years of evolu-tion. Most good horses, you'll find, will have a nice long barrel and an intelligent-looking head."

Because Dan's head is turned to the side in the picture, you can't see the wide space between his eyes, a facial feature that, as we have seen, may have saved his life. When I mention the eye spacing to Campbell, though, he nods enthusiastically. "I don't know that it means a bigger brain necessarily," he says, "but good spacing between the eyes, I've found, is always desirable. Many a horse with a narrow head is stupid and high-strung. The tricky part is, though, intelligence is not always synonymous with want-ing to race. Some horses are too smart, I think, to want to exert much energy. They have figured out what's going on and exactly how much they can get away with. They think they can outsmart you, and often they can. But I'd still take an intelligent horse over a stupid one any time. So would probably anybody. When horses are smart, we humans like them better."

I had something else I wanted him to see. I had brought my laptop and a DVD showing a minute or so of Dan Patch in action at the Minnesota State Fair in 1906, pacing in a race against the clock and accompanied by two galloping Thoroughbred prompt-ers. This and a few fleeting seconds of Dan walking around and nuzzling M. W. Savage at the International Stock Food Farm, also on the disc, are the only motion-picture scenes of the horse known to exist. The footage is scratchy, jerky, and grainy, and it fades in and out, but Campbell seemed mesmerized by it. He hunched forward on the picnic table bench and gripped the side of my computer.

"Wow," he said again, watching Dan power around the one-mile track. "I can see from this, as blurry as it is, that he went low to the ground in front. That's more conducive to speed because there's less wasted motion. All the good ones go low to the ground, but generally speaking that's a relatively recent development in the Standardbred, something that started to crop up, as a result of selective breeding, in the '40s, '50s, and '60s. To see that low way of going this long ago is really kind of amazing."

It was a cloudy but bright day, which made it especially difficult to see the DVD. Campbell kept shifting the laptop to counteract the glare. "You know, his speed is just unfathomable," he said, after he found a workable angle. "The breed was just so primitive back then. You had to warm them up a lot more, they took a lot more repetitive training to learn how to trot or pace—their muscle memory had to be built up—and you had a lot more horses with a bad temperament, like Dan Patch's sire. Plus, don't forget, there's also the evolution of the sulky to consider. Just in the last ten years sulkies have improved so much in terms of aerodynamics—but back then? You had much slower sulkies, slower, rougher tracks, travel was tougher between tracks. There was just a lot more adversity, and horses, on the whole, don't react well to adversity. You might take one just down the road to another track where the water's a little different and they don't like the taste or smell, and they won't drink and they become dehydrated. But this is a horse who, from all I know, seemed to understand what was happening, who handled it all, who was able to accomplish so much because for some reason he didn't have all those unnecessary problems."

We watched together a bit longer, then Campbell looked up. "I don't know if this helps you or not," he said, "but the horse you're writing about was just a complete freak of nature."

He turned back to the laptop, but the movie had jerked to an abrupt halt. Because of the glare, though, Campbell didn't realize that, and for a little while he continued to move along the bench and tilt the screen, searching for Dan Patch.

CHAPTER TEN

In trying to escape fear men begin to make others fearful, and the injury they themselves seek to avoid they inflict on others, as if it were absolutely necessary either to harm or to be harmed.

—Machiavelli, *Discourses,* book I, chapter 46

It turns out that Myron McHenry, when he told Daniel Messner on that May morning in Cleveland that he might not be interested in training Dan Patch after all, and that the pacer would need to pass a surprise additional test to prove himself worthy of undertaking the McHenry Method of Racehorse Education—a test that, according to the master, most horses failed—he was just messing with the poor owner's mind. And toward no particular end, other than to stir up anxiety and fear and make another man miserable for a few moments, just because he could. McHenry was a jerk, and that is what jerks do.

The truth was that McHenry had wanted Dan Patch badly since he had first heard reports, in late 1900, from experienced horsemen who had seen the "nice-headed," "oddly bred," "duck-gaited" horse decimating the competition at the Indiana fairs. More than that, McHenry rather desperately needed Messner's pacer in his barn. In the early spring of 1901, Dan Patch—though just a promise of a horse, still several months from arrival—was the only thing keeping the Wizard of the Homestretch in the racing business. Dan Patch *was* the Myron McHenry stable.

McHenry's usual cycle of acquisition and loss had played out once again. The year before, while Dan was winning in the small time and becoming a local phenom, the man widely acknowledged as America's best driver had enjoyed another sterling season on the Grand Circuit. "McHenry has been a star in the sulky for a good many years," wrote the well-known turf scribe Henry Ten Eyck White in the *Chicago Tribune* on April 28, 1901. "But he never did better work than that which characterized his driving last season of Anaconda, another California pacer, Bonnie Direct, and the hobbled wonder, Coney. He made a record not likely to be duplicated by the driver of one stable in any season, especially when to this list is added Hetty G., also a pacer, that McHenry marked in 2:05 ¼."

Based on that performance, McHenry should have found himself on top of the racing world, weighing requests from owners attracted by his singular ability to get the most out of every horse he drove. His stalls should have been full to overflowing with the Circuit's best stock. Instead, by the end of 1900 he had as usual squabbled with all of his clients, belittling their opinions about horses and racing and sometimes, for good measure, hitting on their wives. On a morning when he was especially hung over, he might even have screamed obscenely at their kids when the banana-curled, velvet-clad darlings got underfoot and wanted to pet the horsies' noses. For any number of reasons connected to his alcoholism and general orneriness, McHenry's horses were all once again gone to the barns of more prudent, less angry men.

Truth be told, the owners could be hard to like. Then as now, they often fell into the category of nouveau riche twits—egoists who thought that their success in coal or newspapers or patent medicine or penny dreadfuls made them something more than mouthy dilettantes. But McHenry's reaction to these annoying people was self-destructive in the extreme, and his inability to tolerate them defined his career. The pacer Anaconda, for example, was, based on his mile record of 2:01 ¾, nothing less than the second fastest harness horse then in training. (The fastest was Dan's sire, Joe Patchen, still active in an era when stallions routinely sired a few foals in the off-season.) Anaconda, who had been more

or less made by McHenry, would be a big earner for several seasons to come—but for Johnny Dick Dickerson. Anaconda was
one of several champions to slip through McHenry's fingers during the summer of 1900.

Until that year, though, McHenry had always managed to find
fresh meat in the form of innocent new owners. The sport was at
its height of popularity during McHenry's prime, and new people
with money to spend were always coming into the business and
seeking out the man they had read so much about: the reefer of
champions, the Wizard of the Homestretch. Messner was a classic example of the kind of owner who stumbled into the lion's
den that was McHenry's stable. On March 16, 1901, McHenry
told White, for the record, that he would soon begin preparing
"a pacer named Dan Patch" for the 1901 racing season, but with
that initial reference to the horse came at least a couple of utterly
gratuitous jibes at the man who had naively dropped Dan Patch
into his lap. For example, the trainer told White that he thought
so highly of the horse that he had already staked him to races that
summer in Detroit, Cleveland, and Boston, "laying out considerable money from my own pocket" to meet the early deadlines for
entries, the implication being that he had to float Messner a small
loan, or at least that Messner had no idea of either his own horse's
worth or how the racing business worked. McHenry also noted in
that same *Chicago Tribune* article that he had been impressed by
Dan Patch "in spite of the knowledge that owners are apt to be
over-sanguine." Playing along with McHenry's usual line of self-
serving bull, White closed his column that day by saying, "Outside of Dan Patch, McHenry has not decided on his string. He
has under consideration a number of horses, but is not going to
take more than three or four." (Ultimately, McHenry would start
the 1901 season with just one horse besides Dan Patch, the pacer
Aegon's Star, who was owned by M. H. Tichenor of Oconomo-
woc, Wisconsin, a millionaire cattle baron new to harness racing.
Within a few months, Tichenor would sell his pacer and stalk off
angrily into the Thoroughbred game.)

One of the myriad ways in which racehorses can cause anxiety and misery in human beings, without any help from a sadist like McHenry, is in their decided lack of what might be called continuity. You never know from one racing season to the next if your horse can start from where he left off the year before. Some horses improve after being put away for a long stretch because the rest helps them mature physically, mentally, and emotionally; indeed, many young horses are put away on purpose after a period of training, to ripen. Other horses, however, can take several giant steps backward during an extended down period, often in ways that their handlers find difficult to identify, let alone fix. "He's just not the horse he was at two" is the sad refrain one often hears around Kentucky Derby time, and in fact in the Thoroughbred world only one juvenile champion has ever gone on to win the Derby, or in any way head the class at the age of three. Often what looks like backward progress, though, is merely a case of a horse standing still—failing to develop further while the others in his age group catch up and pass him by. If the trainer can't find anything wrong, it may well be because there is nothing wrong, beyond the great leveling force of the universe taking its toll.

The thought that Dan Patch had merely been an early bloomer weighed on Messner and the horse's supporters back in Oxford over the winter of 1900–1901. They talked about it in the taverns, at the after-church socials, and in other places where the *Oxford Tribune* could overhear them and note their anxiety. The idea that Dan's magic had somehow been killed off by the midwinter cold was especially popular: those behind this theory said that Oxford was not the sort of town that produced nationally known champions and that Dan would turn out to be just another horse, just as Wattles's once equally promising Prosperity Bill had turned out to be. Whenever Wattles was asked what he thought of Dan's chances as a five-year-old, he would smile thinly, shrug, and hobble away on his cane; it was a hard question for several reasons, and now somebody else's to answer. Even McHenry could not say how good Dan would be as a five-year-old—was he the fastest horse in the world or the biggest counterfeit?—until he was tested in a race.

Dan relieved some of the suspense by going 2:09 ½ in a training mile for McHenry a few days after he arrived in Cleveland; the clocking was slightly faster than his last workout in Terre Haute the autumn before, and he achieved it with shocking ease. Still, even if he was getting stronger and faster, there was the question of desire, of a smart horse's tendency, as driver John Campbell has noted, to figure out that he is going to get fed and watered and brushed whether he goes in 2:05 or 2:20, and therefore not try so hard. Horses get this wrong, of course, and unless they have value as breeding stock, they could, if they stop winning, find themselves doing hard labor or, in those days, being sold for meat. But a little knowledge is a dangerous thing, and Dan might have just decided, as many horses had before and have since, that he simply didn't want to race anymore.

The Grand Circuit would open as usual with a glamorous five-day meeting in Detroit, starting that year on July 15. Bands would play, local dignitaries would turn out, and everyone would wear their finery in honor of the best harness horses in the land. Dan was entered to make his big-time debut at Detroit on Wednesday, the seventeenth. But McHenry didn't want that high-profile race to be Dan's first after a long winter's layoff. If the horse faltered and made him look foolish for raising expectations, he wanted to keep the witnesses to a minimum. He preferred to take his horse on a shakedown cruise, preferably in a somewhat out-of-the-way place.

His best option was fairly obvious. As every experienced horseman then knew, the track at Windsor, Ontario, conducted a five-day meet each year just prior to the Detroit Grand Circuit races. The timing was strategic for Windsor, just across the river from Detroit, which could count on an unusually large number of superior horses coming into the area, and it was good for trainers like McHenry who sometimes wanted to get in a tightener before the Grand Circuit started its three-month, ten-to-twelve-city tour of the eastern United States. Scanning the ads in the horse journals a month or two earlier, McHenry had spotted a race at Windsor that he thought would be perfect for Dan Patch. It was a 2:15 class event on July 10, exactly seven days before the Detroit stake. The purse was only $600—county fair money—but it looked, on paper, like just the sort of relatively low-key scenario he was seeking.

As the appointed day drew close, however, Windsor wasn't turning out to be such a soft spot. For one thing, the five days of racing there coincided with the worst heat wave on record in the eastern half of North America; temperatures hovered in the mid-nineties every day, with humidity to match. (The week before, 880 people had died from heat-related causes in New York City.) Even in an era when racehorses and human athletes routinely, and sometimes foolishly, pushed themselves to the limit, that weather was recognized in the racing journals as dangerously extreme. On top of that, Dan's race had shaped up much more competitively than McHenry could have imagined. A speedy four-year-old pacer from Colorado named Winfield Stratton had entered, and though the Rocky Mountains have never figured prominently on the harness scene, he did show two wins at Overland Park in Denver and another in Minneapolis, at the Minnesota State Fair, where the racing was always first-rate. Also in the field was the scrappy little Canadian pacer Captain Brino, who, whether he went straight to the front or hung back in the early stages, always showed some kind of potent stretch kick.

But if McHenry was worried about either the weather or the competition as race day drew close, he didn't show it. His mood seemed uncharacteristically light. On the ferry from Detroit to Windsor on July 8, the first day of the meet, the trainer fell in with the reporter from the *Horse Review* and cheerfully gave him a tip in the second race on a trotter named Metallus, a gorgeous black stallion handled by a little-known horseman named Richard Eldridge. A few hours later, Metallus won in three straight heats and paid off (for those who were betting on the overall race result, as opposed to individual heats) with the (legal) on-track bookmakers at odds of about 3–1. McHenry, we can assume, had a wager down himself.

Wednesday, July 10, dawned the hottest day of all that week—the temperature reached 97 degrees. A promising trotter named Zarco had dropped dead on the racetrack from the heat the day before. Later that previous afternoon, according to local newspaper accounts, a mare named Ruth Ardelia would expire from "heat distress," and the promising pacer Sidney Pointer would suffer from the "blind staggers," another heat-related condition, after crossing the finish line in victory. Good times.

As if it wasn't already uncomfortable enough in the grandstand, Messner found himself sitting next to Harry Haws, the Johnstown, Pennsylvania, brick magnate who had bid against him by wire for Zelica eight years before, and who, in 1899, had sent an agent to Oxford to try to negotiate a deal for Dan Patch. The two had never met, but Haws started the conversation by informing Messner that he was a fool for not taking the $2,000 he had offered for his horse. Messner, taken aback, said that the way he remembered things, Haws had offered $1,200 and wanted Lady Patch, Dan's daughter out of Oxford Girl, thrown in for good measure. "If your man hadn't asked for the filly you could have had Dan Patch for your price," Messner said. Haws responded by pronouncing him full of shit, and the two men never spoke to each other again. It was aggressive, vulgar men like Haws and McHenry that made Messner wonder if the racing game was really for him.

At least things started smoothly on the racetrack that day: there were no scratches in Dan's event, and the field of six horses got off successfully on their first try. Rather than adapt to the heat and race more conservatively, several horses moved out aggressively at the word "Go," and the race began to develop in an odd way, with the six starters splitting into two equal-size groups. The lead trio—Dan, Winfield Stratton, and Captain Brino—roared ahead with what seemed like reckless abandon, especially considering that the race's conditions allowed for as many as five one-mile heats that afternoon. Around the first turn, the Colorado horse hugged the pole with Dan sitting to his immediate right and the Canadian horse parked three-wide, just off to the right of Dan. They passed the quarter-mile marker in 32 seconds, with Stratton a nose in front.

At the half-mile pole, reached in 1:04, it was Dan who had the nose advantage—but both the pace (faster than Dan had ever gone before) and McHenry's strategy (hung out and uncovered—that is, without a horse in front of him to break the wind) seemed to preclude anything good happening from that point onward for

Dan Patch. If the usual racing dynamics obtained, the leaders, having gone too fast too soon on such a hot day, would presently slow down and fall back, allowing the second-tier horses to pick their way through the staggering pacesetters in the homestretch and divide the spoils.

But very little about this first heat was normal. With the drivers of Dan and Captain Brino both refusing to back off and take a breather, the trio remained fanned out across the track at the three-quarter pole, where the official timer caught them in 1:36 ¼. Their three-abreast formation was now a game of chicken, which couldn't go on for much longer. And it didn't: suddenly, a step or two into the final quarter mile, the formation broke. "At that distance," the *Horse Review* said, "McHenry drew away with Dan Patch."

In truth, he only "drew away" about half a length, winning by that margin in 2:07 ½, but it was the kind of stubborn, spirit-breaking half-length that speaks of complete dominance. His two main rivals, said the *Review,* "put up a bruising finish for second place, and not more than an eyelash apart at the wire." The bizarrely macho mile had gutted them, though; they had no more to give. In the next two heats, Dan jogged away from the pair, and the three others in the field, by open lengths, winning in 2:10, then 2:09.

The raves for Dan Patch were unanimous. "What bids fair to be a remarkable career was begun at Windsor, Ontario, last Wednesday!" said the *American Horse Breeder.*

"A grand performance!" cheered the *Horse Review.* "Dan Patch cleverly defeated his field with a reserve of speed at the finish! He is the great pacer that his owner and breeder, D. A. Messner, Jr. claims him to be!"

The *Review*'s breathless account of the race made Dan 16 ¼ hands high, nearly two inches taller than he actually was. It also gave credit, of a sort, to "a local Oxford (Ind.) trainer named Mr. Waddell [sic], now seventy-four years old [Wattles was in fact seventy-three]," for not ruining the pacer before McHenry came along and worked his magic.

The kicker of the *Review* story was a quote from McHenry on the subject of Dan Patch. "I think," he said, "he is about the best all-around young horse I ever drove!"

McHenry's is a true but curious statement. As even casual racing fans know, trainers, by unspoken racetrack tradition, usually
don't discuss their horses in such hyperbolic terms. Those who
don't consider it bad form consider it bad luck. Horsemen know
how fast fortune shifts in their game and that there is nothing
to be gained, and much to make worse, by raising expectations.
In the running-horse world, trainers usually won't admit a three-
year-old is anything more than "a nice colt" until he's won the
Triple Crown, come back and taken the Travers at Saratoga, then
gone on to win the Eclipse Award as the champ of his division.
McHenry's strangely effervescent statements—to the *Review,* the
Chicago Tribune, and other journals—need to be set in perspective.

That McHenry was genuinely impressed by Dan Patch cannot
be doubted, but one reason he was being so quotable, so over-the-
top on the subject, was that he needed the media exposure, and
the fresh clients, that exposure brings. Even if you have a potential
champion in the barn, it is hard to get by with just two horses.

Money was also at the heart of McHenry's other reason for
talking up Dan to whoever would listen: he wanted to get the
horse sold. From the beginning of his relationship with Messner,
McHenry felt that Dan Patch was the kind of horse who figured
to change hands, maybe sooner rather than later. The situation
just set up that way: there were plenty of rich men who would
like to own a first-class animal that still had his palmiest days
ahead of him—and Messner seemed like just the sort of big fish
from a small pond who, as much as he loved his horse, probably couldn't resist the temptation to cash out and make a killing. (Indeed, rumors that Messner had already turned down offers
of $5,000 and $10,000 for the horse were making the rounds,
and these rumors had probably been leaked to the papers, and
perhaps created from scratch, by Messner himself.) If McHenry
could arrange the sale of Dan Patch, he would, in accordance with
the time-honored racetrack custom, extract a healthy commission
from both the buyer and seller. He would most probably also take
a share of the horse himself, if only to ensure that it would stay in
his stable and continue earning him training fees and a percent-

age of the purse money. Thus it was in McHenry's best interest to turn interviews into infomercials about "the best all-around young horse I ever drove," not just to talk about Dan Patch but to actively sell him to the racing community through the industry journals and the newspaper sports pages.

He rarely missed a chance.

"Some enthusiastic people are predicting," McHenry said, a few days after the Windsor race, "that Dan Patch could make a clean sweep of the Circuit. It is safe to say that the Indiana pacer can go in 2:06 if not better, at the present time."

Dan Patch's first Grand Circuit race, contested in Detroit—or more precisely, Grosse Pointe—one week after that stifling day at Windsor, was the $2,500 Wayne Hotel Purse, for pacers who had not won in 2:15 or faster when the entry box closed, several months earlier. The heat wave was ongoing. ("The weather is intense," said the *Davenport* (Iowa) *Daily Republican,* which reported numerous deaths and "prostrations" in Chicago; St. Joseph, Missouri; Sioux City, Iowa; Minneapolis; and Lincoln, Nebraska.) Ladies especially were being cautioned to stay indoors—good advice, since the outfit typically worn by women to the racetrack in those days (high-necked blouse; ground-length skirt; whalebone corset; huge, veiled hat) would have passed muster with the Taliban. But despite conditions that were borderline deadly, more than 5,000 came out on a Wednesday afternoon to see the trotters and pacers.

The vagaries of racing were on full display that day. The beautiful Metallus, a week after winning at Windsor and being sold for $5,000, got sick during warm-ups—if not from the heat itself, then probably from something caused by the plague of flies that come with a long heat wave—and had to be withdrawn from his stake; he would never return to top form. The feature race, the $2,500 Free-For-All pace, was a ballyhooed showdown between Anaconda and Coney, both of whom, as we have seen, had been in McHenry's stable the previous year, and had continued on without him as prosperous stars of the Circuit. In mid-afternoon, with the temperature reaching its peak, those two geldings put on a thrilling show. The jet-black Coney, looking very much the "hobbled wonder," won the first heat of the best-two-out-of-three race in the sensational time of 2:02. But in the second heat he broke stride, and though he got back on gait and nearly caught the leader, it was Anaconda, a strapping bay, who won in 2:02 ¾. Racetrack crowds, so knowledgeable and time-conscious in those days, would roar their approval when a fast time like Anaconda's was posted on the infield board. Indeed, the reaction Anaconda got for winning the second heat exceeded the ovation that came when he sewed up the race in the next heat at 2:03 ¼. For most Americans then, the idea of seconds and fractions of seconds mattering was a new, exciting, and very twentieth-century sort of thing. As for McHenry, he could only watch glumly from the backstretch—until a reporter approached and asked his reaction to what the *Fort Wayne Sentinel* would call "one of the most sensational races ever made in harness." McHenry looked at him, turned on his heel, and walked away.

But perhaps we can forgive the Wizard's rudeness this one time. He was a busy man—with a horse in the next race.

Dan Patch always made a good first impression. Henry Ten Eyck White of the *Chicago Tribune,* seeing him for the first time at Detroit, wrote, "He is a rugged looking stallion with the best of feet and legs, shod with five-ounce shoes all 'round and does not wear a boot or weight, except light quarter boots. He has a bold way of going, very much like his sire, although not gaited like him behind. His manners are simply perfect."

The turf writers loved Dan Patch, even though he challenged their powers of description by turning each race into a rout. We have already seen how he dominated the Indiana fair circuit in his rookie season, and his Grand Circuit debut proved that he would still need to move far up the classification ladder before encountering horses that could make him sweat. One cannot honestly bring drama to what happened on the track that day in Detroit, when Dan Patch won the Wayne Hotel pace in straight heats of 2:08 ¼, 2:08, and 2:09 ¾, leading every step of every heat, going so swiftly and surely that no challenger, including a highly touted colt named Capt. Sphinx, dared even to make a bid for the lead. One paper described the event simply as "a featureless race."

But the ease of his victories, a problem for turf scribes then and now, was of course no problem at all for McHenry or Messner. Dan was turning a profit. It cost more to keep a horse on the Grand Circuit (about $5,000) than it did to send a son to Yale, but if you could dominate your division, the rewards could be substantial. Grand Circuit purses exceeded those at the county fairs by a factor of five, and on top of that, at least in the early stages of Dan's career, the owner and the trainer could realize a small fortune from betting.

At Windsor, Messner and McHenry had gotten down bets on Dan at 5–1, and they probably each won more than a thousand dollars on that first heat. (In the subsequent heats, Dan, who looked too much like a sure thing for the bookmakers' taste, was barred from the wagering.)

At Detroit they had a chance to make another score, as a lot of supposedly smart money went down on Capt. Sphinx, and Dan's odds in the early betting drifted up once again to 5–1. Before they could lay bets at that price, however, Messner made the mistake of expressing his supreme confidence in Dan to one Aaron Ecock, a sharply-dressed young man whom the storekeeper took to be just another curious fan. Ecock, however, turned out to be a professional racetrack tout who tipped off so many people to Dan (in hopes of getting a kickback if they won) that the horse's odds sank to 2–1. That was still a sweet return for a virtual sure thing, but the difference significantly reduced Messner and McHenry's killing, and may have marked the beginning of the end of their relationship.

Betting was, and still is, an important part of life to many horsemen; along with training fees and purse commissions it constituted one of their main income streams. Dan's owner and trainer were doing nothing illegal or unethical when they backed their horse with the licensed bookmakers who paid a fee for the right to conduct business on the track apron in states that permitted racetrack gambling. Trainers, drivers, jockeys, and owners have never been prohibited from betting on their own horses, the theory being that they are supposed to be trying to win, and the wager is merely an affirmation of that intent. But the system is easily abused, and horsemen have always been happy to abuse it. We have already seen how in Lafayette, Indiana, the year before, John Wattles had pulled the common trick of "laying up"—purposely not winning in order to raise the odds for a subsequent heat and perhaps create a plum betting opportunity on another horse in the heat that he knew he would not be winning. Sometimes in more elaborate schemes, a fixer would bribe one or more drivers of the favored horses to lay up, then make a score by betting on several or even all of the longer-priced horses who weren't being held back; the winner might not even know a fix was in.

Ringers were another problem in those days before horses were tagged with lip tattoos that matched a number on their registration papers. The weekly horse journals routinely reported cases of faster horses being passed off as slower ones, sometimes with the aid of shoe polish or paint. Drugs, though, were the most worrisome threat to racing integrity (as they are today), if only because they jeopardized the health of the horses while making a sham of the sport. To mask pain, to slow a horse down or speed him up, trainers doped them with morphine, laudanum, and cocaine as well as rye whiskey, sherry, and other alcoholic beverages, all of which were in many states technically legal (in 1905 the National Trotting Association, or NTA, passed an "anti-drugging" rule that forbade trainers to give their horses champagne between heats). In the end, what you had at the racetrack was an honor system enforced by a community that hadn't shown much interest in being honorable since the days of the Roman chariot races, when the problem of drugging horses first surfaced.

As a manipulator of outcomes, McHenry fell in the vast middle ground between the straitlaced, nonbetting trainers and the outright crooks. For the most part he played by the rules, pulling down big purses with fast horses, if only because he could usually make more money that way with less hassle and risk. (Not even a fixed race is a sure thing; accidents happen, horses break stride or break bones, and fortunes can be lost in the process.) Yet McHenry also had been called to the judges' stand on more than one occasion to be admonished for his lack of effort in a particular heat. In 1896 he had been questioned closely by the Board of Review of the NTA, which was investigating whether a match race held at Philadelphia's Belmont Park between Joe Patchen and John R. Gentry, who was being driven by McHenry at the time, was fixed. (After hearing Belmont officials say that the 4,000 in attendance had found the contest "disgusting," and noting that the racing association had fined Jack Curry, the driver of Joe Patchen, $500 for "driving to not win," the NTA took the matter "under advisement" and never acted.) McHenry's mean-spiritedness made the idea of a betting coup especially tempting to him; apart from the money to be made, he found the idea of hoodwinking the public irresistible. Years later, when someone asked his favorite from among all the horses he had ever driven, he rhapsodized not about Dan Patch but about an obscure pacer named Prince Direct. More about him later, but the Prince was so skilled at feigning lameness that McHenry often said, "I made more with him than I ever did with Dan Patch."

A horse like Dan Patch had limited use as a gambler's tool. His form and his reputation were such that, after his first few starts, he never went off at anything resembling attractive odds. So he couldn't, in a rigged scenario, play the role of surprise winner, upsetting the field and paying $100 for $5. The only role he might play would be that of surprise loser. You could lay him up, as Wattles did, then bet (illegally) on somebody else in that heat, and bet on him in the next heat, when he would probably go off at higher odds than if you hadn't lost with him. Of course there might be consequences— howls of outrage from the public, maybe even a fine or a suspension. As with any business decision, a trainer had to factor all that in and decide whether the risks outweighed the rewards.

The Grand Circuit that summer was, as all horse racing has always been, intriguingly impure—part grand opera, part *Threepenny Opera*. Cries of fraud went up only when greed pushed one of the participants past an invisible (and ever-shifting) line of decorum. A week after the Detroit meet, at Cleveland, the *New York Times* complained about "the usual queer driving in the annual events." It seems that in the first race on July 23, the trotter Dr. Brook won the first two heats easily, and then finished third in a manner the judges found suspicious. They bawled out his driver, one "Durfee," fined him $100, and denied him his position on the pole in the next heat. When Dr. Brook finished second in the subsequent mile, the judges invoked their right to dismiss Durfee from the sulky and replaced him with "Kennedy," who, perhaps in an effort to show the judges that it was the horse, not the driver, who was the problem, drove Dr. Brook to a dull fifth-place finish. The race by this time had devolved into a war of attrition involving tired horses, petulant drivers, and judges determined to make a point. Ultimately a mare of unknown origin (her registration papers said simply "no breeding") named Palm Leaf brought an end to the messy affair in the sixth heat by winning a race-off of previous heat winners.

The second race that day was even more of a scandal. In the third heat, the judges decided that most of the eight-horse field was trying to lose—the time was 2:11 ½, four seconds slower than the previous heat, and almost all of the drivers had a choke hold on their horses. Their object, apparently, was to set up a victory for a long-shot gray mare named Eyelet, who despite all the help she got barely made it to the wire first. In a highly unusual move, the out-raged judges replaced the driver on the held-back favorite, Riley B., and scratched five other horses before they allowed the race to con-tinue. (With only three horses left in the field, Riley B. easily won.)

The next event, the $2,500 pace, was a more straightforward affair. The *Times* summed it up in a single sentence: "The third race went to Dan Patch in straight heats." The unthrilling miles were timed in 2:10 ½, 2:11 ½, and 2:11 ⅓. The Associated Press called Dan's performance "no more than a stiff jog."

Back in Oxford, no one was bored by these easy wins. At Wind-sor, Messner had started a routine of getting a telegram off to his father an hour or so after each race. As soon as it arrived, Dan Sr. would stride briskly out of the front door of his store and across the street to the little town square park, where he would shout, "Hear ye, hear ye, hear ye," until a crowd gathered. Then he would read the race results and announce Dan's times to cheers and applause. By the Cleveland race, people had started gathering in anticipation of the hear-ye's (the elder Messner shouted them anyway), and if Messner was tardy with his telegram they stayed into the evening hours and waited for news of Dan Patch, often, the *Tribune* noted, "to the chagrin of their supper-warming wives."

In a staunchly Protestant community like Oxford, however, worry permeates everything. The townsfolk and the Messners were together savoring a moment that all suspected could not last. Life in a farming community had taught them that everything is cyclical, and much more goes wrong in the world than goes right. Even as they cheered, they wondered when the correction would come.

Rumors of a possible sale of Dan Patch kicked up again after the Cleveland victory. Messner, who may have started them, denied them, sort of. "It is unlikely," he said, as he boarded the train for Columbus, Ohio, and his horse's next race, a $2,000 Grand Circuit stake.

Out west, meanwhile, another man was talking with great certainty about all the horses he intended to buy. The name of M. W. Savage first surfaced in the pages of the *Horse Review* in April 1901. The occasion was an announcement by Savage in a letter to the correspondent for the magazine's Western Department that he intended to get into harness racing in a big way. "The light harness horse has come in for a full share of his affection," is the how the correspondent phrased this dubious bit of news. (In the long off-season that stretched from roughly November till June, the horse journals filled their pages with saccharine poems, pictures of dead stable cats laid out in little satin-lined caskets, and fluff from their faithful advertisers.) Savage, the owner of the International Stock Food Company, a manufacturer of food supplements and animal elixirs, had a plan to buy a lot of horses and change their names to International This or International That, as he matter-of-factly told the *Review,* "for advertising purposes." Such blatant commercialism would not be allowed today, but back then the rich men who controlled racing got away with it. The great Anaconda raced for one year as Knox Gelatin King. (Savage soon changed his mind about the renaming plan. Had he not, you might be thrilling to the story of International Worming Remedy or International Hog Cholera Cure.)

From Cleveland, the Grand Circuit moved on to Columbus. It was the fourth city Dan had raced in that month, and assuming he won in straight heats, the race there on July 29 would encompass his tenth, eleventh, and twelfth competitive miles in nineteen days. But he showed no signs of fatigue. Said the *Fort Wayne Evening Sentinel*: "The last race, the 2:10 pace, was a gift to Dan Patch, the handsome son of old Joe Patchen, who tiptoed the field and was never forced to the top of his speed at any stage of the race." The fastest of Dan's three heats went in 2:10 ¼. It was wonderful to win so easily, but McHenry worried that Dan wasn't getting the fast miles that he needed. Early in the morning after his victory in Columbus, McHenry brought Dan out and worked him a mile in 2:05, with the last half made, with supreme ease, in 1:01 ½. Next stop: Fort Erie.

At that Canadian racetrack just across the border from Buffalo, New York, on August 8, McHenry told reporters that Dan was "the greatest horse I ever pulled a rein over," a cliché that never fails to impress turf scribes. But McHenry admitted to one concern: the possibility that the public might be getting bored with Dan's easy wins. To make things more exciting, he announced that in the Empire City Stake, as the race at Fort Erie had been christened, he would take Dan back to dead last in each heat and not make a move until the top of the homestretch.

It was a good time to try such a stunt. The larger public hadn't yet warmed to Dan Patch, who with a record of eight mostly unthrilling victories in eight starts was still something of a horseman's horse. Meanwhile the field in the 2:14 class at Fort Erie was a truly motley bunch, a mix of horses Dan had already had his way with in his previous Grand Circuit stops and some overmatched local long shots. In the first heat, timed in a tardy 2:17 ¼, McHenry did exactly what he said he would, slowing Dan almost to a walk at the start so everyone else could pass, then, after moving wide at the top of the stretch, circling the field with what one writer called "an electric burst" and winning easily. The crowd was thrilled, but the judges were not amused by the trick and sent word to McHenry that, since this was a betting race, he should stop fooling around. In the next two heats Dan led from start to finish in businesslike fashion.

From Fort Erie, McHenry, Dan, and Messner moved on with

most of the other Grand Circuit horses and trainers to Brighton Beach, Brooklyn, for a race on August 16. This was the first harness racing meet ever held at Brighton Beach, which had been operating since 1879, presenting Thoroughbreds and, in the off-season, dogs for the public's betting pleasure (even during periods when betting was prohibited in New York State). Thus it had the aura of a major event on that year's racing calendar. One of three tracks in the Coney Island resort area, Brighton was the grandest of several attractions—hotels, vaudeville theaters, and an open parkland where in 1883 William "Buffalo Bill" Cody had staged his Wild West show—clustered around the then-famous New Iron Pier. With its infield of tall marsh grass and warm sea breezes, its cheap grandstand, and its exclusive clubhouse, the Brighton track always drew well from both the working classes and the fashionable set of New York City.

Brighton was not, however, a place for racing purists. One problem involved the track itself, which in the opinion of many trainers too closely resembled the nearby Atlantic beaches. Runners require a deeper, softer cushion than Standardbreds, but the Brighton track was so loose and sandy in places that horses, said the *Times,* would often "sink in to their fetlocks." Some top trainers avoided the track, fearing their horses would slip and injure themselves. Jockeys sometimes had to swerve their mounts violently through the homestretch, searching for the firmest footing.

But it was another kind of crooked racing that gave Brighton its more telling reputation. About half the races there, it sometimes seemed, were as tightly choreographed as the Florodora girls. Riders brazenly held back their horses so long shots could pass them by; trainers drugged horses to make them go faster or slower; and in the grandstand, touts, speaking in stage whispers, dispensed false insider information. Track officials tended to look the other way, either because they had been bribed or because the prospect of cleaning up the place was just too daunting. Brighton went beyond the conventional kinds of racetrack corruption. On several occasions at Brighton, writes the racing historian Jeffrey Stanton, "arrests were made that involved [people] taking rivals' horses from the stables in the dead of night and galloping them almost to exhaustion to ensure their defeat the next day." George Gershwin's father, Morris Gershovitz, a fairly recent immigrant from St. Petersburg, Russia, spent a ruinous three weeks at the Brighton track at around this time, trying to make a go of it as an honest bookmaker before the sharpies did him in. On at least one occasion the *Times* raised its editorial voice, calling for a new era of "fair racing at Brighton Beach," and occasionally a higher racing authority would dole out fines to jockeys and judges. But these were little more than an annoyance, the cost of doing monkey business.

At Brighton Beach, McHenry had entered Dan in a 2:08 class race that carried a purse of $1,500. This was the stiffest level of competition Dan had faced so far, and for the smallest prize he had pursued since Windsor. The conditions reflected the newness of Brighton's harness meet; there hadn't been enough time to collect the stakes payments that would have swelled the purses. But it would not be unreasonable to wonder what Dan was doing there. Brighton seemed like a very missable date, especially for a horse who had earned a break and who might have skipped the long trip south and moved on from Buffalo directly to Readville, Massachusetts, the Grand Circuit's next stop. But McHenry had his own agenda, one that made Brighton necessary. All would be apparent shortly.

The management at Brighton warmly welcomed the Standardbreds on opening day, Tuesday, August 13, with a spruced-up plant and a track surface that had been dragged and graded until, said the *New York Times,* it was "as dry as gunpowder and as smooth as ice." Large display ads in the *Brooklyn Daily Eagle* and the *Times* bid gentlemen ($2 admission) and ladies ($1) to "Come and See the Flying Sulkies." The Landers Orchestra, set up trackside, played the trotters and pacers on and off the track. It was still a good time to be a horse.

Dan's 2:08 pace was scheduled for Friday, August 16, the penultimate day of the meet. It was a slot well suited to a fast-rising wunderkind known to the cognoscenti but still lacking the credentials to mix with the racing royalty on Saturday afternoon. Dan's first appearance at Brighton, however, was an unannounced cameo: on Tuesday, he came out on the track to help warm up his sire, Joe Patchen, who later that afternoon would engage in a match race with Anaconda. Old Joe looked a bit plump and logy as he toured the oval alongside his fast-rising son. In both heats that day, Anaconda whipped Joe soundly. It was time for him to go off to stud permanently.

On Friday there were 16,000 at Brighton, and "the plunging," said the *Brooklyn Eagle,* "was extraordinarily brisk." Dan Patch was the favorite from the moment the betting on his race opened, thanks to "a bid of $1,300 from Sturges in the auction pool." The reference was to Manley Edward Sturges, who will weave back into our tale.

As post time drew near, the two horses receiving the most betting action were Dan (the 1–10 choice) and Martha Marshall. This made sense. Dan, after all, was unbeaten and Martha, though a small, hobbled mare, was coming off wins at Cleveland and Columbus in faster-class races than Dan's.

In the backstretch, Dan Patch found himself surrounded by a three-deep circle of gawkers as McHenry and the grooms made their final preparations. The encroaching mob bothered McHenry more than it did his horse. John Hervey, the Pierce Egan of the harness-horse turf, was among the curious. "The mental picture of Dan Patch as I first saw him is as vivid as though it were of yesterday," Hervey later wrote. "The impression that he instantly made upon me was the profound one that only a very great horse can produce. He stood as quietly amid the throng pressing around him as if oblivious of its presence; with an expression of innate power, of tremendous but unostentatious individual force, such as, I suppose, Daniel Webster, among men, must have posed. Instinctively, as I gazed at him, I felt that this horse, merely in repose, surpassed all the expectations that I might have of him in action."

Any expectations of a great day of racing, though, were quickly shattered. After the Landers Orchestra played the pacers onto the track, it took almost an hour to get the first heat off, thanks to the star-crossed 100–1 shot Paul Revere, who snapped his hobbles during one score toward the start wire, and then, after a long interval in the barn for repairs, came back out and promptly snapped his sulky axle, causing another lengthy delay. By the time he returned from the stables again, the crowd was booing and catcalling, partly because of the tedium caused by the delays and partly because people couldn't help but notice that Dan was not being particularly aggressive in these abortive starts. Hervey noted that Dan "didn't seem to be getting away well . . . McHenry made no effort with him." Well, now. If something smelled fishy at Brighton Beach, it was not because of low tide.

When the starter finally said "Go," Dan Patch got away slowly once again, and dropped in fourth; Martha Marshall toddled to the lead, where she was allowed to proceed, unchallenged, at a comfortable clip. What happened next strains credulity—because nothing happened. As the quarter-mile poles flew by, all seven horses held their positions along the rail. Boos began early and rose in volume as the race progressed, and they reached a crescendo as the field passed under the finish wire in the exact same positions they had held the entire race. Martha Marshall was the winner, Patsy K. second, Major Muscovite third, and Dan Patch fourth. As fixes go, it was shockingly heavy-handed, even by Brighton Beach standards. The time, said the *Review,* was a "suspiciously slow" 2:09.

The spectators at Brighton were not merely suspicious, however; they were convinced that they had just seen a "boat race." The mob roared its displeasure and tossed debris. When the noise did not abate after a few minutes, and an especially vocal group of perhaps two hundred men gathered near the finish wire and began surging against the fence, demanding that McHenry be thrown out, or lynched, a squadron of police suddenly appeared in the homestretch holding billy clubs. The scene was a kind of Brooklyn version of what had happened in Lafayette, Indiana, when Wattles had dabbled in the art of "laying up." More money and more anger fueled the situation now, however, and when the crowd caught a glimpse of the little sandy-haired McHenry, who had been summoned by the stewards to explain his actions, emotions boiled over. Several outraged horse players vaulted the fence and tried to run across the track, apparently intent on doing the driver harm. The police, swinging their clubs, beat them back until the entire mob turned and retreated. From his seat in the stands, Messner watched the battle ebb and flow.

Some of My Early Memories.

The muddy and rutted Chiquesalonghi track, built in 1871, where the septuagenarian trainer "Uncle" John Wattles (right inset) first trained Dan Patch and where, in 1900, he demonstrated to Oxford, Indiana, storekeeper Dan Messner (left inset) that Dan Patch had racehorse speed.

Birthplace and Mother of
Dan Patch, Oxford, Ind.

HOME OF DAN PATCH 1:55.

An unidentified man (circa 1907) displays Dan Patch's dam, Zelica, outside the Oxford, Indiana, barn where the great horse spent his early years. Dan Messner bought her—by accident—at an Indiana country fair. She had many foals, but none besides Dan Patch ever amounted to much. The barn was boarded up for almost a century before Dan Messner's grandson decided to see what was inside.

3

Dan's sire, Joe Patchen, was known as The Iron Horse. He made 100 starts in his career and won fifty-three of them. Though extremely popular, he was, in sharp contrast to his most famous son, dangerous to be around; toward the end of his life, he was kept in chains.

Dan Patch in his prime, with his third and last trainer, the meek but methodical Harry Hersey, in the racing sulky. While many of his rivals needed hobbles and other equipment to keep them on stride, Dan was a natural-born pacer. He once fled a stable fire on the parallel gait.

4

5   The hard-living, preternaturally cranky Myron McHenry, the "Wizard of the Homestretch," was the most famous of Dan Patch's three drivers, and the best.

M. W. SAVAGE AND HIS GREAT DAN PATCH 1:55¼

M. W. Savage, who made a fortune selling an essentially worthless animal food supplement, worked hard and spent heavily to project an image of unqualified success. Dan Patch was an important part of his plan, but Savage pushed the horse beyond reasonable limits.

6

M. W. Savage thought big—much too big. Soon after his Three Feeds For One Cent food supplement made him a millionaire, he purchased The Most Wonderful Horse in the World—and took over the cavernous Exhibition Building in downtown Minneapolis, a structure with eighteen acres of floor space.

The train depot in Savage, Minnesota, directly across from M. W. Savage's International 1:55 Stock Food Farm. Although the location was considered too remote in the early 1900s to sustain a first-rate breeding operation, tourists came from as far away as Russia to see Dan Patch and the famous barns and training tracks. The depot, built in 1880, has recently been restored.

Savage designed a luxurious private railroad car for his barnstorming star. A thick rubber floor cushioned vibrations and the inside walls were lined with plush red velvet. "Dan is an intelligent animal," Savage said, "and he likes pleasant and comfortable surroundings." (The Taj Mahal turret of Dan's barn is visible in the background.)

8-213 · COVERED RACE TRACK · SAVAGE · MINN.

For a while, no horse had a better life than Dan Patch. Even as his business empire crumbled, Savage spent a fortune to build an enclosed half-mile track on his 700-acre Minnesota spread. The track, which had 1,600 windows to admit natural light, allowed the horse to train comfortably during bad weather.

12

As Dan got older and could no longer go record-breaking miles, M. W. Savage hatched a plan to have him "compete" in staged match races with another great pacer he owned, Minor Heir. Here Savage (left) takes Dan on his training miles over the mile track at his International 1:55 Stock Food Farm. Harry Hersey handles Minor Heir.

13

M. W. Savage in 1916, the year Dan Patch died. Savage's financial troubles were taking their toll, and the worry is evident in his face.

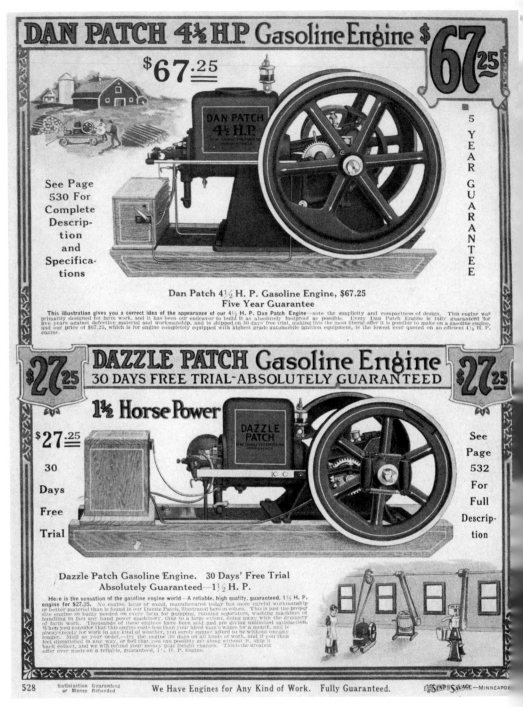

DAN PATCH 4½ H.P. Gasoline Engine $67.25

$67.25

5 YEAR GUARANTEE

See Page 530 For Complete Description and Specifications

Dan Patch 4½ H. P. Gasoline Engine, $67.25
Five Year Guarantee

This illustration gives you a correct idea of the appearance of our 4½ H. P. Dan Patch Engine—note the simplicity and compactness of design. This engine was primarily designed for farm work, and it has been our endeavor to build it as absolutely foolproof as possible. Every Dan Patch Engine is fully guaranteed for five years against defective material and workmanship, and is shipped on 30 days' free trial, making this the most liberal offer it is possible to make on a gasoline engine, and our price of $67.25, which is for engine completely equipped with highest grade automobile ignition equipment, is the lowest ever quoted on an efficient 4½ H. P. engine.

$27.25 DAZZLE PATCH Gasoline Engine $27.25
30 DAYS FREE TRIAL-ABSOLUTELY GUARANTEED

1½ Horse Power

$27.25

30 Days Free Trial

See Page 532 For Full Description

Dazzle Patch Gasoline Engine. 30 Days' Free Trial
Absolutely Guaranteed—1½ H. P.

Here is the sensation of the gasoline engine world—A reliable, high quality, guaranteed, 1½ H. P. engine for $27.25. No engine, large or small, manufactured today has more careful workmanship or better material than is found in our Dazzle Patch, illustrated here in colors. This is just the proper size engine so badly needed on every farm for pumping, running separators, washing machines or handling in fact any hand power machinery, thus to a large extent, doing away with the drudgery of farm work. Thousands of these engines have been sold and are giving unlimited satisfaction. When you consider that this engine costs less than your hired man's wages for a month, and is always ready for work in any kind of weather, you surely cannot afford to be without one any longer. Mail us your order,—try the engine 30 days on all kinds of work, and if you then feel dissatisfied in any way, or feel that you can possibly get along without it, ship it back collect, and we will refund your money plus freight charges. This is the greatest offer ever made on a reliable, guaranteed, 1½ H. P. Engine.

528 Satisfaction Guaranteed or Money Refunded We Have Engines for Any Kind of Work. Fully Guaranteed. SEND SAVAGE—MINNEAPOLIS

14   In the first decade of the twentieth century, America could not get enough of Dan Patch, who drew crowds of 100,000 on several occasions. Dan made more money endorsing breakfast cereal, cigars, washing machines, gasoline engines, and other products than he did on the racetrack.

CHAPTER ELEVEN

THE STORY I JUST related to you—I mean the part about the judges calling McHenry to the stand and the makings of a riot that was squelched by the Brooklyn police—may not have happened, at least not exactly the way I have just rendered it. Or it may have; alas, we just don't know. Although Dan Patch lived only a century ago, it sometimes seems that we possess more certain knowledge about Alexander the Great's strapping black stallion Bucephalus, who died (and received a state funeral) in 326 BC.

The problem is not peculiar to Dan Patch, of course. In the early twentieth century, the most prominent figures in American life, if they came from the low cultures of sport or popular entertainment, tended to be chronicled unreliably, when they were chronicled at all. Literary journalism had not yet been invented, and even its quotidian cousin the feature story was still inchoate. Newspapers had long since recognized the demand for scores and highlights—William Randolph Hearst's *New York Journal* introduced the sports section in 1895—but stories about athletes of both the two- and four-legged kind were usually short and shallow. Worse, they were polite, often steering clear of conflict and bad behavior, in accordance with proper etiquette, painting a grotesquely bland portrait of American life. Muckrakers like Lincoln Steffens and Ida Tarbell aside, reporters did not travel down paths on which they weren't invited. They hardly went down paths at all.

The price we have paid for this reticence is a very patchy early pop history. In his smart and poignant biography of Babe Ruth, *The Big Bam*, Leigh Montville periodically falls back on a device he calls "the fog" to explain why he can't provide his reader with certain key scenes and details. What dire circumstances led little George's parents to deposit him at a sort of Baltimore Boy's Town at the age of six or seven? Forget it: that's fogged over. Something about Ruth's first wife? Sorry, she's socked in, too. But at least Ruth reached his prime in the age of film and radio, and at a time when baseball writers were molding myths out of safe truths and half-truths. The story of Dan Patch, as told by the newspapers of his less evolved day, is as wide as the North American continent (he was front-page news in Alaska) and (for the most part) as deep as a dime. The coverage of the Brighton Beach brouhaha strikes me as typical. Sifting through dozens of accounts of Dan's lost heat that day, I could find only a few mentions of McHenry getting a dressing-down from the judges, and absolutely nothing about a fan revolt. Yet I believe it happened. Why? Here again I fall back on Mary Cross's refreshingly naive *Two Dans* book. When she was interviewing Oxfordites in the 1960s and '70s, Cross found aging earwitnesses who told her that they heard the story from Dan Messner Sr. on the very day it would have occurred. (Messner *père* no doubt learned of the incidents from his son's usual postrace telegram or phone call.) On my own trips to Oxford, I heard the descendants of these people talking about "the trouble McHenry caused," and describing the scene in some detail.

As for why the papers of that day would pass up a juicy riot story, that can be easily explained: the scoundrels who ran the Brighton Track wanted them to—like baseball, racing was trying hard to draw a family crowd—and since so many turf scribes were on the take in those days, the scoundrels got their way. Farfetched? Hardly. The bribing of writers and editors was a venerable tradition in racing—and boxing (ask Damon Runyon)—that lasted well into the twentieth century.

For what it's worth, *The Autobiography of Dan Patch* treats the Brighton Beach incident this way:

My faith in [McHenry] was somewhat shaken [Dan Patch writes] on August 16th. In a race with seven starters I was forced to take the other horses' dust all the way around and, despite my efforts down the stretch, I finished fourth in the slow time of 2:09, being beaten by Martha Marshall, Major Muscovite and Patsy K. I was indignant that my driver should have made me lose a heat that I could have won so easily.

I could not understand it at the time. How could I have understood? I knew nothing of pool-selling. I remember now that Mr. McHenry was called to the judges' stand and he was there, evidently in very earnest conversation, as I was led away to the barns. My owner was also on the grounds and he looked cross and worried but did not talk much.

Obviously, Dan Patch was no E. B. White. Although the *Autobiography* mimics Anna Sewell's popular 1877 novel *Black Beauty*, another tale told from a horse's point of view, and it pioneered the coauthored celebrity memoir form that reached its zenith in the late 1980s with my (and Donald Trump's) *Surviving at the Top*, the seventy-nine-page book is basically a flatulent exercise in facade maintenance commissioned by M. W. Savage and banged out by Merton E. Harrison, an early PR hack who was not above getting a reporter drunk so he couldn't file a negative piece, and who would survive to do advance work for the Dan Patch movie of 1949. One must admire for its understatement, however, the sentence that follows the section quoted just above:

"McHenry's interview with the judges must have been very much to the point, for matters were entirely different in the next heat."

They certainly were: the *Horse Review* called the next heat "a clinker," using the term in the British sense to mean something first-rate. Dan Patch left quickly ("McHenry was out for business," said the *Review*), but then surrendered the lead to the suddenly explosive Major Muscovite, who looked liked he had been given a snort of cocaine between heats (not an unheard-of practice at Brighton Beach). The Major appeared to be running away with the heat until, just past the half-mile pole, Dan pulled off the rail and began a steady advance—closely followed by another seemingly possessed outsider named George. The leaders battled three abreast around the final turn as the crowd stood and screamed. At the top of the homestretch, however, McHenry shook the reins and hollered at Dan, and he dug in and pulled away from the others, winning by two lengths in 2:04 ½, the fastest clocking by a pacing stallion that year. (Martha Marshall finished third, six lengths back.) The *Eagle* said, "Dan wore nothing but the simplest rigging and proved to be what he is—a magnificent natural-gaited pacer, as steady as clockwork and with the speed of the wind." John Hervey, who was seeing Dan in action for the first time that day, trotted out his trademark purple. He called the mile "indescribable" and compared Dan to "a knight of invincible prowess, sweeping through the tournament and scattering all who dared oppose him as a whirlwind scatters chaff."

Dan was keyed up now, and more than ready to go the two more heats needed to seal a victory. But it was getting late. All the delays and disputes had caused the program to fall far behind schedule, and in the gathering dusk of 7:00 p.m. the judges announced that the rest of Dan's race would be contested the following afternoon.

The next day was Saturday, the getaway day, and the featured attraction was a match race between two of the best-known horses in the nation: the hobbled pacer Prince Alert and the brilliant, coffee-colored Anaconda, who had whipped Joe Patchen four days earlier at the same track. Reading just the result, you might think it was a lopsided affair: Anaconda won both the heats, going the second in 2:01 ¾, the fastest time of the year. Yet both miles were closely fought tests of speed, heart, and strategy—what was known in those days as "magnificent sport." In the final "both horses, tired to the point of dropping, stoutly fought on, the drivers . . . lifting, leaning, yelling and whipping tried to push forward for the last inch of advantage." The *Eagle* declared Anaconda "King of the Pacing World!"

As pure spectacle, Dan's Saturday race fell far short of that battle of the titans. The third heat of the interrupted $1,500 pace was the first event on the program, and with Martha Marshall clearly laying up and the others looking worn from the previous day's racing, Dan zipped to an easy wire-to-wire win in 2:07 ¼. He needed only one more win to clinch a victory.

Before that heat could get started, Martha Marshall delayed the proceedings for about forty-five minutes by repeatedly losing her gait during the attempted starts, and galumphing along, said the *Eagle,* "at something between a trot and a lope." When the field finally got away, though, she was all business, racing just off Dan's shoulder for a half mile, dropping back to the pole, then coming on again in the homestretch before suddenly running out of steam. "As the mare wearied," said the *Eagle,* "Dan was pulled down almost to a walk, winning by three lengths in 2:05 ¾." Almost twenty-four hours after it had begun, the race was finally over, and Dan Patch had his tenth consecutive victory.

The large Saturday crowd stood and applauded. Like Ruby Keeler in *42nd Street,* Dan had gone out a youngster but come back a star. In his first trip to New York City, he had not only overcome a long journey and the confusion that resulted from being held back by the man who usually urged him forward, he had beaten a tough field and lowered his mile record three and a half seconds, a drop that deeply impressed the time-conscious public. Some were saying that the modestly bred horse from Indiana, and not Anaconda, was the true pacing king.

Before the contingent left Brooklyn, Dan Messner spoke to a reporter from the *Chicago Record-Herald,* saying that he had been offered $20,000 for Dan Patch from a person he cared not to name. Unlike some other offers that Messner had alluded to, this one was probably real. Feelers for Dan had started to come in, and Messner, never comfortable in his role as prominent horse owner, was beginning to seriously consider cashing in his chip and parting with his prize. Meanwhile, McHenry, assuming a confiding tone, told a writer from the *New York Herald* that he thought he could have gotten down close to a 2:00 mile with Dan Patch at Brighton "had I chosen to go that fast." Given that only one Standardbred had so far broken or even reached the so-called two-minute barrier—Star Pointer, an ugly and chronically sore pacer who went a freakish mile in 1:59 ¼ at Readville, Massachusetts, in 1897—McHenry's boast sounds dubious at best. Still, as the group headed off to Boston for their next race, it was clear that both the career—and the marketing—of Dan Patch were gathering momentum.

On August 22 at Readville—a handsome track on the western bank of the Neponset River that is now the site of a Stop & Shop warehouse in Boston's Hyde Park neighborhood—Dan drew 15,000, a remarkable crowd in those days, when major-league baseball games were routinely witnessed by 2,000 or 3,000 fans. No one could bet on him, though; in an unusual move that could very well have been a reaction to security problems at Brighton, the management barred him from the auction pools. The goal of the staid Bostonians who ran the Readville meet was to get Dan on and off their track with a minimum of fuss (kind of like Ed Sullivan's approach to Elvis), and this they accomplished. Facing a not-bad field of four, Dan won easily in straight heats—the fastest was 2:07 ¼—and picked up the winner's share of a $3,000 purse.

By the time word of the victory reached Oxford on that Thursday evening, the leading citizens had made their way through a soaking rainstorm to the town's Opera House, where something called the *Dan Patch Musical Entertainment* was underway. For this no-expense-spared celebration of their once-scoffed-at horse, "talent from Fowler, Otterbein, Pine Village and Attica strengthened the Oxford band," wrote Mary Cross, "and formed as fine an aggregation as ever played in Benton County." It was on this occasion that James W. Steele, head carpenter of the Opera House, directed the band in the first public performance of his "Dan Patch Two Step." (Not to be confused with H. G. Trautvetter's "Dan Patch March" and "Dan Patch Two Step," the sheet music for which often sells on eBay for $25 or so. Steele's "Two Step" has apparently been lost.)

The following week the Grand Circuit roared into Narragansett Park, about five miles south of Providence, in Cranston, Rhode Island. There Dan would face the largest and fastest field he had yet encountered. His ten rivals—"all his seniors and of ripe experience," said one paper—included the highly touted Canadian gelding Harold H. and the fast mare Mazette. The odd thing about Dan's race, though, was that it was an ordinary 2:08-class event, worth $1,500, and not the $10,000 pace, one of the twin highlights of that year's Narragansett meet, along with the $10,000 trot. Why, the racing world wondered, wasn't Dan entered in the richer and more prestigious event?

In the *Chicago Tribune,* White professed amazement at McHenry's passing up the $10,000 pace, which, he pointed out, had shaped up to be an easier race than the cheaper one. "There is certainly nothing in the field that on form compares with Dan Patch," he wrote. "Were the son of Joe Patchen in the big Providence stake it would be at his mercy. There has been some question," White concluded, "as to why [Dan Patch] was not named last spring when the entries closed."

Was White suddenly being tough on his old pal McHenry? No, as it turns out, he was just setting up the trainer to give his side of the story.

"Well, it's like this," McHenry says in the next paragraph. "At the time the entries to the race closed I knew little about Dan Patch except that he had raced well last year and at the close of the season was good for a mile at Terre Haute just a shade better than 2:10. Now, to put such a horse into a stakes open to every horse with no record better than 2:10 at the close of the 1900 campaign would have been a foolish move, and every horseman knows it. That Dan Patch has, since the entries closed, developed from a 2:10 pacer to one that has a mark of 2:04 ½ cuts no figure in the matter. I staked the horse everywhere it looked reasonable for him to be put, making the entries in my own name, and thereby committing myself to a considerable sum in entrance money, but I was not looking for any 2:10 stakes with Dan last spring."

McHenry's point, as usual, was that anyone who questioned his judgment was that lowest of God's creatures: the something-less-than-a-real-man who knew diddly about horses. It was also very much his style to whine—for the second time in the *Tribune*'s pages—about having to front his owner for stakes payments, not caring if that made Messner look bad. Yet the fact remained that Dan, in his $1,500 race, would be meeting a better bunch than were competing for the ten grand. It was an embarrassing situation for a trainer, who should always position his horse to gain the most from the least effort and risk. And yet for fans of magnificent sport, who were eager to see Dan finally tested, the situation at Narragansett was a blessing. The 2:08 pace was shaping up as such an intriguing race, in fact, that it was moved to the final day of the meet, where it would share the bill with an attempt by the trotter Cresceus to lower his record for the mile by going in a time trial with Thoroughbred prompters. The Chinese minister to the United States, Wu Ting-Fang, was among the dignitaries who turned out on a sunny but windy Saturday to see the American Standardbred at his proud apogee.

Over in the McHenry barn, however, all was not well. The day before his race Dan had started coughing, and when McHenry took his temperature it was, he would later admit, "far above normal." Instead of scratching him, though, the trainer thought he would take a wait-and-see approach. Telling his new groom Chester Landerbaugh to keep mum about the fever, McHenry set up a cot outside Dan's stall, where he spent the night. Dan at first was restless, but then he seemed to sleep, and at about 5:00 a.m., when McHenry looked up from his cot, he saw Dan looking back at him "clear-eyed"—and no doubt surprised to see his sourpuss of a trainer, a man who tended to show up for work a bit on the late side and smelling like fermented hay, stretched out in front of the stall door. McHenry rolled off his cot, looked Dan over, and decided he was fit to race.

If he was, it was only by the standards of an age when horses and human athletes were expected to sweat out sickness and limp off lameness as best they could. During Dan's warm-up miles, McHenry could sense that the pacer was sluggish, his puppylike enthusiasm gone. A few weeks later, White reported that Dan had been suffering from "a touch of rheumatism" that day. To the *Review* correspondent in the press area at Providence, Dan "looked a trifle stale" after winning twenty-two of twenty-three heats in nine cities, in just over six weeks. More likely the problem was a cold or flu that racehorses pick up routinely. But whatever was wrong, the other trainers, who were taking their warm-ups at the same time as McHenry, may have noticed a difference, for when race time arrived, they went at Dan fiercely.

The Canadian champion Harold H., second choice in the betting, was the horse who concerned McHenry most going into the race; when the starter said "Go" he left at full speed, but it was the feisty mare Mazette who showed real moxie in the first heat: even after Dan outmuscled her for the lead at the quarter pole she hung tough the whole mile, never quite getting by him, but pushing him to a clocking of 2:04 ½, the second-fastest mile of his career.

Would the exertions of that first heat wear him out, or would they open his lungs and help him feel better? Dan got off to a reasonably good start in the second heat, racing in second or third position in the early stages. But at the three-quarter pole, as Major Muscovite came on, the pacer did something he had never done before: he started to fade. "It looked like Dan was beaten," the *Lincoln* (Neb.) *Evening News* said. An alarmed McHenry first shook the reins, then yelled, and then, for the first time, flicked the horse with the whip. "That was all Dan needed," said the *Tribune*. Gallantly, and indeed almost miraculously, he came on again "and in the last few strides he stepped ahead of the others and won" in 2:07.

Despite his weakness Dan wasn't just winning the heats—he was wearing the others down, physically and mentally. In the third mile, he took the lead without a challenge and appeared to be home free when another mare, Maxine (bet heavily despite finishing eighth in each of the first two heats), made a huge move from far back around the final turn and came within half a length of catching the all-out favorite in 2:06 ½. "It was a hard race for Dan Patch," the *Review* said, "and that he was able to win it stamps him as a greater racehorse than he had been counted before. In both the second and third heats it looked as though he was beaten, but with the stout heart of his sire he kept fighting and finally paced his rivals into the ground."

"To my notion," McHenry would say months later, "Dan showed himself a great horse, and a brave one, at Providence. When I asked him for speed, he took hold like a bulldog looking for a fight."

Before returning to his stall, Dan did one more thing that day, something people would remember much longer than his victory in the $1,500 pace. After McHenry drove him back to the finish wire to pick up his purse and a trophy, the horse turned to the grandstand and bowed deeply, seeming to acknowledge the applause. It was a gesture he would repeat, when he was moved to do so, for the rest of his public life. "I never taught him to do that," McHenry would always say.

On the town green in Oxford that evening, keeping up what had become a weekly ritual, Dan Messner Sr. gathered a crowd by crying his hear-ye's, then related the story of the race; this time he mentioned how, after winning for the twelfth straight time, Dan had taken a bow. A murmur of astonishment rippled through the hundred or so who had assembled. Then Charles Shipps, the Swedish immigrant who owned the furniture store, stepped forward to say that he was not surprised to hear about Dan's bowing. When he had gone to see the Grand Circuit races in Buffalo a few weeks before, Shipps noted, Dan, "like any a well-raised Oxford lad," had nodded politely in the direction of anyone who called his name.

The sporting press now occupied itself with the question of how fast Dan would ultimately go. White, in his *Tribune* column, speculated that "he will go a mile close to 2:00 before his turf days are over." Some people said 1:59 was possible—a shocking number in a business where, not all that long ago, a 2:25 horse paid the bills. There were, after all, still plenty of people who thought Star Pointer's record was the result of a timing error, and that sub-2:00 miles were beyond the physical limitations of the Standardbred horse.

All the talk about records stirred up more inquiries, feelers, and offers from potential buyers. The most serious offer—again, for $20,000—reached Messner by telegram just before he boarded the train for the short hop to Hartford's Charter Oak Park. Twenty thousand was not a record price for a Standardbred—in 1891 J. Malcolm Forbes bought the trotter Arion from Leland Stanford for $125,000—but no one had ever paid that much for a pacer. Messner mentioned the offer, and the amount, to a reporter for the *Indianapolis News,* once again without mentioning the would-be buyer's name. Before long, though, the gossip had it that the bidder was Manley E. Sturges, the high roller who had gotten the betting started at Brighton Beach by plunking down $1,300 on Dan Patch.

Messner wired Sturges back saying he was not ready to sell. McHenry, for once, agreed with him. The trainer told Messner that he believed Dan could beat Star Pointer's record of 1:59 ¼ by the following summer, and that if they showed a little patience they could get a lot more than $20,000 for the fastest horse who had ever lived. "We're in a good position," he assured Messner. It certainly seemed that way to the rest of the world. In the next issue of the *Horse Review,* the cartoonist Robert L. Dickey drew a picture of the trainer sitting on a mountain of money bags and smoking a long cigar. "Myron McHenry's Latest Photograph," the caption read.

Dan's performance at Hartford did nothing to change the general assumption that all was perfectly well. In a $3,000 stake there on September 5, Dan, again barred from the betting, won "as he pleased," said the *Hartford Courant,* in straight heats, the fastest being 2:08 ¾. McHenry, though, wasn't happy with what he saw. To him, Dan was not as sharp as he had been, and he couldn't say why. The cough and fever were long gone; Dan was eating well, and in his usual high spirits; he just didn't seem to be grabbing hold of the racetrack the way he had earlier in the season. McHenry didn't mention his concern to Messner; he just told the owner that they were going to follow the circuit on its swing west, for another $3,000 stake at Oakley Park in Cincinnati. Depending on how things went there, he said, he would decide on how Dan would finish up the season.

Things went smoothly at Oakley, or at least they seemed to: Dan easily beat a motley quintet of rivals in the minimum three heats, the fastest going in 2:07. That evening, though, McHenry surprised Messner by saying, "We're going to give your horse a couple of weeks away from the track. The break will do him good. As long as we're this far west, you should bring him home to your place in Indiana. Just turn him out and let him graze for a few days. You'll meet me in Lexington a week before the races there."

Messner, as always, did as McHenry said and took his horse back to Oxford. After following the Grand Circuit for a month, it felt good to be home, but it also felt strange: Messner was being treated like a celebrity by some of the same people who had ridiculed him practically to his face, first for buying Zelica, then for breeding her to Joe Patchen, and yet again for keeping the foal. Messner couldn't complain, though, especially since he was unaware of the change in Dan that was worrying McHenry. When a reporter from the local paper asked him why his horse was always so sharp and ready to race, Messner said, "Because he's a happy horse. Only happy horses make good performers."

Around the thirtieth of September, Messner sent Dan ahead to Lexington, accompanied only by Stephen, his local groom. The race was still a week away, and he had a lot to do in Oxford, between catching up on his store business and signing a contract to build a new house. What Cross called "the finest residence in Benton County" was perhaps something short of that, but with its wraparound front porch and large, shaded yard it represented a significant upgrade from the strikingly modest house, hard by the Presbyterian parsonage, where he had lived since he and Maud had married. The *Tribune* assured its readers that once the Messners' house was finished, "Dan Patch would be a privileged guest in the parlor."

In their first workout mile at Lexington, a week before their race, McHenry saw to his dismay that Dan had come back to the track exactly the way he left it. The horse felt heavy on the bit, maybe even heavier than before his brief vacation.

The common rap on McHenry was that he cared mostly about race driving—something even his critics admitted he did better than probably anyone else—and little about training horses. He was, after all, the Wizard of the Homestretch, not the Houdini of Husbandry. The great Hervey himself backed the conventional wisdom, pointing out in a 1930s reminiscence of Dan Patch that McHenry had earlier been more of an all-around horseman who operated a large stock farm, and had in fact been the first man to breed, own, train, and drive a winner of the Kentucky Futurity— the mare Rose Croix in 1896. Since then, though, excessive drink and related declines in health and character, Hervey suggested, had caused McHenry to settle for being just "a consummate virtuoso of the reins. He lacked by a considerable amount," Hervey contended, "the more solid and humdrum faculties that go to make up the commander-in-chief of a great stable and the many-angled abilities and aptitudes that one must possess to achieve success." As the writer saw it, McHenry's horses "often 'trained off,' what looked like coming stars lost their sparkle, and when they did so he lost his interest in them."

Hervey's opinions must be respected, but the evidence suggests that McHenry's reputation for being a poor trainer may have been in part a reflection of his cold and off-putting nature. A trainer is a caregiver, and that phrase on most days did not seem to suit the misanthropic Myron. Yet, as the story of his sleeping outside Dan's stall at Providence shows, his animals sometimes saw a softer, more paternal aspect. Along with that carefully rationed sensitivity, McHenry, the record shows (and even some of his detractors admitted), had a prodigious ability to diagnose and fix a horse's problems, applying his encyclopedic knowledge with care, creativity, and humility. When the mood struck him, in other words, he could be a trainer of the first rank.

On Dan's second morning at Lexington, McHenry told Stephen to take the horse out of his stall so he could have a good long look at "Dennis"—the stable nickname that Dan had recently, and inexplicably, acquired. Dennis looked terrific. He stood calmly as McHenry made a full circuit, inspecting him from every angle. Dan's coat shone with dapples in the white October sunlight, his eyes were clear; you would have never known he had been sick. Nor did he seem to be experiencing problems with his sulky or his rigging; unlike the many other Standardbreds who needed some physical assistance to keep their heads straight or their legs moving in the proper sequence, Dan wore no special equipment, no headpole, no blinkers, no shadow roll, and of course no hobbles, so there were virtually no straps or other paraphernalia to be in need of adjustment. That left Dan's feet as the possible problem area. McHenry had been thinking seriously about them for several weeks, and he had come up with a possible plan of action. But mightn't he want to leave well enough alone? On the downside he could ruin the horse or maybe make him several seconds slower; but if he was right, he could make Dan even better. After a few more minutes of silently circling and staring, McHenry grabbed Dan's lead shank and walked him over to the shed of a horseshoer named Ren Nash.

Shoeing and balancing—the adding and subtracting of boots and toe weights—are critical arts in harness racing because a horse who is off-kilter and not addressing the ground properly is also bound to be off gait. Dan Patch was a gorgeous individual, and a natural pacer, but from a shoer's perspective he was a peculiar and challenging specimen. Let's start with conformation, for how a horse is constructed determines how his feet hit the ground and how he will move forward. Dan Patch, for a pacer, was conformed oddly. He did not display the classic "pacing slope," defined as high front shoulders with a back running downward toward a relatively low-slung rear end. Star Pointer, Pocahontas, and all of the previous champion pacers were built that way, taller in the front than behind, and this led horsepeople to believe that the slope was somehow conducive to the parallel gait (though no one could explain why). Dan, in contrast, was pitched like a trotter, perhaps because he was bred like one; he was slightly higher in the rear (15.3 ½ hands) than ahead (15.2 ¾). It is a measure of how popular harness racing was that when John Hervey measured Dan in December of 1904 and found that his back tilted in the unlikely direction, the revelation became major news. Picked up by the Associated Press, the story ran in hundreds of newspapers, and for a week or so it was as hotly discussed as the New York Giants' refusal to play in the fledgling World Series or any sports story of the day.

Of course Dan had an even more pronounced physical eccentricity than his trotting pitch—his deformed left rear leg, which required the special sulky and the orthopedic shoe, and which left him, as horsemen say, "duck-gaited," "sloppy behind," and basically unable to fully translate his extraordinary power into speed. Thomas Fenton, the remedial blacksmith from Pine Village, had made radical progress with Dan's shoeing before the horse ever came under McHenry's care. But had he thoroughly solved the problem? At Lexington that fall, McHenry began to question whether Dan's feet were properly trimmed and shod after all.

Nash, McHenry's preferred horseshoer, was one of about half a dozen smittys who traveled with the Grand Circuit and were patronized by a more-or-less-regular group of trainer-clients at each stop. The son of a Union Army blacksmith named Philander Nash, Ren came from a family described by one of its own members as "a bunch of big, strapping, hard-drinking Irishmen"— though his branch of the clan had been in what is now Massachusetts and upstate New York since the 1600s. Before Dan Patch came along, Nash was not among the most famous harness-racing horseshoers, some of whom were genuine celebrities for the work they had done to get a certain 2:20 horse down under 2:10, or for merely being the man who shod the great Lou Dillon, Star Pointer, or Cresceus. If you were one of the elite Grand Circuit shoers, you were like Muhammad Ali's cornerman, Bundini Brown—you could walk into any halfway decent bar in any half-sophisticated city in the nation and someone would shout out your name and buy you a drink.

One reason Nash had been eclipsed by some of his colleagues was that he was a modest sort. He took little credit for Dan Patch, saying in an article he wrote years later in the *Horse Review* that he only followed McHenry's orders. That day in Lexington, McHenry told him to shorten Dan's toes dramatically. The trainer had the idea that Dan needed the equivalent of women's high heels; otherwise, to keep his balance, he leaned into the bit and at times felt like he was going to pull his driver out of the sulky. Nash picked the horse's feet up one by one and filed them down as directed.

The improvement was instantaneous. The next day McHenry worked a much more sure-footed Dan at Lexington in 2:04, a quarter of a second faster than his official record. And on October 8, over the same track, the horse won his fifteenth consecutive race, the $3,000 Tennessee Stake, leading every step of every heat in times of 2:05 ½, 2:05, and 2:07 ¼. He looked simply awesome. By the third heat, so much was being bet on Dan Patch, and so little on anyone else, that the pool sellers made the unusual move of not only barring McHenry's horse, but giving back all of the money that had been wagered on him.

Something even more remarkable happened just after the race. Messner, on his way to the telegraph office to wire home news of the latest victory, was stopped in the stable area by several well-dressed strangers who did not introduce themselves but asked if he had been considering Sturges's offer of $20,000. Before he could answer, the men advised him to take the offer, and to move quickly on it. Twenty thousand was a lot of money for a storekeeper from Indiana, one of the men said, and Dan Patch was a big responsibility, and becoming more so each day. "You can't keep a horse like that in a little barn in some little town. It's not safe—it's a crazy world today," the man went on, pointing out, as if Messner hadn't heard about it, that the president of the United States, William McKinley, had been shot to death just the month before. (The assassination by the self-described anarchist Leon Czolgosz had occurred in Buffalo the day after Dan's victory at Hartford; Czolgosz would be executed for the crime within a few weeks.)

"It's a crazy world," the man repeated. "If the president isn't safe, nobody is. You'll sleep better if you sell the horse now."

As Messner mulled over those odd and troubling words, a different sort of threat loomed up in the form of Harold H. The Canadian champ had faced Dan Patch before, at Narragansett, and had been highly touted that day—but badly beaten. He was a different horse now, though, or so the insiders said. His trainer, Al Proctor, had made some adjustments of his own, and turned the gelding into a speed machine. While Dan was back in Oxford resting, Harold H. had won impressively at Terre Haute, going one of his miles in 2:04 ¼, which tied him with Dan's fastest time. More telling, his supporters said, was that the last quarter of that heat had gone in a world record :28 ¾. The *Brooklyn Eagle* was now calling the seven-year-old Harold H. "one of the most remarkable colts ever foaled," and saying that he, and not Dan Patch, was the horse to beat at Memphis, the Grand Circuit's next and final stop. Proctor clearly had McHenry's horse in his sights; he had made the bold move of sidestepping Lexington so his pacer would be rested and ready for Dan at Memphis, where the two would cross paths at Billings Park before a grandstand packed with prominent owners, breeders, and racing officials in town for the climactic meet. "Harold H. is the hardest proposition McHenry's bread-winner has been asked to meet this year," wrote Joe Markey in the *Horse Review*, "and Dan's most ardent admirers admit that the fur will fly, as the Canadian horse is the real thing."

But horses play mind games as much as people do. Harold H. and his trainer were both outpsyched that day, just as many of Mike Tyson's opponents were outpsyched by his reputation and his gladiatorial bearing as he strode from the dressing room to the ring. As Dan Patch stepped proudly onto the Memphis track, the crowd rose to see him, and the Billings Park announcer stood in the infield and, raising a megaphone to his lips, proclaimed the pacer's accomplishments. "Starting from the pole, the great Dan Patch! He has won fourteen straight races since his first start at Windsor in July, and lost but one heat!" At that veiled reference to Brighton Beach a smattering of boos—for McHenry—mingled with the growing roar. Dan, who was leading the parade to the post, stopped, looked about, then bowed, effectively doubling the intensity of the ovation. To Henry Ten Eyck White of the *Chicago Tribune* in the press area, the horse appeared "in perfect condition, not at all drawn from the effects of the long campaign."

While the mob roared for Dan and pressed against the barrier for a better look, several of the other horses—including Harold H.—became skittish. Proctor's horse, a nervous sort to begin with, broke into a sweat. When the first heat finally started, Dan glided smoothly to the lead; Harold H. dropped to third. There was virtually no movement for the first three-quarters of a mile. Then the Canadian pulled out to make his bid. As he crept from third to second place, said the *Horse Review*, "the crowd rose, hushed, waiting for the struggle that was to come—but there was none." The gelding, under heavy urging by his driver, faded back to third. His day was effectively over. (It had actually ended in the parade to the post.) In the other two heats, both won by Dan, Harold H. was fifth, then third again. Dan had not needed to go faster than 2:05.

When the third heat was over and Dan returned to the winner's circle, McHenry flashed a rare smile, and Dan "turned his head to the stand . . . and seemed to understand it all, and looked for more when they led him away."

A small contingent had come from Oxford to see their hero, who with this race became a true national figure, as well known across America as heavyweight champ James J. Jeffries, baseball players Cy Young and Christy Mathewson, strongman Eugene Sandow, or any coeval celebrities of the sporting world. Missing from the Oxford cheering section, however, was John Kelley, the livery stable owner's son who, with the veterinarian Frank Scott, had passed out drunk and botched their assignment of assisting at the birth of Dan Patch five years before. Kelley had set out with the Oxford contingent, but in keeping with his Falstaffian tendencies, had gotten off the train in Paxton, Illinois, to seek refreshment, and somehow never gotten back on. When Kelley finally made it to Billings Park, Dan's race was already over. He was just in time, though, for a party that night at a Memphis hotel to celebrate Dan's undefeated season, during which he'd won $13,800.

At that gathering Messner encountered the same three well-dressed men who had spoken to him after the race at Lexington. They repeated their advice to sell Dan Patch to their very generous friend from New York, and once again commented on the craziness of the modern world.

CHAPTER TWELVE

ON NOVEMBER 2, ELEVEN days after his victory at Memphis, Dan Patch, his five-year-old season in the books, returned home to Oxford and a hero's welcome. His brief drop-by five weeks earlier had not seemed to diminish the eagerness of the townsfolk to see him. A crowd of perhaps two hundred waited at the station, and when the train finally came to a halt and the door rolled open, Dan threw back his head and neighed loudly, and the people cheered. The horse had been sorely missed in Oxford that summer, his first away from home. At the Benton County Fair, balloons bearing Dan's name had been sold for a nickel apiece, but they had only tended to make people pine for the hero who would never grace the hometown track again.

After they'd seen so much about Dan Patch in the newspapers—one Oxford resident had filled a collection of scrapbooks with 672 clippings—it was hard for the townspeople to believe that he was back among them again in the flesh. He looked more mature than when they had last had time to study him; he had filled out through the ribs and rump; his chest muscles rippled. But he seemed completely unfazed by his long campaign. McHenry, when he put Dan on the train for his trip home, had marveled at the horse's condition after nearly three months of racing and traveling. "He looked like a horse just starting out in the spring," the trainer would reflect about a year later. "His hair was as bright as you ever saw on a horse, there was not a puff or a pimple anywhere, and he felt like a colt." A man waiting at the station when Dan arrived back in Oxford said the horse looked "as slick as a mole."

Several in the mob also noted that Dan knew where he was the minute he came down the ramp—home. Indeed, the horse began straining so diligently in the direction of his barn, about a block away, that Stephen had difficulty keeping him at a walk. When at last Dan reached the no-frills green-and-white structure on South Michigan, he proceeded directly to his usual stall—the second of three, on the left—going in headfirst and then turning around so he could see the people who had followed him there. Almost immediately, Messner's four-year-old son Daniel Kingston ran up, and the horse lowered his head so the boy could pet him. The welcoming entourage cooed its approval.

Signs were already out announcing Oxford's upcoming Dan Patch Day—the first of an annual series that, thanks to Bob and Thelma Glaspie, continues into the present. "A typical November day with a cold raw wind sweeping down from the north did not prevent a large crowd from gathering" on November 14, 1901, Mary Cross wrote in *Two Dans*. The ceremonies started with a parade around the town square. One half of the town watched the other half march. First came the Oxford High School band, playing Steele's "Dan Patch Two Step." Then came Dan himself, pulling a wagon driven by Stephen. "The horse has changed considerably this past season," the *Oxford Tribune* would report. "His coltish form has disappeared and he has straightened up into an animal of wonderful beauty and symmetry. His gentle disposition adds considerably to his value."

Dan was followed in the parade by Zelica, all dolled up in her German silver, and then came Lady Patch, a black beauty of a two-year-old filly, the daughter of Dan Patch and Wattles's mare Oxford Girl. Lady Patch was there in part to remind people that Dan Messner intended to breed Dan to a few mares the coming spring before sending him back to the races. Bringing up the rear were two more of Zelica's offspring, both of whom might have been more "Messner's Folly" material, were the townsfolk still in the mood to mock. The first, who had been christened Messner, was a colt by Allerton, a trotting sire of dubious merit whose stud fee was nevertheless one of the highest in the nation—$1,000—and who was at best an eccentric choice to mate with Zelica, a proven producer of pacers. The other was a still-unnamed colt by another overpriced, destined-to-be-obscure trotting sire, Respond.

Yet even these latter horses were greeted—like Dan—with silent awe. Cross wrote that some in the crowd "stood under the bare branches of the . . . maples inside the park through which the bitter wind sighed. Others stood along the sidewalk . . . and a few in the shelter of the doorways . . . but they felt no moment like this would happen again in their lifetime." Wishing to extend the day as long as possible, many, when the parade ended, seemed to forget about the raw weather and, said the paper, "lingered to pet Dan Patch."

That winter, town rivalries were put aside, to a degree, and all of Indiana wanted to claim Dan Patch as their own. At Christmas, the editor of the *Lafayette Call* sent Dan a box of cut flowers. Oxfordites thought that strange—"I'm sure he'd prefer a bushel of oats," one said—and they thought it even more annoying when state office-seekers came to town shaking hands, kissing babies, and passing out Dan Patch cigars. Dan was *their* horse. On New Year's Day 1902 the *Oxford Tribune* ran an editorial that stated: "The town is one mile square; the town has the best looking girls in the world; has the best racing horse in the world; the best location of any city in western Indiana; and has more bachelors than should supply a congressional district."

This was, of course, a classic case of whistling past the graveyard. Under the new rules of the twentieth century, Oxford was destined to be the kind of place one got the hell out of if one wanted any kind of a future. The palpable insecurity of the town made Messner feel that he could not sell the only hero it had ever had; but whenever he came to the decision not to sell, another telegram from Sturges would arrive, reminding him that his record-setting offer was on the table. The New Yorker was charming, never failing to include his regards to Messner's family in his almost weekly wire, but he had a New Yorker's troubling persistence, and, as we have seen, mysterious friends who helped him keep up the pressure. Messner agreed with him that $20,000 was no small amount of money, but on balance he probably wished Sturges would just go away.

While Messner assumed an attitude of silence toward the outside world, M. W. Savage was braying for attention again. In a letter to the *Horse Review* timed for inclusion in the well-read Christmas issue, Savage announced that he had turned down an offer of $25,000 cash for Directum, the trotting stallion he had bought for $12,100 at the Old Glory horse auction in Madison Square Garden just weeks before. Savage said that the offer had come to him "within two hours after the bidding stopped" and that he told the parties, "I would not take $50,000 in cash for him. We believe Directum to be the greatest combined race horse and sire that the world has ever known." That statement was embarrassing for two reasons: firstly, the tossing around of big offers from unnamed potential buyers fooled nobody; second, it showed that Savage, in his horse dealings, was the quintessential sucker, an egotistical owner whom a slick horseman could play like a parlor piano. The twelve-year-old Directum, who in his heyday had been known as the Black Rascal, had already flopped as a stallion at the upstate New York farm where he had been standing for the past several seasons; in Minnesota, then an outpost on the margins of the racing world, where quality broodmares were rare, the poor old trotter hardly figured to burnish his résumé. Veteran trainers, turning the pages of the Christmas *Horse Review* as they sat by their stable stoves, must have chuckled at the pronouncements of such a pompous rube. Directum, indeed! McHenry, coming upon Savage's letter in the *Review,* would probably not have known whether to laugh or scream.

McHenry at that very moment was using the media (meaning the horse weeklies and the newspapers) to stage a propaganda campaign of his own. His object: to get the Grand Circuit to change its rules for Dan Patch. The Circuit at that time had no racing class between 2:06 and the elite free-for-all division, meaning that the following summer Dan, with his record of 2:04 ½, would be classified with, and forced to race against, the best older pacers in the United States. McHenry knew that Dan could probably beat any free-for-all-er in the land, but as the horse's trainer he wanted as soft a season as possible, and he thought that Dan, who had proven to be a powerful draw in the latter months of 1901, might give him the leverage to dictate his terms. He demanded the creation of a 2:05 class, in which Dan would be allowed to beat up the lesser opposition. McHenry never consulted Messner about his plan, but in interviews in the *Review* and with Henry Ten Eyck White of the *Chicago Tribune,* he spoke as if reading from a prepared statement:

> Of course I believe Dan Patch is the best pacer in the country. I believe he will eventually beat the record of his sire Joe Patchen [2:01 ¼]. Dan is the most perfect-mannered horse I ever saw. You can place him anywhere—race in front or behind, just as you like. He lets me do all the driving. He has never met a horse that he didn't have safely beaten at the seven-eighths pole. As to his present speed I know very little about that. I have driven him a mile [in training] in 2:04, and a quarter in :29 ¾, and have never asked him to step faster.
>
> But it would be asking too much of him, great as he is, to pit him against such old stagers as Prince Alert and Anaconda in the free-for-all class next year. He isn't used to racing at the clip they go, and [author's note: bring up the violins here] a young horse might get discouraged, or he might not be able to carry his speed far enough to win if suddenly asked to drop from 2:06 or 2:05 to 2:01 or thereabouts. If Mr. Messner heeds my advice [being offered for the first time via this article] he will retire Dan Patch rather than race him in the free-for-all class next year.

In the cold heart of winter, in January and early February of 1902, a thawing occurred between Dan Messner and John Wattles, and on most mornings Wattles, at Messner's request, drove Dan Patch for an hour or so around Oxford's town square. Wattles might have taken the horse out to the Chiquesalonghi track, just over two miles distant, where he had given him his first training, for this daily work, but Messner wanted to have Dan where he could see him just by stepping out the front door of his store. Owning a famous horse was making him increasingly nervous, and it didn't help that customers kept mentioning how strange it was to see a horse they had read about in the papers, a horse that had been places and seen things that they themselves would never visit and see, circling the center of their little town.

On February 15, 1902, Lady Patch collapsed in the stall next to Dan Patch and, a few hours later, died. The veterinarian first said she was suffering from lockjaw, or tetanus, a disease of the nervous system that a horse might get from a bacterium commonly found in farm soil, but after further examination he changed his diagnosis to poisoning. "You should know," the vet said to Messner, "that this was no accident." More than sixty years later, an Oxfordite named Kenneth Wilkens told Cross that he remembered the jet-black filly who had just started training for a possible racing career "lying outside the barn on a stone boat waiting to be hauled away."

Was the killing of Lady Patch meant to frighten Messner into selling Dan Patch? If so, the plan worked perfectly. Less than two weeks later, Messner announced that he had accepted Sturges's $20,000 offer, and the horse would soon be moving to New York City. The amount topped by $100 the amount paid for the famous "Little Red Horse" John R. Gentry in the depression year of 1896, the previous record price for a pacer. Still, many people in Oxford and beyond thought that Messner could have gotten more for Dan Patch had he been willing to hold out. Messner was aware of that sentiment, and in an effort to avoid explaining himself repeatedly, and to put his own spin on the situation, he drew up five reasons for the sale of Dan Patch that the *Oxford Tribune* was happy to publish:

1. Because I lost his first colt [sic; it was a filly] which was a great prospect and was the only one I had from him at this time.
2. Because I have a better colt coming on in his half-brother Messner, by Allerton. He is a trotter and very promising.
3. Being in the dry goods and lumber business, I do not have the time to develop so many horses.
4. My principal reason for selling was that I got the record price for Dan Patch when I sold him for $20,000.00 [note the gratuitous zeros, no doubt for added impact].

5. Because I'll still own his mother and I think I can raise several Dan Patches.

In hindsight, this is piercingly sad, for nothing would pan out the way he predicted. It was pathetic in the moment, too. Messner's five-point plan is clearly the work of an unquiet mind. He puts his "principal reason"—profit—fourth out of five, and leads with an emotional motive that doesn't quite make sense: I sold him because I lost his only child. Although he would later attempt to portray the sale of Dan Patch as a smart business move, and the sensible, Hoosier thing to do—he went out of his way to stress that the $20,000 did not include the horse's harness or sulky—Messner at this point was feeling overwhelmed by events and their ramifications. Rather bizarrely, he had a lap robe made from Lady Patch's jet-black hide and showed it off to people—for what reason, they weren't sure—saying, with a frozen smile, that it was "the most expensive blanket in Indiana."

A sad month separated the poisoning of Lady Patch and the departure of Dan. Midwesterners came from hundreds of miles in every direction to say good-bye to the horse, some of them choking back tears as they rubbed the white star on his forehead and patted his nose—it was as if Dan Patch was a revolutionary hero awaiting his moment on the guillotine, not a racehorse in his prime, preparing for another season. Letters of condolence—not so much for the death of the filly as for the sale of the stud—poured into Messner's store from people who mistrusted and feared the city where Dan Patch was headed. On Tuesday, March 18, a group of Oxford grade-school girls had a class outing to bid adieu to Dan, who, as always, allowed himself to be petted and even lowered his head so Stephen could snip off some hair from his mane for each awestruck child. The girls were still clutching the hair—now in scented envelopes, or tied with a ribbon—two days later, when the Chicago-bound train came to take Dan Patch away. Many in the crowd of about two hundred sobbed and shouted as the horse moved toward his designated boxcar. When Myron McHenry clambered down the ramp to grab Dan's lead shank and walk him on board, those who recognized him gasped.

In the Dan Patch community, people still differ over the causes and effects of Lady Patch's poisoning. Mary Cross seems to lean toward Messner's public position—that a "jealous person" in the community who resented the success of Dan Patch and all the attention he was getting tried to kill Dan but botched the job. Messner may have actually believed this; he was certainly aware of the phenomenon of horse envy, which, like road rage, can make monsters of seemingly ordinary folk. Another reason he may have liked this scenario is that in it he is the victim, and not a hood-winked Hoosier.

Most of the evidence, however, points to Messner having been played by a couple of cold-blooded horsetraders named Sturges and McHenry. During the winter of 1901–2, McHenry seems to have struck up a friendship of sorts with Sturges, and, over a series of dinners and other meetings, hatched a plan with him to buy Dan Patch from Messner for the primary purpose of selling the pacer to someone else. Thus McHenry in a few months' time had swung from being a staunch opponent of selling at Sturges's price to being Sturges's agent and partner. In *The Autobiography of Dan Patch,* the first-person narrator notes that it was McHenry who negotiated the deal, meeting Messner in Chicago in mid-March to sign the papers. The book also says that McHenry "was in Oxford to take possession of me" on March 20. McHenry probably put up no money of his own but took a percentage of Dan Patch in exchange for facilitating the sale—a service that involved arranging to have Lady Patch poisoned (perhaps by that envious rival horse owner, who might find the task anything but distasteful).

Strangely, in 1827 an earlier Daniel Messner, perhaps a relation, lost a bay colt with a white face marking and a white splash on one hoof, and advertised a "handsome reward" in the *Ohio Repository* for "the return of the stray." The ads, repeated numerous times over the course of several weeks in early 1828, speak of a man pining for his lost horse, calling out into the wilderness and feeling both foolish and sad. Now the same thing had happened again, to another Dan Messner: a beautiful stallion had slipped away. In the days following the sale, Messner tried to portray it as something good for both sides. He had, he stressed, avoided

the situation that he had come to fear most when he had started
to worry about Dan's safety—that he would wind up with neither
the horse nor the money he represented. But was he really at peace
with himself? John Messner, the golf pro, says he doesn't believe
his grandfather harbored any bitterness about the transaction, yet
Dan Jr. kept only one small picture of Dan Patch, in the office
at the store, and spoke seldom of the horse in the ensuing years.
John's father, Richard, who died in 1993, said once in the 1970s,
"My father regretted selling Dan Patch, but he didn't regret that
he may have saved his life." Dan Messner's friends and supporters
gave lip service to the notion that Oxford was too small to hold a
potential world champion, but the town was stunned when Dan
Patch left. The editor of the *Boswell Enterprise* came to Oxford
soon after to do a story about the populace post–Dan Patch, and
reported that everyone was in "a semi-dozing state."

The dozing has only deepened as time washes away the evidence
of Dan Patch. Handsome black hitching posts, each topped with
the famous horse's head, disappeared in a World War II scrap iron
drive. Kelley's Livery Stable came down a long time ago (the nondescript stone house that replaced it is eighty-five years old), and
a plaque identifying the spot as the birthplace of Dan Patch was
stolen sometime in the 1980s. Kelley's Tavern, where stablehand
John Kelley ran to get a bottle of rye on Dan's birth night, was
doing business until recently, though as a combination laundry/
tanning parlor called Sudz and Sun.
    Some pieces of the Dan Patch era were especially hard to lose.
In the late 1940s, when the state was putting in Highway 52,
its engineers plotted a path down the middle of Chiquesalonghi,
which was still part of the Paul Kennedy farm, and still a busy
training track for farmers who were then fantasizing about getting in on the postwar harness-racing boom. Kennedy believed
that Dan's connection to the place, as well as the fact that it had
for years been part of the Benton County fairgrounds, effectively
sanctified the soil—and he fought the plan through the bureau-
cracy. He lost, appealed the decision, then lost his appeal. "Plow

that track up!" he screamed at his hired hand, James Newell, the day the bad news arrived, choking back tears. "I can't bear to look at it any more knowing that it's doomed." But just as Newell drove his plow into place, Kennedy hollered for him to stop. "I can't watch!" he said, running into the barn, where they found him, passed out drunk, the next morning.

The barn at the original Benton County Fairgrounds, where Dan had his first race, lasted until 2003, when the dilapidated structure was leveled by a tornado. On an overcast winter's day in early 2006, Bob Glaspie and I walked the stubbly soybean field where the racetrack used to be. Nothing is more forlorn than an Indiana farm in February—and then right on cue, a funeral wreath blew in from the cemetery just across the road. The hoop of red and green plastic flowers rolled along for a while like, I suppose, an errant sulky wheel. Then it slowed, wobbled, and fell fake-blossoms-down in the mud.

There are no Oxfordites left who laid eyes on Dan Patch, but I did meet a man, a retired high school teacher named George Cross (Mary's brother-in-law), who worked for Dan Messner Jr. in the late 1920s, not in the store but on a farm Messner owned south of town. In his nineties now, Cross still shuddered when he remembered the day he was assigned the job of hauling water for the horses. The farm manager pointed him toward a docile old mare named Bird, one of the many foals of Zelica who didn't grow up to be a racehorse, and told young George (he was about twelve) to hook her up to a strange, high-wheeled vehicle standing inside the barn. "But be careful," the boss said. "That's the very cart they used to break Dan Patch!"

Cross got about halfway to the creek when Bird inexplicably grabbed the bit, bolted, and ran into a fence, injuring herself slightly but smashing the old breaking cart to bits. "I don't think I've ever been so scared, before or since," Cross told me. "It was like an antique, very old-fashioned, you sat in and your feet hung down—and it had belonged to Dan Patch, whose name was still holy around here."

The farm manager immediately drove Cross to Messner's store and told him to go to the owner's office and explain to him what had happened. "I remember being so scared waiting for him," Cross said. "Then he came out and I told him what had happened. He listened, didn't say anything and walked away. I didn't know what to do, so after a few minutes I got up to leave. But someone told me not to, and a few minutes later he came back, looked down at me sitting there and said, 'Well, guess I won't pay you for today.' I was making a dollar a day, and I was glad that he felt that resolved it. But for me, it didn't resolve it. I couldn't get over that I had been responsible for destroying something that belonged to Dan Patch. It still makes me sad."

Bob Glaspie, whose eyes sometimes well up when he talks about Dan Patch, once didn't give a lick about the horse. "As a young man," he told me, "I cared only about women and automobiles." Then, in 1970, Thelma's father gave her a picture post-card of a full brother to Dan Patch called, with typical Hoosier flair, Dan's Brother; it had been sent with birthday greetings to her great-grandfather by Dan Messner in 1910. Bob thought that was interesting, and so a buff was born. The Glaspies soon purchased a print of Dan's head they found at a local antique show; they picked up a Dan Patch tobacco tin while tooling around the country visiting their four children; and Bob bought a 1972 Dan Patch liquor bottle from a bowling buddy in Lafayette. From the start, however, they were collectors with a cause—keeping the memory of the horse alive. They displayed their items (by 1990 they had more than fifty) at the Lions Club's Dan Patch Days, and Bob made an annual appearance at the Oxford Elementary School, where he talked to the children about Dan Patch and tried (in vain) to persuade the principal to change the nickname of the school teams from the Blue Devils to the Pacers. He also loaned the school a large print of Dan hitched to a sulky, which got hung in a prominent spot.

For a while it looked like the Glaspies were making headway. Their ever-expanding exhibit, put on display at the Dan Patch

Days each year, fanned the embers of interest in the horse, and Coonie Morris, the town supervisor, hired an artsy-seeming sign painter—"a man whose first name was Hazel and who had only one arm," he told me—to climb 110 feet up to the water tower and paint "Birthplace of Dan Patch" on the side. The words are still up there, though fading. But at some point the Dan Patch revival movement seemed to stall. Bob knew he was in trouble when he went into Oxford's little Dan Patch Café a few years ago, struck up a conversation with the waitress, and realized about five minutes in that she thought Dan Patch was a baseball player. "Shameful," he says.

Dan's old barn was the closest thing to a permanent Dan Patch memorial in Oxford. Dan Messner Jr. had boarded it up even before he bought his first automobile, a Marmon "48" touring car, in 1914, and although his son Richard never went inside, he kept up the exterior, repainting the roof every few years with the words "Home of Dan Patch." After Richard died, John Messner kept up the tradition of maintaining the facade without ever entering.

"Never had any occasion to, I guess," he said on that autumn day in 2005 when I first met him, and we were standing in his front yard, which is essentially the backyard of the barn.

I had already come to suspect that Dan Patch has always been a complicated and perplexing subject for John. The horse can be accurately described as both famous and forgotten; Dan Patch made a fortune, but John's ancestor didn't; the barn was a national treasure in the (strong) opinion of (a very few) people, but passers-by seldom stopped to read the plaque outside, and the upkeep was expensive. Kibitzers constantly told John that he should cash in, the way "the Seabiscuit people" did—but what, he wondered, did that mean, exactly? The truth is that he felt it was an honor to be associated with Dan Patch, and also a pain in the ass.

I didn't want to add to his problems, but I couldn't resist asking, "Do you ever wonder what it looks like in there?" He responded by motioning me toward the back door and dragging an old table from a pile of junk that had accumulated nearby. The area just behind the barn had been dug out and covered with a roof in the 1950s to allow for the storage of farm equipment; as a result, the back door was now about four feet above ground level. I had to stand on the table to reach it.

"Step over there," John told me, pointing to a cement block and extending a hand for me to grasp. "Then step up here on the table. The door's broken, but if you lean hard you can pull it open a crack."

I did, and I saw the past. A shaft of yellow sunlight came in through a gap in the roof and struck the door of the largest and, judging by the latticework on the door, most luxurious stall. A rusted pitchfork lay in the middle of the floor, its tines curled upward, and near it was a thick green glass bottle. This was the room where Dan Patch and Zelica had lived and Lady Patch had died and men in celluloid collars and women in hats trimmed with ribbon rosettes had come, first to snicker, then to gawk. It looked as though everyone had fled the scene in a hurry and no one had disturbed it for nearly a hundred years.

Getting down from the table was a little tricky; while I was peering into the previous century, and raving about what I was seeing, John Messner had wandered away.

CHAPTER THIRTEEN

MYRON McHENRY HAD A cold. The trainer caught the bug on his way west from New York to pick up Dan Patch in Oxford, Indiana, and his symptoms only worsened as he headed to Chicago with his increasingly famous racehorse in tow. The ailment was a mixed blessing: It had allowed him to beg out of a side trip with his wife, Ida, to see her parents in Geneseo, Illinois. But it also kept him confined to his room at the Palmer House, the luxurious, glitzy hotel on the corner of State and Monroe that he favored in flush times like the present.

Not everyone appreciated the Palmer House, a hostelry very much of its time and place. Rudyard Kipling, while touring the States a decade before, had found it "a gilded and mirrored rabbit-warren" with "a huge hall of tessellated marble, crammed with people talking about money and spitting about everywhere." Kipling complained that "barbarians charged in and out of this inferno with letters and telegrams in their hands, and yet others shouted at each other. A man who had drunk quite as much as was good for him told me that this was 'the finest hotel in the finest city on God Almighty's earth.'"

I go on a bit with Kipling because the flaws of the Palmer House as perceived by the visiting Brit mirror those of McHenry, who was vulgar in a particularly early-twentieth-century-Chicago sort of way. Indeed, Kipling's inebriated interlocutor could have been Myron E. McHenry. The Wizard was inclined to hobnob, harangue, and walk about hung over. On a typical morning-after, McHenry liked taking a hot towel and a shave in the Palmer House's lobby barbershop, where he might cross paths with lightweight champ Joe Gans, escape artist Harry Houdini, or Mayor Carter Henry Harrison on a floor famously lined with silver dollars.

But not on this chilly morning in late March of 1902. Today he would sit propped on a couch in his cavernous room and talk to a reporter from the *Horse Review* while dosing himself with brandy. Even with his cold, McHenry was intent on going ahead with the interview. He had things he wanted to say—and pointedly not say—to the influential horseman's weekly about the sale of Dan Patch, which was still very much in the news a week later. (That morning the Associated Press had moved a story in which an unidentified horseman declared, "No horse is worth $20,000, especially not a pacer.") Some excerpts from the *Review* piece:

On the record sum that he and Sturges had paid for Dan Patch:
"Well, the price may seem a trifle high," McHenry said, flicking imaginary lint off his lap blanket. "But I think I know the horse and his worth as well as anybody, and if I am not mistaken, his next sale, if he is ever sold again, will be for a higher price than he cost us."

On Dan's potential as a racehorse:
"The public knows nearly as much about him as I do. He was never asked to step to his limit and only on a few occasions did he ever appear to me to be busy, and then for only an instant. The fastest clip he ever showed me was in a workout with a runner, when he stepped the first eighth away from the wire in fourteen seconds. One thing is certain; that is, that he will never go any faster than he has to go."

On his preferred style of racing:
"I have seen him rush from behind with the speed of a locomotive and when he passed the other horses settle down to a slow clip, give a confident toss of his head and just about say, 'Well, I have settled this race.' I found it just as hard to drive him a mile in 2:17 as in 2:04. His fastest

mile was in flat 2:04 at Lexington in his preparation for his
Memphis race."

On Dan's whereabouts at that moment:
"I'd rather not say. For Dan's own safety all that I can tell
you is that he is definitely not in New York City, as has
been widely reported."

The last response was a lie; Dan had been stabled in Harlem
for several days. But the point was not the answer; it was that
McHenry had to be seen as not answering. The element of secrecy,
he felt, enhanced the horse's mystique and hence his value.

This was an early—but masterful—media manipulator at work.
Virtually everything the trainer said in this interview was meant
to further his (and Sturges's) plan of getting Dan Patch resold as
quickly and profitably as possible. McHenry here was not speaking to the kids who followed Dan's exploits in the papers, nor was
he addressing the average racing fan who paid his $1 admission
to cheer for, and bet on, his great pacer. Instead his words, though
read by many, were aimed at a mere handful of potential buyers, a
demographic he both loathed and thoroughly understood.

If McHenry had learned anything since coming out of Pink
Prairie, it was that racehorse ownership was all about ego. When
a horse performed well, his owner felt like a genius, a master of
the equine arts, and deserving of all the credit, even if all he was
doing was paying the bills. McHenry and Sturges tried to work
this tendency toward self-delusion to their advantage. They did
this by positioning Dan Patch as an almost but not quite ready-
made champ—a pacer likely to blossom into one of the fastest
harness racers of all time under the stewardship of whoever might
step forward and pay the price. True, buying the six-year-old Dan
Patch did not offer the deeper, more soul-nourishing satisfactions
of having bred him, or bought him as a yearling, but that would
have involved years of waiting and uncertainty. Dan was custom-
made for the go-go businessman of the ragtime age: already very
good, likely to become great, and if you acted quickly, your name
could be on the papers when he reached his peak. Buy Dan Patch

Now! Look Brilliant Later! That was the message that McHenry craftily wove into his *Horse Review* interview that day.

Despite his extreme difficulty in keeping up business relationships, McHenry, in a sales operation, was a damn good outside man: natty, confident, knowledgeable, and capable of saying exactly what a buyer needed to hear. The inside guy, Sturges, was something else again. While quite pleasant-seeming, especially for a fellow who could conspire to kill one horse in order to facilitate the sale of another, the New Yorker was harder to get a handle on, and thus harder to warm to. Only slightly taller than the barely five-foot McHenry, but much more corpulent, Sturges exuded urbanity and charm. To the world beyond the racing cognoscenti he remained a mystery. Where did his money come from? What did he do away from the track? Few knew, but as long as he was spending thousands on horses and stakes payments, few in the sport ever asked.

Manley Edwin Sturges (usually spelled, incorrectly, as Sturgis) was born in 1850 in Sodus, New York, a town that, lacking other distinctions, would later pride itself on being the birthplace of Arbor Day. (It is one of several towns to make that titillating claim.) Sturges descended from a family that traced back to the Plymouth Colony; his mother was a Delano, meaning Manley was a distant relative of a certain future first couple. But the Sturgeses of Soldus were hardly Brahmins; they fitted squarely into the merchant class. As a young man Manley worked in his father's grocery store and later moved on to manage several upstate inns and taverns. One senses a story arc forming: a rising young man coming into his own in late-nineteenth-century America, and eventually becoming the Marriott of Middletown or the Hilton of Herkimer. But then something happens, Sturges's biopic suddenly breaks, and after a patchy edit we see him in portly middle age, smiling thinly beneath a graying mustache and clutching a silver-tipped walking stick as he plays the role of "prominent sportsman, broker and breeder."

Those, as some knew, were newspaper euphemisms—as was "bachelor," a term applied to him frequently in journalistic accounts in which the marital status of others went unmentioned.

Although he was married briefly to a much younger woman named Sarah Martin in the late 1880s, about whom almost nothing is known, turf writers made a point of stressing Sturges's singleness while also noting that he dressed impeccably, attended the races with his adored spinster sister, and dispensed exquisite gifts of jewelry and china to his many racing acquaintances. He was very often called "urbane" and "sophisticated." It didn't mean he wasn't a nice person.

And Sturges (as his small but effusive obituaries would eventually note) was indeed an exceedingly kind and generous man—provided you did not get between him and one of his high-stakes stings or betting schemes. "One might have spent interminable time in his company," John Hervey reflected many years later, "and never for a moment suspect that he was of the profession to which he belonged."

"Sportsman, broker and breeder," in Sturges's case, were winking code words for "professional gambler." As the reader may know, there are two kinds of those. There is the kind who studies trends and probabilities and perhaps has a keen eye for horseflesh, and who, operating aboveboard if not exactly on center stage, uses his knowledge to outwit the oddsmakers. And then there is the pernicious punter who survives by maneuvering behind the scenes, bribing and threatening to shift the probabilities in his favor or set up a sure thing. Sturges was the latter sort. He sometimes raced horses whose drivers were under orders not to win even if every other animal in the field dropped dead before the finish line—and at other times his horses, despite sorry-looking records, literally could not lose. Sometimes he conspired with the other owners and trainers to ensure a particular outcome in a race, and sometimes he and his trainer operated independently of their rivals. Money often changed hands before a race so that more money could change hands later. If racing officials made too much of a stink about his means and methods, money could solve that problem, too. He did what he had to do to get what he wanted, the late Lady Patch being a case in point.

Sturges's name first surfaced in the press in 1901, when the *New York Times* reported that he was caught up in a complicated lawsuit involving a bad chit passed by someone else in a private Manhattan casino. He did bet on roulette, blackjack, and dice, and probably cockfights and dogfights, too—but he preferred horseracing because it appealed to his aesthetic and was a fairly simple game to rig. Anyone who owned a horse in a given race automatically had inside information about at least one of the animals, and from there the owner could, if he was so inclined, start to work some angles.

Year after year Sturges had a stable that sportswriters described as "middling." His horses were always losing when they appeared primed for victory, or coming off a string of bad performances to score at big odds; if that added up to mediocrity, that was fine with him. He made a handsome living from what is known at the racetracks as "reversals of form."

No horse ever served Sturges's purposes better than a runty pacer named Prince Direct, who as we have already seen was McHenry's all-time favorite racer as well. Indeed, Prince Direct was the kind of horse trainers loved to tell stories about as they huddled round the stove on winter nights, an animal that came along once in a lifetime.

Sturges found him by accident. A few weeks after he paid $20,000 for Dan Patch, it seems, the fifty-one-year-old sportsman/breeder/broker/bachelor sent one of his handsome young gentleman associates, Harry Lawrence, to the West Coast on another horse-buying expedition. Sturges told Lawrence that he was primarily interested in Sir Albert S., a California pacer with a record of 2:08 ½. But when Lawrence finally got to San Francisco, where the horse was stabled, he learned that Prince David Kawananakoa, a member of the Hawaiian royal family, was also interested in Sir Albert S. and had offered $9,000 for the stallion. That price was not outlandish, but Lawrence was looking for bargains, so he moved along to Seattle, then a rowdy lumber town barely fifty years old. One night he found himself in Clancy's Saloon on Seattle's Second Avenue South, the home of an illegal high-stakes blackjack game. When the proprietor, Tom Clancy, found out who employed Lawrence, and why the dapper young blade had come to town, he immediately took

him to the stables out back and, by lantern light, showed him a
pacing horse named Freddie C., an animal that would later be
described in the *Chicago Tribune* as "a midget," "gross," and
"fat."

"Now here is an animal," Clancy said, "who could serve you
well."

Despite his cosmetic shortcomings, Freddie C., then six, was
a well-bred horse. The son of the respected stallion Direct, he
was, unlike many racehorses from the Far West in those days,
"blooded" on both sides of his pedigree—that is, his dam, Rosie
C., wasn't some Indian pony or unnamed range mare; she was
a registered Standardbred from Oregon. Clancy pointed all this
out as he moved the lantern around Freddie C.'s fireplug body,
and added that the horse was a fine natural pacer who needed no
hobbles to keep him on gait; he had a record, the barkeep said, of
2:14 ½, and the price was $8,000.

"Whoa. Lotta money for a little horse who's never gotten
near 2:10," Lawrence said. Clancy acknowledged that Freddie C.
didn't come cheap, but said that if Lawrence met him in the morning at a nearby training track, he'd show him what made the horse
so valuable.

Lawrence arrived at the appointed hour but couldn't believe
what he was seeing. Clancy had Freddie C. harnessed and hitched
to a racing sulky, but the fat little pacer looked dead lame, favoring at least one leg, maybe two or three, as he walked gingerly
from the finish line to the top of the homestretch. At one point
he stopped completely and refused to go on until Clancy hollered
and repeatedly whacked the sulky shafts with his whip. Lawrence
wondered if Clancy wasn't just crazy, but then the barkeep called
out to him, saying, "Now watch what happens when I turn him
around in the direction that they go to race."

What happened was that Freddie C. metamorphosed suddenly
into a different horse, a healthy and willing racer who took off
smoothly and paced a quarter mile in thirty seconds flat, and a
mile in something far faster than his official record. "Freddie here
is just a really, really lazy horse and never wants to race," Clancy
explained later. "He puts on an act to try and convince you that he's

not fit to go; he acts terrible so you'll take him back to the barn. I fell for the act the first couple of times myself. Then I realized that if you turned him around and just forced him to race, he gave up and went along with the idea, and he can go pretty fast."

Lawrence, seeing the possibilities, immediately wrote a draft on Sturges's account for $8,000 and later that day made arrangements to ship the horse to McHenry in New York.

Sturges's first move was rechristen Freddie C. as Prince Direct; apart from thinking the name more elegant and more reflective of the pacer's fine breeding, he wanted to erase any reputation that the horse may have acquired out West for his ability to feign lameness. (The changing of a racehorse's name, then a routine matter of filling out paperwork and paying fees, is no longer permitted, owing to the obvious opportunities for skullduggery.) A few months later, Prince Direct limped onto the track at Windsor, the fans took note and placed their wagers elsewhere—and Sturges and McHenry wound up cashing huge bets. Because there were no formal past-performance charts in those days, the scam worked many times that summer before word of mouth gradually ruined a good thing.

McHenry's claim that he made more money with Prince Direct than Dan Patch may not be true, but the former Freddie C. was certainly a better fit for Sturges's stable than the more famous horse. When Sturges struck his deal with McHenry, he allowed the trainer to keep 100 percent of Dan's earnings, which meant the only way Sturges could profit as the horse's owner was in the auction pools. But how to do that? One thing a scoundrel can do with a betting favorite is to hold him back and bet on somebody else. But that scheme had already been worked twice with Dan Patch. To keep doing it would achieve diminishing returns, and eventually bring down the value of the animal as well as the wrath of racing officials (not so much because you were cheating but because you were doing it so blatantly on their watch). A scoundrel's only other choice, when stuck with a truly great horse, was to sell the bastard as quickly as possible.

Once he'd sweated out *la grippe,* McHenry felt refreshed and eager
to get back to business. And why shouldn't he? A year before he
had been facing the racing season with an empty stable and putting up a bluff front while scuffling for whatever horses he could
get. Now he was not just the trainer and driver but also a minority owner of the most talked-about horse in America, a coming
superstar hailed in headline type by the *Brooklyn Daily Eagle* for
being not just "marvelous" but "only six years old." (Since he and
Sturges had only a verbal contract, his exact share of the horse can
never be known, but it is not unreasonable to guess that he took
a 40 percent interest.)

The mass media—meaning the densely woven web of newspapers that covered the contiguous states—was developing a serious
crush on McHenry's horse. "Dan Patch's Limit Unknown!" said
the *Chicago Tribune.* Dan's sale had made national headlines, and
ever since then papers had carried ginned-up items about sightings
("Dan Patch is training at the Empire City track"); jokes that piv-
oted on his prodigious abilities ("Dan Patch can get an entire day's
work done in just over two minutes!"); and tables that showed
where Dan fit among the champions of the previous year (he was
the fastest five-year-old pacer and the fastest pacing stallion of the
season, but not the fastest pacer overall—that being the eleven-
year-old gelding Prince Alert, who had won a race in 2:00 ¾).
Turf writers that winter proposed a match race between Prince
Alert and Dan Patch, and McHenry wasn't saying no, even if he
noted that it was certainly beneath a great natural pacer like Dan
to share the track with a nag dressed in "the Indiana pajamas," as
hobbles were sometimes derisively called.

It was a palmy time for McHenry: besides Dan Patch he had
Freddie C./Prince Direct and another horse, a stallion called
Early Reaper, who could also be played around with to cash a
few bets. McHenry's "genius" with horseshoes and rigging, as
well as his homestretch wizardry, was commented on frequently
by journalists who also passed along his terse pronouncements
on racing matters as if he spoke ex cathedra. Some of McHenry's
statements were clearly self-serving, such as his belief that racing officials needed to create a time class between 2:06 and free-

for-all to accommodate a developing star such as Dan Patch, a speech he would make, and newspapers would publish, at the drop of a manure chunk all that winter. But he also proffered more general wisdom that at times could be genuinely prophetic: the *Syracuse* (N.Y.) *Post-Standard* of April 28, 1902, carried a story in which McHenry called for the abolition of multiple-heat racing in favor of the simple, decisive, and less taxing single-dash system the Thoroughbreds had adopted a generation before; in espousing this line the man celebrated in poetry for savagely "reefing" Phoebe Wilkes stressed that single dashes amounted to more humane treatment of racehorses. On still another occasion, McHenry used his influence with the press to issue a challenge to the mighty Anaconda. Feeling feisty one day while he was talking to reporters in the lobby of the Rossmore Hotel (a horseman's haunt on Broadway, just below Forty-second Street) McHenry said, "Dan Patch would like to take on the so-called snake horse in a match race, at $10,000 a side!" The statement, picked up by the AP, ran in several hundred newspapers, sometimes on the front page, and the nation braced for the reply. But the Anaconda camp kept mum. McHenry probably knew that the famous older pacer, who was notoriously difficult to get into racing shape each spring, was having an especially hard time of it that year, bucking and thrashing and otherwise being "a crank," as the *Review* had reported, as well as a danger to the horses trying to train alongside him on the Harlem Speedway. Deep into the spring, Johnny Dick Dickerson, the man who had replaced McHenry as Anaconda's trainer the year before, couldn't control the stallion sufficiently to give him any serious conditioning miles. Dickerson's understandable refusal to pick up the gauntlet left McHenry feeling as triumphant as if Dan had whipped Anaconda in straight heats. Stepping lively through the lobby of the Rossmore soon afterward, he piped to the milling scribes, "Well, I reckon Mac and Dan will race some this year!"

An increasingly sports-crazed nation couldn't wait. America wanted to see Dan Patch face—and beat—Prince Alert and Anaconda, and whoever else might emerge as a star that coming year, but to fans as well as the public beyond the racetrack fence, Dan's ultimate opponent was time. More than seeing whom he could beat, people were eager to see how fast he could go.

It sounds counterintuitive that an abstract concept would trump a flesh-and-blood foil. But one reason the clock was king in that era was precisely because it was such a cold machine. It couldn't be "laid up" a heat, fed cocaine or champagne, or otherwise fall prey to the chicanery that was such a large part of racing. The watch told the truth. Either you beat it, or it beat you; end of story and no bullshit. By the end of 1902, everyone felt, the watch would reveal just what kind of horse Dan Patch really was.

But that's not to say that the measure of a horse was pure speed, devoid of context. To the sports fans of that era, what the watch truly gauged was Progress—specifically, the inexorable march to the two-minute mile.

It would be difficult to overstate the importance, in the late nineteenth and early twentieth centuries, of that conveniently round number that for years seemed to shimmer and dance just beyond the Standardbred's grasp. It was more like the sound barrier than the four-minute track-and-field mile. It signaled the success of a great American experiment—in this case the light-harness horse, or Standardbred, and even with the automobile coming on strong, it continued to hold out the promise, through a trickle-down effect on the breed, of faster travel, a quicker work commute, more errands in less time. It was that rare, perhaps unique sporting achievement that made observers feel hopeful about themselves and their futures.

People started debating whether a Standardbred could achieve a two-minute mile in 1849. That was when Flora Temple, the tiny "bob-tailed nag" of "Camptown Races" fame, became the first horse to break the 2:20 barrier with a mile in 2:19 ¼. In 1874 Goldsmith Maid, a mare who had run unbroken on a New York State farm for the first eight years of her life, surpassed 2:15 (at age seventeen), and in 1884 Jay-Eye-See—the seemingly rare harness horse who did not have a colorful or dramatic or freakish backstory—dropped the record to 2:10. A good number of intelligent, horse-savvy observers believed 2:10 was, roughly speaking, the bottom for the breed, and that 2:00 was science fiction.

One such conservative thinker, a Maine physician named George H. Bailey, became known as "Anti-Two-Minute Bailey" after he began publishing a series of articles in the horse journals "proving," John Hervey wrote, "by a series of mathematical gymnastics and algebraic equations, fearfully and wonderfully made," that the two-minute barrier was unbreakable.

Bailey's calculations were upset, however, by the rising popularity of the pacer and the introduction of the low-wheeled, relatively lightweight "bicycle" sulky in the early 1890s. All three of the record-setters mentioned just above were trotters—if pacers were breaking any barriers in those early years of the Standardbred's evolution, no one noticed. But when at last the pacer gained acceptance—slightly and grudgingly from the eastern sophisticates, wholeheartedly from the levelheaded jes-folks of the Midwest—2:00 began to look more like a reachable, and in fact arbitrary, point on the continuum. (No one ever disputed that pacers were faster than trotters, the difference being traditionally factored at two to three seconds per mile.) Meanwhile, the "racing bike"—which turned on its head the once widely held theory that the greater your wheel diameter, the faster you would go—sped up every horse who used it by several seconds. (The old-fashioned racing vehicles had wheels seven or eight feet in diameter and weighed as much as one hundred pounds; the bike sulkies had wheels about two and a half feet across and weighed roughly half as much.) In 1892, the year the bicycle sulky appeared on the scene, virtually every track and world record, and a plethora of personal-best marks, fell.

The horse who finally pushed over the two-minute line, Star Pointer, was not well cast in the role of hero. He was, of course, a pacer. He was sketchily bred, especially on his dam's side (his maternal grandmother is listed on his pedigree merely as "saddle mare"). And he was ugly—or rather, and more strangely, he started out perfectly fine-looking, then devolved, says Hervey, into something "gross, ill-shaped and beefy. . . . His great frame was loaded with flesh and muscle in layers and bunches; his head . . . became coarse and heavy; his paunch bellied down; his neck . . . too heavily crested for beauty." On top of all that he was badly gaited, tending to whack himself with his own hooves at slower and medium speeds. As a result he was often sidelined due to injury or, in keeping with the merciless mores of the day, racing in obvious pain. He passed through many owners in his lifetime, which only means that for every seller there was a buyer fascinated by his sole asset: occasional blinding speed. If you could get him through the gearbox and into overdrive, Star Pointer was, despite his poor construction and chronic aches, one of the fastest horses alive.

The proof came on August 28, 1897, at Readville, Massachusetts, when his trainer, David McClary, rubbed the horse's legs with cocaine, warmed him up, then turned him loose. McClary had remarkably little faith in Star Pointer that day. "He seemed out of condition, drawn and nervous," the horse's owner at the time, James A. Murphy, told the *Horse Review* four years later. "McClary had to work him 12 stiff jogging miles before he could get him warm, and then his perspiration was not free. When he turned him around for the word, he had no hope of doing anything." Nevertheless, in what must be seen as a testament to the hard-knock nineteenth-century training methods (cocaine rubdowns! a full dozen warm-up miles!) the "Pinter Hoss," as he was rather too cutesily known, stopped the watches in 1:59 ¼. To the assembled this felt like history in the making, and the crowd nearly killed McClary congratulating him.

But the hero's role didn't stick. By 1902 Star Pointer had changed hands a few more times for increasingly less money, broken down on the racetrack, and been turned out to stud, where he was in the process of flopping miserably. America very much wanted the handsome, gallant Dan Patch to lower the record and eclipse embarrassing Pinter Hoss.

The early reports were encouraging. In March, the *Horse Review* said that McHenry had Dan at the stable of John J. Quinn, on 124th Street near Seventh Avenue, and that he was working him daily "in the parks of Manhattan," presumably Central (which had its own speedway) and Morningside. In April, McHenry moved Dan onto the Harlem Speedway, which stretched from 155th Street, the site of the Polo Grounds, northward to Dyckman Street, for some conditioning miles in the 2:30 range.

Later that month he moved Dan to the Empire City Track (now Yonkers Raceway) and worked him daily in 2:15. On Sunday, May 11, Dan returned to the Speedway to work a mile alongside his sire Joe Patchen, who had been brought down from a stud farm in Orange County, New York, for the occasion. More than 10,000 people came to watch.

These were indeed happy days in harness racing. Though the balance would soon shift, many more people still owned horses than drove cars in 1902, and the Standardbred had become the most popular breed in America. The country was then bouncing back from the depression of the not-so-gay mid-1890s, and rich men were getting into the racing game. M. W. Savage was typical of the new breed of owner, a man with more money and self-confidence than was good for him. The *Davenport* (Iowa) *Daily Republican* seemed amused by the ascent of Savage, a former West Branch boy who had amassed a fortune in Minneapolis, it reported, "with a product [International Stock Food] that he tried to push on the market when here"—without success. In the meantime, however, Savage had changed venues, and was now buying into the harness game with both fists. About a month before the sale of Dan Patch to Sturges, Savage bought—or rather had foisted upon him by a slick Indiana lawyer named Joseph Lesh— a once-fast pacer turned disappointing stud named Online. The price was $10,000. Placed on Savage's Minnesota farm among other ill-advised purchases, Online promptly dropped dead of a heart attack while jogging on a preposterously expensive one-mile training strip built by Seth Griffin, the I. M. Pei or Frederick Law Olmsted of racetrack design. Savage took the loss in stride. Boom times it was.

The Canadians, perhaps because they read different newspapers, didn't know that Dan Patch was the Anointed One, a gift sent down from Diana, goddess of sport, and they thought they had a horse who could beat him. The horse was the same pacer they'd thought could beat Dan the year before: Harold H. That had not worked out, to say the least. Yet the idea that Harold H. might be the pacer who knocked Dan off his throne was not as irrational as it may sound. "Canadian" in 1902 was no longer what one called horses who were swaybacked, knock-kneed, and without pedigree papers. The breeders up north had in the last decade done their part to refine the Standardbred, and if their horses were still a bit coarser and "grouchier" and needed more time to come into full control of their own bodies, they were also obviously faster and capable of carrying their speed farther than their counterparts of a generation or two before. Harold H., seven years old in 1902, had been slow to reach physical and mental maturity, but he had taken a record slightly faster than Dan's (2:04) in 1901, and, said the *Manitoba Morning Free Press* on June 16 of the following year, "he never looked so well in the eyes of horsemen as he does this year."

Canada's fastest Standardbred was indeed training well for the veteran horseman Al Proctor: around the first of July he worked a mile in 2:07 ¼ at Windsor, with the last quarter in :30. "There is no question about the Canadian possessing as much speed as any horse in the world," said the Manitoba paper, and Proctor must have agreed because he telegraphed McHenry and proposed a match race with Dan Patch at Windsor on July 8 for $500 a side. (That was the stated amount, to make the proceedings look relatively gentlemanly; almost everyone understood that when high-profile match races were made, the owners of the horses agreed to divvy up the gate receipts with track management, with each party getting a third.) Dan, for his part, hadn't started in a race that year, and McHenry hadn't gone faster than 2:11 ½ with him in a training mile. On one hand, he might not be ready to go fast enough to beat a finely honed Harold H. On the other hand, how frightened can you be of a horse named Harold? McHenry was willing to overlook that Dan may have needed a tightener—and even that Proctor's horse wore hobbles. He wired back immediately to accept the challenge. Turf writers speculated that $100,000 would be bet at Windsor on that single two-horse race.

But a lot of people didn't buy into Al Proctor's dream, or as the *Horse Review* put it, "Even among the Canadians there was a suspicion that their champion was not equal to the task cut out for him." The crowd was merely respectable—a bit more than

5,000—on a warm, clear day at Windsor, and the betting, said the horse papers, was fairly heavy, but not as spirited as anticipated. Dan Patch, who looked anything but rusty in the warm-up miles, was the 1–2 favorite in most of the auction pools. As McHenry swung into the sulky for the first heat (the winner would be the first horse to win two heats), he remarked to no one in particular, "I'll have it won by the first half mile."

Aiming to keep his promise, he was overly aggressive at the start and twice got Dan's nose in front of Harold H. (who had drawn the pole), causing restarts. On the third try they got away evenly and stayed side by side, with Dan making the longer trip on the outside, and reached the quarter pole in :30 ½. At the half, timed in a torrid 1:01, Dan was still on the outside but now a half length ahead. McHenry didn't see the rail until the three-quarter pole, by which time Harold H. was cooked. Said one paper: "McHenry pulled Dan to a jog in the stretch and almost walked in, in 2:06 ½." In the second heat, "the driver of Harold H. decided to reserve the horse for the final quarter," wrote Henry Ten Eyck White, "and in consequence the pace was a slow one the first part of the journey. Dan Patch was loafing in front all the way, but in the last sixteenth McHenry shook him up a little, and the heat was won in 2:10."

If Harold H. wasn't disheartened by the experience, his owner was: the next day's papers noted that John Swartz of Wingham, Ontario, had sold his pacer to "the McLaren boys" of Winnipeg for $8,000, probably less than half of what he could have gotten a couple of days before.

Dan's next race was nine days later—on Thursday, July 17—in Grosse Pointe, Michigan. Since McHenry and his horse had been at the Grand Circuit's season-launching "Blue Ribbon Meet" exactly one year earlier, the Detroit Driving Club had banked the turns of its handsome one-mile oval to accommodate automobile racing. McHenry, like some other horsemen, might have seen that as an ominous sign, but he had other worries. Only three other horses had ponied up the stakes payments and entry fees for the chance to chase Dan Patch. The reluctance of other trainers to send their horses against McHenry's was understandable, but small fields usually meant dull races, and while he normally didn't give a rat's ass about disappointing the public, McHenry wanted, for selfish reasons, to ensure that Dan remained a popular attraction. Fewer horses also meant fewer entry fees and hence fewer dollars in the pot: Dan's race at Detroit had a purse of $1,500, or $1,000 less than he had raced for the year before at the same track in the 2:14 class.

The three in the field that day, God bless their moldering bones, gave it their best shot. In the first heat, Searchlight, who had a faster record than Dan (2:03 ¼), powered to the front and Dan, who was 1 to 4 in the betting, sat second, an open length behind the leader. Coming off a year's layoff, Searchlight looked sharp. Said the *Horse Review:* "Many thought that the unbeaten son of Joe Patchen had met his match at last."

Searchlight's driver, Thomas Keating, was probably not one of them. After a fast half mile he tried to give his horse a rest, slowing the third quarter to 33 seconds. But soon he felt the hot breath of Dan Patch on his neck. Around the turn for home, McHenry pulled to the center of the track and jogged by Searchlight, stopping the clock in 2:05. The second and deciding heat was a repeat of the first, but a half second slower. The *Chicago Daily* wrote that "Dan Patch, the champion pacer, has added a new scalp to his collection."

After the race, when Dan had been cooled down and McHenry was supervising his leg-wrapping, the trainer looked up and was surprised to see Dan Messner standing in the stable door. McHenry braced himself, wondering if Messner was bitter about the deal, or perhaps even had found out, or figured out, what had happened to Lady Patch. But Messner only smiled politely and congratulated McHenry on his latest victory as he patted Dan on the nose. Then he was gone. Messner would go home and tell the *Oxford Tribune* that Dan looked well-cared-for by his new owner and that his mahogany coat "felt slick as satin." He would never see Dan Patch again.

At Cleveland five days later, the same three masochistic opponents showed up, joined by Riley B., another brave but overmatched animal. Dan started out at odds of 1 to 4, dropped to 1 to 5, and then was barred from the betting. Once again the purse was small—only $1,500, the lowest offered that afternoon. As for the race itself, it was, to borrow words from the newspaper coverage, "dull," "moot," and "featureless." The last is a bit unfair. McHenry did what he could to liven up the proceedings, hanging back in third place behind Riley B. and Searchlight in the first heat, then pulling out at the top of the stretch and powering to the front. Though one account said Dan was "just loafing" through the mile, he stopped the clock in 2:03 ¾, a new personal best. The second heat resembled the first except for a slower time (2:05 ¼).

Although Dan Patch had added another victory to his string, the day, from McHenry's perspective, was something less than a success. Dan's performance was buried in the next morning's newspapers beneath stories about the blind trotter Rhythmic, who was on an eight-race winning streak, and a scandal that had erupted right on the racetrack, when driver George Spear was ordered out of the sulky and fined $250 for not trying to win with his trotter Lord Derby. (The stallion, who had finished last in his first heat, won the second with his judge-appointed replacement driver.) About all Dan had accomplished, thanks to his fast first heat victory, was to eliminate himself from the 2:04 class, which at McHenry's insistence had been set up in the pacer's honor. With the season just begun, McHenry, Sturges, and the pooh-bahs of the Grand Circuit suddenly found themselves looking at a long hot summer of small fields, paltry purses, and quiet crowds.

McHenry saw only one way out of this untenable situation: he would stop racing against other horses, at least for a while, and match Dan against the clock in a series of exhibition miles that would occur between the races at the Grand Circuit stops. The spectacle of a single trotter or pacer attempting to beat a pre-announced time, often in the company of one or two galloping Thoroughbred prompters, was not an unusual sight at the harness tracks of that day. Because of the widespread obsession with time and the two-minute mile, those contests were often the most prominently advertised and avidly anticipated events on the card. They could, in fact, unfold quite dramatically by the standard of any era, with the featured horse giving his all at the behest of his driver, and the crowd roaring each time an official flipped over the numbers that displayed the fractional and final times. At most tracks, patrons could bet on whether a time trialer would achieve his goal. No horse-and-driver team had ever raced the clock on a full-time basis—but McHenry wasn't certain he was doing quite that; all he knew was that there were no decent opportunities for traditional races on the horizon. So with Dan Patch having won all of his nineteen races, and fifty-four of fifty-six heats, McHenry would now take things a week at a time, using the speed shows to keep Dan's name in the news and, if he could take a few ticks off his horse's personal best, increase his resale value. If the public got behind the exhibitions, McHenry knew he might eventually be able to negotiate appearance fees for Dan, the way the owners of Anaconda and Prince Alert had done on several occasions when their horses went against the clock to tremendous fanfare. Those horses had commanded $500 to $1,000 just for showing up.

McHenry didn't have to wait long to gauge the public's reaction to the time trials. For the next Grand Circuit stop, in Columbus, he had come up with a fresh promotional idea—on August 2 Dan would attempt to beat the record of his sire, Joe Patchen (2:01 ¼, as most racing fans knew). About 7,000 people, or almost 50 percent more than had seen Dan compete in a traditional race in Cleveland on July 22, showed up to see what would happen. Still more people would have come, the *Horse Review* noted, had more believed the goal to be within Dan's grasp. But Joe Patchen's hallowed mark looked to many, the paper said, "like too far to go in one stride." After all, the racing season had barely begun, and Dan Patch had already knocked a full second off his own personal best. Records did not normally fall until late September, after the horses had raced themselves into peak form, and the air became warm, wet, and still in a way that seemed to favor speed. Star Pointer didn't go his 1:59 ¼ until the twenty-eighth of August, and the only other horses to flirt with 2:00—John R. Gentry (2:00 ½ in 1896) and Prince Alert (2:00 ¾ in 1901)—did so in September and October, respectively. Dan

Patch might get his sire's record, said the wise ones, just not this quickly.

What almost no one knew, however, was that Dan had gone 2:01 ½ in a private workout mile over the Columbus track on July 31. This bully performance actually worried McHenry, who felt that Dan was so "on the bit" that he might just blow right past a few milestones that the trainer would rather reach one at a time over the coming weeks and months, to maximize publicity and bonus money. Nor was Dan's extreme sharpness the only thing that weighed on McHenry. The trainer noticed that the pacer was slowly reverting to his old habits of sprawling out behind and simultaneously leaning forward into the bit—displaying, in other words, the same tendencies that seemed to have been cured the summer before when horseshoer Nash shaved Dan's hooves. Dan's bad habits were obviously not preventing him from going some wickedly fast miles, but the trainer wondered if he should ask Nash to increase the already extreme angle still more. Ultimately he decided to use the Columbus time trial as a test of just how "off" Dan was.

The track was fast, but the weather was unseasonably mild on August 2, a distinct disappointment to McHenry, Sturges, and all of Dan's fans, who had hoped for a sultry day, humid air being thought of then as especially oxygen-rich and thus conducive to speed. But if the trainer considered calling off the attempt, he was dissuaded by the size of the crowd (no official figures were reported, but the *Newark Advocate* called it "an immense throng"). With so many doubters, and the weather turning against him, McHenry was also able to lay down thousands of dollars in bets at relatively favorable odds. Too much money was at stake to pine for ideal conditions; the show would go on.

Later, Dan Patch's races against time would be more slickly packaged in terms of production values, with the track cleared of horses during the elaborate introduction by a smartly dressed master of ceremonies, and bands playing throughout the show. But that first time trial at Columbus was a no-frills affair. Dan slipped onto the track almost unnoticed, and his name alone (and none of his accomplishments) was announced as he paced in a clockwise direction, taking a final, slow warm-up mile with a single running-horse prompter loping behind. Then, as the crowd grew quiet, McHenry drove him to the head of the stretch, turned him in the racing direction, nodded to the head judge and shook the reins to get Dan rolling. As he passed under the start wire in full stride, the three official timers clicked their watches.

McHenry was determined to be conservative and to go only as fast as he had to, but this led him to make uncharacteristic mistakes. The first quarter, timed in :31, was too slow by quite a lot; it put Dan on a 2:04 pace. When the numbers were posted, the crowd moaned with disappointment; the day already seemed lost.

But the next quarter, in :29, showed that McHenry at least hadn't given up hope. A half in 1:00 flat meant that Joe Patchen's record, and even a sub-two-minute mile, were within reach. McHenry kept up the pace. By the time Dan reached the three-quarter pole in 1:30 ¼, with no urging, the crowd was up and cheering. But about fifty yards before the finish line something odd happened. McHenry inexplicably tapped on the brakes by pulling back on the reins and, said the *Chicago Tribune,* "succeeded in partially stopping Dan Patch before the mile was completed." The final time, caught identically on the three judges' stopwatches, was 2:00 ¾. Dan had surpassed his sire's mark and equaled Prince Alert's best performance, which was also the third-fastest mile in history. But clearly he could have gone faster.

McHenry's strange tactic of slowing Dan in the stretch confused the turf writers and (one of them suggested) angered the horse, who "seemed displeased at being pulled up." The experience appeared to have jangled McHenry's nerves as well. Afterward, he was both effusive and cotton-headed, seeming to forget, when he talked to the *Tribune*'s White (an inveterate quote polisher), that Dan had already raced his way out of the 2:04 class:

> "My intention," McHenry said, back in the stable area, moments after the exhibition was completed, "was to drive Dan Patch a mile close to 2:01 ¼, but not quite reaching that mark, thus escaping the penalty of the record and leaving the horse in the 2:04 class. He was so good, however, and paced

so easily, that we made faster time than I intended. When I saw that he was certain to beat old Joe's mark I tried to stop him, but could not slow him up in time. I am sorry now that I did not drive him out, for I am sure he could have come the last quarter in :29, equaling or lowering Star Pointer's record of 1:59 ¼. He will do it before the season is over."

McHenry's clumsy postrace spin-doctoring didn't go down well with at least one turf writer, the anonymous *Horse Review* columnist who signed himself Trotwood:

"I admire Dan Patch as much as anyone," he wrote in the next week's edition,

> but it always makes me tired when a lot of fellows tell what a great horse "would have done if—." McHenry is the cause of it all this time by intimating that if he had not pulled the great son of old Joe down in the last quarter, he would have broken Star Pointer's record. It is easy enough to talk all of that, but doing it is another thing . . .
>
> Well, Dan Patch starts again Thursday [August 14th] against Pointer's mark, and on the Brighton Beach track, and if he does the trick I shall be as proud of it as anybody. . . . It may, however, be safely bet on that no horse born yet is going to beat Star Pointer's record.

McHenry, it was true, had driven an erratic mile, going slow, then fast, then slow again, no doubt confusing his horse. But despite his bad driving, and worse explaining, the outcome fit his plans precisely. By beating Joe Patchen's record, he had enhanced his horse's image and collected on his bets. But the two-minute-mile barrier and the Pinter Hoss's record could still be broken one at a time. If there had been any doubt about it before, there wasn't now: McHenry held the reins on the hottest property in American sports.

CHAPTER FOURTEEN

THE WESTERN UNION MESSENGER in Columbus was getting to know Myron McHenry very well—not a good thing for the middle-aged "boy" who delivered the wires to the horseman staying at the Deschler Wallech Hotel, because the Wizard was a pathetic tipper. Even before Dan Patch's first race against time, telegrams had begun arriving from officials at the New York Trotting Association, which ran the Brighton Beach harness meet; after Dan's celebrated mile at Columbus, the uniformed delivery boy found himself in McHenry's presence five or six times a day for three or four days running, and piling up quite a collection of nickels. The NYTA had been trying to pull together a dream race on August 16, just two weeks hence: Anaconda, Prince Alert, and Dan Patch squaring off for $3,000 and the title of pacing king, a distinction that, as hard it may be to believe today, once stirred the hearts of sports fans.

At first McHenry had seemed at least vaguely interested in the proposition, which after all carried a cash prize twice the size of Dan's most recent purses. But once he had the Columbus time trial behind him, the trainer thought he had the leverage to wangle a better deal, one that minimized the risk and maximized the glory and cash. What he boldly proposed to the Brighton Beach boys was an attempt by Dan to lower Star Pointer's record on their seaside track. He and Sturges would split $5,000 if the horse succeeded, on top of a guaranteed $1,500 for appearing. The NYTA put up a show of hemming and hawing, but within forty-eight hours it had accepted McHenry's terms. Nor was this the only deal that McHenry, in his new capacity as booking agent, was negotiating from his room in the Deschler Wallech. On August

12, the *Review* reported that "the Indianapolis management has practically closed a contract for the appearance of Dan Patch to go against his record at the approaching Indiana State Fair in October." Because the Hoosiers ultimately refused to guarantee anything above $1,000 for Dan's appearance, that deal never got made, but "closed a contract for an appearance" is a locution worth noting, for it signaled a sea change in the horse's career: Dan Patch was, for the time being at least, no longer a racehorse— an equine athlete who lives by his performances and competes under established and standardized rules. Now, and for the foreseeable future, he was an attraction, something to be negotiated and contracted for, scheduled strategically, and advertised well— something a bit like the W. H. Barnes Show's famous diving elk, an 800-pound beast that leaped from a forty-foot platform into sixteen square feet of water for the pleasure of the fair-going set.

As an attraction, Dan kept a different schedule from the horses in the traditional racing game. Normally, he would have appeared at Brighton Beach on Saturday, August 16, the Grand Circuit's getaway day, when the most prestigious races took place. But NYTA officials, as part of their discussions with McHenry, said they wanted Dan instead on the fourteenth, a Thursday, when attendance could use a boost. Dan had not only become a marketable commodity; he was also now a marketing tool—high-priced bait, like the bananas given away at the Benton County Fair. McHenry didn't care. Since Dan would have had twelve days' rest at that point, almost twice as much as usual between his stiffer efforts, it was all the same to him as long as their check cleared.

The Brighton meet got off to an interesting start. On the first day of racing, August 11, the blind stallion Rhythmic, who had been tearing up the Grand Circuit since Detroit, won the $10,000 Bonner Memorial Trot, and his trainer, Scott Hudson, explained to the New York reporting crew, which even then thought a story was never told until they told it, that no, he wasn't scared to drive the horse; Rhythmic, he patiently explained for the thousandth time, sensed where the other horses and the rail were, and kept himself out of trouble. (Several months later Hudson would be amazed to discover that the speedy Rhythmic was deaf, too.) The

next day, the "noted plunger" (and perfectly named fin de siècle
rich guy) E. E. Smathers made headlines in the *New York Times*
by betting $40,000 on a horse in what was considered a wide-
open 2:20 pace (there was no place or show betting in those days,
so everything went on the horse's nose). The object of Smathers's
affections, a future champion named Direct Hal, won in straight
heats, giving his backer a profit of $20,000.

On August 13, a large display ad appeared in the *New York
Times*: "Tomorrow, DAN PATCH, The Unbeaten Pacer, to Beat
The World's Record!" In smaller type the ad noted: "Special Race
Train at 1 p.m. from New York side of Brooklyn Bridge." The
Brooklyn Eagle said, "Flying Sulkies at Brighton To-Morrow."

No exact attendance figures were reported for Dan's second
appearance at Brighton, but the crowd was described by various
sources as "immense," "exceptionally large," and "tremendous."
A good guess would be ten thousand people. To be able to say you
had been there when Star Pointer's record fell was no small thing,
and unlike the prerace mood in Columbus, there was hope in the
Brooklyn air. Said the *American Horse Breeder*: "If the conditions
are at all favorable, he stands a chance."

One troubling thing, though: it had not been a good week for
speed. Instead of the usual ocean breezes, stiff winds buffeted the
track from several directions, whipping up the tall sea grass in the
infield. On August 14, said the *Chicago Tribune*, "the flags on the
grandstand were snapping and the air was distinctly chilly. It was
far from the day a stallion likes for speed work—still and sunny.
In addition to the cool breeze, light clouds obscured the sky." The
consensus was, said another paper, "that 2:02 would be an excellent mile on such a day."

Dan Patch's time trial was scheduled for 4:00 p.m. The star
attraction first appeared on the track, unannounced but to a huge
ovation, at shortly after two, when McHenry drove him a warm-
up mile that was timed by sportswriters in 2:28 ¼. A half hour
later, he appeared again for a mile in 2:10, and at shortly after
3:00 he went another "pipe-opening" mile in 2:11. All seemed
well enough, but when McHenry came back to the stables after
that final warm-up, he wore a look of concern. Instead of stay-

ing at Dan's stall to oversee the final preparations, he strode purposefully to the backstretch offices of the NYTA and told officials there that he wanted to alter their agreement. "I've never felt such wind gusts as I have today on this racetrack," he said. "We must announce that because of these conditions there has been a change of plans and now Dan Patch will attempt to beat his own mark of 2:00 ¾, not Star Pointer's."

The racing men were shocked. "And the $5,000 bonus?" one of them wondered.

"That now becomes the prize for beating his own mark," McHenry said. "It's a new day and a new deal, and if you have any argument with that I will take my horse and leave right now."

A few moments later, the starting judge picked up his megaphone and announced to the throng that because of the winds Dan Patch would now be aiming to beat 2:00 ¾.

The fans didn't seem to mind the change, but most people were standing and roaring so loudly at that point that they might not have realized what was happening. The track management, which possessed more show-biz flair than its counterparts in Columbus, had whipped them into a frenzy. After a musical fanfare, the star was grandly and elaborately introduced by the man with the megaphone, and then the band played Dan onto the track. The strapping pacer, his brown coat glistening, was immediately followed by two prancing Thoroughbreds who would be his prompters that day, one running ahead of Dan, the other urging him on from behind.

As McHenry brought Dan to the top of the homestretch and slowly wheeled him around, the crowd fell silent. McHenry held Dan still for a long moment, then nodded to the starter to indicate his readiness. "Away went the head runner," said the *Tribune,* "and after him went Dan, with his ears pricked and his legs moving with the regularity of piston rods."

Dan paced the first quarter in :30 ¼ and the second in a flat :30. The prompters, galloping between the shafts of a sulky, looked awkward compared to the smoothly pacing Standardbred, but they were doing their jobs well (one was driven by one of Dan's grooms, Frank Chamberlain; the other by a Manhattan-based trainer named

Charley Thompson); a two-minute mile, and maybe better, was in sight. The wind until the half-mile pole hadn't been much of a factor, but when Dan rounded the turn at the three-quarters, fierce gusts kicked up, hitting him directly in the face. McHenry bent his own head forward, took both reins in one hand, and yanked down the peak of his driving cap so it wouldn't blow off. For all that, the third quarter was a better than respectable :30 ¾. Straightening into the stretch, Dan dug in and picked up the pace. The *Tribune*'s Henry Ten Eyck White wrote that "Dan's sprint to the finish, a point where most horses in their trials against time falter perceptibly, roused the crowd to cheers, and from the lower end of the crowded grandstand to the wire there was an outburst that sounded like musketry." The last quarter had gone in :29 ¼; the final time was 2:00 ¾, the same as at Columbus.

The *Review* would call Dan's effort "an honorable failure." It was certainly a better than respectable time, but McHenry sullied the moment by making what was becoming his standard excuse. "I could have gone that third quarter faster than I did," he said, "but I wanted the horse to go good right to the wire, so I took him back."

Hervey, writing in the *Review* under his nom de course of Volunteer, called the Wizard on his whining. "In the flush of enthusiasm it is one thing to talk about beating 1:59 ¼, but it is quite another affair to do it," he said. "While I know the present belief of many is that Dan Patch is greater than Star Pointer, I have yet to be convinced of that fact." Hervey strongly suspected that McHenry had blown Dan's chance to go down in history by holding him back in Columbus. "In every horse's career there comes a time when he is better than he ever was before or ever is again," his column went on. "Very often it comes unaware, even to the best and most skillful trainer. . . . I do not pretend to say that at Columbus Dan Patch was better than he ever again will be. He is young, strong and sound and he ought to train on and improve. . . . But the fact is that he has lost one golden opportunity which may never come again. All the conditions favored at Columbus, and the horse was on the verge of the supreme accomplishment—and McHenry took him back! To use a hibernicism, if he had to do it over again I don't believe he would do it—at least I hope not."

The criticism of his horsemanship stung McHenry, who had barely spoken to Hervey before, and now stopped completely. What hurt the Wizard worse, though, was the realization that if he had gone just a quarter of a second faster at Brighton Beach, he would have picked up the $5,000 prize.

Still, there was no time to dwell on the negative. The *Review* had written "Dan Patch, 2:00 ¾—it looks well in print, does it not?" and called Dan's breaking 2:00 "a moral certainty." Besides, the automobile racers were moving into Brighton, and Dan and all of the other pacers and trotters had to vacate their stalls and move on.

Overall, things were not going badly for McHenry. In the last few weeks his life had changed in a fundamental—and for him, enjoyable—way. He was now spending most of his day sending and receiving wires, writing letters, and making telephone calls. He liked the feeling of power that came with controlling a hot property, and saying no to people (when Dan had a scheduling conflict or if they offered something less than the stated fee) had always been one of his most intense pleasures. What he didn't like was the time it took away from his training. Dan Patch's mechanics still needed tending to—he was getting increasingly "sloppy behind," and he was leaning into the bit harder than ever. Was this one large problem or two (or more) distinct ones? He needed to figure that out; if the problems got worse, Dan could be sidelined and miss out on thousands of dollars. Normally, McHenry would have been constantly observing a troubled horse, and spending solitary afternoons smoking cigars over his various options. But now he had so much else on his mind. He kept telling himself that he would focus on Dan's problems at the next stop, when things had settled down a bit.

The dangers of that approach became evident at Readville, Massachusetts, where Dan had his next race against time on August 23. The early part of the day did not augur well. "A high, cold wind swept in from the northwest," White reported, and the horse made a rare—and sensational—misstep during his first warm-up mile, losing his stride and briefly breaking into a panic-stricken

gallop. The early arrivals at the track could hardly believe what
they were seeing. Was there a master of ceremonies this time? A
band? Since McHenry did not have full control over the staging
of Dan's appearances, and the newspaper coverage is so inconsis-
tent on these points, it's impossible to say. The *New York Times*
did note, however, that at precisely 5:00 p.m. the horse, after the
usual warm-ups and the nod from McHenry to indicate his readiness, "started at a terrific clip and was well settled into his stride
at the half mile." Indeed, McHenry had Dan flying; he reached
that marker in a phenomenal :59 flat. But at the five-eighths-mile
marker, his always troublesome left rear leg struck the sulky shaft,
and for the second time that day he broke stride, something he had
never done before in a race or time trial. The sight of Dan galloping down the backstretch must have been disturbing to fans. We
can safely assume the crowd gasped. We know with certainty that
a mortified McHenry instantly pulled him up and finished out the
mile at a slow jog.

McHenry didn't want to open the next day's *Boston Globe* and
see "Dan Patch Breaks Stride, Fails." So he sent word to the Readville management that he and Dan would return in a half hour and
try again. The consensus along the backstretch was that this was a
mistake; although Dan Patch had raced three heats on many occasions, that extremely fast half mile and the physical trauma involved
in striking the sulky shafts and going off stride had probably taken
too great a toll. McHenry, as always, had no interest in what his
fellow horsemen thought. Still, in the second attempt, which started
promptly at 5:35, he drove his horse more conservatively, reaching the half-mile pole a second and a quarter slower than in his
earlier attempt. Ultimately it was a blissfully uneventful mile, and
Dan's four nearly identical quarters added up to 2:00 ¼, a new
personal record. "A better-rated mile was never driven," said the
Horse Review. Indeed, McHenry had deftly threaded the needle,
collecting the $5,000 for lowering Dan's personal best but leaving
the two-minute mile for another day.

"Dan Patch Is Getting There," read a front-page headline in
the *Davenport* (Iowa) *Daily Republican* that appeared between stories about President Theodore Roosevelt's New England tour and

a lengthy Pennsylvania coal miners' strike that had left the country dangerously low on fuel for the winter. "Getting there" was good enough for McHenry and Sturges. By drawing out the suspense, Dan Patch was only encouraging interest in his quest. Robert L. Dickey, the famed illustrator for the *Horse Review,* drew a cartoon of a kingly but dazed-looking Star Pointer, his crown askew, saying, "That boy of Joe Patchen's seems to have taken up his father's fight against me—a few more jolts and that crown is gone!" "Dan Patch is the pacing marvel of the year," exclaimed the *Portsmouth* (N.H.) *Herald.* "Patch lays back his long ears, his mane and tail straighten out in the wind, his muscles contract to the highest tension and of his own volition he strains every nerve to attain his limit of speed. Quarters better than thirty seconds do not seem to distress him. He gamely follows the fence to the half-mile pole at top speed, rounds the last turn like clockwork, and gamely fights the watch to the wire. It is not necessary for Driver McHenry to urge him."

The *Oxford Tribune* continued to report on Dan Patch, but in a somewhat morose way, noting that the horse was "very much missed" at the Benton County Fair, even though, on the day of Dan's performance at Readville, three colts Dan had sired with nondescript local mares had won red ribbons (the equivalent of blue ribbons today) in the prize ring. Neither those living images of Dan, nor the knowledge that Free Banana Day was just twenty-four hours away, could assuage the locals' feeling of loss.

At Providence on August 29 weather conditions were perfect at last, and Dan Patch came out flying—"squatting low in a long stride," said the *Elyria* (Ohio) *Daily Chronicle,* "and cutting through the air so that his ears were bent back and his mane was straight out." When he reached the three-quarter pole in 1:29 ¾, the Wizard went to work, shouting, bouncing in his seat, rattling the reins, waving the whip madly. "McHenry encouraged and roused him for the final brush," White wrote. "The runner was taken back, and with a fleck of the whip on his withers, Dan Patch darted under the wire in 1:59 ½." And so he had at last made it past the two-minute barrier, but not quite past Star Pointer. "The crowd gave a great cheer as the horse returned to the wire," said the *Fort Wayne* (Ind.) *News,* "and McHenry also came in for like attention. Dan Patch was not in the least distressed, and on being taken to the cooling tent was ready in half an hour to go another good mile had it been required." Manley Sturges, on hand for the first time in weeks to witness one of Dan's performances, endured back slaps sufficient to loosen his teeth fillings.

There was no bigger story in the nation that day. The *Idaho Daily Statesman* noted, "From the performance of Dan Patch the pacer, one is justified in concluding that records made by the automobile have inspired the horses to do something to show that they are still in the running." The *Times* was no less enthusiastic, saying that Dan Patch, by getting down below 2:00 and earning another $5,000 for his handlers, had "closed out the Narragansett meet in a blaze of glory." The *Horse Breeder* ranked the occasion with "the great dates in American history." The *Horse Review* lost control of itself, excreting a hideous poem called "To Dan Patch 1:59 ½":

> *Here's to you, Danny Patchen, an' yo' tussle with old Time.*
> *It's a devil's job you've got, suh, in any age or clime—*
> *You're shooting at the record of a master in his art*
> *An' the hoss that ever gets there—wel' he kno' he's got a*
>   *heart.*
> *For it's pace—pace—pace*
> *In a record-breakin' swing*
> *And it's race—race—race*
> *Rund a hot and hurtlin' ring.*
> *But the hoss who stops within a quarter second of success*
> *Has missed it jes' the same as if he laid down with the res'.*
> *So here's to you Danny Patchen,*
> *In the marnin'!*

McHenry was sensing, if not exactly feeling, the love. At Philadelphia's Belmont Park, on the overcast afternoon of Wednesday, September 3, twelve thousand people, more than would turn out for any Phillies game that season, came to see the pacer attempt to beat the track record of 1:59 ¾, set by Star Pointer six years earlier. The racing strip at Belmont ran visibly uphill from the half-mile pole to the head of the stretch, making Pointer's achievement all the more remarkable. Another problem for Dan was that the Belmont clay had a reputation for becoming extremely sticky when it got wet—and at three o'clock, two hours before Dan's time trial was scheduled, it started drizzling. On Dan's final warm-up mile, McHenry didn't like what he saw, and when he came back to the barn, he told his chief groom Chamberlain to get the horse ready to go as soon as possible, before conditions worsened. This Chamberlain did, and accompanied by a single running horse driven by the well-known Trenton trainer Scott Quinton, Dan Patch was formally announced to the grandstand at a few minutes before four o'clock.

Later that evening, McHenry would say the Philadelphia mile was "all things considered one of the best Dan ever went"—but then he often said that when the horse fell short of the announced goal. It was certainly a creditable mile—2:00 flat—given the conditions, and by the standards of only a month before it was an extraordinary one. An appreciative crowd "rose and gave the horse and driver a great ovation" as they returned to the finish wire, one paper said. But—and it may be difficult to believe this—some members of the press went out of their way to find a negative angle. A few, twisting reality to suit their pessimistic premise, saw the Providence mile as a near miss of the world record and the Philadelphia mile as a near miss of the Belmont one. To these cynical types, Dan Patch was showing signs of being a big tease, a horse who would seem on the verge of rewriting the records, but never quite do it. "Despite all he's done," wrote one, "Dan Patch could still go down as a disappointment."

CHAPTER FIFTEEN

It takes greater fortune to carry off good fortune than bad.
—François, duc de la Rochefoucauld

THE GOOD PEOPLE OF Syracuse, New York, were not at all cynical or pessimistic about Dan Patch. They wanted him at the New
York State Fair, which had been held annually in their city since
1890 after years of vagabonding about the rustic northern coun-
ties, and in which they took as much pride as an upwardly mobile
city of 108,000 can in endeavors involving hoochie-coochie shows
and who's-got-the-fattest-hog contests. As soon as McHenry
announced that he would be conducting a series of time trials with
his pacer, the managers of the Syracuse midway extended him a
warm invitation to revisit the scene of so many of his racetrack
triumphs. They were thinking conventionally, those poor, sweet
upstate chaps. They yearned for a yes, feared a no—but instead
got a number, or rather a series of dollar amounts from a man
one step ahead of them in the evolution of the celebrity culture.
McHenry wired back that Dan Patch would cost them $5,000 if
he broke his own or Star Pointer's record, with a $1,500 guaran-
tee no matter what happened, plus another $1,000 dollars or so in
travel and other expenses. The Syracusans swallowed hard—they
had never dealt with the issue of appearance money before—and
formed a Dan Patch Fund, asking local businesspeople to kick
in $10 each. They needn't have worried about raising the cash.
Within a week the fund was oversubscribed, and after a flurry of

telegrams a deal was made with McHenry and a welcoming committee formed to meet the famous horse on September 5.

But nothing was simple anymore in the life of Dan Patch—not the securing of his services, and certainly not dealing with the stately superstar in the flesh. Consider that when Dan pulled into the Syracuse depot in what the *Post-Standard* called "a special, well-appointed car in keeping with this aristocratic king of the turf," a kind of clanging, hissing chaos reigned. Earlier that day, fifty boxcars holding the contents of the sprawling Modern Machinery exhibit had rumbled in behind schedule from points west, and crates full of typewriters, can openers, washing machines, lawn mowers, and bicycles were littering the platforms, or being unloaded onto horse-drawn trucks by frantic, shouting porters. Meanwhile the regular Grand Circuit racing stock was disembarking down assorted gang-planks, and some of the stallions, put in a foul mood by their journey and bewildered by the bustle, were snorting and rearing and lashing out with their hind feet. In short, it was the usual, predictable pre-fair mess. But to the designated greeters, put on edge by the prospect of dealing with the most famous horse in America, it all spelled danger; they took one look at the scene and declared it too overwhelming—too vulgar—for the great Dan Patch. Never mind that he was the least panicky stud horse that anyone had ever seen—an easy traveler, always curious and eager for new experiences, a wickedly handsome devil, yes, but a simple, wide-eyed Hoosier at heart. Something, they decided, would have to be done!

And so things got complicated. While Dan's train waited outside the Syracuse station, fair officials spent more than an hour discussing the situation, dispatching messengers, and making phone calls. Ultimately they hatched a plan to uncouple Dan's car from its train and then recouple it to an engine that would take it on a spur of track that led directly into the fairgrounds. This was the kind of treatment only visiting dignitaries like President Roosevelt received. Unfortunately, it took three more hours to effect the switching, during which time, and despite the change of venue, the original welcoming committee of one dozen swelled to about two hundred gawkers and souvenir hounds. When "the great sidewheeler" finally came down the ramp "in perfect condition," said the *Post-Standard*, the mob "crowded around the great horse as he was carefully taken to the stable provided and eagerly looked over the clean-limbed racing machine which has demonstrated power to outstrip the wind."

An hour later, they were still looking. A few tried to swipe a hair from his tail.

Truly, it was exhausting to be Dan Patch.

Dan's retinue that day lacked its two most notable members, McHenry and Sturges. Their absence disappointed many in the crowd, who wanted to gaze upon the men they had lately been reading so much about in the newspapers, but the trainer and owner had pressing business in Hartford, where Sturges's newly renamed Prince Direct was entered in the 2:13 pace at the Grand Circuit meet. The purse of the race was only $1,500, but that's not what concerned them. Hartford was one of the first places where the former Freddie C. would do his trick of looking dead lame in the post parade, so as to drive up the odds—then turn in the racing direction and pace like the wind. The ploy worked perfectly. Prince Direct that day won three straight heats, the fastest in 2:08. For McHenry and Sturges, the victory meant several thousand dollars in auction-pool profits—not coincidentally, more than they would make if Dan broke the record at the New York State Fair.

With his owner and trainer off to the races, Dan came to Syracuse in the care of two full-time grooms—about whom not much is known. Though dual caretakers were a rarity back then, their near-anonymity is typical of the times. Grooms in those days were generally gypsies with nicknames like Spitshine and Shorty, rootless ramblers who were, for various reasons, often not able to maintain steady employment but who, on the backstretch, toiled like slaves. It was an all-male world then, and if the men were white their skin often possessed a strange copper-pewter hue, a combination of dirt, sun, and hepatitis. They slept outside their horses' stalls, brushed, bathed, hotwalked, and fed their charges, and were expected to be on call around the clock (though it was often tacitly understood that they would be dead drunk each evening). In return they received a dollar a day and . . . well, nothing else, certainly no credit. Their bosses, the trainers, almost never mentioned their names to the press, and the turf scribes never thought to ask.

Dan's grooms in 1902 were both white (writers sometimes noted that he was tended by two Caucasians as a way of conveying how incredibly pampered the horse was). The senior man was Frank Chamberlain, a small, wiry racetrack veteran and a good enough driver to handle the second Thoroughbred prompter on those occasions when McHenry wanted two runners to accompany Dan (the primary prompter would usually be driven by a local trainer who knew the track well). Chamberlain had proven himself several years before, when he rubbed the trotting mare Rose Croix, whom McHenry bred and trained and drove to victory in the 1896 Kentucky Futurity in the then-newsworthy time of 2:11 ¼.

The junior groom was McHenry's eighteen-year-old nephew, Chester Landerbaugh, whom the trainer had hired early in 1902 to assist Chamberlain and act as a kind of bodyguard for Dan Patch. McHenry was worried that somebody might try to harm the horse in some subtle and invisible way, the better to cash a bet. He also by nature abhorred the greenhorns who crowded around, asking questions and ooohing with fascination at the sight of Dan Patch emptying his bowels. McHenry knew that keeping the horse's value high meant fanning the flame of Dan's celebrity— and that meant putting up with these people. He just wanted to make sure the idiots didn't get too close.

Landerbaugh, who had just graduated from high school in Geneseo, Illinois, did not wander naively into the position; he had heard stories about his unavuncular uncle. "He knew Myron had a temper," Chester's son Emmanuel said in 1993. "But he wanted some experience, and he thought this would be a good way to get it." Whatever horse wisdom poor Landerbaugh acquired that summer was hard won. McHenry told his nephew he must sleep inside Dan's stall, on a cot set up in the straw. Each morning, wanting breakfast, the horse would wake Landerbaugh before dawn. Emmanuel remembered his father's stories: Dan would start out gently, nudging the groom with his head. If that didn't rouse the young man, Dan would "paw Dad on his shoulder a little harder. And if that didn't work Dan would start pawing Dad over his whole body and boy did that hurt!" The horse was not alone in liking to abuse the fresh-faced farm kid. Once, when their train had stopped briefly someplace in Michigan, and McHenry had sent his nephew into town to get food, the engineer started up just as he saw Landerbaugh returning—then slowed down, only to speed up again every time the kid tried to hop aboard. Finally, with a cruel cackle, the engineer took off, forcing Landerbaugh to wait for the next train. "When McHenry found out that man had left him without one of his grooms," Emmanuel said, "he lit into the man something fierce."

But more often it was Landerbaugh whom McHenry lit into fiercely. Once, in 1902, when he found the boy using as bedding the expensive golden hay that Dan was meant to eat, McHenry berated his nephew so harshly that the teenager made up his mind to quit, and soon afterward returned to Geneseo and the family farm, where he remained the rest of his days.

With McHenry setting the tone, there were not a lot of yucks around Dan Patch's stall. An anonymous writer from the *Syracuse Post-Standard* had to strain for occasional levity in an otherwise nicely rendered account of a visit to the pacer at the New York State Fairgrounds on September 8. In his story, headlined "Nothing Too Good for Dan Patch," the writer begins by noting that Dan exudes "an air of utmost indifference" that suggests that a reporter's call "was very commonplace."

> In the stable he wears as little clothing as possible to keep him warm, for horses, like babies, are not coddled in the present generation, as they are much more liable to take cold when they go out. He wears bandages on all four legs to keep them in proper condition and contentedly munches his hay in the most complacent manner in spite of the curious visitors that throng his stall at the State Fairgrounds. His hay is grown in the uplands of California and it is practically wild oats. It is cut while the grain is in the milk and it is cured by long exposure to the sun. It is the sweetest morsel imaginable and it is only enjoyed by equine royalty.

Dan Patch eats 12 quarts of oats a day in lots of four quarts three times daily. Every pleasant morning he is jogged out. About twice a week and about two days before a race or an exhibition he is given a fast workout, two or three slow miles, and then a warming up mile in about 2:10. After this he is given a thorough rubbing and is cooled out.

Dan, like almost every other horse in the professional ranks, rejoices in a stable name, his being Dennis. It is one of the peculiarities of racing horses that no matter what high-toned name they may go under on the card, one may be pretty sure they are Pat or Jim or Dennis or Pete to the men in the stable who care for them.

Dan Patch is a remarkably good traveler and will lie down in his box car, which is a rare thing for a horse to do; they invariably stand during a journey. He seldom seems tired after a long trip, and comes out as fresh as a daisy. Another good feature about this remarkable pacer is that he never seems to mind a change in tracks. He will go to a new track and reel off as fast a mile as if he had been traveling it weeks at a time. Nothing about the locality bothers him and indeed he is what might be called a blasé horse. He has toured the country so much, has received so many ovations and has become accustomed to vast crowds and many changes of scenes that all tracks look alike to him now.

In the stable he is kind and affectionate. He never nips a groom on the back just for fun and never strikes out just to show he has a lively pair of heels. He is aristocratic and will not notice strangers, but is fond of his trainer and rubbers.

Aside from sweet, clean bedding his stall is lined with either straw matting, made as only a stableman can make it with the wavey-topped straw standing up and neatly plaited, or he has blankets hung up if there is not time or the conveniences to make the matting.

It was the intention of one of the local photographers to take a picture of Dan Patch yesterday, but Mr. McHenry and the rubber refused to let their precious charge venture out of the stable on account of the severe wind. It was too piercing and there was a danger that the horse might have a chill. He was comfortably blanketed and stood in his box and contentedly munched his fragrant hay, guarded by his rubbers from the least draft, they even going so far as to only allow a person to enter by one door, as when the other was open the wind blew directly in, dust and smoke laden. Out on the track in all the fury of the fall gale were the poor trash of horseflesh hooked up to the heavy drags making the track smooth and speedy for the aristocratic equine comfortably stabled and waited upon but a few feet away.

That story only encouraged more of the curious to come to the fairgrounds to see the horse—which one could do in those days merely by walking up to his stall. Landerbaugh himself couldn't handle the crush of the visitors, who reached in to pet Dan and sometimes opened the side door to the barn, admitting the dreaded cross-draft. The next day, after he had worked the horse four miles, McHenry announced that he was barring tourists—but that anyone who wanted to see Dan Patch would find him on exhibit in front of the grandstand on both afternoons remaining before his race day starting at three o'clock. "I do this because we want to satisfy everyone's natural curiosity without injuring the horse by having people bother him in his stall," said McHenry to the assembled scribes. "I fear that if we exhibit him there he will be liable to colds and nervousness and you know a horse that we want to get every ounce of speed out of now that he is on edge to make a lasting world's record cannot be given any chance to fail. I want to impress again on everybody the fact that we are not jealous of Dan Patch, and we want everyone to see him, but we do want to protect the good horse all we can."

On September 10, about 24,000 people poured into the grandstand to see Dan's time trial. It was the biggest crowd he had ever drawn, and the biggest ever at the then-sixty-one-year-old fair. If attendance was boosted somewhat by the other fair attractions, it was also likely diminished by heavy rains that had come the night before and increased the possibility of a postponement. Around noontime, after taking one of his other horses on an exploratory trip around the oval, McHenry did in fact call off the performance, saying he would try again the next day. Oddly, no one seems to have complained, perhaps because the rest of the races went as scheduled, and the paying customers got to see the second-biggest celebrity on the Grand Circuit, the blind trotter Rhythmic. Guided by what his trainer Scott Hudson insisted at the time was a heightened sense of hearing that made him even safer to drive than a normal horse, Rhythmic won the $5,000 Woodruff Stakes that day in straight heats.

More than 43,000 people came to the fair the next day, a sunny Thursday, and about 30,000 of them passed through the racetrack's turnstiles. The *Horse Review* said every seat was claimed by noon, four hours before Dan's trial, and that thousands had taken what was then the unusual step of spilling into the infield. "Every available space from the lower to the far upper turn was occupied by a patient and tireless mass of humanity," the *Review* noted. "Boxes, chairs, benches and in fact any old thing that could be rented to obtain a better view was secured by the more fortunate ones." Though Dan Patch was not formally introduced until he came out for his time trial, the crowd greeted his three unannounced appearances for warm-up miles with "tremendous ovations."

Yet after all the anticipation and hoopla, the mile itself was a letdown. The track was "smooth as a billiard table," said the *Post-Standard*, but because it had baked dry in the sun following heavy rain, the clay surface was also as hard as a cue ball. McHenry blamed the "cement" strip, and the wind, for Dan's "slowing in the stretch" (the final quarter time was :30 ¼; he didn't slow much) and finishing in 2:00 ¼, a second off the record. Dan was cheered anyway, and the fair promoters, thrilled with the gate receipts, considered the day an historic success.

Not everyone was pleased with the direction of Dan's career, though. A core group of racing purists despaired at him ever returning to the American turf as God intended it, with horses racing against each other. These self-styled guardians of sport, many of whom were the sort who could barely tolerate pacers to begin with, criticized McHenry and Sturges for diminishing harness racing in order to create a kind of touring vaudeville act and rake in the cash. They were absolutely right about that, of course. But the time trials would not have continued if they hadn't been so popular. No conventional horse race ever drew 30,000 to the New York State Fair.

Besides, who was Dan Patch supposed to race? The second and third best pacers in the sport, Anaconda and Prince Alert, were both having an inglorious, up-and-down year in 1902, taking turns beating each other in match races. Mart Demarest, the Prince's trainer, was also fending off accusations that his horse was a "hop-head" whose success was attributable to heroin and cocaine. He denied it flatly, saying, "The only stimulant I give him is whiskey and that was only after races when he was thoroughly exhausted."

Sturges called off the match race between Prince Alert and Dan Patch that had been scheduled for Empire City on September 16, before Dan even went his mile at Syracuse. His horse, he said, would instead time-trial at the Yonkers track. (Prince Alert took the week off.) The ostensible reason for the cancellation was that Sturges and McHenry would not deign to race against a hobbled pacer. But Dan, whose undefeated status could be lost with just one misstep, had little to gain and plenty to lose in such a showdown.

Empire City, located about two and a half miles above the Bronx border, was, along with Brighton Beach, considered a New York City track, and McHenry, who was always showcasing Dan for potential buyers, wanted to impress the distinguished owners as well as the important newspapers that were sure to be part of the scene. The prompter he hired that afternoon was a well-known Thoroughbred named Carrie Nation, aka the Kansas Cyclone: the *Brooklyn Eagle* called her "the classiest pacesetter ever to step on a trotting track." It was with Empire City in mind, moreover, that he had, a week earlier at Syracuse, taken the unusual step of bringing Dan Patch back onto the track, unannounced, thirty minutes after his exhibition mile for additional work. With the crowd filing out and few people noticing, McHenry drove Dan a second mile that afternoon, in 2:06 ⅙, "with a view," said the *Review*, "toward keying him up to maintain the high rate of speed necessary to break the world's record at the Empire track this week."

It wasn't just about "keying him up," though. McHenry was also concerned about Dan's continued pulling—or more precisely, his leaning forward against the bit—and he wanted to see how giving the horse extra work might affect that worsening habit. The answer turned out to be not much. Conditions were ideal at Empire City on Tuesday, September 16, but Dan got away only moderately fast, reaching the quarter pole in :30 ¼ seconds. "He was not moving in his usual easy, machine-like fashion," said the *Eagle*, and indeed, before he reached the half-mile marker Dan lost his gait completely and, for the second time in twenty-three days, broke into a unsightly gallop. An embarrassed McHenry pulled him up immediately, guided him back to the barn area, and, as he had after the break at Readville, sent word that the two of them would try again in half an hour. This time, however, horse and driver did not redeem themselves: Dan's second mile went in the shockingly slow time of 2:02 ¼. Said the *Eagle*: "The old gentleman with the hourglass proved invincible."

The auction-pool sellers at Empire City were not surprised; doubting Dan's sharpness, they made him 4–5 to finish in two minutes or above. But McHenry seemed shocked by the slow miles, and the next-morning headlines—"Dan Patch Fails" (the *Eagle*), "Dan Patch Has No Excuse" (the *Chicago Tribune*), and "Old Father Time Proves Too Much for Dan Patch" (the *Atlanta Constitution*)—injured his ego. He first tried to blame the track, which had just been resurfaced, and which he insisted was not sufficiently "settled." Then, seeming to forget his point about the faulty surface, he said that he and Dan Patch would remain at Empire City until Friday, September 19, when they would try again. When it poured rain that day, McHenry said they would go the next. He was getting desperate. The season was growing short, and there were few tracks left on the Grand Circuit schedule as fast as Empire City; his chances of breaking Star Pointer's record in 1902 were slipping away. When Saturday came and the track remained, as the *New York Times* said, "utter slush," his spirits sunk further still. At 1:00 p.m. racing secretary Horace Wilson trudged around the slimy oval in rubber boots, then said there could be no racing until at least three o'clock, when the track might be borderline navigable, but hardly fast. McHenry, with a heavy sigh, told his grooms to pack up and prepare to move on. Encountering some reporters on the way out, he did his usual spinning ("Dan Patch had reached a peak on Thursday. If we could have raced then, I believe we could have broken the record"), but his excuses, to some ears at least, were sounding tired.

Some sports fans—even then an extremely fickle lot—were wondering if his horse wasn't getting worn out, too. Or maybe Dan Patch simply wasn't as good as he was being made out to be. During the last few weeks he had looked like a very good horse, but perhaps not the fastest one ever. Yet the Dan Patch apologists always outnumbered the doubters, and some of them said their hero was still too young to be doing all that was being asked of him. At six, an age when most successful racehorses of today would have been long since retired, Dan, they insisted, was still several years from his athletic prime. (They happened to be right.)

McHenry, though, was not as patient as some of his supporters. He wanted to hang the world record on Dan Patch, as they said in those days, then get him sold, as soon as possible. He did not think Dan had reached his limit. Yet he knew from hard experience that racehorses don't keep getting better forever—that they tend, in fact, one way or another, to break your heart.

Even a son of a bitch like McHenry had a breakable heart.

McHenry wanted to restore Dan's luster with a cranking-good mile, but he wasn't sure what his next move should be. From Empire City, the Grand Circuit swung west, finishing out the season at a succession of relatively rough-hewn racetracks where records were less likely. His best option, McHenry decided, was to break away from the Circuit and visit a newish and generally overlooked meet conducted by the New England Breeders Association. The purses were small, the trappings second-rate, but the timing and location were perfect: the meet took place the following week, in Readville,

Massachusetts, over the track where Dan had recently had a mile in 2:00 ¼ and where Star Pointer had set his record. McHenry wired the Breeders Association (run by J. Malcolm Forbes and a bunch of his fellow Brahmins) and told them that he and Dan would come for free if they would make sure the surface was in prime condition—and promise not to advertise or even leak the secret of the attempt in advance. If this move worked and Dan broke the record, McHenry reckoned, the world would find out about it; if it didn't, the fewer witnesses the better.

Lacking the best horses and falling, as it did, only a month after the Grand Circuit had roared through Boston, the Breeders meet, in its sixth year, teetered on the brink of extinction. Only about 3,500 diehards were present on September 23—a clear, warm and windless Tuesday—to exclaim with disbelief as the starting judge announced to the crowd that Dan Patch was in the house, and would be going against Star Pointer's record that afternoon. At the request of a *Horse Review* photographer who probably could not believe his good fortune at having shown up that day, McHenry posed for a picture, supposedly inspecting the track in dress shirt, high celluloid collar, necktie, vest, and derby—in other words, the way most horsemen, and spectators, dressed for a day at the races. He looks confident and relaxed in the photo, but perhaps he was simply relieved. For after Dan's first, slow warm-up mile, about an hour earlier, he had driven the horse straight to the shoeing shed and told Ren Nash, who had abandoned his Grand Circuit clients to be with McHenry that day, that it was time for a radical adjustment.

"This horse is pulling me a ton," McHenry said. "He's hitting the wheels and sprawling all over the track."

Remembering the afternoon in an article he wrote for the *Review* ten years later, Nash said, "I can take no credit for the shoeing of Dan on that occasion," because McHenry knew exactly what he wanted. According to Nash, McHenry spoke the language of a shoer. "Let's try him with a sharp calk running from the inside toe around the outside of the shoe to the outside heels, as close as you can have the calk," McHenry told Nash. "Then calk his shoes in front and make them sharp; also shorten his toes as much as you can and leave the heels alone."

"The great horse," said Nash, "was shod according to orders."

Swinging into the sulky for the second warm-up mile, McHenry felt an immediate difference: Dan, because of the new and severe angle, was walking rather gingerly, but when asked for speed he found his balance and was no longer pulling on the bit. When the time trial began at exactly four o'clock, the Wizard drove him aggressively. He reached the quarter in :30 ¼ and, said the *American Horse Breeder,* "with a bounding runner at his heel the half came in :59 ¾." Normally, as we have seen, the posting of Dan's fractional times caused the crowd to break out in cheers (or on rare occasions, sighs of disappointment), but the small group of mostly knowledgeable observers at Readville provided a backdrop of sheer silence. Maybe they still couldn't believe that Dan Patch had showed up unannounced, but watching that race must have been a strange experience, like seeing Sarah Bernhardt perform Hamlet before an empty house. The *Horse Breeder* correspondent noted that you could hear "a thousand voices saying 'up,'" the word serious fans said in those days to indicate they were clicking their stopwatches at a particular quarter-mile juncture. Beyond that there was only the pounding of hooves, the cracking of whips, and the shouts of the drivers urging their horses onward.

As Dan reached the three-quarters in 1:29 ¼, the record was in sight and McHenry went to work, said the *Breeder,* "driving one of those terrific finishes which years ago gave him the name of 'the Demon Driver.'" Finally the oddly silent crowd did begin to buzz with excitement—but was immediately told to hush by cranky starting judge Frank Walker, who ordered the assembled to "Keep quiet and give the horse a chance!"—as if it was silence that spurred a horse onward. Most obeyed, though; only a smattering of applause greeted Dan Patch as he passed below the finish wire—in 1:59 ¼.

That was Star Pointer's fabled time, an historic mile, but the crowd didn't know how to react. Did tying the record mean that Dan had succeeded or failed? What's more, many of those saying "up" in the stands had caught the race on unofficial stopwatches in 1:59 or faster. McHenry, back in the stable area, jumped off the sulky in a rage: he too had timed the mile in 1:59 flat. (One of the writers' watches said 1:58.) For about ten minutes boos and catcalls rained down upon the infield judges' stand, where the four official timers (one was Malcolm Forbes) sat. On its editorial page that week, the *Review* would say that Dan's true time was 1:59 and ⅕—and thus a record. Most stopwatches made since about 1880 showed fifths, not quarters, the *Review* noted, while lamenting that such an important mile was not measured "the modern way." In fact, as a subsequent inquiry would show, three of the four official timers at Readville that day were using watches that measured in fifths, and they all timed the mile in 1:59 ⅕. Still, though there was no rule that said a race must be timed in quarter seconds, the National Trotting Association, the governing body with jurisdiction in Massachusetts, stubbornly stuck with tradition, rounded the fraction up to a quarter, and declared that Dan and Star Pointer now shared the world record.

Another controversy soon cropped up. The *American Sportsman* pointed out that Dan's time at Readville technically should not count at all. According to NTA rule 132, that journal noted, if a horse "starts to beat a specific time and fails," the mile becomes a "losing performance" and thus "shall not constitute a [personal] record."

Poppycock, said Henry White in the *Tribune:* "It is universally admitted that Dan Patch is the best pacing stallion ever to look through a bridle." The *Review* agreed, and to illustrate its point, supplied a charming anecdote about a "darky" who is "jailed without a warrant for stealing a chicken." When his lawyer assures him that the authorities can't do such a thing, the darky notes that "in p'int of fact, boss, dey hab alreddy dun it." The *Review* reminded readers that Dan "hab alreddy dun it" and "that fact will be accepted the world over."

Perhaps only Ren Nash was completely satisfied with the outcome of the Readville Breeders Association meet, for it was there that Dan Patch's shoeing problems were finally solved, and the horse cured of his lunging. "He did not sprawl at all, or hit his arms [*sic*] or knees from that day on," Nash wrote. "No one ever experimented further with the stallion's shoeing."

The western swing that ended Dan's 1902 season was in one regard exactly what McHenry and Sturges wanted—a month-long publicity bonanza that seemed custom-made to showcase the horse to potential buyers. Everywhere they went, newspapers fanned anticipation for Dan Patch with front-page advance stories, then followed up with worshipful accounts of Dan's time trials. News about President Roosevelt (who was then intervening to end the previously mentioned Pennsylvania coal miners' strike) and the first sighting of a mountain gorilla by a non-African explorer received secondary play when Dan came to town.

But on the whole the tour was troubling to the trainer and the owner, for unless they actually smoked out a buyer on the swing through Ohio, Indiana, Tennessee, and Missouri, the sojourn would not make financial sense. Truth be told, they had not been able to make all that much with the traveling Dan show even in the Northeast, where track managers could be convinced to spend for a major attraction. (They had collected the $5,000 jackpot they demanded only once, at Providence.) In the Midwest, McHenry and Sturges found themselves among promoters too parsimonious, or too poor, to pay appearance fees; negotiating on the fly, they had to cobble together whatever deals they could, sometimes agreeing to be paid only if they broke the record, once taking only a (small) percentage of the gate, and once or twice performing solely for the chance to set a record and increase their horse's value. In the end, when their expenses were figured in, Sturges and McHenry almost certainly lost money on the fall dates.

Their basic problem was that they were trying to make serious money with a horse in an age when horses did not make serious money. It may seem impressive that Dan and his contemporaries were racing for purses of three thousand 1902 dollars—until one looks closer and sees that (a) such sums were available rarely, and only to the best animals, and (b) virtually all purse money was generated by entry and starting fees. Harness racing may have been America's number-one sport, but it was basically a matter of the masses watching rich sportsmen (on the Grand Circuit) or proud farmers (at the fairs) compete for bragging rights and their own pooled cash. Scandalously large amounts changed hands in the auction pools, but that revenue did not circulate through the sport proper. It would be about four decades before pari-mutuel betting would allow track managers to skim the gambling take for (among other things) purse money. And more than ninety years would pass before corporate sponsorship would morph the Run for the Roses into Yum Foods Presents the $2 Million Kentucky Derby. In Dan Patch's day there was no system in place for producing windfall purses, or any kind of fund promoters could dip into to pay an appearance fee.

Sturges and McHenry had bought Dan Patch in order to sell him, and they had done a fine job of burnishing his reputation. But they still faced one considerable challenge: the high end of the harness horse market tended to want trotters only. Rich men and pacers didn't mix. The kind of buyer who could give Sturges and McHenry a profit on their $20,000 purchase seemed hard to come by.

Except that M. W. Savage was practically stalking them that fall. One of the few men in America who would pay high-class trotter money for a pacing horse showed up in Cincinnati, the first stop on Dan's western tour. He was dressed conspicuously, in a starched white shirt, a long, dark frock coat, and a black derby—the grooms, who noticed him lurking around Dan's stall on the backstretch at Oakley Park, had started calling him "the Parson." Savage spoke to no one, but he was clearly on a mission to observe Dan Patch's daily routine, and more than that, to see firsthand the excitement that the horse caused. The Parson must have been impressed on October 2, when, in the kind of promotional flourish that the western tracks like Oakley weren't known for, Dan was brought out along with Cresceus, the closest thing to his equal among trotters, and the two champions went a half mile at some speed, nose to nose, exhibiting their contrasting gaits to a wildly cheering mob. Unfortunately, it rained hard for the next couple of days, and by the time of Dan's exhibition, on October 6, a cold wind was blowing, the surface was soft, and Dan seemed to tire in the second half, finishing the mile in 2:03. That could not have sat well with the Parson, but this probably did: a crowd of some 5,000—about 40 percent more people than the Redlegs were averaging at their ballpark, the Palace of the Fans—had turned out on a raw Monday afternoon to see Dan Patch pace.

The western press loved Dan Patch, too. McHenry no longer had to keep coming up with excuses when he failed to lower the record: the media had started to do his spin-doctoring for him. "The horse was in fine condition, the track wasn't," said the *Fort Wayne* (Ind.) *Journal-Gazette,* and the *Horse Breeder* praised Dan for his "grand effort" under tough circumstances. The page-one headline in the *Decatur* (Ill.) *Herald* was simply "Cincinnati Track Was Bad." Still, McHenry couldn't resist. The 2:03 outing at Oakley Park, given the conditions, was, he said with a straight face, "the best mile of Dan Patch's career!"

The next day, October 7, Dan arrived in Terre Haute for a time trial scheduled for the following afternoon. Because this had been a last-minute booking, there was little advance publicity. Still, half a dozen men from Oxford (but not Dan Messner) had hurriedly arranged a trip downstate to see the horse who had perhaps once literally brought home their bacon. Upon arriving they went directly to his stall and later reported that Dan recognized them and whinnied. McHenry, if he'd been there at that very special moment, would likely have told them to get the fuck out of the way.

An elaborate, 128-page promotional book called *The Racing Life of Dan Patch* that Savage published in 1913 states that the pacer started at Terre Haute to beat 2:01 ¼ (presumably the track record) and finished in 2:01, which would have made the day a success. The book lies. Dan's time was given correctly, but in truth he was shooting for the 2:00 ½ track record set there by Star Pointer, and thus failed. McHenry at the time complained that the track was a quagmire, "at least two seconds slow"; Dan had to race three lanes out from the rail to find anything like decent footing and even then "his shoes cut an inch and a quarter into the clay." Over the next few days, columnists would enhance the trainer's excuses, writing that Dan's shoes dug into the mean old Terre Haute track an inch and a half, then two inches. Any sort of failure had to be explained away at a time when Dan Patch's name was becoming a synonym for speed. On the day after that Terre Haute trial, in an account of the University of Michigan football team beating Michigan Agricultural 119–0, the *Chicago Tribune* wrote that "Coach Fielding Yost's Wolverines went down the field today at a Dan Patch gait."

McHenry thought he and Dan should try again at Terre Haute, a fast track when it was dry and only slightly yielding. They hung around the better part of a windy week waiting for ideal conditions before finally giving up and setting out for Davenport on Monday, October 13. By the time they arrived, late that same night, the town buzzed with anticipation for the time trial on the sixteenth. "Dan Patch day will be a day of days in Davenport," said the *Republican,* which reported that "the business houses of the city" would close down between two and five o'clock on Thursday afternoon "in order to allow not only proprietors but employees to see the great Dan Patch attempt to break the world's pacing record."

It turned out to be yet another one of those you-had-to-be-there-and-see-the-terrible-conditions-to-truly-appreciate-it miles. Dan, "with a running mate plunging along abreast," said the *Tribune,* paced in 2:01, not the stuff of headlines, perhaps, but more than a second below the track record, and the fastest mile ever paced west of the Mississippi. "A remarkable mile," noted the *Decatur* (Ill.) *Herald.* And the *Humeston* (Iowa) *New Era* said, "He proved himself the king of the pacers."

Around this time the Parson at last emerged from the shadows and awkwardly introduced himself to McHenry and Sturges, whom he had been rather obviously spying on—and who had been looking back at him, wondering when the man they had long since identified as Will Savage was going to step up and say something—for several weeks. The trigger may have been the cheers of the Davenport fans. For it was Iowa that Savage (though Ohio-born) considered his native ground. He had skulked out of West Branch around 1885 as a failure, and now he had the means to buy Dan Patch and make a statement to those Hawkeye hicks. No correspondence concerning the inner workings of the sale has ever surfaced, but we do know that after Davenport, negotiations began to gather momentum. Savage, in one of the subsequent propaganda pieces, referred to "the several proposals and counter-proposals concerning Dan Patch" that continued over the next few weeks.

McHenry and Sturges had no choice but to keep their show going as Dan traveled on to Memphis and the final Grand Circuit meet of the year. It helped their negotiating position to appear to be

moving forward as planned, keeping their eyes on the prize. Still, by
the end of October their swing west had become a slog. The Memphis track, which had been remodeled with great fanfare by Seth
Griffin—the same renowned track architect who had built a one-
mile training oval on Savage's farm a few months before at a cost of
$18,000—was, to the surprise of the racing world, something of a
disaster, a full two seconds slower than it had been before the refurbishing, due to a new racing surface that hadn't yet coalesced. Dan
tried a mile at what was formally known as Billings Park on October
24, but though he came home proudly, with his head high in the air,
and nosed out his Thoroughbred prompter at the wire, the final time
was ho-hum: 2:01.

With the meet still in progress four days later, on Tuesday, the
twenty-eighth, McHenry and Dan tried again to beat the record, only
to wind up going half a second slower. Again, the excuses of wind and
cold weather were trotted out by fawning turf writers before McHenry
could say the words himself. Yet with virtually the entire harness racing world assembled at Memphis for the season's climactic meet, the
trainer was acutely embarrassed by Dan's ordinary clockings, just as
he had been at Empire City. When his hobbled archrival Prince Alert
stole the spotlight—first by winning a weird half-mile match race
against Sir Albert S. in :57 ¼ (the fastest time ever recorded for that
eccentric distance), then, several days later, going a mile in 2:00 ¾,
the fastest time of the meet—McHenry decided to try one final time,
on November 1, the last day of the 1902 Grand Circuit season. To
do this he had to cancel an appearance he had scheduled in Minneapolis around that same date. It would have been nice to display the
horse in Savage's backyard—it might have even brought the sale to a
head—but leaving Memphis and traveling that far northwest, to the
margins of the harness-racing world, might also have looked like he
was running away from the main stage in Tennessee, and McHenry
had no reason to retreat. He still believed that Dan could break the
record that fall, if conditions were conducive. At Memphis on All
Saints' Day the track was dry and fast, and he got Dan off to a quick
start, but, said the *Chicago Tribune*, "the pacer was forced to breast a
gale" in the backstretch—and he could do no better than equal Prince
Alert's 2:00 ¾. This inspired the Prince's owner, Providence brewer

James Hanley, to challenge Sturges to a match race, at $20,000 a side. The harness world drew a sharp breath of anticipation.

Sturges withheld a response. A more pessimistic man than McHenry, he believed that Dan had reached his limit and would probably never beat Star Pointer's mark. It was time, he felt, to cash in; it was not time for Dan to venture back into horseracing. Savage had offered $60,000 for Dan, which would be the most ever paid for a pacer; Sturges had been holding out for $120,000, and thought his price reasonable because J. Malcolm Forbes had paid Leland Stanford $125,000 for Arion, no better than a B-plus trotter, in 1892. Sturges, a few weeks before, had been willing to walk away from Savage's offer. But after Memphis he was worried that his horse was wearing out—and that he almost certainly would never again find a buyer as eager as Savage.

McHenry was just as interested in selling, but only because he was as always in tight financial straits. Still, to get the maximum price he thought the best strategy was to stay cool, to seem aloof, and to keep Dan in action. He convinced Sturges to try one more time for the elusive sub-1:59 ¼ clocking in Kansas City. Previous accounts of Dan Patch's career do not mention this stop, which was rendered abortive by a bizarre incident. McHenry and Sturges for some reason came to Kansas City without a Thoroughbred prompter; they had planned to keep Dan there for the winter, under the care of Kansas trainer Dick Benson, and they had figured they would buy a local runner and leave that horse with Benson, too, until the following spring. But McHenry couldn't find a suitable animal at the right price; he felt the local boys were all trying to gouge his well-heeled eastern client. So he and Sturges arranged a one-day hire of a jumper, probably a retired Thoroughbred racehorse, who belonged to a wealthy young local boy. All went well until the half-mile pole—where the prompter abruptly collapsed and died. Dan startled and pulled up, almost injuring himself in the process. There would be no more time-trialing that day, or that season.

A few weeks later Sturges told that story to a writer from the *Horse Review,* presenting it as a humorous tale of life on the road. He had another good tidbit for the reporter: one night in early

November while he and McHenry were in Chicago, walking back
to their hotel after a late dinner, they ran into . . . Dan Messner. It
must have been an awkward encounter for the storekeep who had
watched his horse's legend grow exponentially that summer, and
whose other horses, including a couple of Dan Patch colts, were
then in the process of failing to pan out. Sturges and McHenry
greeted him with backslaps and boisterous good cheer but moved
on quickly, without mentioning that they had just struck a deal for
Dan Patch with M. W. Savage.

It was a deal in principle at that point. Their smiles would fade
before the papers were signed. Savage, sensing their eagerness to
sell, and perhaps their lack of options, said at the last minute that
he wanted to rework a few details. His terms were now $40,000
in cash and the other $20,000 in breeding rights to Dan Patch. No
contract for the sale of the horse from Sturges to Savage has ever
surfaced, so we don't know how many stud services the $20,000
amounted to, nor do we know how strongly Sturges objected to
the last-minute switch. But by giving him, in this backhanded way,
a continuing financial interest in Dan Patch (the value of his breeding shares rose with the overall value of the horse), Savage ensured
that Sturges would keep mum when he announced the sale as a
straight-up $60,000 deal. The turf scribes, for their part, never
questioned the number, which appeared in hundreds of newspapers around the world.

If $60,000 was a misleading price, it was also, from Savage's
perspective, the perfect one: high enough to make headlines but
low enough to show the Minnesota millionaire as a font of prairie
prudence, a role in which he reveled. Savage liked to say that Dan
Patch was the cheapest horse he ever bought, owing to the tremendous promotional value he derived from the pacer. A month
after the sale he said that he had already received "$20,000 in free
publicity from the purchase of Dan Patch," and the papers would
run with that plucked-from-the-air number, too, because it made
for a good story.

Yet as much as he enjoyed being P. T. Barnum–ish, Savage also
liked to pretend that he was a beyond-wealthy industrialist like
Charles Alfred Pillsbury, the Minneapolis flour miller, or James

J. Hill, the St. Paul railroad man, a cultured capitalist living his dream. He would often pooh-pooh "the popular notion [created by him] that I bought the horse in a sudden rash impulse when I was in an 'advertising' frame of mind." When in this messianic mood he would say, "I have been born with desire to raise high class harness horses" and own "a first-class stock farm"—and no one should ever make the mistake of suggesting that he would bend those noble motives to make a buck.

M. W. Savage was so intent on projecting an image, he sometimes lost track of what it was.

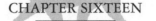

CHAPTER SIXTEEN

ARE HORSES JEALOUS? A. B. Powell, the veteran trainer of horses, who after two patient years actually taught two horses to stand up on their hind legs and box with gloves on, declares that not only are horses jealous but that it was the outcome of an incident arising from the feelings which the green-eyed monster is reputed to inspire which led him to believe he had found a pair of boxing horses.

—*Horse Review,* March 31, 1903

A NEW YEAR, A fresh newspaper, and snapping open the *Minneapolis Journal* on Thursday morning, January 1, 1903, the citizens of the Mill City found the sports world in its usual comforting state of turmoil and flux. The Northwestern Athletic Conference was upping the minimum distance a team needed to advance a football in a given series of downs from five yards to ten (they were sticking with three downs, though); the valet for the well-known Thoroughbred jockey Ted Sloan, the mysterious and mono-monikered Carloz, had been arrested in London for lifting his employer's "$425 diamond sleeve links," and . . . whoa, now (says the *Journal* reader), nothing comforting about this: "Dan Patch, the champion pacing stallion, recently purchased by W. M. [sic] Savage of this city, will arrive in Minneapolis from Kansas City Saturday morning over the Omaha Road. The horse will have a [railroad] car to himself."

For the average Minneapolitan, this was the kind of information that required action. Either one simply had to be there, down by the depot on the Mississippi River, at the end of Nicollet and Hennepin Avenues, craning one's neck, shouting huzzah, and generally buying into the idea that a horse who had never before even visited your town was suddenly its shining hope and emblem—or you wanted to be as far away as possible from what was sure to be a massive traffic jam in an era when traffic shat, peed, and eventually, if gridlock persisted, started kicking.

Many more people than the police expected chose the first option and trudged through the muddy streets of Minneapolis to greet the horse on the zero-degree morning of Saturday, January 5. It was hard to count them all, hanging, in the preferred style of the hoi polloi, off bridges and trestles, perching on ledges and climbing up the facades of buildings for a better look—or standing hip-deep in snow in the railyard and waiting to storm the well-guarded American Express car pregnant with what the *Journal* had called "the mahogany-bay wonder." According to some estimates, three thousand people welcomed Dan Patch to Minneapolis, a most impressive turnout considering the temperature, and that the city's major ethnic groups are noted for their emotional reserve. When the boxcar door at last rumbled open and the assembled glimpsed the animal—"so covered up in blankets," said the *Journal,* "that only a vague idea could be secured of his points"—the crowd "whooped then surged forward." The police moved in, swinging clubs, while the *Journal*'s Newsboy Band played.

In the following days, some journalists writing about the wild reception would see it as proof that, despite all the flap about the internal combustion engine, the horse hadn't been swept into the dustbin of history quite yet. The *Horse Review* asked, "Would thousands have turned out to cheer an automobile?"

The question was cleverly framed, but moot. The horse was doomed. In 1903, 300 out of Minneapolis's 200,000 citizens owned motor-driven vehicles, but the number of "automobilists" was exploding. The city sounded—and smelled—different than it had the year before. Newspapers no longer treated cars as curiosities: stories about duster-clad dentists and their wives driving to Chicago in horseless carriages, once a staple of the *Journal*'s front page, had receded into the sports section, on their way out the back door of the paper. At the state fair the year before, horses had to share the track with car races. Within a decade, the daredevil driver Barney Oldfield would race against an airplane at the Hamline fairgrounds. By 1949, racehorses, an embarrassing reminder of olden times, would no longer be invited to the fair.

Still, on January 5, 1903, the apologists for *Equus caballus* could be forgiven their optimism, for the inevitable had not quite happened yet: Henry Ford was six months from filing incorporation papers, the Wright Brothers were eleven months out of Kitty Hawk, and New York was a full five years from the day when a reporter could call the 120,000 horses still living in the city "an economic burden, an affront to cleanliness and a terrible tax upon human life." Dan Patch could still be celebrated as both an evolutionary leap and a symbol of his ubiquitous and vital ilk. He could also be appreciated as an individual, what former New Jersey governor Jim McGreevey might call "an equine American"—a rare example, perhaps the only example ever, of a pop culture hero who outdid his own hype.

For if the masses projected onto Dan Patch their own fantasies, values, and ideals, he did nothing to contradict, and everything to justify, their faith. Dan Patch was extraordinarily fast, handsome, smart, hardworking, self-motivated, and trusting of human beings. He did truly like to have his picture taken. And while he did not actually count the house at the places where he appeared, he did look back at the people who had paid money and traveled far to look at him, and his gaze, for some reason, lingered.

It only made him all the more loveable, as he prepared to enter Minneapolis, that the small-minded suits who ran racing (and, it seems, every other sport, always) had recently done him wrong. In the waning days of 1902, the *Wallace Yearbook*, the official record of the harness turf, had issued a new edition that listed Dan with a personal record of 1:59 ½, thus taking the strict interpretation that his quarter-second-better performance at Readville, because it had been announced to the crowd as an attempt to beat the world record and not simply to reach it, constituted an unlistable "loss." Aw, gimme a friggin' break, said the Minneapolitans (speaking for the nation). They yearned to show that such bureaucratic hairsplitting did not sit well with them—and that Dan Patch, and not the plug-ugly, poorly bred, shoddily constructed Star Pointer, was the champion in their eyes. To make a statement, in other words, about themselves. They had love to give, this sea of Swedes, Norwegians, Germans, and Yankees that lapped up against Dan Patch's railroad car—and the horse, wisely, let them give it. The newspapermen of that era never analyzed the relationship between Dan and his public—it was too early for such psychological studies—but the turf writers sensed what the public wanted, and shaped their dispatches along the contours of that desire. Here is the *St. Paul Pioneer Press* on Dan's arrival:

"Dan Patch evidently felt very fine after his long journey, a fact probably accounted for by the assiduous care with which his attendants watch every move he makes. No young dandy of the Cashbags aristocracy ever had more attentive body servants than Dan has, while his nonchalant acceptance of every attention indicates that he has been well brought up—with proper comprehension of the divine right of kings."

It must be said that Dan that day also benefited from a communal rush of relief that had nothing to do with him being a horse or a hero. Minneapolis, over the last several months, had managed to flush out a government so corrupt that it had become a national scandal and—this is what really irked the upwardly striving Minneapolitans of 1903—a national joke. In mid-1902 about half of the city's candy stores were fronts for whorehouses; opium dens and unlicensed saloons called blind pigs operated openly along the Mississippi River; and the local gambling kingpin drew a salary as a police detective. In a much-publicized article called "The Shame of Minneapolis," written for the January 1903 issue of *McClure's Magazine*, Lincoln Steffens labeled the administration of Minneapolis mayor Albert Ames the most corrupt in the land. By the time the story appeared, though, justice was in the process of triumphing. Ames had been indicted for bribe-taking, most of his cronies had been tossed out or locked up, and though the authorities still faced the task of tracking down the former mayor (who had reportedly fled to New Hampshire, perhaps because he had the clothes for it), there was reason for optimism. A fresh administration had been elected and (on New Year's Day) sworn in, and the town felt ready to begin again. Dan Patch looked like another sign from heaven of a new and better day.

Once the mob was billyclubbed back, Dan's entrance became a surprisingly dignified and well-choreographed affair. Several dozen members of the Minneapolis Riding and Driving Club—some on horseback, others in their fancy gigs—lined either side of Nicollet Avenue, forming a corridor of unfettered capitalists through which the great pacer walked placidly, with Harry Hersey, Savage's farm manager and "house trainer," holding his lead shank. As Dan and Hersey crested the hill that led up from the station, Robert L. Jones, a wealthy fish merchant who was never seen without a silk top hat, swung his phaeton in front of Dan, the other club members fell in behind, and the parade of the privileged progressed along a route "lined with cheering crowds who sought to catch a glimpse." In what the *Minneapolis Journal* claimed was an exclusive interview with Dan Patch printed in the next day's edition, the horse was quoted as saying, "I should have preferred to enter the city quietly, without any of this brass band racket. However, I suppose that is one of the necessary evils attendant upon being the fastest harness horse in the world." The reporter did not ask Dan why he spoke like an upper-class English twit.

Conspicuously absent from the festivities was Myron E. McHenry. The trainer at that very moment was hurtling away from Minneapolis on a train bound for New York City, where he hoped to spend the winter sipping whiskey, dining at Longchamps and Luchow's, and avoiding the press and its inevitable questions about Dan's future. It was better for everyone involved that McHenry wasn't in Minneapolis that mindlessly merry morning, and that Hersey—a quietly competent horseman virtually unknown to the larger harness-racing world—was leading the horse through the canyon of cheers. Although McHenry had just signed a contract to train Dan Patch for the next two years (his reason for coming to town), he and Savage weren't easy in each other's presence. And cutesy touches like the mock interview with Dan—and the adorable urchins of the Newsboy Band—would only have made the Wizard of the Homestretch retch.

To be fair to McHenry, though, Savage was the horse owner

from hell: he combined strong opinions and big plans with scant horse sense. Specifically, he did not seem to understand that horses had physical and psychological limits beyond which pushing them was pointless, not to say cruel.

Such ignorance, astounding in a man whose fortune derived from a line of animal elixirs, still might be forgivable, or at least understandable, if Savage had come of age in a big city where the closest some slickers came to horses was the forward seat in a livery cab. But that was hardly the case. Marion Willis Savage, born March 20, 1859, was the son of a backwoods country doctor, Edward Willis Savage, who, after putting in some Civil War service, moved his growing family from Marleborough, Ohio, to West Branch, Iowa, when Marion was about four. To supplement his meager income, the elder Savage concocted homemade cures (or more likely "cures") for a variety of human ailments and sold them at the drugstore where he worked part-time as a clerk. Marion later swabbed that same counter (over which he may have served a cherry-lime rickey to young Herbert Hoover, a contemporary West Branchian), but in his teens he forked off from the family business and went into farming, concentrating, despite his poor feel for the subject, on the raising of horses. That venture ended in the late 1880s, when his land was flooded and he was forced to sell out. Next he tried combining his interest in agriculture with his father's profession and, taking a partner, started a company that produced patent medicines for animals. That didn't work out, either. Proving what Jesus said about no man being a prophet in his own land, young Savage, peddling his potions house-to-house, saw his remedies ridiculed and rejected by neighbors to whom he was the local soda jerk. When his partner absconded with the company funds one day, Savage closed up shop and took his wife, Marietta, and young son, Erle, to Minneapolis, then becoming a minor hub for pharmaceutical firms. There in 1891, with an investment of $400, he founded the International Stock Food Company and came up with a catchy slogan, "Three Feeds for One Cent." Partly because he was now an Oz-like figure, issuing tall promises of fatter pigs, healthier horses, and more shearable sheep from the upper reaches of a downtown office building—and partly because his ads were much more cunning—people were willing to believe his claims. Despite the Panic of 1893, which undid so many small businesses in Minneapolis and elsewhere, his company flourished.

Savage was a striver and a wannabe, and like most people who fit that description, he tended to think glitzy and big. Long before he needed such space, he moved his growing business into the Exhibition Building in downtown Minneapolis, a structure apparently built by someone who set out to enclose the entire outdoors, and nearly succeeded. (It had eighteen acres of floor space—750,000 square feet—most of which Savage never used.) His torrent of catalogs, pamphlets, and promotional books was graphically impressive, if at times bizarrely garish, and printed by state-of-the-art presses on paper only slightly less fine than Irish linen; they have held up well over the last century. In them one finds, between the solicitations to buy his myriad products, solicitations to believe in a self-created, shameless, and ultimately icky character named M. W. Savage. "He has the energy of a Roosevelt, the heart of a woman and the tenacity of a barnacle," says a character sketch of the boss in a fake newspaper he briefly published called the *Dan Patch Times*. (His great-granddaughter, the novelist Deborah Savage, has said, "The strangest and saddest thing is that this carefully-created, impossible-to-live-up-to image he had was also his self-image. He really bought into his own propaganda.")

His "French-style" mansion on then-prestigious Portland Avenue had cathedral-size stained glass windows and a ballroom on its third floor. He had vague but lofty political aspirations—and now the world's most famous racehorse.

Savage's plans for Dan Patch, once his deal had been struck, became Topic A in America's sports conversation that winter. Some, noting that he detested racetracks and the people who lounged about at them, said that he would use the stallion strictly for stud purposes; McHenry, in this scenario, had fallen into a cushy job as a glorified caretaker. But others, noting that Savage was a master promoter of himself and his products, predicted a long summer of time trials and other sorts of personal appearances that would advance the International Stock Food brand; Savage, they said, might even be making a moving picture of his horse!

Which would it be, stud duty or show business? The answer, needless to say if you knew Savage, was both, only more so. Dan Patch would not simply cover a bunch of mares in Minnesota; he would be the "foundation stone for a breeding industry to rival that of the Bluegrass." "My great desire," Savage said, "is to show the horse world that [Minnesotans] can breed harness racers. Many men expressed the opinion that it was suicidal to bring Dan Patch to this state. It will take time to demonstrate our theory, but when we prove it, it will mean a great deal for Minnesota."

Dan so far had been bred somewhat haphazardly to a total of perhaps a dozen mares, which was more or less in keeping with the custom of the day; some thought a little love-making soothed a stallion's savage breast and made him a better athlete. The practice probably ought to have been kept on that basis, or eliminated, if Dan Patch was expected to break Star Pointer's record, but Savage had other, bigger plans. Dan, he announced, would serve a full spring season, impregnating at least twenty-five mares between January and June—when he would begin training in earnest for several months of speed exhibitions at who-knows-how-many far-flung stops. "I have purchased Dan Patch largely to use for exhibition purposes," Savage said to one newspaper on the very same day that he had announced to another that Dan would transform the breeding industry in Minnesota. "Since there is no horse left to go against, Dan Patch will be tried out on various tracks, and Mr. McHenry believes that under favorable conditions he can reduce his record to 1:57 flat."

Savage was improvising here, or, as it's sometimes called, lying. McHenry, reading those statements in the New York newspapers, could barely contain his anger. 1:57? He had never predicted anything below 1:58 for Dan Patch, even privately, and in any case what point was there in raising the public's expectations? Now if Dan went in 1:57 ½—a clocking that sounded like something out of H. G. Wells—he might be considered a failure. But how was he going to break any records with a horse who was likely to have his edge worn smooth by several months of stud service? Off the record, McHenry told some of the writers he encountered in New York that he thought Savage was a fool for trying to "breed and circus the horse all over America."

But publicly the Wizard stayed mum. He had succeeded in getting the horse sold; his object now was to stay attached to Dan Patch, reaping whatever benefits he could for as long as possible. To do that, he had to play the game, or at least not spoil the game Savage was playing. A month-long party was in progress back in Minnesota, and he would only look bad if he popped any balloons. On January 29, more than 20,000 turned out for the Riding and Driving Club's first Winter Horse Show, in which Savage had entered Dan Patch in the "single light harness" category. The whole event—indeed, the whole Winter Horse Show—was a trumped-up excuse to celebrate Dan Patch. On the day of the "competition," all four of his rivals dropped out as if on cue, and at 4:00 p.m., the judges declared Dan the winner and festooned his bridle with numerous blue ribbons. With great ceremony they also presented Savage with the $2 first prize—a sort of rich guy's joke that the city's WASPy founding fathers never failed to find amusing. According to contemporary accounts, the horse, hitched to a sulky, was then brought outside the hall, where, with "a police squad clearing a path ahead of him," Dan "stepped majestically down the avenue, the blue streamers flying in the breeze."

It is not as if people did not need security in the ragtime era— after all, the presidents of the United States and France, the king of Italy, and Lady Patch all were assassinated between 1894 and 1901—it was just somehow not yet the moment for them to have it. More than half a century would pass before gated communities, pope-mobiles, and bulletproof presidential limos increased and emphasized the distance between the famous and their followers and ratcheted up the tension in the celebrity culture. In the winter of 1903, everyone in Minneapolis knew that Dan Patch was living in a large stall in the stable behind Savage's house at 2600 Portland Avenue. His owner soon started driving him around town and, on weekends, taking two- to four-mile jaunts, hitched to a sleigh when there was sufficient snow, with his sons Erle and Harold bundled up beside him (the cutter is on view today at the Harness Racing Museum in Goshen, New York). "Harold, who is only eight, often drove him," Savage wrote in a letter to the *Horse Review.* "Dan is so gentle that any lady could drive him through the crowded streets." When Dan stopped at intersections, people would pet him and children would run beneath his belly (one of those children was W. R. Frank, who, about forty-six years later, would produce *The Great Dan Patch*). But Dan's winter idyll didn't last long. In early April, when it came time to start his breeding season, he was loaded into a horse-drawn truck and driven ten miles south to Savage's "summer property" in a rural area then known as Hamilton.

The International Stock Farm has been called "lush," "paradisiacal," and "futuristic," but "over-the-top" or "ridiculous" would be equally serviceable descriptives. A few years before, Savage had purchased 700 acres of Minnesota River bottomland at $100 per, and begun construction of a gargantuan stable (the main part of it was another downtown exposition building that had been broken down and reassembled in the wild) that featured five oblong barns radiating, like 160-foot-long wheel spokes, from an octagonal structure ninety feet in diameter. This central building was crowned with an onion-shaped "Oriental" dome. Locals referred to it, with varying degrees of sarcasm, as the Taj Mahal. Out back of this sprawling complex, which housed 200 horses, was a one-mile training track so precisely graded and perfectly surfaced as to shame the strip at the Minnesota State Fairgrounds. A couple of years later, Savage would, at the cost of an additional $25,000, add a completely covered and fully heated half-mile track with 1,600 windows—the first of its kind ever built in the United States—so Dan Patch and his other horses could train in rain and cold weather.

To give Savage his due, the design of the place was in some ways ingenious, with the pure, cool spring water of the farm stored in the tin onion turret, which had been painted silver to reflect the heat. Strategically placed louvers allowed stale, damp air to travel upward and out of the dome, ensuring that the entire hub-and-spokes complex stayed dry and well ventilated. The whole place was kept hospital clean, and the tourists, who started coming by almost daily in the spring, commented on how well the horses were cared for by the many grooms, who always wore shirts, ties, and hats. On a bluff overlooking the Minnesota River at the farm's north end, Savage built a mansion with fluted columns and an Italian marble staircase that he christened Valley View. In fine weather, he could sit on his front porch and, with field glasses, look down upon an operation functioning with clockwork precision. Savage claimed the place cost him $500,000.

And yet the primary function wasn't to raise horses, or even to give its wealthy master a place to get away from it all. It existed to impress people. The International Stock Farm was not half so valuable to Savage as the story of the International Stock Farm, told and retold in his myriad publications, in speeches, and in letters to customers and distributors of his products. In a typical sales letter, aimed at getting just another Pennsylvania sodbuster to take a $7.50 three-month trial offer of his Three Feeds for One Cent supplement, Savage goes on for four single-spaced pages (the letter, one of thousands sent from his offices each day, is typed, not printed), attempting to disarm the rustic addressee with facts about "The Most Famous Harness Horse Breeding Farm in The Entire World." He mentions how it dazzled a recent Russian visitor who said, "The famous stables of the Czar and the stables of the Emperor of Germany are nothing when we compare them to those owned by the proprietor of Dan Patch!" He asks, rhetorically, if his correspondent "realizes the magnitude of this great farm and what it means for the horse breeding interests of the entire United States?" Self-deluded though he may be, this is a master snake oil salesman at work, speaking slickly and trading on the effect of outward appearances while providing a dizzying diversion from the product itself—which gets hardly a mention. And no wonder. Savage frequently said that "after careful study and long experimenting I select a certain combination of Roots, Herbs, Barks and Seeds," and that he used "only the highest grade of quality for every ingredient." He refused to list his ingredients for International Stock Food on the label, saying it was a secret formula. But later tests showed the stuff to be a compound of bone meal, charcoal, salt, pepper, chalk, baking soda, a flowering plant called gentian that was used as a flavoring in Moxie soda pop, and trace amounts of strychnine, or rat poison, which was then thought by some (crackpots) to have a cocainelike effect. Savage's fortune, in other words, was built upon a handful of useless, and somewhat toxic, dust that unsuspecting folks sprinkled on their animal feed. His core claim—that International Stock Food would allow animals to digest 70 to 75 percent of their food, instead of the usual 55 percent—rang false with scientists (who in a few years would begin a campaign to discredit him), but it resonated with the tens of thousands of Americans still trying to make a go of it on family farms. Some reports say that Savage's privately held company turned a profit of $4 million in 1900.

But was Savage savvy enough to think he could coexist with McHenry? It is easy to see the ways in which the trainer and the owner were opposites. Savage, a pillar of the Wesley United Methodist Church, was a teetotaler who abstained from tobacco and detested gambling. McHenry chain-smoked cigars, frequently drank to the point of illness, and, like so many of the trainers of that era, routinely rigged races so he could cash a bet.

But they were alike in some ways, too. They both appreciated women. McHenry found his in hotel bars and oyster houses and, more than once, on the arms of his soon-to-be-ex-clients. Savage projected the image of a loving husband and father (especially the latter), but he employed more than 200 women at the height of his success (out of about 300 total employees), and he took a special, and not exactly paternal, interest in them, providing afternoon and evening musical entertainments and readings at which he was usually the only male attendee. He also played host to all-girl employee picnics at the stock farm and generously took time to mentor a succession of strikingly pretty private secretaries. If he heard the rumors about his personal life, he didn't acknowledge them; he may have even thought they were good for his image. What his wife thought—about anything—we don't know; she escapes mention in all of Savage's self-published biographical sketches. He remained married to the former Marietta Bean, a plain woman not quite five feet tall, but in 1903 he did list his address as the West Hotel.

Both men were also loners. Savage and McHenry knew many

people but were known by none—which is how they liked it. Neither wanted to take advice, and both were constitutionally unable to take orders. That McHenry signed a two-year contract to continue training for Savage says something about his need for money, but it speaks even more of his deep fascination with, and inability to separate from, Dan Patch. Nothing other than this once-in-a-lifetime horse could cause him to cast his lot with a man whose presence he could barely abide. McHenry didn't give a damn that Dan Patch posed for pictures, but he did care that he was the best animal—the fastest and the smartest—he had ever seen. If you're a horseman, you don't ever walk away from a horse like that.

The two men had an agreement of sorts that Savage would make all decisions regarding Dan Patch in the winter, spring, and early summer, when the horse was in stud mode, and McHenry would be the day-to-day boss during the late-summer-to-fall time-trial season. I say an agreement "of sorts" because it was unwritten, to a great extent unspoken, and Savage violated it at will. For example, when McHenry showed up in Minnesota at the beginning of June to begin preparing Dan for the 1903 season, Savage informed him that there would be a delay in the horse's training because he had accepted "a few additional mares" (actually, fourteen additional mares) into Dan's book (at $225 per service, live foal guaranteed, a mid-level stud fee that reflected both Dan's prominence and lack of any track record as a sire). McHenry thus got a sense very quickly of how the arrangement was going to work.

When Dan Patch finally reached McHenry at his Cleveland headquarters in late June, the trainer had less than a month to prepare him for his first time trial of the year, in Columbus, on July 17. Even though Dan had been logging eight to ten slow foundation miles most days that winter, and seemed no worse for his sexed-up spring, that was not enough time. So instead of the goal at Columbus being Dan's personal record of 1:59 ½ as originally proposed, McHenry advised the management that they would instead shoot for the half-mile record of :57 ¾, set by Prince Alert the previous fall at Memphis. And so it was that Dan, with ears back and nostrils flared, sprinted halfway round the oval in exactly Prince Alert's world-record time on that Friday afternoon, serving notice that even if, as the *Horse Review* said, "he is nowhere near ready to give his best," he was still at bottom the old Dan, maybe better.

For McHenry and Savage, the Columbus experience yielded a less obvious but no less intriguing lesson: not every speed exhibition needed to be geared toward the almighty mile mark. They could mix it up. They needed to mix it up, in fact, because given Dan's travel schedule and the rough condition of some of the tracks he would be visiting (his bookings that year occasionally took him far afield of the Grand Circuit), there would be times when lowering his own record, and breaking Star Pointer's, would be out of the question. Why not give the spectators a thrill by going for a record that was venerable and impressive-sounding, yet still within reach? At the bumpy half-mile oval at Erie, Pennsylvania, where Dan stopped next on August 5, the advertised matchup was Dan versus the track record of 2:10 ¼. Dan glided around the oval twice, stopping the clock in 2:09, and everyone went home happy.

After the race McHenry told a reporter that he wanted to set all sorts of records that year. He wanted to start with the record for a pacer pulling a four-wheeled vehicle, he said, "and possibly the pacing team record if an available mate can be found for Dan." He also mentioned going after the record for a mile with a Currier & Ives–era high-wheeled sulky (2:06 ¼), and the two-mile record of 4:19 ¼. "These things may seem an arduous task," McHenry said, using the stiff speech that people of that era seemed to fall into when they addressed reporters. "But remember the greatest pacing horse the turf has known is the one that will be asked to accomplish them."

All those eccentric feats would have to wait, though. Empire City, which came up next on their schedule, may have been in Yonkers, but it was "New York" to the racing world, perhaps the single most prestigious stop on the Grand Circuit, and thus not a venue at which to dabble in odd distances or other gimmicks. Even though McHenry knew Dan was not yet in peak form—and that the first turn of the Empire City track had recently been found to be running slightly uphill—he had no choice but to get serious and attempt to shoot for at least a new personal best. On Monday, August 10, the first day of the meet, he took Dan for a public workout in 2:03

¼ and spoke of "perhaps wiping out all existing records" in his formal attempt two days later. On that Wednesday, though, he was in a different frame of mind, showing himself yet again to be like George B. McClellan, the Civil War major general who drove Lincoln crazy by waiting endlessly for ideal conditions to attack. Despite glorious weather, McHenry complained about the wind (again) and the looseness of the track, which he said was more suitable for running horses than pacers. The time trial had been scheduled for one o'clock, but he kept pushing it back, waiting for what he called "the near gale in the homestretch" to subside. Finally at 5:00 p.m. he asked the announcer to tell the 10,000 people who had come to see Dan that he was dubious about making history but he would try his best. Dan turned in an excellent mile, but—"not surprisingly given that he had only 75 days of preparation," said the *Minneapolis Journal*—"tired perceptibly" in the final stages and stopped the clock in 2:00 ¼. Still, there was no cause for despair. A reporter from the *New York Telegram* took a straw poll of trainers at Empire City that day and found them "much impressed by Dan's mile," which they tended to see as a tightener that would set him up sweetly for his next stop.

At Brighton Beach a week later, on the morning of the next time trial, McHenry did not seem to share their optimism. Just after 8:00 a.m. on August 19 he led a gaggle of reporters on an exploratory walk around the track and began making his usual excuses. "It isn't hard enough for him," he said, kicking the surface with the toe of his boot. "I don't look for a mile faster than 2:02, even if the wind should die down."

It was in fact a flukey late-summer day, cloudy and almost cold. Just after noon, a shower fell, a development that would diminish the size of the crowd; many fans, looking at the sky, guessed the finicky McHenry would cancel. And he nearly did, but at four o'clock, as the dedicated faithful sent up a rousing cheer, Dan and his two prompters appeared on the track and walked slowly up the stretch from the paddock. McHenry, the *New York Times* noted, looked like "he was anxious to have the race over."

Perhaps because they thought their chances of breaking the record were so slim, the three drivers—Doc Tanner, a trainer for the wealthy set, and the journeyman Lou Banta handled the prompters—decided to try something different that day. Instead of one Thoroughbred hanging just off Dan's right flank and the other galloping behind, Tanner took his horse in front of Dan, and Banta hovered at the pacer's side. In this configuration the lead horse, besides giving Dan something to strive toward and eventually pass, might serve as a windbreak. The danger was that Dan might feel boxed in and unable to fully extend himself. Yet from the word "Go" he seemed to enjoy the new arrangement. "With a swift, frictionless stride," said the *Lima* (Ohio) *Times-Democrat,* "he shot from the wire, and seemed determined to push his nose into the flying sulky ahead of him." Dan, to the surprise even of McHenry, seemed particularly eager that day, leaning in on the turns like a bicycle racer. "The pacing champion made the first turn so close to the pole," said the *Times,* "that his sulky wheel almost grazed the fence." The first quarter went in :29 ½, "and when the judges hung out the sign the watching crowd gave a cheer." The half-mile posting of :59 ¾ "showed Dan was crowding Father Time hard and the applause was renewed." Then came the relatively slow three-quarter time—1:29 ¼—which seemed to suggest that Dan was tiring, and turned the applause to muttering. All week long the final quarters of races had gone slowly; the track may in fact have been too loose, as McHenry suggested. In any case, said the *Horse Review,* at this point "the knowing ones among the watching thousands lost hope."

Fortunately, the three drivers didn't. Instead, the Wizard of the Homestretch got busy, using every tactic short of the whip, while Tanner, driving the lead prompter, pulled his horse wide at the top of the stretch, turned his head back toward Dan and "let loose a series of war whoops that were eventually smothered in the cheers as Dan was seen finishing like wildfire." The time, on all three of the officials' watches, was 1:59.

The *New York Times* carried the story on page one, above the fold. "The unbeaten pacing champion astonished patrons of the turf," it said, "by overcoming a combination of unfavorable conditions and covering a mile in time a quarter of a second faster than the distance ever covered by a harness horse before."

A year after the crowd had stormed onto the Brighton Beach track, calling for McHenry's head, "the grandstand was emptied," said the *Review,* "and a mob of cheering men gathered around the judges stand. Hats, canes and umbrellas were tossed skyward, and it was with difficulty that starter Walker could find quiet to proceed with his little speech. Dan trotted back to the stand . . . and wisely cocked one ear back and for the moment seemed fully conscious that he was the object of the splendid ovation."

McHenry at length was introduced to the crowd. "I was indeed surprised at today's mile," was all he could manage.

Savage had missed the race, but he announced from Minneapolis that he was "flooded" with congratulatory telegrams. He neglected to mention that most were addressed to the horse. He also threw in the news that he had just turned away a prospective buyer. W. W. Gentry, the proprietor of the semifamous Gentry's Dog and Pony Show, had offered $93,000 for Dan, Savage said. In fact, Savage and the poor man's P. T. Barnum were pals of sorts, partners in publicity seeking, and they no doubt enjoyed getting their names in the paper with a story that was probably bogus.

But anything about Dan Patch was news. The papers were starting to realize that Dan Patch was more than just a racehorse and a sports-page story. Because he had overcome so much, because he was a living testament to American ingenuity—and because he was such an American beauty—he was an American hero. The day after Dan's mile at Brighton Beach, the *Chicago Tribune* published this editorial:

DAN PATCH, CHAMPION

Dan Patch is only 7 years old, but he has thousands of friends who will be rejoiced to hear that by pacing a mile in 1:59 he has established a new world's record.

It is no wonder that Dan Patch has friends. He is not only a great horse. He is an amiable and sociable horse. He likes people. He likes to turn his head and look at people when he is on the track. He likes to listen to the band. He likes things in general. He has a good time. He is a good mixer. That's why he has friends as well as admirers. That's why, when the news goes out that Dan Patch has paced another wonderful mile, one will find that all of Dan Patch's human acquaintances are visibly, and sometimes bibulously, gratified. Dan Patch is a good fellow.

Also, Dan Patch has never lost a race. This makes him unique among pacing champions. Other champions have sometimes lost. Dan Patch has never lost. He has been on the track four years and has never seen another horse go in ahead of him.

He was first driven when he was a four-year-old. How gentle a disposition he has is shown by the fact that, although he is large and powerful, he was broke to driving by a man 74 years of age. In that first year of his track life he went a mile in 2:16 ¼. During the next year he brought his record down to 2:04 ½. In the following winter he was sold for $20,000.

At the opening of the 1902 season, therefore, he was a six-year-old possessing a 2:04 ½ record and a $20,000 label. He was destined to treble his value during the season. The way he did it was by going a public mile in 1:59 ¼. He was then bought by Mr. M. W. Savage of Minneapolis for $60,000. It is an indignity to Dan Patch to buy and sell him. There are many human beings who, if they were bought and sold, would appeal less to one's sentimental feelings. Dan Patch is only an equine being, but he is too noble a being at that to be made a commodity. However, if men will insist on making him a commodity, it is only fair to say that they ceased some time ago to do it any price under $60,000.

In the future they will not be able to do it except at a price far above $60,000. That quarter of a second which Dan Patch knocked off his record day before yesterday had a distinct money meaning. It made him a more valuable commodity than he was before.

But let us forget that he is a commodity. Let us remember only that he is the most magnificent and the most magnanimous horse that ever put on harness. May he live long and prosper.

N.B.—He is a champion that doesn't talk.

CHAPTER SEVENTEEN

Fast horses are true hard money.

—Frank Forester

THE *New York Times* said in its page-one story about Dan's record mile that the horse had earned $2,500 for his effort at Brighton Beach. Marion Savage—a student of the press, albeit not always an A student—must have found that amusing. That sum (the equivalent of about $50,000 today) may have been the bonus he received for Dan breaking the record, but it is only a fraction of what he made for taking his horse to racetracks in the summer of 1903. Although most of Savage's business records and correspondence have been lost, it appears from the available sources that the base price for a Dan Patch time trial was a guaranteed $2,500, plus a percentage of the gate, plus the bonus for setting (or sometimes merely equaling) a record of any sort. The gate receipts were especially significant: Savage sometimes negotiated for 50 percent of the admissions, and sometimes he received 100 percent of the increase above the entrance fees that had been collected on the equivalent date the year before, when Dan had not been present. In the 1903–4 period, promoters of Grand Circuit and state fair meets often wound up owing Savage $5,000 to $10,000, which, even at the low end, was more than any professional baseball player made in a year.

It is not difficult to see, then, why Savage was never seriously tempted to quit barnstorming and return to racing, where the most he could reasonably expect to realize from winning a Grand Circuit stake was $2,500, minus several hundred he would have had to pay in starting fees. Even a brief dip back into the sport's mainstream (for a winnable match race, say, or a soft free-for-all stake) could actually wind up costing him money, because if Dan ever lost—and every trainer will tell you that if your horse keeps racing, he will lose (stuff happens: ankles twist; horses drop dead in front of you; shoes fly off; protesting suffragettes swarm onto the track; you just never know)—he would perforce no longer be "The Undefeated Dan Patch," and his diminished luster would depress his drawing power and thus his appearance fee. Racing other horses wasn't worth the risk, and Savage knew it. The Parson may have proved an easy mark for a trainer with an impotent or semi-fertile stallion to unload, but for a while at least, he made a good business out of what for Sturges and McHenry had only been a sporadically successful traveling show.

Yet the money he derived from circusing and stud fees was, Savage felt, only the beginning of how he might profit from Dan Patch. The horse was still getting accustomed to the Minnesota winters when his name began appearing in advertisements for Savage's International Stock Food, aka Three Feeds for One Cent. An early advertorial in the *Horse Review*—a fake article that fades in and out of mock farmer-speak—says that Dan "commenced to take the food last November," meaning just after Savage purchased him, and now "eats it regular. It keeps him in good appetite, makes solid muscle, and is undoubtedly helpful to him in the procreative sense. It serves in toning the system, improving the digestion and purifying the blood." Left in its packing crates, it could also be stacked in such a way as to build a barrier between the horse and his admiring public—which, to Savage's chagrin, was the only way that McHenry, a stickler about what he fed his horses, ever actually used the stuff.

Savage would eventually work the horse's name as hard as he worked Dan himself. In 1903 Dan Patch White Liniment and Dan Patch Stable Disinfectant became the first products in a brand line that would grow to include Dan Patch watches, Dan Patch washing machines, Dan Patch hobby horses, Dan Patch engines, and

the Dan Patch railroad, to name just a few of the dozens of Dan
Patch products with which Savage was directly involved. Collectors of Patchiana like to describe Savage as "a man ahead of his
time" because of the vigor with which he exploited his horse. But
in many ways he was just another of the hucksters who spontane-
ously generated in an age when rising literacy rates (for the first
time, more than 90 percent of the population could be misled by
print ads) and increased personal wealth (the economist Thorstein
Veblen introduced the term "conspicuous consumption" in his
1899 book *The Theory of the Leisure Class* to describe the way
Americans were handling their excess cash) made suckers plenti-
ful. The slickest of the slicksters hid behind celebrities, who were
discovering that they could cash in on their athletic prowess or
theatric talents in new and lucrative ways. Connie Mack said he
told his Philadelphia A's to drink Coca-Cola because "I think it
is good for them." Sweet-faced John Wessels, an accomplished
Indian club swinger, age nine, lent his image to Mecca cigarettes,
as did Charles P. Blatt, "Champion Cannon Ball Catcher." Buffalo Bill Cody swore by a horse liniment called Reservitol. Ty
Cobb proclaimed his love for Ty Cobb cigarettes. Sarah Bernhardt
boosted Carter's Liver Bitters. Even Queen Victoria and Pope Leo
XIII pushed product, the former lending her name to several supposedly healthful tonics, the latter endorsing something called
Mariani Wine, a cocaine-laced patent medicine said to ease both
the temptation of onanism and the pain of menstrual cramps.

Some celebrities were doing more endorsements than they
knew. It wasn't entirely clear, based on the vague, loophole-rid-
dled Trademark Act of 1881, if anyone in that suddenly ad-mad
age owned their own name and likeness. In 1892, Bernhardt sued
an absinthe company for appropriating her image in its ads. In a
landmark 1909 case, Pittsburgh Pirates shortstop Honus Wagner
forced the American Tobacco Company to stop issuing trading
cards with his picture—either because he didn't want to promote
smoking among the younger set or because he hadn't been paid
to do so (accounts vary); his victory over Big Tobacco, in any
case, resulted in the withdrawn-from-circulation, and famously
rare, T-206 card, examples of which have sold for as much as

$2.35 million. Savage inherited a similar problem regarding the unauthorized use of the name Dan Patch. At the time he bought the horse at least five different companies were making Dan Patch cigars, and none was paying a royalty to him or anyone else for the privilege. The merchandising of Dan Patch, after all, had begun back in Oxford, where before the horse had ever raced, the local blacksmith was publicly boasting about providing Dan's shoes, and panatelas were being rolled in the pacer's honor. That was innocent, small-time stuff, though. So was most of the pirating that went on in the early years of Savage's ownership: besides the spurious stogies (all small regional brands), the Capewell Horse Nail Co. and a Cincinnati tack-trunk maker named C. W. Phellis used Dan's name without permission in homely ads that the horse journals relegated to their back pages. But later, when the horse's fame reached its zenith, Savage couldn't quash or control all of the several dozen more sophisticated manufacturers who appropriated the name for breakfast cereal, toys, and stable equipment like the Dan Patch manure spreader. No one should feel too sorry for Savage, though: what Dan Patch products he marketed himself, or managed to control, probably brought him about a million dollars annually between 1903 and 1908.

Savage prospered on several fronts during that stretch. He had the perfect business for the first few years of the twentieth century, when the horse was still king and America still encompassed many thousands of small family farms whose owners—open to the idea of scientific agriculture, but not well-off enough to afford agronomists or veterinarians—scarfed up his cheap and miraculous-sounding elixirs. But the perfect business of 1903 would be a lousy business in 1913, when the trend in America was strongly toward fewer, larger farms and the kind of transportation that did not rely on worm powder, louse killer, and harness soap. His other, equally large problem was that he spent far too much on image enhancement. He didn't just maintain a half-million-dollar horse farm, which would have been extravagance enough; he published numerous heavily illustrated, 100-plus-page books, as well as posters, catalogs, and pamphlets, mythologizing the property and his role as its master. This literature he sent, along with full-color lithographs of

Dan Patch, to anyone who asked—and after reading about them in his ads, hundreds of thousands did. Each promotional piece went out with a letter individually typed on fine cotton stationery. Savage also distributed without charge a number of ersatz newspapers (the *Dan Patch Record*) and magazines (*Illuminated World Life*) that allowed him to express his (increasingly paranoid) views about life and business (especially "the Eastern money powers") at unsettling length. Even in his best years, ego-related expenses cut deeply into his profits.

That the company was only rarely and briefly as prosperous as he pretended it was may help explain the coldhearted way he plotted Dan Patch's career. Despite Savage's occasional professions of love for the animal, Dan was basically a horse for hire. He went where the money was, and when the clients wanted him to go. After his Brighton exhibition in 1903, Dan was shipped to Readville, Massachusetts, for a time trial on August 17 (he paced in 2:00 ½ over a track that was "wet and lumpy" from several days of rain), then boarded a train for a date at the Minnesota State Fairgrounds (1,400 miles away) four days later. The horse, accompanied by his new groom, a laconic, haunted-looking Englishman named Charlie Plummer, traveled in the same car as his two prompters, taking the Boston and Maine railroad to Chicago, where in the middle of the night they changed trains for the final leg of the two-day journey. It was late in the afternoon of Sunday, August 30, when they reached the fairgrounds in Hamlin, a bit less than twenty-four hours before the time trial. Dan, the rare horse who got plenty of sleep when he traveled, appeared in good fettle, yet he still could have used some quiet time, given the next day's agenda. Instead, McHenry found that Savage had erected a large tent in one corner of the barn area ("at considerable expense," the owner told the *Horse Journal*) under which stood a freestanding box stall with "an extra roof and well-padded sides." There, Savage had announced without consulting McHenry, the horse would be "exhibited at no charge" until the time for his assault on the mile record.

A crowd was already waiting when the travel-weary trainer came upon the scene; as soon as word got out that Dan Patch had arrived, the mob swelled further. McHenry, seething at the sight of all this unnecessary hoopla, sent his grooms to head off gawkers at the stable gate. More than sixty years later an Indiana farmer named Phares White remembered how, as a boy of eleven, he was turned back, even though he had spoken up to say he had come all the way from "Dan's home in Oxford" to see his favorite horse. "Yeah, well, everybody's got some goddamn reason they think they deserve to see Dan Patch," said the grouchy swipe as he pushed little Phares away.

The next day, more than 60,000 came to the fairgrounds track, many arriving on special trains sent in from Iowa, Wisconsin, and the Dakotas. The opening-day crowd was exactly double what it had been the year before, when there had been no Dan Patch to cheer for. McHenry and Savage spent the prerace hours at their usual task of tamping down expectations, a tactic that they hoped would heighten the impact of whatever Dan might do, and generally make the customers more appreciative. It was an exquisite late-summer day; there was no breeze to call a gale, no drizzle to describe as a drencher, and so both men directed their criticism at the Hamlin track itself, which in fact had never been particularly fast and which that year had been badmouthed by other horsemen for the poor grading of its turns. "Most of the experts said Dan would do well to negotiate the distance in better than 2:02," said the *Horse Journal*. Savage, looking worried and perhaps even feeling so, said he thought a mile in 2:04 would be "commendable," given the conditions.

In the event, the mile went, without incident, in 2:00, a sisterly kiss of a clocking but a nice, round, and until recently magical number that the Minnesotans applauded enthusiastically. "Dan Patch finished so easily, that those of the spectators who had no watches did not realize they were witnessing a really sensational mile until the final time had been hung up," said the *Journal*. "Then the crowd vented its enthusiasm in long cheers." The *Minnesota Times* was more succinct: "The mob went fairly crazy." A "handsome floral horseshoe" from the Lake of the Isles Driving Club was presented to Dan by President W. B. MacLean, who said, "O, king of light harness horses, to, in a small way, show the esteem in which yourself, your owner, your driver and your caretaker are held by the people of the Northwest . . . I present you with this floral emblem, and with it our best wishes for your future success."

A handsome check for $5,500 was also presented to Savage, but he was dissatisfied, thinking that fair officials had manipulated the figures from the year before to minimize what they owed him. His feelings were probably justified. Yet rather than create a controversy that might result in his appearing greedy and strain relations with a fair board that he would need to do business with in the future, he didn't pursue his complaint. Later, the papers would report that Savage had spent the shocking sum of $3,000 to promote Dan's appearance at the fair in newspapers and on flyers—which raises the question of whether he was really a marketing genius, as his supporters claim, or some kind of advertising addict.

For all the space Savage bought in their pages, the local papers couldn't entirely hide their glee when it came to light in August 1903 that he had filed documents assigning Dan Patch a value for tax purposes of just $261. In his defense Savage noted that it was common practice in those parts to list all livestock as being worth $40 a head, no matter what the circumstances, implying that he was actually being magnanimous. He added that any further investigation by the Minneapolis assessor would be essentially moot since the horse resided on the farm (in Scott County), rather than in town (Hennepin County).

Other rich men lent their support. "The value of any horse to his owner is to a certain extent fictitious," said MacLean, the presenter of the handsome floral emblem. "I have a friend who recently bought a blooded bulldog from London. He values that dog at $1,000—you wouldn't give 25 cents for him probably." That argument did not impress Minneapolis officials, who raised the evaluation to $12,500. When Savage countered by restating his argument that the horse lived on the farm, the Scott County tax man stepped in and, to the obvious delight of reporters covering the story, raised the assessment to an unprecedented $22,500.

Meanwhile, the horse and his trainer were working their way back east. At Lima, Ohio, on September 7, Dan went against the track record of 2:04 ¼ held by his sire, and beat it by a quarter sec-

ond. Two days later he started against his own world record at Hartford, but, having traveled more than 4,000 miles in ten days, he was,
said one paper, "a trifle tired," and finished in 2:01.

On the same card that day at Charter Oak Park, in the $2,500
Hartford Futurity Pace, a three-year-old full brother to Dan
named Silver Patch was, said the *Chicago Tribune*, "hopelessly
distanced" by two fillies in the first heat and barred from further
competition. Silver Patch was owned by Dan Messner, but not
driven by John Wattles. The trainer, now seventy-five, remained
back in Oxford, where he still raced a small stable. A few days
earlier, at the Benton County Fair, he had finished fourth with a
trotting mare named Gail Smith in a race than went in 2:34. His
share of the purse had come to $1.56.

Dan Patch was tired, and McHenry knew it. While Savage was still
working the phones and telegraph wires and firing off letters in an
attempt to add dates to Dan's schedule, the trainer wanted nothing more than to coast through the rest of the 1903 season, keeping his horse sound, and picking up checks at the seven remaining stops on an itinerary that took them back to the Midwest,
then down south, where Thoroughbreds still ruled and champion
harness horses seldom ventured. It had been a long year for Dan
Patch, who had serviced thirty-nine mares that spring, traveled
thousands of miles, and set several records. McHenry, who had
seen Star Pointer fall apart when that pacer was pushed too hard
too often, took the classic horseman's view: he felt it was better to
be conservative, keep Dan within the known limits of his ability,
and survive to do it all again the following year.

The problem for both McHenry and Savage was Prince Alert.
Dan's whiskey-drinking, hobble-wearing nemesis couldn't tempt
them into a match race, but he did bedevil the owner and trainer
by duplicating, and sometimes improving upon, Dan's feats. Less
than two weeks after Dan set the half-mile track record at Lima
with a mile in 2:04, Prince Alert zipped twice around the half-
mile track at Bethlehem, Pennsylvania in 2:03 ½. Then on September 23—the same day that Dan was clocking a 1:59 ½ mile

for a crowd of 10,000 in Columbus—Prince Alert stole his thunder by lowering the world record to 1:57 at Empire City. Horsemen debated the legitimacy of that mile: not only was the Prince wearing his "Indiana pajamas," as well as enough buckles, straps, and restraining devices to stock a store called The Erotic Equine, his lead prompter had pulled a sulky rigged with a large canvas windshield. Defending Dan's honor, the *Minneapolis Journal* ran an editorial cartoon showing its hometown hero with his ornate "pacing crown" on perfectly straight. "And it doesn't need any wind shield to keep it there," the caption read. Still, all that meant little to the average fan, who read "1:57" and thought "wow."

Both McHenry and Savage wanted badly to reclaim the title of World's Fastest Horse. Neither thought Dan ought to go into the long off-season as the dethroned champion—the second-fastest horse of all time by a full two seconds. It would be bad for broodmare bookings, and for the Wizard's sleep. In late September Savage, aware of McHenry's tendency to think of the longer haul, wrote to his trainer, urging him to get the record back from Prince Alert before the end of the season—and offering him a $500 bonus if he did. The incentive was both insultingly small and unnecessary.

Before they could think about records, though, they first had a commitment to keep at Oakley Park, a painfully rutted and rocky track in Cincinnati where history-making speed was out of the question. Dan showed up on the muggy afternoon of October 1, paced a mile in 2:01 ¾, McHenry checked his dental fillings, and the caravan moved on. (Prince Alert, now brazenly duplicating Dan's every move, went a mile at Oakley the next day in the exact same time.)

Lexington was next on Dan's agenda, two weeks away. By an arrangement made months before, the advertised goal at the Breeders Track was the mile record to wagon, 2:01 ½, set by the obscure pacer Little Boy in 1901. Given that wagon racing had fallen out of favor during the Grant administration, and virtually no horses tried for that record anymore, this should have felt like a low-pressure gig. But McHenry viewed the Lexington stop with grave concern. The trainer had not liked the way Dan finished up his mile in Cincinnati, and wondered if he wasn't in a downward spiral. "When we came out for the warming up heats," McHenry would say later, "he shook his head and acted as he always does when in right trim, but by the time those miles were over he was dull, and I saw that his playfulness was a bluff and that he was really not feeling as chipper as he would make me believe. Dan is a horse that will always do his best. But between his own feelings of lassitude and the poor track, his performance that day did not suit me. I knew right then that he had been given a little too much fast work and had trained off—in other words he was a little stale."

Confident in his diagnosis, McHenry decided to make a radical move: he canceled all workouts for the next eight days, giving Dan what he later described as "a complete let-up. He was walked and handled in the usual way," McHenry explained, "but there was no harness work." The risk in doing this was considerable: Dan might lose his mental edge—his "raciness"—as well as a critical portion of his aerobic capacity. He might, after more than a week off, assume he was being put away from the season, and balk at a return to the daily workouts and the restricted racetrack routine. He was, in the end, a horse, and that was the way a lot of horses acted.

It wasn't until his warm-up miles at Lexington on the day of his time trial that McHenry felt his gambit might have worked. Dan, he said, "appeared oblivious" to the much heavier and less maneuverable wagon he was being asked to pull; he grabbed the bit smartly and moved along with true eagerness, not just the animal version of positive thinking he had displayed in Cincinnati. The first time McHenry turned him for a score to the starting point he got away flying. All things considered it was, many horsemen at the Breeders Track agreed, Dan Patch's most impressive mile so far. His time was 1:59 ¼, more than two seconds below the old wagon mark. "Dan was given a Kentucky ovation," wrote Hervey, "which means a lot to the initiated." A few days later the *Chicago Times* ran an "Open Letter from Father Time" to Dan Patch and Lou Dillon, a mare who had just become the first trotter to go a mile in 2:00. "Dear Enemies . . . ," it began.

But the season was now growing short. Mart Demarest, the

trainer of the twelve-year-old Prince Alert, took one last shot at tempting Dan Patch into a match race, saying that the horse's owner, Providence brewer James Hanley, the man behind Narragansett beer, was willing to bet Savage $25,000 man-to-man. McHenry scoffed at the offer, saying that he had nothing to prove against Demarest's horse, but that "Dan would break him in two within an eighth of a mile." Savage again responded by saying he would never put Dan on the same track with a hobbled pacer. The *Tribune*'s White used his column (at the suggestion of his drinking partner McHenry) to rekindle the rumors about Prince Alert being "a dope horse."

That was too much for Demarest, who called White to say he was tired of reading those charges. He wanted to settle the matter once and for all, he declared—then launched into a semicoherent explanation that today would bring down the wrath of PETA. "Here are the exact facts," Demarest said. "One day at Memphis I did get some extra strong coffee and some good whiskey and mixed them. The drink was administered to the animal in small doses, say a couple of ounces at a time, but it was a stimulant for a specific purpose." White didn't ask, and Demarest didn't say, what that purpose was. "You can say that not one drop of stimulant has been near the Prince this season"—you can say that, yes, but would you be correct?—"but if I thought the horse would be improved by a drink of champagne," Demarest said in conclusion, "I would see he got it!"

McHenry and Savage agreed on this much: they needed to put the subject of Prince Alert aside and assess their circumstances. The two-week Grand Circuit finale at Memphis loomed just ahead, followed, for Dan, by dates at the half-mile track in Birmingham, Alabama, and at Macon, Georgia, where he had been engaged to go against two eccentric records: one for high-wheeled sulkies, the other for two miles. If he was going to take back the mile record—the only one that mattered—before the end of the 1903 season, Memphis would be the spot.

Dan's appearance at Memphis on October 22 in some ways followed the usual script. The press was waiting at the train depot when Dan arrived a few days before the race, and when he stepped out of his boxcar the *Horse Review* said he looked "every inch the king." As part of the welcoming ceremony, racing secretary Murray Howe made a speech in which he teased McHenry about the trainer's never-ending quest for perfect conditions. "You see we imported the sky from Italy," said Howe, "and the ozone which you notice in the air was gathered and bottled in the middle of the Atlantic Ocean." A unnamed "Southern Colonel" praised Howe for the fineness of the racing surface at Memphis's Billings Park, comparing it to "a toddy mixed with just the right amounts of whiskey and water and the right amount of stirring." Then the colonel did some mixing of his own: "The track is as smooth as glass, ductile as rubber and when you walk over it feels, beneath your feet, like a piece of velvet carpet."

On the morning of the Thursday time trial, McHenry, as usual, was carping about the weather ("it's muggy") and the track ("Dan keeps catching his toes in it"). This time, though, he was just going though the motions, barely suppressing a smile as he whined. He seemed to have an unusual nervous energy, a giddiness, almost, that could not be entirely attributed to the fact that Dan Patch had warmed up brilliantly and appeared to have what horsemen then called "the feather edge."

In fact, McHenry had a secret that he could barely keep: he and Savage were parting company after the 1903 campaign. The two men had finished working out an arrangement, which probably involved a lump-sum but partial buyout of McHenry's contract, the evening before, and the trainer, brimming with relief and excitement, was wondering just when and how to drop his bombshell. He said nothing at first, but when he came back from his final warm-up mile with Dan he could no longer contain himself and mentioned, almost casually, to the scribes still milling around the stable that he and Savage had negotiated a divorce and that he would be playing out the string for the season, then leaving the harness-racing business to train Thoroughbreds. He seemed to be focused only on the fact that he was getting away from Savage, for he was, by all accounts, uncharacteristically bubbly.

In the sulky, though, he was the Wizard of old. McHenry could compartmentalize with the best of them, and that morning he put

his emotions aside and drove Dan Patch as well as any man had
ever driven a Standardbred racehorse. "The pace was so perfect,"
said the *Review,* "that Dan's nose was never more than three feet
behind the back of Scott Hudson," driving the lead prompter.
Every quarter but the third went in exactly :29, and the third went
in :29 ¼. Powering toward the finish line after McHenry had
touched him lightly with the whip, Dan had nearly run over his
two Thoroughbred prompters. "He sprinted home like a deer,"
Hervey wrote. Hats and walking sticks once again flew. While the
excited racing judges fumbled for the correct numbers to post, an
excruciating pause ensued. Finally the sign went up: 1:56 ¼.

"The cheering continued," wrote White, "long after the horse
had jogged back to the stand and McHenry had received the congratulations of hundreds of men who rushed out on the track
to shake his hand." Said the *Record,* "Mac was greeted as only
southerners can pay tribute to a popular idol. Dan turned his head
toward the stand in the old familiar way, and never did a horse
appear more conscious of the admiration bestowed on him than
did this splendid brown champion."

"The one thing to be regretted in connection with this champion," concluded the *Review,* "is the announcement that he and
Mr. McHenry are apt to part company soon."

The precipitating cause of the rupture between McHenry and
Savage is something we will never know. The polite newspapers of
the day completely avoided the subject. McHenry's drinking was
almost certainly a factor—the sheer numbing routine of it or one
especially lengthy or embarrassing binge may have finally pushed
the moralizing, teetotaling owner too far. But that's just an edu-
cated guess. McHenry sober could be an impossible man.

And yet the split was not inevitable. Savage and McHenry
would no doubt have muddled through at least another year
together, setting records and making money, if Savage had not had
an ideal replacement in the wings. Harry Cook Hersey was the
anti-Wizard: a nervous man, meek and moderate enough to be the
inspiration for the comic strip character Caspar Milquetoast. The
son of an Elmira, New York, grocer, Hersey had learned the harness-horse trade while working for a journeyman trainer named

Lou McDonald, who apparently taught him, by example, never to do anything that would excite notice. When Savage hired him as his farm manager in 1900, Hersey, then thirty-four, didn't even have a reputation for being nondescript. Not one jot of newspaper ink confirmed his existence.

Savage liked that about him, and he found refreshing the idea of a trainer who would do the bidding of the man who signed his paycheck. Savage didn't require a wizard. All he wanted was a solid horseman who would stay out of the spotlight and actually feed Dan Patch the little packets of worthless grit that supposedly made him great.

CHAPTER EIGHTEEN

Each day brings us nearer to the time when the auto will be a thing of the past, and those buildings used as repositories for automobiles will be turned into stables for fine horses.
—*American Horse Breeder*, April 19, 1904

THOSE WHO CARE ABOUT Dan Patch should, I suppose, thank God for Harry Hersey, who, in his desire to be accommodating, always answered questions about the horse fully and straightforwardly, with no self-serving spin. Asked once to divulge the secret of Dan's success, he replied that it was "due largely to the care he receives both in the winter and during his campaigns"—then launched into an earnest 2,000-word disquisition on Dan's four daily feedings, six weekly joggings, frequent brushings, careful leg-wrappings, nightly walkings, regular hoof-pickings, postworkout coolings—a laundry list that at once provides the scholar with precious, intimate knowledge and puts him to sleep. ("After he eats a meal," Hersey reveals, "the feed box is put away and washed.") The only interesting parts are the way he begins—"Dan's day starts at 5 o'clock in the morning . . . when he is fed four quarts of well-screened oats with two tablespoonfuls of International Stock Food, one of the ingredients in the champion's every meal"—and his revelation that "Dan is never left alone," by which he means not even for a fraction of a minute. Trainers, assistants, and grooms are either working him or watching him all day long, and at night he is double-guarded: "His untiring groom Charles Plummer" sleeps in the stall with him 365 days a year, Hersey says, "and the night watch goes on at 7 p.m. and remains until 6 a.m."

The size of the answer says much about the man: Hersey knew he wasn't a brilliant horseman and could never make himself into one. But he believed that if he were extraordinarily diligent, vigilant, and thorough, he might be able to hang on to his once-in-a-lifetime job, which paid about $8,000 a year and came with the perk of a modest house on the Savage property that he shared with his wife, Fannie. Hersey, like most of America, was shocked when Savage offered him the job of being Dan Patch's chief trainer and driver. He knew he wasn't at all cut out, in terms of his self-image, to be a partner to a charismatic horse like Dan Patch, whose triumphant return to Minnesota at the end of the 1903 season had been listed by *Collier's* magazine as one of the significant events of the year, along with the signing of the Panama Canal Treaty and the prewar maneuvering between the Russians and Japanese. But ready or not, Hersey had gone, in a few weeks, from unknown farm manager to the focus of newspaper articles and barbershop debates. And public opinion was running strongly against him. Sports fans were citing his promotion as proof that Savage wasn't so smart after all, and may even have been a touch crazy. People in places where Hersey had never been, who until a month ago had never heard his name, were saying, as they passed the mashed potatoes to their wives and children, that he was in over his head and unworthy of this golden chance. It wasn't easy being Hersey. Or as his hometown *Minneapolis Journal* often called him, Harry Hershey. Or Herschey. Or, once or twice, Herschel.

But Hersey was not the reason that the post-McHenry era got off to an inauspicious start. Late one evening in early February 1904, while Dan was sleeping in the stable behind Savage's house on Portland Avenue, a defective flue sent a spark down a chimney and started a fire in the unoccupied adjoining stall. The stable quickly filled with smoke. Plummer, in his usual spot on a cot next to Dan, jumped up, unlatched the stall door, and allowed Dan to pace safely into the street, where he wheeled around and watched the humans deal with the conflagration. "Horses are notorious for their unmanageableness at such perilous times," said the *Review,* "but once again Dan, who has so often demonstrated his marvelous intelligence, showed his perfect mental balance by pacing out with unruffled calmness. The alarm had reached Mr. Savage, who hurried to the scene just in time to see Dan emerge in safety."

For the horse business in general, early 1904 was a somewhat unsettling time. With the stock market slumping and automobiles becoming ever more attractive to wealthy men both as an investment opportunity and a form of personal transport, the annual auctions of Standardbred stock suffered. At the Old Glory Sale in Madison Square Garden, 429 horses were sold for an average of $624 per head; though year-to-year statistics were not kept, the number sounded, and was, said the *New York Times,* "unusually low." Savage picked up a few broodmares in the $400 range and his annual acquisition of an infertile, shy, and possibly gay stallion—in this case the fourteen-year-old Arion—set him back a mere $2,500. Were these sensationally low prices a cyclical thing, many observers wondered, or a sign of the equine apocalypse?

The depressed market had an effect on Dan Patch. After the fire, he moved, earlier than scheduled, to the farm, where to the casual observer everything would at first have seemed perfectly in order. The sign on the train depot just across from the Taj Mahal barn had just been changed from Hamilton to Savage, Minnesota, in honor of the esteemed humanitarian who also happened to be the town's biggest employer and taxpayer. Plummer, in his scant spare time, had decorated Dan's stall in the Victorian style with lace curtains and, at the doorway, an embroidered red velvet portiere. A forty-four-year-old career groom who had previously rubbed the Thoroughbred champions Firenze and Salvatore, Plummer also built shelves in the stall for a few of Dan's more impressive trophies and hung up glass cases containing the shoes the horse wore at Brighton Beach the year before. As a final homey touch, just before Dan arrived, Plummer added a framed portrait of the pacer's sire, Joe Patchen.

What the scene lacked, however, was a parade of fecund broodmares queuing up to present themselves to Dan Patch. Savage had increased Dan's stud fee from $225 to $500 since the previous season, on the not unreasonable theory that the fastest horse of his breed ought to be among the most expensive to breed to. But the high price, the poor market, and the remoteness of the locale combined to produce a quiet winter. Not that Dan ever went lonely. Savage compensated for the lack of outside business by sending about two dozen of his own mares to the stallion, figuring he would sell the babies at yearling auctions and through his increasingly Sears-like catalog. Meanwhile, huckster that he was, he boasted to the horse journals that Dan's breeding season was an unmitigated success and that the stallion's book was "full and closed"—though he quickly added that if someone *really* wanted to breed to Dan Patch he would "do his best" to get them a service. This may have fooled some people; M. W. Savage always had a knack for doing that. But racing insiders saw the situation for what it was: proof that Savage's plan to have Minnesota eclipse Kentucky as the cradle of the racehorse was running slightly behind schedule.

Just how slow business was at the farm that spring can be illustrated by a transaction that occurred one afternoon in late April. A husky rustic of Swedish descent—"red-shirted and pink-whiskered," wrote the *Horse Review* reporter who happened to be there to witness the scene—rode onto Savage's property on an ungainly black mare that had the stout build of a draught horse and "feathery legs" that suggested she might have been at least part Percheron. The Swede said in heavily accented English that he had just traveled seventeen miles from his home and wanted to breed the mare he sat astride to Dan Patch. The Savage farmhand to whom he was telling this was skeptical. "Do you realize it takes $500 in coin of the realm to breed to that horse?" he asked. At this the Swede reached into his overalls and, said the *Review,* "brought up a roll of bills big enough to choke the firebox of an Atlantic liner." Hersey, who by this time had wandered onto the scene, promptly took the $500 offered by the man and told him to go around the back of the barn to the breeding shed, where he would have Dan Patch ready to go in few minutes.

Hersey, though unlike Savage in so many ways, possessed an unerring sense of what the boss wanted. At the same time, he was honest, truly caring about horses, and willing to play a supporting and sometimes thankless role in the Dan Patch drama. In late May he stood by calmly as he heard Savage utter the words that would make any trainer's blood run cold: "I plan to devote all my spare time to assisting Mr. Hersey in the working of the horses this year," the owner told the *Review*. "And at Memphis [in the fall] I plan to drive Dan against the amateur driving record of 2:01 ½." This move to participatory ownership, like so many things Savage predicted, never came to pass. Still, Hersey not only took the proclamation with grace and equanimity, he talked down the fifty or so other stock-farm workers who had threatened to quit rather than deal on a daily basis with Savage or anyone else who had the energy of a Roosevelt, the heart of a woman, and the tenacity of a barnacle. Hersey's colleagues were extremely fond of him. When Savage announced that Hersey would take McHenry's place in Dan's sulky, they were so delighted that they presented the owner with one of those "handsome floral horseshoes" that Minnesotans seemed to slip each other like Tic-Tacs in those days. Hersey was a fine trainer, a decent man, and the ideal employee. His one drawback was that he had, as they say in the harness racing business, heavy hands; he tended not to make horses go faster.

That Hersey—a birdlike man who weighed barely 130 pounds—felt like a millstone to Dan Patch in those early months of 1904 was not a matter of opinion. Savage routinely dropped by to observe workouts; like every other man of that era who had even a passing interest in racehorses, he owned a stopwatch, and the stopwatch did not lie. Could there have been something wrong with the horse? That seemed unlikely. Dan Patch by all accounts never looked more magnificent than he did that spring; he had slimmed down some, going from what the *Review* called his "high-flesh time" of 1,500 pounds in the fall to something closer to 1,200; he had simultaneously "broadened through the chest and was showing greater muscle." In attitude, moreover, he remained, at age eight, coltish yet calm; when hitched up for speed work, he seemed as eager as ever, but as June turned to July his progress lagged and his clockings were a full two or three seconds slower than they should have been. Just to be sure he wasn't becoming "track stale" after jogging countless miles around the same farm course, Hersey drove him occasionally through the streets of Savage, then a town of about 200 souls, and as word spread that he was on his way, people would pour out of grocery stores and barbershops and the infamous Budweiser Club to cheer him. Dan obviously enjoyed the change of scenery, and the encouragement. But whatever the distance or the route, the pacer's times with Hersey in the sulky remained stubbornly un-Patchian.

Savage may have panicked at some point that spring and reached out to McHenry, asking him to come back for one more season. In mid-May McHenry told several reporters that he was abandoning his plan to "go with the Thoroughbreds" and would be once again driving Dan. But nothing came of that. McHenry may have been in his cups when he spoke, and may have made up the secret as well as leaked it. But even if it were true, Savage, upon reflection, had to realize that he was stuck. After making such a bold decision, and taking so much public criticism for it, he could not back down. As Dan's first public appearance of the season approached—at the Indiana State Fair, in Indianapolis on August 11—he stayed with Hersey. McHenry took his one runner, an untested two-year-old filly named Maritana, to the tracks around New Orleans. As the *Horse Review* put it, "Mr. M. E. McHenry will sit behind the brown horse no more."

Partly because of his absence, the Dan Patch traveling road show was suffering from the same slack demand as Dan's stallion services. The economy and the automobile could be blamed for the slow bookings, but a bigger problem was the attitude of racetrack promoters, who doubted that they could sell the public on the idea of Dan possibly going faster than he had already, especially with Savage's hand-picked flunky in the bike. Savage, just a few months before, had been optimistic enough about the new era to lease a baggage car from the Chicago and North Western Railway and transform the sixty-five-foot specimen of rolling stock, which had room for fourteen horses and a dozen men, into Dan's private Pullman. "Dan is an intelligent animal," Savage told the *Syracuse Post-Standard,* "and he likes pleasant and comfortable surroundings." The outside of the boxcar, painted gleaming white with gold trim, had an almost lifesize "framed oil painting" of Dan on either side. Two-foot-high red letters spelled out "Private Car for Dan Patch, Champion Pacing Stallion of the World," beneath a four-foot-high bucket of Three Feeds for One Cent stock food. Inside, the floor was covered with thick black India rubber padding and the walls upholstered in red plush velvet with moldings repeating the gold-and-white motif. It looked like a Terre Haute whorehouse.

Yet as spring became summer there were not many places for the gaudy new car to go; none of the big tracks in the East where Dan had put on historic performances had made so much as an inquiry about a speed exhibition. Savage, disappointed but hopeful he could still turn the season around, did what he always did when business was poor: he announced that business was great, and said what looked like trouble was actually the manifestation of his master plan. He had decided not to "make those long trips to the East" that year, he told the press, and "would favor the fans of the Western states," where Dan hadn't ventured before, while "slowing down on the horse's commitments a bit and giving Dan a break."

At Indianapolis—his first time trial with Hersey in the sulky— Dan raced very much like a horse who needed a vacation. After a week of heavy rain that caused two postponements, Dan finally started on Friday, August 12. Traveling a sulky-width off the rail to avoid the wettest part of the strip, he missed his own record by six seconds, finishing in 2:02 ¼, his slowest clocking on a mile track in two years.

Dan's next appearance, at Des Moines on August 26, was a last-minute booking for which the Iowa State Fair board drove a hard bargain: fair officials wanted Dan to "do his fast stunts" (as the *Humeston Advocate* said) on that Thursday—and appear before the grandstand during the races on Monday through Wednesday afternoons. Savage, eager for bookings, accepted their terms, and all went as scheduled the first two days. But on Wednesday, Hersey, who was busily attending to a slight swelling in one of Dan's front legs, neglected to bring him out for his well-advertised bow. At two the crowd began to grumble, and the racing secretary sent word back to the barns that Dan was overdue. When at four there was still no sign of him, and the 15,000 in the grandstand had begun chanting his name, "Superintendent Cameron of the speed department," said the *Lincoln* (Neb.) *Evening News,* "promptly dispatched the marshal over to Patch's barn to ascertain the cause of the delay. That worthy brought back the news that Dan Patch would not appear and Superintendent Cameron was very wroth." This was an extremely rare case of Hersey failing to be accommodating, but the Iowans didn't know that. "That's a crusty bunch over there at Patch's stall," a fair official told the paper. "They've got the swelled head and something ought to be done for it."

The next day, a record 40,000 spectators squeezed into the grandstand that had looked about to burst the day before with 15,000. "Spectators were lined up 10 deep" around the half-mile track, said the *Evening News,* "eager to see the lightning wonder." Dan's assignment that day was to beat his own record for a half-mile oval of 2:03 ¼. The track was dry and fast, and he went the first of two counterclockwise laps in 1:02 ½, which put him in a position to succeed, but coming around the last turn Dan's left rear leg struck the sulky wheel and he broke into a gallop. A few steps later he was back on the pace, but his time was 2:06, and Hersey, unlike McHenry in similar circumstances, made no offer to try again. The Iowans cheered anyway, and the next day's *Des Moines Capital* celebrated the horse for lowering the state record.

But Savage was worried about Dan Patch; if his value as an attraction was to start moving upward again, if he was going to continue to set speed records, someone had to address whatever may have been bothering him and start fixing it. Was Hersey up to the task? Savage wasn't sure, but to eliminate the possibility of an embarrassment on his home turf, he canceled his plan to drive Dan himself over the state fairgrounds track at Hamline on August 18 in what was to have been an attempt at the amateur driving record. (Savage didn't know which he feared more: failing to beat the record, or driving a faster mile than the horse had been going with Hersey; both outcomes played into his critics' hands). Instead, Dan would ship directly from Des Moines to Lincoln, Nebraska, where, on September 1, he would attempt again to lower the record for a half-mile track.

At first, the visit to Lincoln looked like it might be a repeat of the Des Moines debacle. Dan missed a well-advertised "work-out appearance" on the day before his time trial, disappointing a record crowd of 25,000 that had come just to see him circle the track. They hissed and booed when it was finally announced that he would not be coming over from the barn area, and not quite as many turned out the next day to see the actual time trial. That went off without incident, and Dan turned in a clocking of 2:05 ¼, a track and state record. Maybe it was simply because Dan had not broken stride, but despite the unspectacular time, Hersey was encouraged by the performance. Dan, he felt, had responded to him better than ever before. The difference was subtle, but real; just possibly, they were getting in sync.

They had a week until the next exhibition, at the Wisconsin State Fair in the Milwaukee suburb of West Allis. Automobile racing had made its debut there the summer before, but the *Plymouth Reporter* noted that this was the first year that the fair would be "gorgeously lighted with electricity" after dark. The fair board even tried night harness racing on the half-mile track. That glamorous-sounding experiment, however, was short-lived. On opening night the trainers decided, after a few heats, that they and their horses "could not get their bearings" under the lights, and the program was abruptly canceled; the remainder of the races, it was announced, would take place as usual on the mile track in the sunshine. That included Dan's time trial, which had been scheduled from the start for Wednesday afternoon, September 7, as part of a day-long program that included Mademoiselle Zoar the Slack-Wire Walker, Dare Devil Tilden the Bicycle High-Diver, and a balloon ascension by the Celebrated Belmont Sisters. "Patch," the *Milwaukee Journal* noted, "is the great attraction."

It was an eventful fair, even before Dan Patch Day. On Tuesday, September 6, Colonel Francis Ferari, an animal trainer best known for his work with Big Frank, the Hoochie-Coochie Bear, was seriously injured by one of his lions, which reached through the bars of his cage and gave Ferari "a terrific blow on the shoulder." Assistants rushed to Ferari's aid and beat back the lion, named Barnum, "with clubs and irons." That night a concert by a band of Filipino policemen, brought from Manila at the controversial cost of $3,500, was plunged into darkness twice when the gorgeous electrical lighting failed. "But the Filipinos either have cats' eyes or know most of their music by heart," said the *Milwaukee Journal,* "for they played on undisturbed."

Dan Patch Day dawned murky, and by 10 a.m., as Governor Robert "Fighting Bob" La Follette was delivering a stirring speech about the unfairly high price of shipping corn through Wisconsin, the skies opened. La Follette, though on an uncovered podium, kept speaking as the rain poured down, supplying illustrative anecdotes "on his favorite theme of railroad rates," said the *Journal,* "at length and with much detail." By eleven o'clock he was soaked through, and so was the racetrack. Organizers hung a large banner saying "Dan Patch Race Postponed Until Thursday" on a Milwaukee-bound streetcar as a way of spreading the word.

On Thursday the sun came out, along with a record 53,016 fairgoers. The track, never especially conducive to speed, was still wet, but Dan took to it well, and Hersey rated him with an evenness that might have impressed McHenry: the first two quarters went in :31 ½ seconds, the third in :30 ½, and the fourth in :30 ¼. The time—2:03 ¾—wasn't spectacular, but the performance cheered Hersey and Savage, who was in the grandstand that day; both men felt that horse and driver were continuing to make progress as a team. That evening Savage got off telegrams to the newspapers in Topeka, Kansas, Dan's next stop, saying, "If the Topeka track is as I have heard it is and if weather conditions are favorable I feel certain Dan Patch will break the world's pacing record for a half-mile track when he comes to your fair."

Even before that, the Kansas fair board was eagerly anticipating Dan's arrival. A fair spokesman told the press that the horse's appearance "in the home of his ancestors" (Joe Patchen had been born in Peabody, Kansas) demonstrated that the fair had come a long way from the days of nearly forty years ago, when racing once had to be canceled because grasshoppers covered the half-mile track "from one to three inches deep" all the way around. The fair had built a special thirty-by-twenty-five-foot stable for Dan. Though they intended to use it also for "the other great horses who are sure to be making a pilgrimage to this city," Dan Patch's name and "1:56" were painted on the roof in gold numerals and letters six feet high. From a pole planted just outside the door flew "a silken flag bearing a picture of the great pacer." The floor was rubberized, and there were curtains and fly screens on the windows. One-quarter of the floor space was given to "a room for Charles Plummer, fitted up with a bed, washstand, mirror and everything that pertains to comfort, such as might be found in a good hotel." Plummer, as quoted by the *Topeka State Journal,* does not sound much like a man born in Newmarket, England: "Lordy, ain't this rich," he said as he led Dan Patch into his posh quarters. "Guess they must think we're all right. Nice, ain't it, Dan? Better than anything we've had in some time!" Hersey was also impressed. As Dan had his blankets and ankle bandages removed, the trainer walked around inspecting the premises. "Say, this is fine!" he said, patting the horse's nose.

Less than twenty-four hours later, however, misery reigned. Hersey had no idea that anything was wrong until he took Dan for a well-advertised warm-up mile just before three o'clock the next afternoon. The horse was extremely lethargic. While the crowd, oblivious to the problem, whooped and hollered, Hersey tried in vain to get Dan going at something faster than a three-minute-mile clip. Finally he steered the horse back to the track entrance ramp, where a worried Plummer waited. "He just won't go on," said Hersey. Plummer noted that Dan hadn't "emptied out" in quite a while, meaning moved his bowels. Dan hadn't even defecated during his warm-up miles, which both men agreed was highly unusual. "I'm going back out and giving him another mile and see if that loosens him up," Hersey said. The crowd was confused when Dan reappeared so soon, but the tactic worked, and Dan returned to his stable in what seemed like an improved state.

When Plummer fed him a short while later, however, Dan devoured his supper ravenously, displaying what would later be diagnosed as pica, or depraved appetite, a condition that the manufacturer of the Three Feeds for One Cent food supplement might have been interested to learn most often resulted from nutritional deprivations or imbalances. Pica can manifest itself in the eating of dirt, gravel, wood, or some other nonfood stuff as the animal attempts to acquire one or more trace minerals missing from his diet. Because those materials resist digestion, they can easily clog the intestines of a horse and cause severe colic and even death.

Dan tore through his supper of oat mash and hay in an unsettling fashion, then began devouring his straw bedding; before Plummer could stop him he had wolfed down enough chaff to create an impaction in his small intestine. Almost immediately he began to sweat. A few hours later, at eleven o'clock that night, Hersey was summoned from his room at the Copeland Hotel and arrived to find the horse "in terrible condition." One fairgrounds vet was on the scene; Hersey had phoned another in Chicago and wired Robert Moore, a prominent veterinary surgeon in Kansas City, to come quickly. Otherwise they followed the standard procedure of the time, which was to walk the horse as much as possible in order to loosen the impaction. All night long, in a driving rain, Hersey and Plummer made slow circles with Dan around the fancy little barn that bore his name.

After around 4:00 a.m. Dan could walk no more. The men brought him inside where, said the *St. Paul Globe,* he lay "propped up on a bed so soft as any in the land, with shaded lanterns casting their shadows over him. Always strangely intelligent, Dan Patch in his sickness is almost human, and when he raises his broad, bony head and surveys the group around him, the rough and ready stable boys sob and weep."

As Tuesday dawned, his condition remained poor. Reporters stationed outside the barn could occasionally hear Dan groaning. When this happened, "they gazed at one another as if some human being was in his last agonies instead of a horse." At about 7:00 a.m. Hersey emerged to make a statement for the assembled press: "Dan is a very sick horse. For him to race again this year is practically out of the question and the question is now will he live. . . . This is terrible news to send to Mr. Savage. Not only that he may lose a valuable horse, but because of his love of the horse, who is just like a member of the family. There is no horse in the world who can take his place." Hersey paused to gather himself, then added this postcript: "He never was sick a day before in his life. Not a bit of food is given him that is not screened, nor a wisp of hay that is not carefully first looked over. I cannot imagine what caused the trouble. We have cared for him every minute."

At around 3:00 p.m., as Hersey would say later, "Dan commenced to get worse, with a rising temperature." Savage, rushing to Topeka by train, was napping in his Pullman berth when a porter brought him two telegrams from Hersey. The more recent one said that the owner should gird himself for bad news upon his arrival because there was little cause for hope. At five o'clock both attending veterinarians sat Hersey down and told him that Dan Patch had no chance. Dr. Moore later would report that Dan's heart "grew so feeble that the pulse could not be taken at the jaw and the rate could only be determined by listening to the heart beats. A cold perspiration covered the entire body much of the time and the pain was almost continuous . . . the prognosis was very unfavorable." Plummer, in tears, told a reporter, "I don't believe he will live until Mr. Savage gets here."

By now the news of Dan's illness had spread across America. From down in New Orleans, McHenry sent a tasteless telegram to one of the attending vets: "Strike up a band and yell Go! over him," said the wire. "He'll get up!" His black humor, had people known about it, would not have resonated with the rest of America. In Oxford, citizens flocked to Messner's store and asked what he had heard, even though he had heard no more than anyone else and kept saying so. Elsewhere people hunkered on stoops and curbs near the closest newsstand. Some Dan Patch fans stayed all night, waiting for the particular clip-clop of the horse-drawn truck that delivered the papers.

Exactly what happened in Topeka during the critical evening hours of September 13 is still not known. The less sensational, and far more likely, version of events is that Dr. Moore arrived from Kansas City and, through a tube inserted in Dan's throat, administered mineral oil, which, in combination with gentle massage, broke up the impaction, allowing for a rapid and dramatic recovery that left Dan weak but essentially well. Thanks to Savage's publicist Merton Harrison, however, most people heard a tale that involved Savage swooping in at about 7:00 p.m., rolling up his sleeves, elbowing aside the bumbling vets, and administering his International Colic Cure, an "old Indian remedy" that was "the only colic cure sold with a cash guarantee." This story comes with a choice of Hollywood endings: either the reporters burst in to find Savage calmly slicing a carrot and inserting the slivers into the mouth of the recumbent horse, whose head rested in his master's lap; or, as a large crowd of well-wishers waits outside the barn, the door suddenly swings open and a Dickensian stable urchin sticks his head out and says, triumphantly, "Anyone got any apples?"—indicating a hungry horse within.

For the obvious reason that it sounded better, the press didn't question the Savage version of what had transpired behind closed stable doors. Likewise, none of the contemporary accounts addresses the mundane but important question of whether Dan Patch was insured. He was, for $50,000, but the subject never came up with the journalists filing from Topeka, probably because they felt that Savage having a financial hedge against Dan's loss deprived the story of some drama.

Savage was willing to talk about money, though, or anything else that would give the reporters a better, and therefore bigger, story. Shortly after he arrived in Topeka, someone asked him how much his seriously ill horse was worth. The question caught him off guard, and it is instructive to watch him fumbling for an answer as he simultaneously spins the ideas of Dan's being worth a fortune but not for sale. "Well, I hardly know," he starts off. "If anyone were to offer me $150,000 for him I would not look at it. . . . However I presume that that figure about represents his commercial value. . . . But I would not take twice that amount for him. It is a matter of sentiment with me, and I have never tried to estimate the amount that would buy the horse."

The press was also not shy about the touchy matter of Dan's appearance fee. Fair finances were always a good story, and the papers, in Kansas and elsewhere, typically played the role of public watchdog, scrutinizing expenses, reporting on gate receipts, and constantly assessing whether the annual agricultural fests made financial sense. "Unless Dan Patch makes a miraculous recovery and can appear before closing day on Saturday," said the *Topeka Daily Herald,* as soon as the horse had passed the critical point, "his fee will need to be renegotiated."

Savage was having none of that. Dan might not be able to go against the world record in Topeka—indeed, Hersey was suggesting that he might never race again—but by almost dying he had delivered the fair a huge publicity windfall, the owner felt, and the fair board had no excuse for giving him less than the $2,500 minimum. Savage would make it even more difficult for the fair to renege: on Thursday, September 15, he announced that the following afternoon Dan would make a short walk from the stable area to the grandstand to greet the public and show them that he was all right. In fact, said Savage, Dan would appear twice, in the afternoon and in the evening.

That announcement, coupled with the story that Savage himself had cured the horse, made the owner an almost mystical figure in Topeka. Later that afternoon, he and Hersey visited a downtown barbershop for a shave and a shoeshine. When Savage rose to leave, a "negro porter," said the *Herald,* rushed over with Savage's trademark long black parson's coat. The reporter recorded the scene:

"Are yo' Mistah Savage?" said the porter.
"Yes," replied the amused horse owner.
The negro stared in actual reverence.

But Savage deserved no reverence for the way he was handling Dan Patch. That he was asking too much of the horse too soon became evident when, as the hour for the first appearance drew near, Dan lay prone on the straw of his stall, far too weak to make even the quarter-mile walk to the grandstand. Yet instead of saying that the show could not go on, Savage said that it would go on a day later instead. The owner—who seemed almost embarrassed by his horse's inability to bounce back, especially after he had been doused with the full complement of International Stock Food products—even threw in the bizarre promise that Dan would go a mile on Saturday "hitched to a sulky," so his Kansas fans could "see what he looked like on the move." The supposedly sentimental and caring owner was leaving for business in St. Joseph, Missouri, but the *Topeka State Journal* said that he had given "trainer Hershey" strict instructions to "entertain the crowd." As usual Savage was overplaying his hand and overestimating the limits of his horse. Twenty-four hours later, on what the fair had months before designated as Automobile Day, Dan could still not come out of his stall.

A Niagara of further evidence would follow, but all one needed to know about Savage's failings as a horseman and a human being were on display in his management of Dan Patch in the latter months of 1904. Several months of rest and recuperation were clearly in order, even by the lights of the relatively unmerciful trainers of that day. Savage himself had said before leaving Kansas that the rest of the year's dates would be canceled. ("He will not be going to Memphis or Oklahoma City.") But then, with a minimum of fuss, the cancellations were withdrawn and the horse was taken back to the farm in Minnesota with an eye toward getting him ready so he could keep as many commitments as possible.

Hersey would later admit to the *Horse Review*'s John Markey that Dan looked "gaunt and thin as a greyhound" when he arrived back in Savage, Minnesota, around September 20. "His flesh," he told the writer, "seemed literally to wash off him in chunks." Nevertheless he was, at Savage's direction, almost immediately put on a regimen of a few slow training miles every day with "a brush of speed on the end." By the last week in September he was up to five miles a day, and on October 1 Savage shipped Dan to Springfield, Illinois, to keep a booking to race against his world record of 1:56 ¼ at the state fair on October 5. The reader will perhaps not be surprised to learn that he failed to lower that mark. Not that it was a disappointing performance by any means. With more than 50,000 people—including even Governor Richard Yates Jr., an ardent opponent of legalized horse racing—cheering him on, Dan went a smooth but slow mile, finishing in 2:04. "Though the horse did not break any records," said the *Springfield News*, "he is still a national pet." To Savage he looked "as good as ever."

He did not; he was still down in flesh, but he was recovering quickly. Savage shipped him immediately to Memphis, where his next start was scheduled for October 24. The seventeen-day interval would at least give Dan time to continue building his strength. Dan had shown a liking for Memphis. The managers of the Memphis track liked Dan, too, and when they offered him a second date, on the twenty-sixth, Savage eagerly accepted, saying he was doing it to satisfy "the public's demand to see Dan" in this comeback period. Hersey would eventually rebel against Savage's hard use of Dan and other horses, but for the time being the trainer was, however grudgingly, complicit in his boss's plans. He said nothing, and even drove Dan aggressively in the first of the trials, finishing the mile in 2:00 ¼.

Two days later, Dan Patch surprised everyone, not least the bookmakers, who had made him a strong favorite to finish slower than 2:01. With nostrils flared and mane flying, Dan paced the fastest mile of his life. The performance, moreover, demonstrated how exciting a time trial can be: after he reached the three-quarter pole in 1:26 ½, his prompters, Cobweb and Mag the Rag, parted before him and, with their drivers turning toward Dan to shout "Indian warwhoops" and a small but vocal crowd on its feet, the pacer came home in 1:56. Hersey, who had driven in a hell-bent fashion, hugging the rail so closely with Dan, said the *Memphis Scimitar*, "that it seemed as if he would scrape the paint off the fence," was lifted out of the sulky by the surging crowd "and almost carried off on the shoulders of his admiring friends." When they finally put down the little man in the very heavy jacket, Savage, "wreathed in smiles," according to the *Minneapolis Journal*, "wrung his hand."

Did the world record justify going so hard with a horse who had almost died less than two months earlier? Clearly Savage thought so. Although he would later insist that he never used Dan's illness to sell his products, or made claims that they had saved his life,

the owner did just that shortly after the Memphis mile, design-
ing a full-page ad for his Three Feeds for One Cent food supplement that carried the dramatic headline "Dan Patch Given Up to
Die—What Restored Dan Patch in Six Weeks?" The copy extolled
"the remarkable vegetable preparation" that "gave Dan the extra
constitutional strength to withstand his severe sickness." It also
prominently featured a letter from Dr. Moore that is framed as
an endorsement but which is really just a perfunctory note saying
the horse had been very sick but had gotten better. This was all
laid out around an "actual photograph of Dan in action" that is
patently a drawing.

Whatever: onward. On November 4, Dan was expected at the
Louisiana Purchase Exposition, more popularly known as the St.
Louis World's Fair. It was an honor to be one of a string of star
attractions that, since the fair opened several months before, had
included John Philip Sousa, Scott Joplin, Helen Keller, Thomas
Edison, and Beautiful Jim Key, a performing horse who could
allegedly read, write, cite Bible passages, sort mail, and much
more, owing to "the power of kindness" (he eventually became a
spokeshorse for the burgeoning Humane Society movement). But
neither Savage nor Hersey looked forward to the St. Louis date.
The fair paid only a small honorarium, and the exposition's ballyhooed Delmar track had been built for running horses and thus
had a deep, loose surface not suitable for sulky wheels. The prospect of racing where there was no chance of capitalizing on Dan's
razor-sharp current form made Savage cranky. When fair officials
asked him, just before Dan left Memphis, if he would mind switching dates from Saturday, November 5, to Sunday the sixth to help
them resolve a scheduling conflict, he wired back, "Sorry, but Dan
Patch joined the Methodist Church two years ago" and thus did
not race on Sundays. The telegram, leaked by his publicist Harrison to the press, got Savage an extra round of headlines, and back
in Minneapolis, Savage's Wesley United Methodist Church soon
issued Dan his own set of contribution envelopes, making him an
official parishioner. But St. Louis was not harness-horse country,
and the time trial, before a crowd of just 4,000, went in 2:01 ¼
and received only cursory coverage.

At Oklahoma City on November 17, the crowd was estimated at 5,000, but that was, said the *Horse Review*, "just about every one in the town." (As part of the promotion, each woman in the crowd got the sheet music to "The Dan Patch Two-Step.") This booking demonstrated that Savage never said no to anyone who could pay Dan's appearance fee, for here was perhaps the slowest racetrack in North America, a half-mile ring of ankle-deep sand. The $2,500 bonus hinged on Dan's beating the track record of 2:05 ¼, and after a warm-up mile the day before Hersey thought they might have a shot at that—but only if they fixed the sulky of the lead prompter, Cobweb, with a three-by-one-foot canvas screen that he and Cobweb's driver, Charley Dean, rigged up on the spot and fit under the cart to cut down on the dirt that the galloper would naturally fling up in Dan's face. The "sand shield," as they made sure to call it in order to distinguish it from a windshield, a similar device thought by some to provide an unfair edge, "did not," Hervey noted, "work like a charm." Dan got off to a sensational start, reaching the half in 1:00 ½ and the three-quarters in 1:30 ½. But despite the shield, said Hersey, "the dirt and sand thrown back was so blinding I could scarcely see the time my watch recorded." At the seven-eighths pole they reached a spot so loose that Dan stumbled and, while trying to right himself, made a break. "He seemed just as anxious to land himself as I was to land him," Hersey said. "We lost several seconds, and Dan seemed so angry about that, and about breaking, that after the finish I had difficulty in preventing him from going around the track again." The eventful mile went in 2:03, not just a track record but, bizarrely, the world record for a half-mile track. Savage called it "the best performance of Dan's career," and though he said that after every time trial, he was probably correct this time. "I see no reason why he should not beat his own world record of 1:56," Savage told the *Daily Oklahoman* after the race. "He is a young horse, being eight years old, and there is not a pimple on him. I expect him to winter well in Minnesota."

And after a stop in Dallas, Texas, where the horse paced in 2:01, taking six and a quarter seconds off the track record and picking up another $5,000, Savage finally did take Dan Patch home. The Newsboy Band had its trumpets waiting.

CHAPTER NINETEEN

'Tis the pace that kills.

—old hunting adage

THE BIG WHEEL TURNS and jerks softly to a stop. We are at the top. Look. To the west lie the snow-capped Rockies, beyond which Dan Patch will eventually, alas, go. Closer by, we see the Celebrated Belmont Sisters ascending in their balloon. Behind us are Messner, Wattles, poor Myron McHenry. And ahead?

Ahead means down.

The car swings slightly.

Taken in combination, the years 1905 and 1906 constitute a span between the upward and downward paths of the career of Dan Patch and thus can be called the peak of his professional life. Nothing essential changes during this period, but everything settles into place with an almost audible click. Hersey and the horse sync up as never before, and go some sensational miles. Savage expands the Dan Patch brand line to include Dan Patch breakfast cereal and Dan Patch engines. And a Dan Patch appearance becomes a slicker, more efficient spectacle. The public—advised of Dan's imminent arrival by a team of advance men Savage sent ahead to each stop—queued up at the appointed hour; paid a $1 admission; received printed propaganda about Savage, his products, and his proto-Disneyesque stock farm; filed past the man selling

$1 souvenir horseshoes (the forerunner of the concert T-shirt); and took its seats in the stands, where another member of the troupe, shouting through a megaphone, introduced Dan with a spit-shined, applause-inducing spiel. *He began his career on the turf in the most modest of circumstances . . . the son of the Iron Horse . . . undefeated . . . world champion . . . one minute and fifty-six seconds . . . purchased by Mr. M. W. Savage for the record sum of $60,000. . . . Ladies and gentlemen . . . the King of the Pacers . . . the Most Wonderful Horse in the World!*

For the promoters, fair boards, and track managers who booked the show, a Dan Patch exhibition became a more refined thing as well: easier to profit from but harder to make a killing on, owing to the kind of bargains Savage was now able to strike. He raised the base price of an appearance from $1,000 to $3,500, asked for and usually received a larger percentage of the gate, and invented a slew of new records for Dan to break—the state record, the record for a mile without a prompter, the record for the mile without a prompter in front of you, et cetera—so his horse would almost always be assured of making news (useful for promoting future appearances) and earning a bonus check. During this time, Savage also came up with another gimmick: a public demand that betting and alcohol be banned wherever the horse appeared. "Dan Patch Is a Methodist!" he would thunder, then wink; Savage loved to tell this joke, and the newspapers never got tired of printing it. What the turf scribes conveniently failed to note, however, was that for a fee of $3,000 or thereabouts he would waive his demand for a viceless venue.

This all worked very well for a while. From a single speed exhibition at the Minnesota State Fair in early September of 1905, Savage, thanks to a huge turnout of Dan Patch fans, realized $21,500—Sarah Bernhardt or Enrico Caruso bucks. The figure was so shockingly high that the fair board took a stab at getting him to renegotiate; loosening their celluloid collars, the jowly and mustachioed managers of the midway said they needed to talk turkey with him before he left the grounds about being a good Minnesotan, a reasonable man, a friend of the fair, and so on. But remembering how they had chiseled him (or so he believed) two years earlier, and that in 1904 Dan had suffered the indignity of not being invited to the fair until the last minute (he ultimately did not appear), Savage not only laughed in their faces but leaked the story of his laughing to the papers. Why should he feel sorry for the fair board? Savage wondered; they were making plenty off his horse. Their Dan Patch Day crowd had been 77,000, up from 16,000 the year the horse's invitation got lost in the mail.

Dan's popularity in 1905–6 reached frightening proportions. Crowds had built steadily since the days when Dan was the buzzed-about "Indiana horse" whom all the trainers and grooms wanted to see. By 1905 he had become an idol not just to the regular run of racing fans (who were legion in those days) but to women and children, too, and attendance at some of his time trials surged past the point of safety. At the Minnesota State Fairgrounds that year, Plummer had panic in his eyes when, after Dan's mile of 1:59 ½, several thousand people poured onto the track, surrounding Dan so closely that they were pushing against the delicate white shafts of his sulky. Minneapolis cops came running and, said the *Horse Review,* "cut a corridor in the mob" for Dan's escape. Five days later, having learned from the near-disaster, police were already lining the homestretch when the pacer whizzed by in 1:57 ½, a track and state record.

It's a wonder no one was killed. At Indianapolis on September 13, 1905, 50,000 surged against the rail, broke through, and kept coming as Dan barreled down the homestretch. Hersey had to weave around errant spectators but still finished in 2:00 ½, a track record.

The intensity of adoration only increased the next year as Dan Patch turned ten and people began to realize that, given the fragility of racehorses and the vagaries of the barnstorming business, they might never see him again. At the first of Dan's two appearances in Minnesota in 1906, on September 4, authorities found themselves overmatched. "Despite the efforts of policemen," said the *Minneapolis Journal,* "the immense crowd surrounding the track . . . had broken over the fences in their attempt to see the world's greatest pacing stallion, and in the last 100 yards of the final quarter, Hersey

drove Dan Patch through a lien [sic] of spectators. The horse, however, apparently intent on nothing but speed, never swerved from his
course, and flashed by the grandstand in 1:56 ½." By then, Hersey
was accustomed to seeing ecstatic fans in the homestretch when he
swept around the final turn. The week before at Galesburg, Illinois,
"the crowd swarmed on the track and it took the entire police force
to keep them from interfering" with Dan's mile in 1:57 ¾, an Illinois record. The press was also finding it hard to control its emotions. From the *Lima* (Ohio) *Times-Democrat* of September 29,
1906: "His performances speak more eloquently than can words
about his supreme power as a pacer, the likes of which has never
worn bridle or been subject to the will of man. As Mr. Webster in
his great debate of Hayne proudly exclaimed, speaking of Massachusetts and her history: There she stands, behold her as she is! So
can Americans point to Dan Patch with just pride and ask the world
to produce his superior in fame, endurance and speed!"

It needs remarking, though, that besides coming from the
heart, these sentiments were coming, almost exclusively, from the
heartland. Savage, during 1905–6, fielded no inquiries about his
horse from the big cities, and when Dan appeared in Chicago on
September 30, 1905, he could draw no more than 5,000 fans. If
he had been a trotter—or a car—things might have been different: that's what the eastern sophisticates preferred. But at the time
when he was pacing his best miles, Dan's days as an attraction
at places such as Brighton Beach, Readville, and the West Side
Driving Club were already done. That wasn't so easy to notice,
though, because in the next tier of cities—Indianapolis, Minneapolis, Memphis, and the like—Dan was still visiting royalty. And
in small-town America, he was a god.

Consider Allentown, Pennsylvania. Just nine days before his
disappointing Chicago stop, when Dan appeared at the fair there,
the place had come alive in a way that Billy Joel might not believe.
As the horse stepped on the track, said the *Horse Review,* "Trees,
the roofs of sheds, anything that overlooked the track was thick
with humanity." Dan broke the half-mile track record that day,
pacing in 2:01, and the gleeful crowd rushed down to the finish
wire, pulled Hersey from the sulky, and tossed him around like

a rag doll. When finally set down, Hersey bowed, tried in vain get out a few words, then wobbled back to the stable area on foot. There Plummer, in accordance with the contract, had already hitched Dan to a racing wagon for another time trial. Hersey then steered Dan back out and together they went "the fastest mile ever in Pennsylvania by a four-wheeled vehicle on a half-mile track." The announcement of that absurd record set off a solid half-hour of whooping and hollering; Savage, though not present, must have been happy, too: the feat also earned him an additional $4,000 above the $4,000 he was already getting. While that was surely a high price for humble Allentown to pay, the fair board could afford it: when officials tabulated the gate receipts that evening, they counted 115,000 paid admissions.

Like most objects of adoration, Dan became the subject of wild rumors. A man from Iowa piped up to claim that the pacer was not a son of Joe Patchen. Messner and Wattles, the man alleged, had been given a fast shuffle when they took their mares to be bred to the Iron Horse ten years earlier and Zelica had instead been impregnated by an obscure stallion named Dineen. Apart from a round of headlines, nothing came of the tale. Not long afterward, a Canadian trainer named John Thompson claimed that Dan Patch had been stolen from his stable and was actually a thirteen-year-old trotter named Arrin, apparently coerced by his kidnappers to pace. Savage, who was always glad to be talked about, even by a crackpot, called in a veterinarian in response to this allegation; the vet examined Dan and determined that he was definitely not thirteen. Messner, meanwhile, wired the horse magazines to say that Dan Patch was exactly who he was supposed to be. One week later the *Horse Review* carried news of Messner's death. This, too, was not true.

Savage, in these heady days, was making some extravagant claims of his own. Ratcheting up the ads for the Three Feeds for One Cent supplement, he began saying it gave horses "Courage and Nerve Force," and suggested that the strychnine-laced concoction increased sexual potency and "could be taken into the human system." He also made up, and leaked to the press, a story about Manley Sturges begging to buy back Dan Patch for

$180,000, and him spurning the offer. Savage in these peak years seemed a bit tipsy with success. Without knowing why, exactly, he bought the seedy and struggling Gentry Bros. Dog and Pony Show. According to Fred Sasse's book, Savage also, around this time, loosed thousands of colorful gamecocks on his International Stock Farm, thinking they made the place even more fantastically beautiful—but then promptly ordered the birds to be rounded up and disposed of after a woman to whom he had given one complained that they were not sufficiently meaty. Sasse says this anecdote shows Savage's commitment to excellence. I think it shows that both he and Sasse were a bit nuts.

Success made Savage feel omnipotent, and that miscalculation, combined with his obsession with Dan Patch setting new records, led him to cheat. Dan, in 1905, had already been racing for about two years with one pacesetter running in front of him, serving as both a rabbit and a windbreak. This angered some observers, who thought Savage was violating the spirit of the rule that said that no shields or other blocking devices could be employed to help a horse lower his time. But about halfway through the 1905 tour, Savage went a step further, telling Hersey to equip the lead prompter's sulky with the "dirt shield" they had used once at Oklahoma City the year before. When the reporters questioned him about it, Savage said the approximately three-by-one-foot piece of framed canvas, affixed to the axle of the front-running prompter, was "to prevent soil and clods from being flung up in Dan's face." Although somewhat smaller than the typical outlawed windshield, the dirt shield was basically the same device that Savage, and the hometown Minneapolis newspapers, had vehemently criticized Prince Alert for using in 1904. Savage pooh-poohed that idea, but there can be no doubt that it helped his horse go faster, and violated not just the spirit but now the letter of the rule as well.

It took a while, however, for Hersey and Plummer to figure out how to use the device. At the Lexington Breeders Track on October 5, 1905, they hung it too low, and, wrote Hervey, "instead of fulfilling its office of dirt-screen properly, it raised a cloud of dust that was blinding." When Dan and his two prompters came around the final turn, "all that was visible was a momentary glint of Hersey's white satin jacket." As Hersey said, "I could hardly see the horse I was driving." The driver of the outside prompter, Doc Tanner, said, "the only horse that could have made it through that choking dust was Dan Patch." He made it smartly, too, going in 1:56. Afterward Tanner suggested that Hersey raise the dirt shield six inches, an adjustment that caused "visible improvement."

That was putting it mildly. Two days later, on October 7, Dan returned to the Breeders Track in Lexington for the fastest official mile of his career. Dan Patch was at his physical peak that crisp fall day, eager to get going and "plunging like an engine in a mad race" all the way around the track, according to the *Lexington Leader*. He reached the quarter in :29 ½, and the half mile in :57 ½ with the crowd chanting, "Come on, Patch! Come on, Patch!" Hersey could have left his whip at home; he was "sitting like a statue," the paper said, when he passed under the wire in a world record 1:55 ¼.

"Never before in the annals of light harness achievement has such magic speed been attained," said the *Leader*. The fans this time didn't rush onto the track until the race was over, but then they came by the thousands. Said the *Kentucky Farmer and Breeder*: "Had it been possible in any way to pick Dan Patch up and carry him on their shoulders before the exultant thousands, they would have done it." Instead, "they contented themselves by patting his silken coat, caressing him, paying him a tribute that he deserved, giving him an ovation that his kind never knew before."

John Hervey was there to witness it. "I was one of the crowd that swarmed upon the stretch when Hersey drove back to weigh out," he wrote in the next week's *Horse Review*. "Hundreds of men and boys mobbed the horse in their effort to touch him, or even his blanket or sulky. I worked my way to Dan's side with difficulty, and also laid my hand upon him, but it was for a different purpose. I wished to discover whether the tremendous effort had exhausted him. I found him with his nostrils no more distended than after a 2:10 workout mile; there was no convulsive heaving of his flanks; he lifted his head in the air, and his eye was as bright as a star."

But not everyone was so enraptured. Many voices rose up to say it had been an unlawful, windshield-aided mile and thus should be stricken from the books. Hadn't the accounts in Savage's own hometown paper said that Dan had lowered his record "behind a wind-shield, without a skip or break"? They had, and Savage, in a letter to the *Journal*, had objected strenuously, saying that the correspondent "who telegraphed the report must have known that it was absolutely false," and obviously didn't know shield from Shinola because only a mere *dirt* shield had been employed. He also pointed out that "the trotting association ruled over two years ago . . . that a dirt shield would be allowed." This put the National Trotting Association in a awkward position because the body had indeed ruled that, but now, because the rule was being abused by Savage and a few others who used it continually, it wished mightily that it hadn't. For the time being, the NTA said, it was allowing the record to stand, but in the *Wallace Yearbook* the performance would be recorded with an asterisk to indicate the NTA's "concern."

Dan Patch finished out the year visiting Toronto and Memphis and never going faster than 2:00 while using the dirt shield in every start. Early in 1906, after winter-long debates, the NTA banned dirt shields as well as front-running prompters. They allowed all current records to stand, but said that any miles raced the way Dan had raced at Lexington would no longer be acknowledged. Savage shrugged off their decision, claiming it meant nothing to him or the paying customers who spun the turnstiles. He would continue to race Dan Patch any way he pleased, he said, because "the people get excited when they see horses going fast."

He was right about that much, of course. And that is why September 4, 1906, was once an important date in the popular culture, and why it still means something to the members of a small church called the Dan Patch Historical Society.

In 1906 Dan Patch Day at the Minnesota State Fair was preceded by a palpable sense that something big was about to happen. "I remember the day well," Archie "Pode" McColl said in 1963. "It was a Saturday afternoon. I took the Omaha train to St. Paul and then went to the fairgrounds. I got there rather late

and found a large crowd already gathered around the racetrack."
McColl had trouble seeing, but then noticed, "There were several
boys around with pails they used to pick up bottles. I asked one
of the boys how much he wanted for his pail; he sold it to me for
25 cents. By turning the pail upside down I could stand on it and
look over the crowd of people in front of me. A fellow standing
next me suggested placing a length of board across the top of the
pail; that way both of us could make use of the pail. After that the
boys were doing a good business in selling pails. When the race
began the horses made three starts before they made the proper
one. Then they flew around the mile track."

They flew, in fact, faster than any Standardbred horse had ever
flown before. Dan Patch's time that day was 1:55. Huzzahs went
up. Hersey was lifted on the shoulders of the crowd, and Savage
was ushered into the judges' stand to make a speech. ("Dan does
all my talking for me," is all he could manage.) A few days later,
the worst poem ever written appeared in the *Review:*

> *We hail thee proud monarch of the turf*
> *and yield to thee thy laurels fairly won*
> *Dauntless is thy courage! Matchless is thy worth!*
> *By thee all kings before thee are undone.*

But the mile wouldn't count because Cobweb, the lead
prompter, had been toting a dirt shield. When the unsurprising
ruling came a few weeks later, Savage ignored it, henceforth citing
Dan's record as 1:55 and even changing the name of his breeding
operation to the International 1:55 Stock Food Farm.

"Mr. Savage was a headstrong guy, yes siree!" said George Augustinack, pointing to an old photograph of the farm that he happened to be carrying around with him. George—vice president
of the Dan Patch Historical Society, collector extraordinaire, and
chief twenty-first-century apologist for M. W. Savage—would
have said a lot more, but he was needed just then on the podium.

The ceremony held at the Minnesota State Fairgrounds on

September 2, 2006, to commemorate the hundredth anniver-
sary of Dan Patch's "record" mile at the Hamline track was not
grand. At just after noon, unbeknownst to multitudes of fairgoers then busy eating cheese-curds-on-a-stick, hot-dogs-on-a-
stick, walleye-on-a-stick, deep-fried-Twinkies-on-a-stick, pizza-
on-a-stick, teriyaki-ostrich-on-a-stick, deep-fried-Snickers-on-
a-stick, and Scotch-eggs-on-a-stick, several official-looking men
stood on a slightly raised platform in a small tent near the grandstand, and one of them, State Representative Duke Powell, read
a proclamation from Governor Tim Pawlenty declaring the day
Dan Patch Day to an audience of perhaps two dozen people. It
began, "Whereas Dan Patch was owned and bred by Marion W.
Savage . . . ," and probably contained other factual errors, but
like the exhibition of ephemera and Patchiana put on throughout the tent by the Historical Society, it was instructive even
when fallacious, and on the whole, just right. In the thirteen
or so hours it was open to the public, several hundred filtered
through the tent, just a deep-fried-bratwurst-on-a-stick's throw
away from the spot where Dan had crossed the finish line in
1:55, many entering as Dan Patch neophytes and exiting with a
friendly handshake from one of the eight M. W. Savage descendants who had come from as far away as the East Coast. The
twenty-first-century Savages were not likely to know a trotter
from a pacer, and some hadn't met one another previously, but
they were united in their knowledge that the family fortune had
dried up several generations ago.

One could see signs of a crumbling empire, and its desperate
king, in the clippings that George had laminated and hung in a
part of the exhibit meant to lionize the master of the International
1:55 Stock Food Farm. These articles, all from around 1912–14,
showed that Savage had announced the formation of the Savage
Motor Company and the advent of the Dan Patch Automobile,
which he described as coming in three models, all featuring Dan
Patch Ignition. So far, so good for George, who the reader will
remember is the Bernard Arnault of Savage-related stuff, owner of
what may or may not be the tail of Dan Patch, dyed red. If one read
George's yellowing articles closely, though, one would gather that

the Savage Motor Company was something of a Ponzi scheme, with Savage selling distributorships, not cars, and distributors taking deposits on nonexistent autos. Savage may have intended to manufacture the Dan Patch car someday after his pyramid plan generated enough cash; still, this episode ended—at least in the Historical Society clips—with the indictment, in 1914, of three Cincinnati men for using the mails to accept deposits "when they had no cars to deliver and no factory in which to make them." George, who cheerfully admits to having drunk the Savage Kool-Aid, interprets this contretemps as "Detroit going after Mr. Savage because they were worried about him giving them competition."

When I mentioned to Deborah Savage that M. W.'s sleight of hand and misdirection was still working on some people a hundred years later, she smiled and shook her head. Deborah, a great-granddaughter of M. W. who lives in western Massachusetts (she wrote an award-winning young adult novel involving Dan Patch called *To Race a Dream*), does not nurse any illusions about her ancestor. "M. W. made a tremendous mask for himself, which he hid behind his whole life," she said. "There must have been a lot going on behind the mask. His son Erle became a drug addict, his other son Harold was estranged from his own son—my father—for eighteen years. But very little of anything—money, information—was passed down. It is an odd family."

Not so Dan Patch's family, which was happy in the usual way. You could see that in another part of the exhibit, which displayed a rare picture of Zelica, back home in Indiana. She is standing before the Messner barn; an unidentified man holds her lead shank. At her right flank is a handsome two-month-old colt who has just turned to look at the camera.

CHAPTER TWENTY

A whole lot of corn around Danbury is where a frost would do no damage, and the balance of the crop is getting there at a Dan Patch gait.

—the *Danbury* (Iowa) *Review*, 1907

Git! Go! Haw! Giddyap! Go, you son of a bitch!

Presenting the world-champion trotter Cresceus, the latest purchase of M. W. Savage, in a little production that might be called *All Dressed Up, No Place I'm Willing to Go.*

Git! Go! Haw!

A small crowd of farmhands gathers at the edge of the training track. The men lean on their shovels and hay rakes, push back their hats, chuckle.

Hee-yaaah!

It is a principle of the theater, timeless and universal, that, like the pie in the face, the foot in the buttocks, and the anything-at-all in the crotch, the sight of a horse refusing to move despite the angry exhortations of one or more human beings will never fail to get a laugh.

Git! Go! Haw!

This is better than vaudeville.

All of you—get back to work!

M. W. Savage had purchased Cresceus—once the second or third most famous racehorse in America—for $21,000, against the advice of just about everyone. And now, everything the knockers had been saying—that the old stud was sour, jaded, and uninterested in sex—was proving true. After a disastrous breeding season (Cresceus was "shy" about mounting the few mares that had been led before him), the owner's plan to bring the trotter back to the races had devolved into low comedy. Cresceus would tolerate being harnessed, he would walk to the track, but once he got there, he would refuse to move.

This was the third time in the last week that Savage, Hersey, and Cresceus had performed their little trackside *sketch satirique* for the amusement of the troops. But today they were trying something new. George Ketcham, Cresceus's former owner, had agreed to come all the way from Toledo, Ohio, to assess the situation and see if he could proffer advice as to how the Minnesotans might get Cresceus off the dime. A carriage was carrying Ketcham from the Savage, Minnesota train station, just outside the gates of the International 1:55 Stock Food Farm, at that very moment.

Ketcham, then forty-three, a member of a wealthy lumber and banking family, was an accomplished horseman who had bred Cresceus and driven him in all of his races. He had, it must be said, made his share of mistakes with the horse, the first of which was misspelling the name of the celebrated Roman charioteer "Crescens" on the registration papers. A more egregious miscalculation occurred when Cresceus, as a yearling, severely irritated a spot on his neck while rubbing it along the top of his stall: Ketcham, diagnosing the problem as potentially fatal, had ordered his stable manager to put the horse down. Instead, the man hid Cresceus until the injury healed, then one day surprised Ketcham with a lean but sinewy bay colt who trotted square and fast. Cresceus would win more than $106,000 over six racing seasons, a staggering amount at the time, if true. I must qualify the statement because Ketcham's numbers did not always bear close scrutiny. He had once reported to the National Trotting Association that Cresceus had trotted the mile in the world-record time of 1:59 ¼ at Wichita, Kansas, a clocking that shocked the world and potentially added tens of thousands to the horse's value. But since Cresceus was known to have been in less than peak condition at the time, people were suspicious, and rival owners called for an investigation. It turned out that only a handful of horsemen had been around the track in Wichita to witness Cresceus's very-late-in-the-season feat, and that as chance would have it, every last one of them had been approached, just prior to the time trial, by a man who asked to borrow their stopwatches. Eventually the clocking was disallowed, and Ketcham, though not formally punished by the NTA, was ostracized from the sport—which is one reason broodmare owners would not patronize Cresceus.

Yet even if things hadn't turned out particularly well for man and horse, no one knew Cresceus better than Ketcham. They had raced together on the Grand Circuit for six years, and Ketcham had been the man to collar the horse and calm him down when, one fine summer's day in 1901, he had viciously attacked his groom, who died not long afterward from his injuries. In the matter of Cresceus's intransigence, Ketcham might well have been of some help.

His carriage pulled up to the track right on time, and then Ketcham alighted and walked directly to the scene of the standoff. He looked Cresceus up and down, stared into his eyes, and talked softly to him. He turned to Savage.

"You say you gave my friend here a full breeding season this spring?"

"As full as we could," Savage said. "He didn't cover many mares."

"Well, I'll tell you something I've learned about horses. Breeding takes more out of some than you might think. Covering one mare for this horse can be more depleting than going several fast miles. And now breeding season is just over, and you're asking him to train for speed? He remembers the racetrack and all the work that went with it. He's telling you no, plain and simple. There's nothing wrong with him that rest won't cure. He's just at his limit. He needs some time off."

This wasn't the first time Savage had been told to back off and give one of his horses a break. Hersey, on several occasions, had diffidently broached the idea that horses had their mortal limits and that it was counterproductive to try to push them beyond those bounds. But he always sensed that when he spoke like this

Savage was not listening—just as Savage might peruse a news-paper article suggesting that he was using Dan Patch too hard, and then turn the page placidly, as if he'd been reading about the murder trial of Harry K. Thaw or some other far-off news story of the day. If he acknowledged the voices of moderation at all, it was to dismiss the speaker as short on imagination and—what did the young people call it?—pep. Savage himself had the opposite problem. His defining characteristic as both a horse owner and a businessman was that he was gung-ho to a fault; he lacked all sense of when enough was enough.

Ketcham stayed on until the next morning. His train had barely left the station, bound for Toledo, when Savage told Hersey to harness up Cresceus and try yet again.

Even Savage's most devout hagiographers suggest that Dan Patch should have retired from time trials after the 1906 season. He still had some fast miles in him, to be sure, but he was breaking the rules now; if he lowered his own record using a windshield, it wouldn't count, and in any case he had, as much as any horse before or since, in some ways hard to define but impossible to deny, made his point. The horse, as 1906 waned, was an almost-perfect 10, bearing virtually no physical or emotional scars from six years of travel, adulation, a feast-or-famine sex life, constant training, and intermittent requests for extreme speed. On Christ-mas Eve, he took Savage and his younger son Harold, then eleven, on a nighttime sleigh ride through Minneapolis, past streetcorner carolers and houses whose front windows framed homemade wreaths and hand-dipped holiday candles. The next morning, when a huge silver loving cup arrived belatedly from the Ken-tucky Breeders Track, Savage filled it with apples and presented it to Dan Patch as a Christmas present. How wonderful and wise it would have been to snap the picture right there, freeze the frame, and end the story.

But no. In January, Savage took out ads and printed posters promoting the pre-exhibition-season stud services of Dan Patch for the coming spring. That year he featured a typical early-twentieth-century contest: guess the number of hairs on the body of Dan's yearling son Forrest Patch (whose porcupine-ish image dominated the broadside) and win a Dan Patch colt "worth $5,000" (in Savage's dreams—Dan's yearlings had never brought that much). In early March of 1907 Savage announced that the fair board in Sioux City, Iowa, had become "the first entity to execute a contract" for a Dan Patch exhibition for the coming season. A few weeks later, the Minnesota State Fair signed on as well, and with Savage's help, concocted a rather clunky (for a marketing genius) slogan: "Dan Patch, 1:54 on the Minnesota state fair racetrack in 1907." Read now, it's a poignant slogan, too, because Dan would never again even equal his best times of past seasons.

Signs of a leveling-off of Dan's physical ability became evident in late 1906, when, in his next start after his 1:55 mile at Hamline, he could manage no better than a 2:01 ½ mile over a wet track in Sioux City. The scheduling—there were only four days between the time trials—showed that the bottom line, and not the well-being of the star attraction, was still shaping Dan Patch's career. At Allentown on September 21, the crowd was smaller and more subdued than the year before, and Dan Patch broke stride twice—once at the start, when his front hoof struck his lead prompter's dirt shield, and again in the homestretch, when his left rear leg went askew and he hit his own sulky; the sad spectacle ended in an embarrassing clocking of 2:05 ½. Clearly, it was time to call it quits, at least for the season. But no; he would soldier on for three more paydays, including a 1:59 ¼ mile at Springfield, Illinois, that, said the *Horse Breeder,* "had no flash of unusual speed at any spot."

Savage, and sometimes Hersey, tried to put a good face on the situation. After every one of those slow or mediocre performances, one of the men would step up to say, You know, that was actually one of the best miles of Dan's career, if you allow for the conditions, or look at it a certain way. In June 1907 Savage told the horsepapers that Dan was training "better than ever," and confided to the *Minneapolis Journal* that he believed his horse, at age eleven, could lower the record to 1:52. He almost certainly knew this was nonsense. Even as he boasted of his horse's prowess and popularity, he was thinking of ways to beef up the exhibitions with additional horses or gimmicks—both to counter the notion that there was nothing new to see in the Dan Patch show as well as to take some of the focus off a horse who was more and more obviously not going to do something spectacular. Buying Cresceus and getting him back to the races to compete in a series of trotter-versus-pacer "novelty match races" was one of his plans. He was also looking into fitting Dan with a gold-and-jewel-encrusted harness, and possibly a sulky to match, though he eventually switched to paint and paste versions of the real thing.

Savage's business was also starting to slow around 1907, ending a relatively brief run of boom years. His companies' dependence on a rapidly vanishing world of small family farms was, as we have seen, a major problem, as was the inability of his upstart general-purpose catalog company, Savage Factories, Inc., to make up the slack; he was at best the third choice (behind Sears Roebuck and Montgomery Ward) for a rural America in search of scissors, a church-worthy hat, kitchen canisters, or ice skates. Various proto-consumerist groups had also begun to pester him about his core product, the Three Feeds for One Cent supplement. A few agricultural colleges wanted it taken off the market, saying (correctly) that the only effects it might have on animals would be harmful. The states of Kansas and Indiana tried to force him, under the Interstate Commerce Act, to reveal Three Feeds's ingredients on the label; Savage fought back fiercely, insisting the mixture was a medicine, and thus not liable to the same federal regulations that governed food. He eventually lost the battle in the U.S. Supreme Court. Yet Savage might have survived even such downturns, miscues, and legal setbacks if he had not, in 1907, become involved in—indeed, obsessed with—building a railroad from downtown Minneapolis to his farm, twenty miles to the south. The Minneapolis, St. Paul, Rochester & Dubuque Traction Company, more popularly known as the Dan Patch Air Line, would drain him financially and perhaps hasten his death, but when he incorporated the company in July 1907, he overflowed with optimism, even joy. He was convinced that he had struck upon the kind of cleverly branded twentieth-century idea that would catapult him into the same league as the Pillsburys, the Hills, and other truly formidable Minneapolitans. And who knows where he might go from there?

Savage was a man of sprawling ambition, convinced that his role in history was destined to be something much greater than the owner of Dan Patch. In 1908 he allowed a group of Minneapolis Republicans to form a committee to promote his nomination as a candidate for governor of Minnesota. He called himself "the businessmen's candidate," and his campaign buttons said "Savage will help Minnesota grow." In his stump speech, he insisted that he was not a professional politician, a truth all too apparent from his vapid oratory ("I realize this is an age of commercialism, and that Minnesota, if it keeps to the fore, must push out"). At the state convention in June he lost the nomination by 262 to 235 votes to a stuffy Civil War captain named Samuel Snider, who in turn would lose the general election to the incumbent—and obviously very ill—Democrat John Johnson, who died the next year.

This was a motley field to finish third in. Yet Savage found his dip into politics bracing. Oddly—and tragically, at least from his heirs' perspective—the lesson he seemed to take away from the experience was that he was more than ever a man of the people, and that his God-given powers of persuasion remained intact. Savage was convinced that he could raise the tens of millions he needed for his Dan Patch Air Line by selling stock to farmers and others who lived along the proposed right-of-way for $25 a share; though he was right to assume that he would have gotten nowhere with professional investors, he claimed to be motivated by a desire to share his surefire moneymaking railroad notion with average Joes, not "Wall Street." Caught up in their own misguided enthusiasm, Savage and his fellow board members soon extended the already-too-long line fifteen miles farther to the south. The push into wilderness and open farmland made little sense for a passenger train—until Savage came up with the idea of building an amusement park at the far end, thus creating a destination that would in theory generate traffic. To some, Antler's Park, a modest collection of rides on the shore of a lake that Savage named Lake

Marion after himself, is proof of the founder's Disney-like genius. But when comparing the two entrepreneurs, it helps to remember that only one succeeded.

In pitching his railroad to the public, Savage relied more than ever on the power of Dan Patch as a brand—as an abstract suggestion of quality, speed, and success, and not an oat-munching, manure-making mammal. "Receive $1,000 in Common Stock Free from DAN PATCH," said one early *Horse Review* ad, "if you write to me today for my special proposition on one of the greatest electric railroads in the world." Dan's handsome head appeared in most of the ads, on the gaudy stock certificates Savage issued, and on the sides of the railroad cars he depicted in his literature. While it is doubtful that Savage would have done right by Dan and retired him at his peak even if he hadn't launched the railroad, the Dan Patch Air Line, along with the general decline in Savage's business interests, made a successful Dan Patch road show more important and necessary to Savage than ever. Savage, besides needing what money Dan brought in from his appearances, needed the horse to be out there on the racetracks of heartland America, meeting the people and supporting the brand.

As the decade wore on, and money became an increasingly troublesome issue, a schism developed in the Savage household. The dispute centered on horses. Dan Patch himself remained a profit center almost until the end of his career, but Savage's wife, Marietta, and their older son, Erle, an executive in the business empire, both saw the International 1:55 Stock Food Farm as a hopeless money pit. They weren't falling for any of M. W.'s bull about Minnesota surpassing Kentucky as a breeding capital, nor, under the circumstances, did they care about his treasured childhood dream of owning a first-class stock farm: the horse operation to them was nothing more than a boondoggle, tolerable in flush times, stupidly expensive now. And they were right: Savage by then owned half a dozen overpriced (and still unprofitable) stallions, more than two hundred fancy broodmares, and assorted other horses housed in bizarre buildings set on seven hundred mostly unproductive acres. Several dozen employees were needed to take care of them. In 1908, when he should have been retrenching, Savage built an indoor half-mile track that had over 1,600 windows (a dozen of which seemed to break whenever the wind blew) to go with his expensive outdoor oval. Around 1908, Marietta and Erle began urging him to sell the farm, which that year was almost as big a drain as the railroad on his earnings. M. W. would hear none of it. He and his son Harold bonded over their strong feelings for the horses, but gradually grew estranged from the other half of the household, especially as Erle began to develop problems with alcohol and morphine, and Marietta became his protector.

As Savage's luck would have it, just when he needed to lean harder on Dan Patch, the horse had increasingly less to give. Early summer floods disrupted training on the Savage farm in 1907, forcing Hersey to move the horses (he took Cresceus, too) in early July to Decatur, Illinois, where Dan's first time trial of the year was scheduled for July 31. He wound up getting a last-minute booking in Terre Haute on the twenty-fifth, and went a mile in 2:02 ¼. At Decatur, he went in 2:01 ½, another unexciting time but a track record. Nine days later he could do no better than 2:03 ¼ over the half-mile track at Pekin, Illinois.

Having less to give, though, was not the same as having nothing. There were occasional flashes of the old magic. To the surprise of no one more than Hersey, Dan went a mile at Galesburg, Illinois, on August 15 that ranked with his best—1:56 ¾—albeit with the aid of the now ever-present dirt shield. "He is evidently in the pink of condition," said the *American Horse Breeder.* A week later he broke the track record in Davenport, Iowa, pacing in 1:58 ½. It was getting harder, however, for Dan to sustain his top form. On August 28, on the mile track in Dubuque, the best he could do was 2:00 ½.

Dan's popularity was getting harder to sustain, too. He was still outdrawing most baseball games and prizefights, but his crowds had shrunk perceptibly. Part of the problem was that automobiles were making even 1:55 miles academic (1905 had been the first year more cars were purchased by regular citizens seeking transportation than by goggle-wearing, duster-clad "automobilists"). But Dan's 1907–8 seasons had a decidedly different feel to them from the 1905–6 period—they seemed somehow anticlimactic, vaguely post-farewell-tour. The average fan sensed that the best was over; many felt as if they had already said their good-byes. Yet, because of Savage's stubbornness and circumstances, here was Dan, back again, now being described in the newspapers as "ol' Dan Patch" and "Savage's war horse." "Nothing new developed in connection with the Dan Patch exhibition," said the *Horse Review* after the 1907 Davenport stop. "The same cheering crowd greeted the same phenomenal performance with the same Harry Hersey behind the champion."

And yet some things had changed in the lives of those close to Dan Patch. Scott Hudson, the handsome young Grand Circuit trainer who had driven one of Dan's Thoroughbred prompters from 1903 to 1905, told a Cincinnati reporter that he had "washed out" of harness racing, scuffled to make a living with the runners for a while, but was "down and out" and trying to survive as a mule trader. Hudson, who had handled the famous blind trotter Rhythmic and the fast pacer Audubon Boy, claimed that "failing eyesight" had been his downfall, but the self-contradictory, unfocused nature of the Cincinnati interview suggests there may have been other problems as well. At one point in his ramblings, Hudson even touches on the subject of his old colleague McHenry.

"Myron McHenry is missing!" Hudson says. "I've heard that they tried to locate Myron, but he's done disappeared!"

Also missing in action that summer: the slogan "Dan Patch, 1:54 on the Minnesota state fair racetrack in 1907." The fair, aware that Dan had begun to show his age, had stopped playing up the possibility of records long before the horse returned to his hometown track for an exhibition on September 2. It was just as well. The day was cold, the track was cuppy, and Dan's dirtshield-aided time was 1:58 ¼. While that was far faster than any other Standardbred was capable of going, Dan's 1907 Minnesota clocking would have put him more than sixteen lengths behind the Dan Patch who set the unofficial record there one year earlier. Many

an astute horseman would have looked at his stopwatch after that
mile and sent Dan Patch home right then.

But no. As soon as the obligatory handsome floral emblem
was bestowed, the caravan moved on to Sioux City, where Dan
raced before 45,000 people on September 10 and duplicated his
Minnesota time. Three days later he was in Kalamazoo, Michigan, going 2:01 ¾ over a wet track. The next stop, twelve days
later, was the Ohio State Fair. Columbus that year turned out
to be a calamitous meet. The first shock for most of the Grand
Circuit horsemen was the ghostly sight of Myron McHenry walking the backstretch in his familiar driving jacket on the first day
of racing. It was not exactly a triumphant return to the turf:
McHenry did not look well, and fortune was not completely with
him. In his first race back after more than a year away from the
harness circuit he won a $1,200 free-for-all pace with a gelding
named Angus Pointer in 2:03 ¾. However, in the first heat of his
next race, a $1,200 trot, the mare he was driving, Mae Heart, fell
down at the top of the stretch, and three trailing horses plowed
into the wreck. Two of those horses ran into the infield and had
to be caught, and McHenry was "severely bruised," according
to the *Fort Wayne Sentinel*. Still, the fifty-one-year-old trainer
returned, a half hour later, for the next heat—as did all of the
horses who had fallen and scattered. Further mayhem was in
store, but not for any of them. In the third heat, Thelma, a mare
who had avoided the first-heat accident and won the previous
mile, attempted in the homestretch to take advantage of an opening along the rail, but wound up tripping over her own feet and
breaking into a wild gallop. When Thelma's driver finally pulled
her up, just past the finish wire, said the *Sentinel*, "her left hind
leg was broken square off and hung only by the skin. She was
taken to the infield and shot."

The race, however, went on, with the battered and bloodied sur-
vivors returning for one more heat, which was won by a mare named
Wild Bell, the only horse in the field who had not fallen or died.

It was a disastrous afternoon, too, for Dan Patch, who was at
the Columbus fairgrounds, scheduled to go a training mile in preparation for his time trial two days later. By 3:00 p.m., he hadn't

appeared for his much-ballyhooed workout, and his stall was the scene of intense activity: Hersey and Plummer were rushing about and conversing in urgent whispers, and a squadron of grooms had been enlisted to form a line and keep the public at bay.

Just after noon that day, as he was being led out by Plummer for his training miles, Dan had stepped in a low spot outside his stall and "knuckled over" in his right front ankle, severely spraining the ligaments and tendons. After recoiling wildly, he had tried, instinctively, to walk off the pain. "I did not mind it much at first," says the *Autobiography,* "but as I walked, my leg pained me more and more."

The next day, after Hersey wired Savage the news of the apparently serious injury, several veterinarians were on the scene, one, a Dr. McKillop, from as far away as Chicago. The owner's instructions were to get Dan Patch onto the racetrack the next day by any means possible. Savage, who believed in a way that more enlightened horsemen no longer did that injuries could be somehow "worked" out of a horse, wanted Dan to go some kind of mile, however slowly, so he could collect his appearance fee. And just as much, he wanted to avoid fueling the already palpable perception that Dan was getting too old for the life his owner was insisting that he live.

The ankle was treated with "hot applications and blisters," and the next day Dan was hitched up and brought out at the appointed hour. Says the *Autobiography* (which at least was written by an eyewitness):

> I knew I could try but I believed it impossible for me to do anything creditable and any kind of mile would cause me untold pain. I saw the multitude in the stands. I heard the bands. I knew people were watching and waiting for the world's champion and that they would see only a limping horse. My pride was hurt. I would not go out and parade my weakness before the thousands who expected so much. For the first time in my life I hated the crowds and the music. I would not go. It was rank injustice and I would not submit to it. For the first and last time I balked.

Plummer stepped to my head and asked me to come on. No, I would not. I felt the lines tighten. For almost the first time in my life I felt the sting of the whip. I grew more stubborn. I would not move. I only shook my head, hoping they would understand. A number of the horsemen standing around the gate came closer and stood in astonishment to see Dan Patch refusing to do what was asked of him.

At length, after fifteen minutes of persuasion, someone [probably Hersey] said, "He seems to know that he can't do himself justice and he doesn't want to be humiliated, but we've got to show that howling mob that he's really lame or we'll never live to tell how it happened."

That changed everything. I was only going to be shown. The people were entitled to that. All my resistance ceased and I walked slowly, limpingly, through the gate and down the track past the expectant thousands. I limped painfully, and kept my head down.

It wasn't just the crowd Hersey and Plummer were trying to appease by having the horse hobble back and forth before the 12,500 in the grandstand. They were also sending a message to Savage: they had tried. They had put on some kind of show, and quite possibly earned the appearance fee.

"The oohs multiplied until thousands united in a low, soothing chorus of kindness and sympathy that was most affecting."

Dr. McKillop, however, would not follow the script. He announced to a circle of turf scribes in Columbus that Dan Patch was "very lame" and "perhaps done." The horse "may be able to go 2:04 or thereabout after a few weeks letup," said McKillop, "but I deem record-breaking out of the question."

A few years before, that would have been stop-the-presses news. But in September 1907, the perhaps-career-ending lameness of Dan Patch received little more than a perfunctory mention in most newspapers. A lot of people, especially in the East, may not have realized Dan was still in the exhibition business. Those who did may have thought it was just as well that circumstances were forcing Savage's hand, by giving the owner no options in the matter of Dan's retirement.

But Savage didn't see the situation that way. Although Hersey gently suggested that they call it a season, he brushed aside the notion and said he wanted Dan to go a decent public training mile at Lexington two weeks later, to show the world that the horse still had a few miracles left. This was accomplished, and a week after the stop at Lexington, Dan Patch went against the clock again. The location—City Park in New Orleans, far from the eyes of the harness-racing world—suggests that Savage was experimenting to see if Dan could handle a lucrative double booking he had at the third annual Arizona Territorial Fair on November 11 and 15. Still favoring his right front ankle slightly, Dan turned in a clocking of 2:01 over a rough track in New Orleans and cooled down well. Though that mile was not witnessed by a representative of the National Trotting Association, and thus never made it into the record books (the only source for the time was Savage), it was good enough for the owner, who told his trainer to head directly to Phoenix. There, less than two months after a vet had said that Dan would never come near two minutes again, he paced in 1:57 ¾, and then two days later in 1:57 ½.

A note in the *Nevada Journal* soon after said, "Dan Patch 1:55 will be on tour again next year."

One early April day in 1908, M. W. Savage paid a call to the Boston offices of the *American Horse Breeder*. He had come east to conclude the sale of Cresceus (who was still unwilling to do much more than walk around a racetrack) to a trotting-horse enthusiast in Russia, and he was making the rounds of the turf journals to ensure that the name of Dan Patch remained in print. Pointedly staying away from the subject of Dan's stallion career, Savage told the *Horse Breeder* editors that Dan had had a fine winter, during which the owner, as usual, drove his famous pacer around town. "When jogging along on a loose rein in the city," Savage said, "he will incline his head to one side and cast a glance to the upper windows of the buildings. If

he comes to a place where another street crosses at right angles to
the one upon which he is traveling, he will stop, look first one way,
then the other of the cross street, then, after the inspection, resume
his jog." Savage's message was that all was sweet and good in Dan
Patchland. "I will continue to exhibit Dan," he said, "as long as the
horse appears to enjoy the sport."

Three months later, taking time out from begging farmers to
contribute $25 to his Dan Patch Air Line and organizing his guber-
natorial run, Savage announced that Dan was on the verge of a
1:54 mile. Still, he said he was cutting back on the exhibition miles
the horse would pace in 1908, so that, as the *Minneapolis Journal* put it, "the champion's energies will not be wasted in going
fast miles over poor tracks in bad weather at inopportune times."
The consensus among the cognoscenti was that Dan, at twelve,
was experiencing severe physical problems; why else, they figured,
would Savage be saying, "Dan Patch has well-earned a rest"?

Ultimately 1908 was for Dan Patch a short, odd season, at the
end of which those still following his adventures were left guessing
about just how bad off he was. Not counting a publicity stunt—
Savage brought a crew of reporters to the farm on August 31 to
watch Dan go in 2:00, "the fastest workout mile on record"—he
made only four starts that year: at Detroit, Columbus, and Lexington, twice. But he went respectably fast in each (1:58 ½; 1:58; and
1:57 ¼, in the first Lexington try), and in one he almost made history. On October 11 at Lexington, blazing around the track with
his full complement of prompters and a dirt shield, he reached
the half-mile pole in :56 ½ and the three-quarters in 1:25 ½. Savage's predicted 1:54 mile was in sight. But at the seven-eighths
marker, his longtime pacesetter Cobweb, driven by the recently
reemployed Scott Hudson, suddenly collapsed in a tangle of limbs
and sulky shafts (he had broken a blood vessel in his neck, and
had to be destroyed). Dan was forced to swerve so wide that he
lost all chance of breaking the record, and Hersey pulled him to
a jog. A month later Savage asked Hudson to write a testimonial
about the experience in Savage's promotional booklet *The Racing Life of Dan Patch*. "There is not doubt in my mind but Dan
Patch was faster this fall at Lexington than any time I have ever

seen him," Hudson began . . . and ended, "Dan Patch is certainly a Wonder Horse to improve, as he has, from year to year."

Savage ended 1908 the way he had begun it, by reaching out to the press.

"I have just noticed that it has been reported that Dan Patch has been retired," he said in a statement released on November 30. "This is quite a surprise to me . . . Dan has not been retired. He is at my farm in first-class condition and I expect him to pace miles next year faster than any pacer has ever gone."

Savage concludes the statement by noting that Dan had paced a total of seventy-three race and exhibition miles so far in his career, at an average time of 1:59 ½. "We have hopes" he said, "of bringing that number up to 100."

CHAPTER TWENTY-ONE

All love demands a witness: something "there," which it yet
makes part of itself.

—Kingsley Amis

A BURST OF FRESH enthusiasm for Dan Patch and even more for
his owner M. W. Savage played out across the pages of the Standardbred horse journals in the early months of 1909. In articles
and editorials, and in the raucous cartoons of Robert L. Dickey,
the forty-eight-year-old Savage was depicted as a cunning, raffish
fellow whose adventures augured a bright future for the sport,
even if the attendance figures, the changing nature of highway
traffic, and everyone's gut feeling were telling a different, more
dire story. The long off-season forced publications like the *Horse
Review* and the *American Horse Breeder* to survive for months
on spurious gossip about obscure broodmares, debates over rule
changes, worshipful puffs about major advertisers, and sentimental photographs of dead stable cats—but this was something different. Savage wasn't just providing genuine news in the still of
winter, he had done the most noble and sportsmanlike thing a
sportsman can do: he had written a large check.

The $45,000 that Savage paid for the pacer Minor Heir on
January 4 electrified the harness-racing world almost as much as
Dan Patch's record miles had a few years before. The amount was
the second-highest ever paid for a pacer (or the highest, if you
consider that only $40,000 in cash changed hands when Savage

bought Dan Patch), and some of the more gung-ho turf scribes figured that meant the best trotters must be worth even more, and that the industry as a whole was at last reviving.

But not only were the optimists balancing their projections on the slender reed of one surprising transaction, they were overlooking two aspects of that transaction that, if pondered at greater length, would surely have harshed their mellow. The first was that Savage, with his railroad heading south in more ways than one, and his main business faltering, had made an irrational move in buying Minor Heir; the man had no business spending $45,000 on a horse, something that Erle and Marietta were making abundantly clear to him on an almost daily basis. His purchase, and the price it established for a champion pacer, said much more about his diseased ego than it did about the Standardbred horse market.

The other reason the industry might have tempered its enthusiasm for the deal was what Savage planned to do next—namely, to take the horse out of competition and make him part of the Dan Patch road show, thus depriving the sport of one of its most exciting attractions.

Minor Heir had started the previous season as merely a promising pacing stallion. Blind in one eye—a groom had inadvertently struck it with a corn-bristle brush—he had passed, for a few hundred dollars, from his original owner in Buffalo, New York, to someone out in Winfield, Iowa, before being seen and admired by Charles Dean, a respected trainer who was also one of Dan Patch's regular prompter-pilots. Minor Heir had been in only a few unofficial backwoods races and had never won when Dean acquired him, for $4,500, in late 1907. But he had gone a quarter in 30 seconds (hence the price), and the trainer was deeply impressed by the potential he saw in the pacer's fluid gait. Never the most hardy of horses, Minor Heir nevertheless thrived at Dean's farm in Palatine, Illinois, and as a six-year-old in early 1908 won his first official race in 2:05 ¼. A few weeks later, in a match race against The Eel—a silver-gray Canadian pacer who was that country's ice-racing champion—Minor Heir won a grueling five-heat contest and set four world records in the process. By the end of the season he had a time-trial mark of 1:59 ½. Like Dan, he had a calm disposition and generous ways, and many said that apart from Dan, he was, though decidedly on the small side, the most comely Standardbred they had ever seen. "His head was fine and clean in outline," Hervey wrote, "and his body lines were symmetry itself, lithe, graceful, athletic, yet suggestive of power and speed. His coat was a particularly rich shade of bay that toned off into mahogany and rosewood tints; it was satin-like in texture and when it was heated the network of veins stood out beneath it in exquisite relief."

It was this magnificent, kindhearted animal that Savage would set about ruining in 1909, even as he pushed Dan Patch past the breaking point.

Minor Heir's role in the Dan Patch show was to be a foil for the star attraction: after they were introduced at length and paraded up and down the homestretch, the two would compete in a match race advertised as "genuine races for blood" between (Savage would have the public believe) two champions in their prime. Savage hoped the customers wouldn't notice that Dan's signature time trial had slipped off the program. At the age of thirteen, Dan was still as fast as ever, he insisted, adding that the horse would certainly lower his (unofficial) 1:55 record somewhere along the line, but in the meantime, these showdowns with Minor Heir were being presented as a kind of public service, to give the fans a treat.

No sane observer believed the match races would be legit, and they weren't. The choreography was simple: after the "Go," Dan would drop back and draft behind Minor Heir until midway through the homestretch, when the local driver who had been selected to drive Dan (an effective publicity gimmick; Hersey always drove Minor Heir) would pull the older pacer to the passing lane and breeze on by. The ploy was as subtle as a World Wrestling Entertainment event, but the first time they tried it outside of rehearsals, at the fairgrounds in Grand Fords, North Dakota, on July 24, Ed Hall, the driver of Dan Patch, and Hersey botched things up, or Dan simply didn't have anything resembling his old finishing kick, or both—and Minor Heir was still half a length ahead at the wire, even though Hersey had slowed the race to a crawl. Since this was the one and only heat scheduled, did this mean that Dan had lost the first race of his career? It wasn't clear yet if the *Wallace Yearbook* would consider these races official (it wouldn't), but meanwhile Savage was vigorously insisting that they were. Ultimately, a one-paragraph AP story slugged "Minor Heir Beats Dan Patch" went over the wires, but because of the ambiguous status of the competition and the suspicious brevity of the dispatch, very few papers used it. It might have been a comic episode but for the final clocking: Dan Patch had not been able to pass his alleged rival in a "race" that went in 2:11 ½.

Sensing the need for damage control, Savage laughed off the Grand Forks disaster as "a workout," and sent the *Horse Review* a long account of another match race between the same two on his farm track the following week. This time, with Savage himself driving, Dan Patch, oddly enough, engaged Minor Heir in a thrilling stretch duel before getting his nose in front at the wire. Savage proffered no final time for the mile, but said the last eighth "went in a 1:56 clip." When he and Hersey dismounted, Savage was said to have raised his fist in mock fury and bellowed, "You fellows aren't quite as smart as you think you are. Dan Patch is still Dan Patch."

But of course, he wasn't. On August 14 over the half-mile track in Springfield, Ohio, the two horses reached the halfway point in a pokey 1:04 ¾, and even with Minor Heir making a convenient break in the stretch Dan went all-out to win in 2:08 ½. "As a speed exhibition," said the *Review,* "it was rather disappointing" for the 15,000 who paid their way in.

"Some disappointment was manifested by the crowd at the time in the Minor Heir–Dan Patch match race," wrote the *Review* correspondent in Muncie, Indiana, eleven days later. The time was 2:10 ½, so slow that Hersey, try as he might, could not stop Minor Heir from inching in front of Dan in the last few strides, resulting in another embarrassing "loss" for the star of the show.

A very bad situation would get worse at Dan's annual homecoming at the Minnesota State Fair. Said the *Review:* "There was widespread general disappointment loudly expressed among the great crowds of people, both out at the grounds and downtown, in the cities of St. Paul and Minneapolis, when it was announced that,

owing to a suddenly developed lameness on the part of the champion, Dan Patch, the match race, which all, especially the country
folk, had come to see, would be called off." Instead, Minor Heir
was sent on a time trial to beat his record of 1:59 ¼, and Dan was
"shown in the homestretch" throughout the afternoon. Noted the
Review: "While there were perhaps 20,000 people in the racetrack
enclosure, there was not the same pressure for seats, or even room
to stand in front of the bleachers, as in former years."

Those who had turned out probably regretted it. During one
of his warm-up miles, Minor Heir took a bad step, which "had
the effect of laming him for the rest of the afternoon." Trying to
complete the lap, the little pacer could be seen "nodding perceptibly, as if he were considerably hurt somewhere in front." Savage,
of course, ordered that he go anyway, and Minor Heir, limping
noticeably, hobbled around the track in 2:01 ¾.

This was a star-crossed tour, each stop bringing a fresh disaster.
At the Wisconsin State Fair a week later, Dan was still lame and
so was Minor Heir, but the latter started anyway in a time trial.
Hersey, perhaps eager to be done with the proceedings, somehow
got away before the horse had been "formally announced," a violation of the rules. "To the keen disappointment of the crowd," the
mile didn't count. Not that it mattered, since Minor Heir missed
his personal-best record by a full four seconds.

On September 22 a curious note appeared in the *Review*. Written by John Markey, the item said for the first time publicly that
Dan had been having problems with his right front foot for four
years, but "now that is the best of the four." Chief among Dan's
many leg ailments, said Markey (who had obviously been talking
to Hersey, though the trainer was not quoted directly) was "swelling and pain in his left hind pastern and ankle." The pastern—the
bone that connects the hoof and fetlock—"has dropped about an
inch and Hersey fears that further attempts to train him will cause
a permanent breakdown."

Savage was angered by the report, and possibly in response,
ordered Hersey to go a mile with Dan Patch at Sioux City on
September 21, even though it had already been announced that
because of his lameness Dan would merely be shown there in front

of the grandstand. With no pretense of a race, Minor Heir paced abreast of Dan and the two toured the track in 2:10 ¼. That mile was proof, said Savage in a snappish telegram to the *Review,* that "Dan's pastern had not dropped" and that he remained "the only horse that can beat two minutes today."

But he would never come near that time again. Hersey managed to get Dan and Minor Heir on the track together on October 4 at Sedalia, Missouri, where their mock match race was timed in 2:07. Nine days later in Parsons, Kansas, however, Dan was able only to put on a "one-eighth of a mile speed show" for 3,000 spectators, while Minor Heir went a separate "exhibition mile" timed in 2:05.

At Dallas on October 23, they managed another match race in 2:07. From there they traveled overnight to Shreveport, Louisiana, where someone broke into Minor Heir's stall, and blacksmith Ren Nash and a stable hand spent the night in jail for their too-vigorous assault of the intruder. It was a sad and seamy swing down south; the turnout in Shreveport was probably fewer than two thousand, and the fake race went in 2:09. On November 8 at the always fast track in Phoenix, teamed up for what would be their last pseudo-duel, the two finished almost in tandem in 2:03 ¼. It was Dan's fastest mile that year, but it took the last of what he had to give.

What had started at the Benton County Fair ended in the Los Angeles Agricultural Park, a place described in the *Autobiography* as "rundown, mossy, lonesome and spooky." Said the *Los Angeles Times* on Thanksgiving Day, 1909:

> Dan Patch finished his great career as a racehorse yesterday in a dismal, drizzling rain, on such a day Napoleon should have gone to St. Helena. There is nothing equal to a drizzle in which to end careers.
>
> More than 3,000 people sat in the leaky grandstand with their legs wound around their chair rungs to keep out the puddles; or stood along the fence in the mud and cheered the game old bay pacer's last race.

Dan Patch's press agent announced, anyway, with deep emotion that it was Dan's last race. . . . The water dripped down from his clothes as he said this.

The soggy crowd responded with a yell of applause; and Dan Patch swung out through the paddock gate and onto the muddy track.

A moment later appeared Minor Heir, the young pacer who is creeping up on the world's record.

As they jogged past the grandstand the crowd sent out a mighty cheer. At the familiar sound the old pacer turned his head and looked up at the crowd with an expression of interest and curiosity absolutely human.

The amateur trotting horses who were just leaving the track from the last race were in a white lather—nervous, quivering, sensitive things. But Dan Patch was the old bored professional. When he looked up at the crowd it was like an old soubrette peeping through the curtains. He took one look and jogged on with about as much emotion as a butcher's delivery horse.

Up the stretch you could see them whirl, and the sulkies turned. Old Dan swept down under the wire, his machinery running with the perfect rhythm of an engine. Past the grandstand with a rush, you could see them turn the quarter and glide on down to the half. . . . Finally they loomed out of the fog and swung into the stretch. The time was 2:15 ½.

Just as he swept under the wire at the finish, the veteran at once slowed down without a hint from the rein. He stopped where he saw his grooms were waiting by the trackside. In an instant the straps were off and Dan Patch was hooded and gowned like a monk in a big gray blanket. They led him away. When the groom came to a little depression, he slowed up as tenderly as if he were leading a rheumatic old lady.

Finally, under the picturesque old peppers by the paddock, Dan was led into his stall and was rubbed to take the stiffness from his lame old knees. For an hour or more thereafter, the grooms led him in a circle around the peppers. His promenade was frequently interrupted by women and children who wanted to pet him and feed him sugar. He liked the feel of little soft hands on his face, and gently rubbed his velvet muzzle against the children who were lifted up to him.

After the race, Hersey talked about Dan as a mother might talk about her first born. "His legs have given out—worn out," he said, "I guess old Dan is about all in."

But no. Nine days later, because Savage had worked a deal to have Minor Heir attempt to lower the California record, Dan Patch was back on the track at Agricultural Park.

"Dan Patch, who has a record of 1:55, did not cover himself with glory, for the old stager was not in shape and the cold day was anything but favorable for any burst of speed," said the *Los Angeles Times*. "Dan has had four bad legs for some time, and was not sent a fast mile, jogging around the track in 2:14 ½ accompanied by a runner, and the fact that he pulled up lame was an indication that he was going on his nerve, for he warmed up stiff in front. He is a grand, game old horse and while he did nothing startling there was sufficient satisfaction to the shivering spectators in seeing an animal who has shown his heels to the best of the harness horses in the past."

Once more the hood, the blanket, the women, the children.

Now, finally, he was done.

CHAPTER TWENTY-TWO

All horseplayers die broke.

—Damon Runyon

DAN PATCH'S LAST PUBLIC appearance occurred on September 7, 1914, when he marched down Nicollet Avenue, one of several retired animals enlisted to participate in a tribute to work horses organized by the Minneapolis Humane Society. He was eighteen years old and in reasonably good shape for a horse who couldn't exercise much, or so it was said. While it would be fascinating to see how he looked in the parade, leading, or perhaps mixed in with, a group of horses who had worked, said the *Minneapolis Journal,* for "department stores, express companies, fire and police stations and firms generally," no one took pictures. Except for the disruption it caused to downtown automobile traffic, the event was not big news in the city where, eleven years before, Dan had caused pandemonium by walking the other way down the same street.

Dan Patch had a singular status in Minneapolis in his declining years: famous but also familiar. Even if they didn't see him much anymore, people had become accustomed to having him around.

The morning after his last appearance of the 1909 tour, he and Minor Heir and the prompters had boarded a train that took them through the Rockies and back into the teeth of what one Minneapolis paper called "an old-fashioned winter," though it was still technically fall. While blizzards raged, Plummer had gone to work in earnest on the horse's aching legs, and Savage had started predicting "near two-minute miles" for Dan in 1910, but no one was taking the owner seriously. He knew himself that Dan was through as an athlete, and early the next spring he went shopping for pacers to compete against Minor Heir in another series of semi-official races that would replace the staged Dan Patch–Minor Heir showdowns. The upgrading of the act was part of an industrywide trend at a time when migration to the cities caused fair attendance to soften. The Celebrated Belmont Sisters had started strapping on parachutes and jumping from the gondola of their balloon; and the Gentry Brothers, after Savage sold them back their struggling Dog and Pony Show, hired the widow of General Tom Thumb, Barnum's famous midget, and at every performance had her "marry" the replacement midget she had "married" twenty years before. The problem with Savage's show was that he couldn't improve upon the original. The three horses that he bought for undisclosed amounts—George Gano, Hedgewood Boy, and Lady Maud C.—were among the best in harness racing, but they were no match for Minor Heir, who would have been allowed to win anyway, because, as everyone realized, Savage was using the exhibitions to promote his stallion's career.

Dan Patch came along on the 1910 tour for the first month or so, but he was never "shown at speed," as horsemen then said. The usual routine was that he came out first and paraded before the grandstand, pulling his "gold" harness and "jeweled" sulky in which sat Plummer, stiff with fear (like many grooms, he was not a public person) and wearing a gleaming white suit. As they reached the finish-line area, the permanently leg-sore Dan bowed to the crowd, basked in their applause, and then paced slowly to a point at the start of the final turn, from which the master of ceremonies said he would "observe his colleagues in action." One didn't need binoculars, however, to see he was not fully absorbed by the proceedings, and who can blame him? There was something dreary about a purseless race among four horses owned by the same man. Probably some time in mid-September, Dan Patch left the act and came home to his twenty-by-twenty-foot stall in Minnesota to stay. He wasn't seen much pulling Savage, or his son Harold, through the streets of Minneapolis, but local families, especially if they owned

an automobile, often brought their children to see the great horse at
Savage's farm of a Saturday or Sunday afternoon.

Dan's stallion career wound down early. His sons and daughters—Dana Patch, Hazel Patch, Ed Patch, Agnes Patch, Rena
Patch, Junior Dan Patch, and a couple hundred others—cropped
up in races all over America, but while some were just fine none
was great, and demand for Dan Patch's stud services stalled. Savage tried several schemes to turn things around. He offered to
"crate and ship" a Dan Patch yearling to anyone who requested
one, no money down, the price to be negotiated a year or so later,
when the buyer presumably saw what a world-beater he had on
his hands. He slashed Dan's stud fee from $500 to $275, then
lowered it again, to a price he would disclose if you wrote to
him. Nothing worked; Minnesota was too remote, Dan's breeding record too unspectacular, the Standardbred business in general
too slow. By the time he reached his midteens Dan might as well
have been a gelding for all the names he had on his dance card.

The International 1:55 Stock Food Farm could not have been a
pleasant place to work during this period. Half the Savage family
stood in angry opposition to its very existence, and there was little
evidence to refute their contention that the spread and all of its
horses were a tremendous waste of time. Not only were the stallions
not producing income—Minor Heir's stud services would eventually be offered at the embarrassing price of $75—but the touring
show (which employed eighteen men) was sparsely attended and
often less than an aesthetic success: once all four of the Savage allstars broke stride in the same race, creating what one paper called
"a farcical effect"; on another occasion Hersey became ill in midrace and vomited from the sulky. With Dan out of the spotlight,
the point of all the hippodroming seemed lost. Savage, remaining
true to his belief that people love to see records being set, kept
constant pressure on Hersey to push the horses harder, and, as
always, to "work" the animals out of whatever lameness or illness
they might have been suffering from. The trainer knew this was
often wrong, if not immoral, just as he had known it was cruel to

push Dan Patch as far as Savage had insisted, but for years he did little more than hint that there might be a wiser way to proceed.

Matters finally came to a head in 1911 over a promising son of Dan's named Dazzle Patch. The speedy and strapping colt was, most horsemen who saw him agreed, Dan's best hope of making a name for himself as a sire. Savage printed posters of Dazzle, as well as a booklet telling a contrived and corny story about his life on the farm with a fictional trainer much younger, blonder, and more athletic than Hersey. The owner may have seen Dazzle as the next star of the road show, in which at that time he was just a minor player. The problem was that Dazzle Patch was not a sound horse; he suffered, not surprisingly, from the ligament strains, tendon irritations, and muscle pulls that come from going too fast too soon. When in the early fall of 1911 Hersey told Savage with uncharacteristic firmness that Dazzle was not fit for any more time trials that season, Savage became irritated, and said that if Hersey couldn't solve the horse's problems, he should try half-mile time trials, in order to keep Dazzle's name before the public in some way. These sprints, however, only aggravated his injuries, and by November he was back on the farm, limping severely. When one morning Savage told Hersey to get him on the training track and "work his kinks out," Hersey had finally had enough. He threw his whip on the ground and said he was quitting.

In September of 1912 Dan made his last visit to the Minnesota State Fair, not going near the track but standing in a tent "decorated with his gaily colored silk and wool blankets" and surrounded by "his suit of linen which he wears when not on exhibition" and a collection of trophies. "Dan Patch" was still a household name, even to children who could have no memory of his racing days, thanks to a brand line that included breakfast cereal, washing machines ("the fastest wash in the world"), watches, locks, household thermometers, and sewing machines, all of which brought in money for the Dan Patch Air Line to immediately drain away. But because Dan was unable to move much due to his chronic pastern and suspensory problems, his life was sometimes dull. After Plummer quit in 1912 (he missed the racetrack life, and was thoroughly sick of Savage), workers on the farm began taking turns bringing the pacer home with them for one- to three-day stretches. Kelly Madigan Erlandson, a great-granddaughter of a Savage farmhand named Michael Egan, remembers her grandmother Effie telling stories of walking into the backyard with her girlfriends and finding Dan Patch standing beside her mother's garden, munching on grass. Effie and her sister would sometimes climb onto the horse and ride him bareback. You could always take Dan anywhere.

Savage replaced Hersey with the man who had been his first assistant, the equally meek Ned McCarr. Hersey, the next spring, got a job training horses for Sterling Holt, an ice merchant in Indianapolis. Holt had a medium-size stable with medium-quality stock, and for a few years he and Hersey did all right. When Holt retired and sold his horses, around 1918, Hersey tried to make a go of it as an independent trainer, but harness racing was at its lowest ebb and horse owners were difficult to come by. In 1920 he took at job at the City Shoe Repair Shop in downtown Indianapolis; when he left town, fifteen years later, he owned the business.

Hersey and Savage did not part on friendly terms. The owner bad-mouthed him to newspaper men (who didn't print the slurs), and his publicist Harrison had Dan say in the *Autobiography* that he would have gone as fast and been just as successful for any other halfway decent trainer. Hersey did not return the slights, and those who knew him in his later years said he enjoyed reminiscing about Dan Patch. After answering questions about the horse, he would sometimes give his interlocutor an old-fashioned stick pin crowned with a small, golden image of Dan's head. Hersey died, a day short of his seventy-third birthday, on April 19, 1940, in Newark, New Jersey, where he and Fannie had moved to be near their daughter Louise, a Broadway stage actress who once had a small role in a musical review that starred Al Jolson.

John Wattles also died (on April 14, 1911) surrounded by family and apparently past the point of bitterness about Dan Patch. But Myron McHenry, in contrast to the other men who had trained Dan Patch, came to what Hervey called "a sad and shabby end."

After parting ways with Savage he drifted—no, stormed—in and out of the harness-racing business, always insisting that he was not regretful of anything regarding the great horse, but frequently making obscenely derogatory remarks about the owner to whoever would listen. Whereas Hersey gave out jewelry to people who seemed interested in Dan, McHenry would feign an elaborate yawn when the subject came up, or simply walk away. In 1910, six years after he and Savage announced their separation, he said he was suing the owner for $15,000 for breach of contract. (If he did, nothing came of it.)

Keeping track of McHenry could be difficult. He would lose touch with the horse world for months, only to surface "with a string of fast ones" in Juarez, Mexico, then go back into his rabbit hole until a reporter spotted him at a running track in Ottawa with "a bunch of cheap Canadian platers." "I have never been able to make a living with the runners," he once said, "and I have never had a losing year on the harness turf." This was true, if only because as small as he was, he could not be a jockey, and the Thoroughbred game didn't play into his strengths as a driver. He won the Kentucky Futurity with a trotter called Silko in 1906, and that year and part of the next trained the first-rate stable of Lotta Crabtree, a now-forgotten comedienne who was the Lucille Ball of her day. McHenry drove her trotter Nut Boy to victory in nine prestigious stakes.

But the Wizard never stopped drinking, and so even when things were good they were awful. His devoted—and quite well-off—wife, Ida, finally divorced him in 1905, telling the judge, according to the *Chicago Tribune,* that he "went around the racing circuit with a Mrs. Flynn." McHenry, the paper added, "did not contest the charges." His health declined precipitously after his marriage dissolved; by 1910 or so people found it hard to look at his sunken, yellow face and his tattered clothing. On the morning of September 15, 1911, McHenry, who was fifty-five, collapsed on the racetrack in Detroit and was taken to the hospital, where he was diagnosed with "pernicious anemia." A hat was passed, and he was put on a train to Geneseo, Illinois. There he lived three more weeks, cared for by Miss Mary Hammer, who had been his first-grade teacher at the Old Salem School. The well-known Kentucky breeder John Madden, the owner of Silko, paid for his headstone, which bears the inscription "America's Greatest Reinsman." His old friend Sturges—who was still a high roller then but who would die penniless in his nephew's home in Bay Ridge, Brooklyn, in 1918—did not send flowers.

Dan Patch died on Tuesday, July 11, 1916.

He had started feeling bad on Friday the seventh, a day of ninety-degree heat in Savage, Minnesota, but the stable hands attending him thought they noticed an improvement over the weekend, so they did not call the vet. Monday morning he stopped eating, though, and by the evening he could barely stand. Dr. Charles Cotton came but was noncommittal. At just before ten o'clock the next morning Dan Patch suddenly fell on his side and, according to several eyewitnesses, began frantically moving his legs in a pacing motion. "This continued for several seconds," said the *St. Paul Pioneer Press,* "and then, with a gasp, the noble animal was dead."

Savage was in Minneapolis's Hillcrest Hospital at the time, recovering from minor surgery for hemorrhoids. He may have been purposely drawing out his convalescence to avoid stockholders and other creditors of the Dan Patch Air Line who were clamoring for information about why the railroad wasn't fully up and functioning yet, and threatening to sue. Since his main business was no longer the cash cow it had once been, Savage was more or less broke. His only plan at that point was to stave off the angry mob of small investors—more than 8,500 local people were holding worthless shares in the railroad—by saying he was hospitalized and would deal with the matter when he was able to return to work.

When his farm manager Murray Anderson called to say that Dan Patch had died, Savage took the news with equanimity. He reminded Anderson of a discussion from the year before, as Dan approached the age of twenty. Savage had said that when the horse died, he wanted to stuff and mount his carcass and exhibit him across America. It was a quaint, P. T. Barnum–esque notion that, given the small amount of space Dan's death would command in the nation's newspapers over the next few days, probably never would have succeeded. Dan Patch had lived a life of average length, but like Frank Sinatra and Bob Hope a few generations later, he had lived too long, and had died in a world much different from the one where he had made his bones. His departure did not resonate.

Still, Savage never had an idea that he didn't cling to for too long, and he told Anderson to immediately wire the Minneapolis newspapers, advising that a masterpiece of taxidermy was in the offing. Although that left him only internal organs to bury, he also contemplated a soaring monument to the pacer that would draw paying pilgrims to the farm.

His voice was confident, but behind his mask, he felt . . . what? . . . scared? shamed? cornered? We can only guess, but the next day, following an afternoon-long visit from Marietta, Savage had a heart attack and died. His passing occurred thirty-one hours after the death of Dan Patch. He was fifty-seven. Outside of Minnesota, this was minor news, and the horse journals, out of obligation to a former advertiser, crafted polite-as-possible and rather cunning obits. Said the *Horse Review:* "In the course of many visits to our office, extending over a period of nearly twenty years, during which he discussed exhaustively his plans, his hopes, his ambitions and his successes, we came to know him."

An unofficial autopsy was done on Dan's body as it was prepared for mounting. Dr. Cotton was surprised to discover that the horse's heart weighed nine pounds, two ounces, making it four pounds heavier than he might have expected. The outsize organ, which once served Dan so well, had apparently become distended and inefficient with age. "He had an athlete's heart," said the doctor, "and that is what killed him."

Even in their grief about M. W., Marietta and Erle were calm and clear about his horses. The farm and all the animals, they immediately decided, would be sold off as soon as possible; no gravestones would be erected; there would be no traveling corpse. Erle sent a telegram to trainer Ned McCarr, who was in Peoria with what was left of the Savage racehorse contingent, telling him to pack up the stable and come home.

Marietta called in a group of five or six stable hands and told them to bury Dan Patch down by an oak tree near the Credit River, where Savage had interred other horses, and to keep the location a secret: she didn't want tourists or newspapermen coming around. When one of the grooms asked about a coffin or box of some kind, she said it was too hot to leave Dan's body out while they built one, and besides, she needed to focus on her husband's funeral.

"Just bury him. Go!"

The men, reeling from the two deaths, as well as the rumor that the farm might be sold and their jobs put in jeopardy, grabbed shovels and did what they were told.

A week after Savage's death, the Dan Patch Air Line went into receivership, its obligations outweighing its assets by nearly $11 million. (Another railroad, the Minneapolis, Northfield and Southern Railway, would take it over, and Savages from later generations would work on it, as brakemen.) Savage's other companies were adversely affected because he had issued millions of dollars of preferred stock in them, which he used as collateral for loans he took to finance the railroad. Savage left no will, but after probate, his estate was $65,000 in the red. His family spent the next two decades fending off creditors and living as best they could on the dwindling cash flow of International Stock Food and its related concerns. The last of M. W.'s businesses collapsed during the Depression.

The farm was auctioned off by the Scott County sheriff in 1919 to pay back taxes. The horses by then had all been sold for whatever Erle, the estate manager, could get, which was often as little as $25. The asking prices for George Gano and Dazzle Patch were $850 and $400, respectively, and they probably went for less than half of that; they may have, like many of the others, been given away, such was the lack of demand for Standardbred horses by then. The dairy farmer who bought the property may have noticed that a certain large oak tree near the river had toppled over. Storms had also flattened the indoor half-mile track and severely damaged the Taj Mahal minaret. In 1922, after the dairyman had moved on, a fire brought the rest back to earth.

Epilogue

The magician seemed to promise that something torn to bits might be mended without a seam, that what had vanished might reappear, that a scattered handful of doves or dust might be reunited by a word, that a paper rose consumed by fire could be made to bloom from a pile of ash. But everyone knew that it was only an illusion. The true magic of this broken world lay in the ability of the things it contained to vanish, to become so thoroughly lost, that they might never have existed in the first place.

—Michael Chabon, *The Amazing Adventures of Kavalier & Clay*

WELL, OF COURSE, NOTHING ends quite that neatly.

Several of Savage's horses carried the legacy of his hardheartedness into the motor-driven age, chief among them Minor Heir. Savage, by 1912, had pushed the exquisite and expensive pacer to the point of lameness, but then compounded the problem by beseeching a veterinarian of dubious credentials to perform Frankensteinish tendon-repair surgery on both of the horse's front legs. Instead of patching him up and returning him to full employment—the only reason to incur a veterinarian's fee, as far as Savage was concerned—the procedure left Minor Heir, who lest we forget was already half blind, severely crippled. When Savage died, the horse, still only fourteen, was considered worthless, and rather than bear the expense of feeding him, the estate gave him away. He wound up in Williston, Tennessee, with a man who kept him as comfortable as possible until the day, in 1928, when the former world champion stumbled over a stone, fell, and broke his neck.

Dan Patch products disappeared from stores and catalogs during the World War I years, not because the pacer had died but because the brand was now a liability, evoking as it did the horse-and-buggy age, which sounded, even then, as unmodern as it does today. Would you buy Elvis-Os breakfast cereal if you were not such an ironic cat? Dan Patch sleds and little red wagons, however, hung on until around 1949, the year of the Dan Patch movie.

Erle died in 1942, but Savage's younger son Harold lived even deeper into the twentieth century, always believing that a Dan Patch revival was just around the bend. It was, as you may have noticed, not. But the hope kept him going through tough times, which for him could be defined as times in general. In the 1940s Harold restarted one of his father's corporate entities, the International Sugar Feed Company, which he ran until his death in 1977. For most of those years it was a one-man operation, and Harold was what A. J. Liebling would call a telephone booth Indian, a man who allows the world to think he is the tip of an iceberg when he is in fact but a rapidly melting cube. "Like his father, he was a dreamer," says his daughter Mary Savage Colwell, "but in a kind and gentle way." It pained him when a pacer named Billy Direct (a distant relative of Prince Direct) finally broke Dan Patch's official record of 1:55 ¼ in 1938, but he kept the faith that his father's horse would one day be rediscovered. The mention of Dan Patch in Meredith Willson's 1957 show *The Music Man* moved him deeply, and despite limited funds, he commissioned a playwright to compose a libretto for a Broadway musical based on the horse (nothing came of it). Harold also attended Dan Patch Days in Savage, Minnesota, usually riding in the lead wagon, which was sometimes pulled by a descendant of Dan Patch when one could be found (because of his lackluster record as a sire, it was difficult). Until the end, Harold's company letterhead, though not on the best bond paper, always featured the somewhat enigmatic visage of Dan Patch, cocking his head and looking back across the decades.

The idea of a Dan Patch revival has never once crossed the mind of John Messner. Nor does the grandson of the horse's original owner and the owner of the Dan Patch barn express any desire to be involved with DP enthusiasts and their Patchiana as the curator of a Dan Patch museum. Yet he came to the conclusion one day in December 2005 that the boarded-up Dan Patch barn, which he had been "seeing but not seeing" outside his front door lo these many years, was "on the verge of becoming the Dan Patch scrap pile." So he called his friend Ty Morris, a thirty-something Lafayette firefighter who is adept with wood and wires, and a fairly major renovation was begun.

Naturally, this involved entering the structure, something, as we have seen, that neither John or his father, Dick, had ever done, despite the proximity of the barn to their front door, and which his grandpa Dan didn't do much in the nearly thirty-six years he lived following the sale of Dan Patch in 1902. To refresh the reader's memory, my theory is that the barn has long reminded the Messner men of a troubling truth—not that Grandpa Dan sold the horse too soon, but that other people think he did, or else think the family must have made millions from Dan Patch. Either assumption would be highly annoying to John, who is cranky in a way I respect: he does not suffer fools, or the kind of people who would spend much time wandering around a Dan Patch museum, gladly. It may be only now, in the early twenty-first century, when people have all but stopped making any kind of assumptions about Dan Patch, that the old barn has become for him less fraught and therefore more approachable—in other words, something closer to just an old barn.

Still, he had Morris go in first, check out the place, then report back.

Morris—Scronedog to his Oxford friends—is an agile, energetic man who brought a boyish enthusiasm to the project, and who took less than two days to acquire a basic sense of the structure's condition and contents. It helped that he was oblivious to both the extreme cold and the occasional cat-size rat running between his legs.

Some of what he found was not surprising. Though the inner sanctum had not been penetrated in nearly a century, the Messner family had in the 1960s farmed several hundred acres south and east of town, and a subcontractor they had hired to work the land had used outer portions of the barn to store equipment and house animals. "There was a whole lot of dried sheep poop," Morris told me, smiling broadly, as he, John, and Bob Glaspie took me on a tour of the half-renovated barn one freezing morning in late February of 2006. "And indications of hogs."

It was, however, the roughly sixty-by-forty-four-foot barn proper that serious Dan Patch aficionados, and now even John himself, were interested in. That was tougher sledding for Morris, thanks to a profusion of hay and oats that lay in drifts three and four feet deep in some places. Once he had carefully shoveled and swept that stuff away, Morris found what I had gotten a peek at through a crack in a jammed doorway on my previous visit: essentially the world of Dan Patch, abruptly abandoned. There were pitchforks and shovels strewn about, along with "a hypodermic kind of device for putting a pill down a horse's throat." There were remnants of two sulkies: one the standard forty inches wide; the other, measuring forty-four inches, was almost certainly the custom-made bike built to accommodate the errant left rear leg of Dan Patch. Near a little room that had served as a stable office, five nails, suitable for hanging harnesses, had been tapped into the wall, and designated, in still-quite-legible pencil, for LADY, SON, BESSIE, DAN, JOE. The identity of the second, third, and fifth would be hard to determine (Joe Patchen never lived there), but there was no doubt about the other two.

Along the north wall stood three stalls. One, the middle one, had a shallow but definite indentation in the middle of its floor. "You can tell this was the stall of a male horse," Morris said, pointing to the spot. "Because that's where he peed." The tour stopped and stared.

My friends at the Dan Patch Historical Society in Savage, Minnesota, won't be pleased by my saying this, but if you want to picture the urine spot Dan left behind for us to contemplate, imagine the shape of Indiana.

What really got Morris's heart pumping, however, and sent him running across the yard to find John on the second day of the excavation, was what he found in the rear of the stall: Dan Patch's tack trunk. The box, which bore the horse's name in fancy, faded letters, was sitting on the dirt floor, open and surrounded by a brush, a currycomb, leg wraps, girth straps, and a bottle of Humphrey's lineament. Inside the box were neck sweats (homemade-looking gingham hoods that Dan wore when cooling down after a race or workout), a pump for inflating sulky tires, and a copy of *Western Horseman* magazine dated September 24, 1900. "When Bob Glaspie saw that tack trunk," John said with a wink, "he fell on his knees and rubbed it like it was a twenty-year-old woman."

To a very small number of people, it was an exciting find. For security reasons, Morris and a helper gently placed the loose items back in the trunk and carried it into John's house. About a week later, after the Lafayette paper published a story about the barn renovation, John got a call from the Harness Racing Museum in Goshen, New York, offering him $10,000 for the trunk. He turned it down flat. Exactly why he can't say. Nor does he know what will happen next with the barn and the artifacts, given his position on museum management. "It's wonderful to find all this, I guess," he said. "But I honestly have no idea what I'm going to do with it."

It is rare to find a person who has ambiguous feelings about Dan Patch. To know the horse is usually to want something with his name on it, and to wish you could have been there when he hit the starting line at full speed, leaned into those turns, tore down the homestretch, raced under the finish wire, then came back, stopped, and bowed.

I was a little upset at John for teasing Bob Glaspie the way he had, especially in front of Thelma, but I forgave him about twenty minutes later when, after excusing himself for a while, he reappeared and, with a bit of ceremony, stopped the barn tour, such as it was, and presented Bob and Ty Morris and me with horseshoes that had been discovered during the renovation. Ty and I got front shoes, caked with rust but in the classic inverted U shape; they could have been Dan's, but they might also have been Bessie's or Son's or Joe's or Lady's. What makes them wonderful is that they are from the Dan Patch barn; and even the great collector George Augustinack, who may or may not own Dan Patch's tail, dyed red, would covet them.

Bob got a different kind of shoe. When he held it up for all to see, it was clearly and breathtakingly asymmetrical, with an extra length of iron extending from one of the tines. Everyone in the barn knew what that meant, and we gasped, and when Bob tried to say thank you, he couldn't for a moment because he was crying.

Note on Sources

EACH BOOK HAS ITS own challenges, the chief one in this case being Dan's strange status: a pop cultural hero who is now a kind of entry-level historical figure known only to the experts. Not only are all the eyewitnesses gone, but so, for the most part, are the children who heard their stories of the great pacer. It is only in Dan's birthplace of Oxford, Indiana, and in Savage, Minnesota, where he lived most of his twenty years and where the Dan Patch Historical Society meets regularly, that people still pass along the legend of Dan Patch with passion and, sometimes, embroidery. One Oxfordite I interviewed apologized for only having "barber shop lore," as if that was not something precious. I am grateful that he shared it, and the stories he and other people told me, in Oxford and Savage, constitute one strand in what might be called the book's narrative cord.

Another important source was the newspapers of the day; I paged and scrolled through many hundreds at the Minnesota Historical Society, at the New York Public Library, and online. Ragtime-era sportswriters, as I say in chapter eleven, did not always dig deeply, but they did keep close tabs on the horse as he moved about the landscape. Their stories provided occasional priceless details. Newspaper sources are all cited in the text. So are the horse magazines, all now defunct, that were probably even more valuable to my research. Reading *American Horse Breeder* and (especially) *Horse Review,* I could see the story of an up-from-the-boondocks horse and his flawed human connections playing out in Technicolor and even, in places, 3-D. Some of the novelistic-seeming scenes in this book are less novelistic than the reader might suppose; the details and dialogue having been transported from those gloriously eccentric old journals.

Apart from the books mentioned in the text, I found these sources especially important to understanding the evolution of sports and advertising: *A Brief History of Sports* by Elliot J. Gorn; *A Sporting Time: New York City and the Rise of Modern Athletics, 1820-1870* by Melvin L. Adelman; *American Sports: From the Age of Folk Games to the Age of Televised Sports* by Benjamin Rader; *City Games: The Evolution of American Society and the Rise of Sports* by Steven A. Riess; *The New American Sport History: Recent Approaches and Perspectives* edited by S.W. Pope; *The Encyclopedia of New York City* edited by Kenneth T. Jackson; *The Mirror Makers: A History of American Advertising and Its Creators* by Stephen Fox; *Fables of Abundance: A Cultural History of Advertising in America* by Jackson Lears, and AdAge .com. For more on Pope Leo XIII's endorsement of Mariani wine, see *A Brief History of Cocaine* by Steven B. Karch.

Acknowledgments

It is dangerous to dine with the author of a nonfiction work in progress, for he will start talking about his topic at the coat check and still be gangbusters at grappa time. Grappa may be the only thing that can slow him down. At a restaurant in the West Village, B.K. Loren and Lisa Cech, just in from Boulder, listened so graciously and gracefully to my ramblings about the crazy-good horse they fortified my belief that the story of Dan Patch would resonate beyond the horse and sports worlds. As I sat at my desk in Brooklyn writing this book, I often imagined I was talking to those lovely women across a restaurant table. A pleasant way to work.

It is impossible to thank people in the right order. Most of the Oxfordites and Savage residents who helped me are noted in the text, but some deserve a special mention. At the Indiana end of my research, Bob and Thelma Glaspie were wise, open-hearted, and generous with their materials and knowledge, and Thelma served me some fine Hoosier meals. The Glaspies also introduced me to John Messner and his wife, Pam. John gave me the idea to weave the present day into the narrative, as well as a rusty horseshoe that I shall always treasure. Through the Glaspies I also met Joseph Morris, who allowed me to copy and use the manuscript written by John Wattles's son Ray, one of several fascinating items in Joe's unique Dan Patch collection.

My frequent trips to Minnesota were made more valuable and more fun by Jens Bohn, the president of the Dan Patch Historical Society, and his wife, Joyce, proprietor of the beautiful Peacock Inn, the crown jewel of Chaska. Joyce, who always gave me the family discount at her five-star hostelry, cooks a mean breakfast. George Augustinack, vice president of the society, shared his vast knowledge of all things relating to M.W. Savage, allowed me to view parts of his legendary collection, and gave me honey from his bees. We may not agree on matters relating to Mr. Savage, but I respect George's opinion and admire his passion.

Stan Bergstein, the executive director of Harness Tracks of America, gave me encouragement and guidance thirty-five years ago, and also with this book. He is very special to me, and many others.

Ellen Harvey of the United States Trotting Association helped me immensely throughout the two years I researched this book. She and the USTA's Ken Weingartner made many drives to the Harness Racing Museum and Hall of Fame, in Goshen, New York, on gray winter weekdays to sit with me and page through the old, unindexed horse weeklies. They wouldn't even let me buy them lunch. Gail Cunard, the executive director of that wonderful museum, made its resources available at my convenience. Without her and her staff, this book would not have been possible.

Thanks is also due to, among others, Mary Cross, Diane Kleinsteiber, Catherine Stearns Medich, Lois Cross, Janet Williams, Will Williams, Dean Hoffman, Ed Keys, Don Daniels, Robin Mahoney, Robert Steckman, Deborah Savage, Joe Goldstein, Carol Hodes, the Savage Public Library, Diana Eliazov, Mary Phyllis Cowell, Nicole Kraft, and Terry McDonell.

My editor, Bob Bender, displayed a deft touch with the reins and never resorted to the whip. At Simon & Schuster, Johanna Li, Victoria Meyer, and Elizabeth Mason have also been most helpful. My agent, Kris Dahl, liked this idea from the start, and nurtured it wisely. My friend Karen Schneider was an early and careful reader of the manuscript. Meredith White urged me forward in the first place.

Then there are these people: Adele Leerhsen, Erica Leerhsen, Deborah Leerhsen, Nora Leerhsen. Frankie the Dog taught me much about animals, and Nature's Miracle.

My wife, Sarah Saffian Leerhsen, was the first to read the manuscript, express encouragement, and make wise suggestions. She is just the best.

Index